Because this text is a journalistic review of a controversial medical field, Wine Appreciation Guild submitted review copies to medical, academic and industry authorities. Here are responses from the original manuscript readers and other reviewers which lend support and credibility to Gene Ford's findings.

"With *The Science of Healthy Drinking* Gene Ford again hits the bulls-eye! We are fortunate that he has a special knack for reading and digesting the widely scattered and sometimes pretty heavy literature about the health benefits of moderate drinking, and that he is willing to invest the time, thought, and effort that it takes to "translate" it all into understandable and enjoyable prose. No wonder he was named Wine Writer of the Year – an apt reward for this kind of significant public service, which has long been his forte. **Dwight B Heath, Ph.D.** Anthropology Department, Brown University, author of *Drinking Occasions* (Providence, Rhode Island)

"Thank you for sending me chapters of your forthcoming book. The vast majority of those that drink do so moderately and it should be very helpful to those men and women to have a clear idea of when they are moving into an area of excessive drinking. So, right on!" **Thomas B. Turner, M.D**. Founding director, Alcoholic Beverage Medical Research Foundation, Dean emeritus, Johns Hopkins Medical School (Baltimore, Maryland)

"I have read it thoroughly, and found it was very entertaining, easy to read, and a very important contribution. I know of no other source that is as effective in shaking up the prohibitionist status quo as your book . . . I believe this book should be widely read by health policy advocates, the general public, and by physicians." **Alfred A. de Lorimier, M.D.,** Pediatric surgeon, Professor of Surgery Emeritus, University of California Medical School, San Francisco, Former chair, Society of Medical Friends of Wine (Geyserville, California)

"Gene Ford, devoted lay investigator of the connection between drinking and health has performed a great service with *The Science of Healthy Drinking*. Although it may seem a vast compendium to the uninitiated, he has actually reduced the vast scientific literature into a readable, witty and entertaining, enormously enlightening summary. If you value your health, you should read this book!" **David N. Whitten, M.D., Ph.D.,** Emergency room physician, educator, and co-author of *To Your Health: Two Physicians Explore The Health Benefits of Wine* (Ft. Worth, Texas)

"I have read and commented on your manuscript. I think it is a wonderful collection of the research that suggests that moderate drinking can have a positive health impact. I am enclosing a few of my articles . . . that add other evidence to the points you are making." **Ruth C. Engs, R.N., Ph.D.**, Department of Applied Health Science, Indiana University and author of *Clean Living Movements: American Cycles of Health Reform* (Bloomington, Indiana)

"Gene Ford has once again provided the definitive compendium on the range of reported health benefits from moderate alcohol consumption . . . The government should provide Mr. Ford a grant for his one-man effort to balance the presentation of data on alcohol's costs and benefits." **Stanton Peele**, Ph.D., Researcher, educator and co-author of *Alcohol and Pleasure: A Health Perspective* (Morristown, New Jersey)

"I read and enjoyed your manuscript. What a herculean job you have done in reviewing so much." **Arthur L. Klatsky, M.D.**, Researcher and senior consultant in cardiology, Kaiser Permanente Medical Center (Oakland, California)

"It is well-organized, easily-read, and highly informative. The volume is indispensable for both the practicing physician and the individual seeking information on personal health." **David J. Hanson**, Ph.D., Sociologist, web host and author of *Preventing Alcohol Abuse* (Chapel Hill, North Carolina)

"This book will play a vital role in AWARE's mission to provide accurate and balanced information to physicians and other health professionals about the health effects of moderate consumption." **John P. Juergens, Ph.D.**, Research Institute, University of Mississippi, chair of American Wine Alliance for Research and Education (University, Mississippi)

"Gene Ford shatters the all-American dichotomy which favors labeling substances as either "good" or "bad," documenting that alcohol has the potential to be both "good" and "bad" depending upon how it is used. Readers will likely be astonished – and pleased – to learn of the positive benefits of moderate alcohol use." **Elizabeth M. Whelan, Ph.D.** President, American Council on Science and Health (New York, New York)

"Readers may be surprised to learn that moderate drinking can have health benefits. In this comprehensive review of numerous scientific studies, Gene Ford gives the always fascinating and sometimes startling details." **William Rorabaugh, Ph.D.**, Professor of History, University of Washington and author of *The Alcoholic Republic* (Seattle, Washington)

"Literature on the health effects of moderate drinking tends to veer from sensibility in one direction or another. This stems less from medical conservatism than from an unfounded fear that truthful words will trigger alcohol abuse. A greater fear may be the label of "alcohol friendly." On the other side, many lay writings may be naively simplistic extrapolations of scientific findings. Gene Ford has meticulously avoided both pitfalls and presents one of the best balanced, not to mention compendious, analysis of this important public health and social issue." **Wells Shoemaker, M.D.**, co author of *The French Paradox and Beyon*d (Aptos, California)

"*The Science of Healthy Drinking* is a masterful compilation of the long term effects of moderate drinking. The audience for this book is universal. The general public deserves to know that *not* drinking in a responsible manner — whether by abusive drinking or abstention — can be hazardous to their health. Not informing a patient with coronary disease of the benefits of moderate drinking could be construed as professional negligence. This book allows the patient to make an informed choice." **Donald G. Kilgore, Jr., M.D.** Confrerie de la Chaine des Rotisseurs (Chapel Hill, North Carolina)

"During an era when everyone — including members of the licensed beverage industries — seem to focus on the relatively small percentage of people who misuse alcohol, Gene Ford in a well-constructed publication focuses on the positive aspects for the vast majority of people who enjoy the health and social benefits of drinking." **Morris E. Chafetz, M.D**., Founding Director, National Institute on Alcohol Abuse and Alcoholism, President, Health Education Foundation (Washington, D.C.)

"A proper balance is feasible — restricting alcohol abuse, encouraging moderate alcohol use. This book and Gene Ford's long-time efforts should help us achieve this proper balance." **Norman Kaplan, M.D.**, Professor of Internal Medicine, University of Texas Southwestern Medical Center (Dallas, Texas)

"Overall, this is the work of an energetic, smart, penetrating and hard-working author. It is at times productively and refreshingly brash, but at times it seems to verge on being too enthusiastic for the credibility of its own message, much like Ford's previous books. It will be a useful reference." **Harvey E. Finkel, M.D.**, Clinical Professor of Medicine, Boston University Medical Center (Brookline, Massachusetts)

"Gene Ford has produced a lucid, articulate, extremely well-researched treatise on the scientific evidence that supports moderate alcohol consumption. His work should prove helpful and entertaining to both health professionals and interested members of the public." **Keith I. Marton, M.D.,** Chief Medical Officer, Legacy Health System (Portland, Oregon)

"I'm putting a copy of this book in my office waiting room with expectations I'll be loaning it out until my patients buy their own copy! From my perspective as a practicing physician, uninformed alcohol ambivalence and irresponsible negativism are being slowly replaced in my profession by engaged enlightenment based on scientific fact. Gene Ford's book is an essential early step towards realizing that goal." **Edward J. Ford, M.D.**, Internist, rheumatologist (Milwaukee, Wisconsin)

"Gene Ford has done a great job with the independent research on wine and health. I wholeheartedly commend it." **Robert Mondavi,** Robert Mondavi Winery, (Oakville, California)

"Gene Ford has drawn together key citations from the entire scope of scientific work in this very diverse and controversial field. This is a very impressive and complete synthesis of the complex uses of drinking . . . Caregivers need this type of information to answer the increasing volume of questions by their patients." **Elisabeth Holmgren,** Director, U.S. Operations, Alcohol in Moderation, former research director, Wine Institute (Alamo, California)

"Gene Ford captures a balance between empirical data and practical application of how licensed beverages can be part of a healthy lifestyle. His work documents how moderate consumption can play a role in preventing various illnesses, and dispels the myth that what tastes good cannot be good for you. Cheers to your health!" **David Rehr**, President of the National Beer Wholesalers (Alexandria, Virginia)

"Gene Ford's new, remarkable book *The Science of Moderate Drinking* is just that. He forcefully and convincingly supports two propositions: one, that there exists an impressive scientific literature demonstrating the health benefits coming from responsible drinking: and, two, that the systems currently being used for the communication of health data are indifferent to its dissemination. The main body of this encyclopedia, a word which best describes the excellent organization of this vast effort . . . Ford mentions and quotes Garrison Keillor – and I couldn't help but note similarities between the two. This is not to take anything away from Ford's scientific expertise, nor his intellectual prowess, but rather to emphasize how comfortable Ford seems to want to make us feel." **Ralph E. Kunkee, Ph.D.,** Professor of Enology, Emeritus, University of California (Davis, California)

"Finally! Everybody I know in the beer business has followed the research and knows the benefits of moderate consumption. What has amazed me is the resistance of the media to carry the story. Now with this overwhelming investigation, I am confident that the story is ready for the masses. It can no longer be misrepresented or ignored. Thank you, Gene Ford." **Paul Shipman,** Founder, Redhook Ale Brewery (Woodinville, Washington)

"Gene Ford's passion and dedication to find the truth about alcoholic beverages for the health benefit of all people. This book is a valuable source of information that all health professionals and those who sell or serve alcoholic beverages should refer to frequently." **Brother Timothy Deiner**, FSC (Napa, California)

"This book serves as an excellent resource for health care professionals and the public at large . . . and offers remarkable documentation on the broad range of medical advantages of responsible alcohol consumption. Ford's dedication to providing enlightenment on the positive, healthful qualities of beverage alcohol is to be commended." **Harry G. Wiles**, President, American Beverage Licensees (Bethesda, Maryland)

"If you're a reasonable person and you think about what you eat and drink, then Gene Ford's *The Science of Healthy Drinking* will not only comfort you, but provide sanity to the otherwise insane landscape that has dominated the debate on alcohol and health. I'll toast my next beer in hopes that this book will reach out to the choir in the *other* room and that we can all begin to tolerate the benefits of moderation and admit that pleasure is not an evil sin." **Charlie Papazian**, President, Association of Brewers, Author of *The Complete Joy of Home Brewing* (Boulder, Colorado)

"Gene Ford has produced a seminal work on the wide-ranging health benefits of moderate drinking while, at the same time, tackling some of the most pervasive misconceptions we Americans have about alcohol! This is certain to become a critical reference tool for medical professionals, scientists, researchers, journalists and just about anyone interested in learning why moderate drinking is as important as good nutrition." **David Sloane**, President of WineAmerica, the National Association of American Wineries, (Washington, D.C.)

"I found this work most rewarding and enlightening. To find a voice of reason and common sense backed by thorough research and referenced so aptly is surely awesome. I wholeheartedly recommend your book to my retailers and advise that they provide copies to their school boards, legislators, clergy and their medical advisors." **Fred Guarnieri**, president, South Jersey Package Stores Association (Westmont, New Jersey)

"As is often the case in America, the public policy pendulum can swing to absurd extremes. As with the laws, regulations and public attitudes concerning alcohol consumption. Arbitrary and draconian drinking and driving laws are in concert with misguided campaigns intended to promote complete abstention from alcohol consumption as the path to good health. Gene Ford's *The Science of Healthy Drinking* can push the pendulum into a more rational and constructive arc." **James J. Baxter**, President, National Motorists Association (Dane, Wisconsin)

"For those of us who have spent our lives in the hospitality industry, the incessant slamming of alcohol has grown old and wearisome. Enter Gene Ford with *The Science of Healthy Drinking*. It is an impeccably researched look at alcohol and its impacts on human physiology. The book will cause prevalent misconceptions to fall from the sky as they are exposed to the light of scientific reason and factual explanation." **Robert Plotkin**, Author and consultant, Bar Media (Tucson, Arizona)

"I strongly recommend *The Science of Healthy Drinking*. Because of efforts by groups such as MADD, there are generations who know very little about responsible drinking, believing that Irish are all drunks, that Jews never are, and that any drinking amounts to all seven deadly sins rolled into one. This book can help change the attitudes of the younger generation and even help their parents learn how to deal with their children, as well as with alcohol." **Perry Luntz,** Editor/publisher, Beverage Alcohol Market Report, National editor, Beverage Network Publications (New York, New York)

"Gene Ford's new work reflects 25 years of dedicated study into sensible drinking and health. He was the first in the U.S. to publish news and information on scientific and medical evidence on moderation. In the new work several members of AIM's Social, Scientific and Medical Council have contributed. In thirty-three chapters and 446 pages Ford presents a deeply researched case for moderation." **Peter Duff**, Alcohol In Moderation, (London, U.K.)

"I recommend this book without reservation to any professional in the drinks industry . . . As vital a book as this might be for the health community, it should be the basis of responsible, intelligent and informed actions for the 1.6 million individuals in the manufacturing, marketing, distributing and selling of legal adult beverages." **Mark Silva,** Founding director and publisher, RealBranding.com and RealBeer.com (San Francisco, California)

"In thirty chapters, the book details the firmly established benefits of moderation, explores some of the less well-known protections and introduces avenues for further research. Throughout, Ford shows how the research has either been generally distorted or ignored by those most responsible for disseminating health information. . . those interested in the science and/or debates over alcohol policy and will find the arguments informative and the references helpful." **Eric Shepard**, Alcohol Issues Insights, January 2003 (Nyack, NY)

An Appeal to Physicians

The following endorsement from a prominent physician/journalist practicing in Ega, Denmark captures the focal message of *The Science of Healthy Drinking*. That message – and this book – appeals to practicing physicians around the globe to take personal responsibility for establishing a healthy drinking ethic for the benefit of their own societies. This worthy goal will never be met without participation by the clinical profession.

"As a family physician, I recognize that responsible public health authorities cannot issue blanket recommendations to start drinking for health. The family physician, however, with his or her solid knowledge of the patient's history, is in an excellent position to offer sensible advice on the health benefits of moderate, regular consumption of beer, wine or spirits. With Gene Ford's well-researched book in the office desk drawer, the family physician would have a gold mine of up-to-date, unbiased information on every aspect of alcohol and health at easy disposal. Gene Ford has managed to prove his point that drinks are healthy foods when taken in moderation, but – just as important – he also empahsizes that they should be drunk because they give pleasure and add conviviality. So, just in case, read Gene Ford's book now and learn the science of healthy drinking before your doctor!" **Erik Skovenborg, M.D**. Physician, writer, researcher and author of *Vin og Helbred: Myter og facts (Wine and Health: Myths and Facts)* (Ega, Denmark)

To encourage health agencies and trade associations to schedule a Gene Ford speech, we include the following comment about his recent speech in San Francisco before The Society of Medical Friends of Wine

"We are grateful to you for an excellent talk that was aimed directly at our members . . . the medical community above all others should be in a position to dispense accurate information on the relationship between wine and health. Your talk was a combination of solid research and a wake-up call, in a package that was fun to listen to." **Margaret F. Harding**, Executive Secretary, The Society of Medical Friends of Wine (San Francisco, California)

For information contact Gene Ford by e-mail:
ford@fordvideo.com

Publications by Gene Ford

The Spirit World, audio tapes, 1976
Ford's Illustrated Guide to Wines,
Brews and Spirits, 1978, textbook
Ford's ABCs of Wines, Brews and Spirits, 1987 **
Safe Service of Alcoholic Beverages, server
training program, 1987
The Moderation Reader/Healthy Drinking
bimonthly periodical, 1987 – 1995
The Benefits of Moderate Drinking,
Alcohol, Health and Society, 1988
Drinking and Health: The Good News, The
Bad News and the Propaganda, 1990
The French Paradox & Drinking for Health, 1993**
Ford's One Hour Wine Expert, videotape, 1997 **
Ford's One Hour Beer Expert, videotape, 2002 **
The Science of Healthy Drinking, 2003 **
(** currently in print)

To order books and tapes

Wine Appreciation Guild
360 Swift Avenue, Unit 34
South San Francisco, CA 94080
Phone: (800) 231-9463
www.wineappreciation.com

To book a speech by Gene Ford

e-mail Ford@fordvideo.com

For continuing research and commentary

www.scienceofhealthydrinking.com

Warmest Regards
Gene

The Science of

Healthy Drinking

Gene Ford

Wine Appreciation Guild
South San Francisco, California

Library of Congress Cataloging-in-Publication Data

The Science of Healthy Drinking

Ford, Gene A.

p. cm.

Includes References and Index

1. Drinking of alcoholic beverages– United States. 2. Health
benefits. 3. Temperance culture. 4. Medical practice. 5. Public health. 6. Government health policies. 7 Medical education. 8. Consumer education.
L.C. Number 2003105531

First Edition 2003

Published by Wine Appreciation Guild
360 Swift Avenue Unit 34
South San Francisco, California 94080
(800) 231-9463
www.wineappreciation.com

ISBN 1-891267-47-7
Printed in the United States 10 9 8 7 6 5 4 3 2 1

Contents

Acknowledgments

I will be forever grateful to the following individuals for their contributions to this effort: to Elliott Mackey, my long time publisher for his unwavering commitment to drinking and health issues; to my wife Patricia who has read, edited and commented on everything I've produced over two decades of writing and speaking about this topic; to Elizabeth Warden who copy-edited the thicket of scientific technicalities in these pages; and to the readers below of specific chapters — or entire manuscripts — of the many working drafts of this book. Their advice and counsel are visible throughout. Mistakes or misjudgments remain with the author. Special gratitude also to Byron Canfield and Mac Townsend for their computing wizardry.

Alfred A. de Lorimier, M.D.
Ruth C. Engs, R.N., Ph.D.
David J. Hanson, Ph.D.
Dwight B. Heath, Ph.D.
Elisabeth Holmgren
Man Kim, M.D.
John P. Juergens, Ph.D.
Arthur L. Klatsky, M.D.
Stanton M. Peele, Ph.D.
Charles Stipp, M.D.
Henry and Leslie Sully
Anthony E. Thein
Greg Walsh
David N. Whitten, M.D., Ph.D.

Foreword

Aspirin in regular, small doses is life-giving; aspirin in episodic, large amounts is harmful. Despite this potential harm, low dosage use of aspirin has developed as a major advance in the prevention of heart disease.

Alcohol, like aspirin, in regular, small doses is life-giving; alcohol, like aspirin, in episodic, large doses is life taking. Because it is more difficult to limit alcohol intake, particularly among the one of ten people who choose to abuse themselves or who become addicted to its effects, a broad attack upon the dangerous misuse of alcohol has been instituted.

Unfortunately, as Gene Ford has so carefully documented in this book, the well-intentioned attempt to prevent alcohol abuse threatens to restrict the healthful use of alcohol, throwing out the baby (and the parents) with the bath water.

Both the public at large and the health-care profession must continue to do everything possible to prevent alcohol abuse. At the same time, it is essential not to prohibit or impede the continued healthful consumption of moderate amounts of alcohol – the practice of the overwhelming majority of the people who drink.

There are many similarities but also some major differences between the campaign to prevent abuse but not to totally prohibit the moderate use of alcohol with the campaign to restrict but not to totally prohibit the smoking of tobacco.

The major differences between alcohol and tobacco are that tobacco has no health benefits and is many times more addictive. For good reason, all health-care professionals and a majority of the public are in favor of reasonable restrictions on tobacco use, particularly for the children who are so susceptible to becoming addicted. Few, however, want to totally prohibit the availability and use of tobacco despite the strength of the arguments that the only way to save the 435,000 people in the nation who die each year from tobacco is to do so.

Although alcohol is much less addictive than tobacco, we must continue to protect those who are susceptible to its misuse, particularly adolescents and those who have become addicted alcohol abusers. On the other hand, we should be very careful not to frighten the majority of the population who drink moderately so that they will deny themselves and everyone else the major protection against premature heart disease from regular, moderate alcohol intake.

I am particularly upset by those health-care professionals who are unwilling to advocate healthful drinking because of their mistaken belief that any such advocacy will encourage alcohol abuse. Certainly health-care professionals have, in general, been too timid in their campaign against tobacco. At the same time, I believe they have been too indiscriminate in their campaign against drinking. A proper balance is feasible – restricting alcohol abuse, encouraging moderate alcohol use.

This book and Gene Ford's long-time efforts should help us achieve this proper balance.

Norman M. Kaplan, M.D. *

* This foreword appeared in my third book in this field – *The French Paradox & Drinking for Health* – published in 1993. Dr. Kaplan's comments seem even more appropriate for this expansive manuscript. I asked for and was granted permission to reprint it here without change.

Gene Ford 2003

Epidemiology and the Communication Issue

Epidemiology

Much of the science reported in this book was developed in a number-crunching technique called epidemiology. Epidemiology grew from medical record-keeping during disease epidemics. In the computer era, this archiving discipline vastly expanded from its original model. *The Medical Advisor* published by Time/Life, Inc. notes: *Epidemiology is the statistical study of disease among populations or groups of people. Once dedicated to infectious diseases and epidemics, this specialty has expanded to cover non-infectious diseases such as cancer and heart disease* (The Medical Advisor 1996).

Modern epidemiology evaluates not only sick people but whole populations of individuals among whom are sufferers of one or more identifiable diseases. A variety of techniques are involved. Epidemiologists conduct retrospective studies — asking participants to reconstruct personal histories including life-style habits such as food and alcohol consumption, whether they smoke, exercise routines, levels of education, religious practice, family medical histories and so on. They stage prospective studies — asking individuals to record various aspects of their lives for extended periods. Study participants range from as few as a dozen individuals to the several hundred thousand involved in the two major American Cancer Society surveys.

Epidemiologists eliminate confounding factors which can skew the findings and invalidate analyses and reports. They excise, or analyze separately, data from individuals suffering lingering illnesses and those who have been long-term smokers. In alcohol studies, drinkers and never-drinkers often are distinguished from abstainers who have had previous drinking problems. The studies also compare the health impacts of light and moderate daily drinkers with results obtained from both abstainers and heavy drinkers.

Because self-reporting depends on memory and candor involving hundreds – sometimes thousands – of individuals, epidemiology does not enjoy the certitude of biology, physics or mathematics. In such large groupings, inevitably some respondents are neither candid nor honest. In addition, each study reflects unique demographic and cultural profiles. Studies conducted in Denmark differ from those taken in Mississippi or Alaska. Major variances are found in responses between rich and poor individuals in the same nation or region. When a line of research produces similar results from a wide variety of studies – as do the findings on drinking and cardiovascular disease – a scientific consensus emerges. But oncologist Finkel prudently urges greater diligence on the "fact gathering" end and greater caution on the "analysis" end of the process: *Studies of populations may arouse the first awareness of important relationships, but, because we fortunately cannot strictly manipulate humans . . . epidemiologic information rarely can be conclusive. The large number of studies with super-imposable results, in men and women, in blacks and whites, in Europe, in North America, and in Japan, Australia, Israel, and Iceland, in various age groups, lend great weight to their conclusion – the J-shaped curve* (Finkel 1998).

The byword in epidemiology is caution. Caution is suggested about findings in many chapters. Consensus among scientists is reported for some cardiovascular benefits cited in Chapters 1-7. In other chapters, J- and U-shaped curves show moderate drinkers at less risk than abstainers and abusers. Some findings are limited to a handful of studies since less serious diseases don't get the research funding of the hot button issues. When taken as a whole, the "evidence" cited here constitutes an impressive epidemiological affirmation that responsible drinking is compatible with human health. You can take that to the bank before reading a single chapter.

While prudence is warranted, oblivion isn't and that's where the communication controversy arises. Medical and public health critics of the alcohol-favorable epidemiology argue that the findings do not have sufficient definition and certitude to support widespread dissemination to the public. They argue that rigorous prospective trials similar to those required of pharmaceuticals are necessary before the results can be supported.

This book counters that an overwhelming and diverse epidemiology justifies support of responsible consumption, as is the case in most other western nations. Studies in many of these nations report moderate drinkers among the healthiest individuals. The imputed benefits in beer, wine and spirits consumption exceed those of any other foods in the larder.

The hundreds of scientific quotations in these pages were chosen from the over 1,400 articles listed in the Reference section. The first draft identified forty-eight separate human conditions in which researchers identified either direct benefits or less harm from drinking than that perceived in popular culture. This large reference section will be a useful tool for researchers and physicians looking for additional answers. The quotes derive from multiple sources. Most come directly from the original published studies. Some are taken from abstracts and summaries published in survey periodicals such as *Alcohol Research* (The Netherlands), *Alcohol Issues Insights* (Nyack) and *The Alcoholic Beverage Medical Research Foundation Quarterly* (Baltimore). Still others derive from popular medical newsletters such as *UC-Berkeley Wellness Letter* (University of California), *HealthNews* (*The New England Journal of Medicine*) and *Harvard Health Letter* (Harvard Medical School).

Though epidemiology may be a somewhat chancy tool, it has been responsible for significant medical advances. Its findings have stimulated biomedical and animal-model experimentation in dozens of fields which have either confirmed the original data or sent researchers off in new directions. Feinstein in *Scientific standards in epidemiological studies* says this:

> *Many substances used in daily life, such as coffee, alcohol and pharmaceutical treatment for hypertension, have been accused of "menace" in causing cancer or other major diseases. Although some of the accusations have subsequently been refuted or withdrawn, they have usually been based on statistical association in epidemiologic studies that could not be done with the customary experimental methods of science . . . . Until the new paradigms, methods, and data are developed,*

*however, non-epidemiologic scientists and members
of the lay public will have to use common sense and
their own scientific concepts to evaluate the reported
evidence. If war is too important to be left to military
leaders, and medicine to physicians, the
interpretation of epidemiologic results cannot be
relegated exclusively to epidemiologists. The people
who struggle to understand those results can be
helped by recalling the old adage that statistics are
like a bikini bathing suit: what is revealed is
interesting; what is concealed is crucial.*

Feinstein, A., Scientific standards in epidemiologic studies, Science, Vol. 242, December
2, 1988

This book testifies to Feinstein's theory that the findings of
epidemiology are too important to be left completely in the
hands of medical and public health systems which are smitten
today with a "risk" mentality, even for responsible drinking. The
book reveals some bells, many books and a profusion of candles
on how *favorable* drink benefits are repressed.

The Communication Issue

An important theme of this book holds that American medicine suffers under Temperance rubrics established a hundred
years ago – a dry philosophy buttressed today by a committed,
anti-drinking federal health bureaucracy that, incidentally,
holds many of the major purse-strings for medical research
funding. The evidence demonstrates that alcohol conservatism
extends far beyond the normal give-and-take debate that is
essential to the research enterprise. A pattern of omitting drink-
positive research in disease articles and the tendency to over-
state the risks of abuse and addiction will be shown again and
again in medical and government publications.

This presumption does not mean that some evil conspiracy is
abroad in the land. Far from it. Conservative physicians are the
best physicians. Some physicians concur with the federal health
bureaucracy that reducing all drinking would be an effective
way of fighting abuse. Some believe in a prohibitionary agenda.

But, there is little coverage in medical education of parallel research developed in sociology and anthropology. These other disciplines often define and clarify true alcohol abuse risks.

Studies in the social sciences refute the presumption that every new drinker is at serious risk of over drinking. Some are, of course, but only a small percentage of any drinking population becomes addicted and most abusers have psychological or social problems underlying their abuse. This book identifies traditional temperance myths and perceptions about drinking within medicine as the critical problem. The irony is that polls indicate that far more physicians drink than does the general population. Few clinical physicians are personally adverse to responsible drinking. Most imbibe comfortably, with little risk.

Here is an example of how this ultra conservatism can confound a person seeking definitive advice. Journalist Jonathan Rauch found nothing but confusion when he sought advice about therapeutic drinking for his 69 year old father, a rare social drinker, who was experiencing mild hypertension. In "Temperance Kills," he reports that his father's physician had never mentioned any drinking benefits. Skilled in digging-out the essentials of a story, Rauch contacted a prominent Harvard researcher, an American Heart Association official and other medical authorities. After these interviews, Rauch concluded: *I think the message most people would get from (these) sources is: Drinking isn't all bad, but eschew it anyway . . . Presumably an avoidable heart attack is equally tragic whether the cause is too much alcohol or too little. To continue today's policy of muttering and changing the subject verges perilously on saying not just that too much alcohol is bad for you but that ignorance is good for you* (Rauch 1998).

Examples of communication failures are cited in nearly every disease chapter. The most common technique is omission. Articles on how to avoid diabetes, kidney stones, osteoporosis and other illnesses omit any mention of studies which report moderate drinkers at least risk. This mischief bleeds over into the popular media shortchanging the clinician and confusing the public. Consider the coverage of a study which found that frequent drinkers enjoy the lowest heart attack risk which was published in the January 9, 2003 in the *New England Journal of Medicine.* The study analyzed data on 38,077 men over twelve years in the Health Professionals Follow-up Study. In "Roles of Drinking Pattern and Type of Alcohol Consumed in Coronary Heart Disease in Men" Mukamal found that: 1) alcohol consumption was consistently associated with lower risk of coronary heart disease; 2) that daily drinkers had lower risks for heart attacks than casual or light drinkers; 3) that benefits accrue from all types of drinks; and 4) that among this group – physicians, dentists, veterinarians, optometrists and other medical professionals: *The associations were strongest for beer and liquor, intermediate for white wine, and weakest for red wine* (Mukamal 2003).

This does not amount to a plug for the consumption of beer or liquor in preference to red wine. Indeed Mukamal reveals that this particular grouping favored beer and spirits and that: *Our findings support the hypothesis that the beverage most widely consumed by a given population is the one most likely to be inversely associated with the risk of myocardial infarction in that population* (Mukamal 2003). Many studies in the book support this assumption such as in Denmark (page 228), Germany (pages 65,66) and France (page 230).

Mukamal's frequency findings were headlined in the media along with some "muttering" and "changing of the subject" from a Goldberg editorial in the same journal. In "To Drink or Not to Drink?," Goldberg suggests that: *Epidemiologic studies provide initial insights into the relation between lifestyle and disease. They suffer, however, from the impossibility of eliminating confounding differences between groups* (Goldberg 2003). Fair criticism but Goldberg then speculates: *Thus one wonders if the alcohol -consuming groups also drank more tea, ate more nuts, or consumed more fish – all lifestyle factors associated with reduced cardiovascular risk.* Goldberg's epidemiological reservations are appropriate but since he fails to relate this new finding to the corpus of several hundred other similar cardiovascular studies, the reader lacks a critical frame of reference to evaluate this particular finding.

While exercising prudent caution about epidemiological data, Goldberg ignores a profusion of *biomedical* research which does credit drinks with balancing of fibrinogen, cholesterols, folate, platelets, blood clotting, triglycerides, homocysteine, B-vitamins, and bone density, not to speak of improved mortality, less stress and cognitive benefits. The "Types and levels of drinks" category in the Index points to dozens of studies which have explored frequency levels in healthy drinking. Mukamal's study expands on these findings. Goldberg ignores these data.

Proper referencing would relate the frequency of consumption finding beneficial influence. Mukamal's study amplified this one important aspect of a large, developing body of literature. It must be related to other data for informative perspectives.

This deliberate narrowing of the research horizon in medical commentary limits the perspective appearing in popular media reports. Here are two examples. *Time* magazine's coverage of Mukamal's study by Gorman appeared as "Where's the Proof?" It echoes the negative Goldberg line: *Even if moderate drinking does confer health benefits, which it probably does, they are rather modest – certainly not stronger than the effect of small daily doses of aspirin on heart health . . . the effect may be more in line with the apparent cardioprotective benefits of eating a modest portion of nuts each day* (Gorman 2003). Probable? Modest? Many studies from many nations show responsible drinkers with better risk odds than abstainers who also employ admirable lifestyle habits, not only for heart attacks but for several dozen illnesses. This broader correlative perspective is absent in most coverage.

A similarly narrow focus was seen in the grilling of Mukamal and Goldberg on the Lehrer evening television news on PBS. Reporter Margaret Warner fleshed-out the key differences between epidemiological and biomedical studies but her questions – and Goldberg's answers – failed to place this study into the larger context of global findings favoring responsible drinkers.

One can hardly fault media commentators and journalists since the medical sources they rely on fail to clarify the depth and diversity in healthy drinking findings, as they do for other controversial research such as hormone replacement.

Another study published in the January 27, 2003 issue of the *Archives of Internal Medicine* illustrates why medical authorities need to provide unbiased perspective on the stream of drinking studies that are released to the public. This project involved the Nurses' Health Study consisting of over 70,000 female medical professionals who were, like the men in the Health Professional's Study, tracked for over a decade. The study reported that women in this study who averaged five hours sleep at night were at much higher risk for a heart attack than those who averaged eight hours. Such sleep influence is interesting new data but it does not enjoy, at this time, a range of confirming studies. By comparison, Mukamal's finding on drinking frequency enjoys several hundred correlations as Types and Levels of Drinks in the Index demonstrates. Goldberg and others in medicine should provide this broader perspective to the media and to the public. Repetition is the required path in epidemiology for enabling a scientific consensus.

Epidemiology demands common sense. Nowhere does this writer claim that drinking alone prevents heart attacks. None of the scientists quoted in this book attribute the risk reduction among moderate drinkers exclusively, or even predominantly, to alcohol intake. But they do observe and report a favored status. They note a synergism arising from good dietary practices, adequate exercise and stress-free lifestyle factors – along with drinking – as keys to the maintenance of good health. The reality is that clinical physicians and the public currently are very poorly informed about this growing volume of favorable drinking research. With drinking science, medicine suffers atherosclerosis of its communication arteries. The data is extant and profuse. It simply isn't discussed in polite circles.

This book points to archaic temperance myths and anti-drinking public health bureaucracies which deter medicine and nutrition from treating drinks as common foods. Pure alcohol is a psychoactive drug. But drinks are much more than pure drugs. Drinks originate in the soil as do other plant foods. After they mature into fruit and grain, they undergo natural fermentation into beer and wine. Some of each are distilled into liquors. Drinks provide many nutritional and therapeutic benefits aside from their dangerous alcohol toxicity. Drinks provide calories and numerous vitamins, antioxidants and minerals. Drinks have nutritional and therapeutic merit. Even if it could be proved that all benefits associated with drinks derive from other lifestyle factors, it would be absolutely undeniable that responsible drinking is no *impediment* to good health. Dozens and dozens of studies find moderate drinkers the healthiest group.

This imbroglio would alter dramatically if the public would demand that scientists, physicians and nutritionists cease the pretense and classify drinks as inexpensive and wholesome foods, not as street drugs or questionable medicines. Goldberg's editorial opines: *If alcohol were a newly discovered drug (instead of a drink dating back to the dawn of human history), we can be sure that no pharmaceutical company would develop it to prevent cardiovascular disease* (Goldberg 2003). Pharmaceutical companies will never support alcohol research because they have no way to retain proprietary (profitable) ownership of drinks. Goldberg cites the "dawn of human history." From that very dawn, drinks have been highly valued foods and reliable companions in medical therapy. America's alcohol ambivalence rejects this rich history and reduces drinks to a nether world, denying their historical status as healthful foods. Keep in mind that this book addresses exclusively factors involved in responsible consumption.

Narrowing the discussion to solitary, unrelated studies or exclusively to the cardiovascular diseases deprives the public of pertinent discoveries about diabetes, the common cold, cancer, gallstones, mortality, Alzheimer's, cancer, stress and many other conditions. Physicians and patients cannot make informed drinking decisions from such a narrowed base. The proclivity in medicine today is "Don't ask; and we won't tell."

Fortunately, over the last year or so, some medical newsletters and medical journalists have gravitated to a broader recognition of a health role in responsible drinking. Remember that this book speaks *only* to responsible consumption. The popular media are exhibiting increasing interest because of the cascade of new, favorable studies. However, few media outlets have reporters with sufficient research backgrounds to place a critical perspective on the reports. This book speaks also to the media.

For proof of the nascent media interest, consider the remarkable series of articles by Abigail Zuger in the *New York Times* in December 2002. In "The Case for Drinking (All Together Now: In Moderation!)," Zuger writes: *Thirty years of research has convinced many experts of the health benefits of moderate drinking for some people. A drink or two a day of wine, beer or liquor is, experts say, often the single best non-prescription way to prevent heart attacks, better than a low-fat diet or weight loss, better even than vigorous exercise. Moderate drinking can help prevent strokes, amputated limbs and dementia* (Zuger 2002). That's good, comprehensive reporting.

Zuger quotes Dr. Curtis Ellison, one of the panelists on the CBS-TV "French Paradox" program: *The science supporting the protective role of alcohol is indisputable; no one questions it any more. There have been hundreds of studies, all consistent.* Few authorities in medicine openly deny such benefits but they are practiced in muttering and changing the subject.

I personally classify the *60 Minutes* French Paradox program right up there with the Biblical Wedding at Cana in terms of effective drinking communication. Researchers Curt Ellison and Serge Renaud didn't transform water into wine, but their calm and scholarly presentation convinced the majority of the twenty million viewers that red wine consumption could help to reduce cardiovascular problems. What healthy drinking science needs is more calm and sophisticated communication of a remarkable body of scientific literature, without overselling the benefits or understating the risks of abuse.

Mukamal's study joins many others establishing a real advantage in frequency of consumption: *Among men, consumption of alcohol at least three to four days per week was inversely associated with the risk of myocardial infarction [heart attack]. Neither the type of beverage nor the proportion consumed with meals substantially altered this association* (Mukamal 2003). Dry advocates do not favor this conclusion. Yet, to resolve alcohol ambivalence in our land, American medicine must face this research and discontinue the mumbling and dissembling, the efforts which discourage the clinical practitioner and the public from gaining a deeper understanding of the developing science.

For this metamorphosis to occur, clinical medicine needs to openly embrace the demonstrated *positive* relationships of drinks while continuing to discourage excessive consumption. One study (see Chapter 31) concludes that moderate wine drinkers save society up to $1 billion in annual medical costs compared to nondrinkers. Since beer and spirits were not part of this study, total savings would be much, much greater since beer consumption is much higher than spirits and wine combined. This evidence has real dollar and "sense" logic to consumers as annual medical expenditures soar over $5,000.00 per person.

A scientific warning and disclaimer

This book consists of a journalistic foray through hundreds of scientific papers. The author has no medical credentials. Therefore, this text should not be utilized as a medical advisor. Medical advice should be sought from a physician or other professional caregiver. Not from a polemical text. If anything found in these pages seems relevant to personal or family conditions, refer those findings to your family physician for commentary and advice.

So, if good health interests you, read on, exercising the caution and good sense about epidemiology suggested by Finkel and Feinstein. For this reading, it will help to put aside any reservations about the merits of epidemiology until a perusal of the many findings assembled here is completed. Few things are absolute in scientific research, but some are obvious. That being said, the breadth of epidemiology favoring responsible drinking is uniquely impressive. It deserves a thorough airing to the American public.

Gene Ford 2003

Prologue

Two scientific conclusions are indisputable. First, no one needs to consume alcohol to conduct a healthy, happy life. Second, epidemiology has revealed that those who consume in moderation (as confirmed in many nations) are less disease prone than those who abstain. No one disputes the first of these scientific realities. Medicine and public health authorities in the United States generally ignore the second.

This book presents generous evidence of the efficacy of healthful drinking across a wide spectrum of illnesses. Yet, it does not suggest that everyone drink. The book seeks to inform physicians and health-conscious lay people of potential health benefits in responsible use. The book:

1. Sets forth credible findings of health benefits in responsible consumption for thirty common health conditions

2. Explains why most doctors and few among the general public are aware of these and other beneficial, peer-reviewed findings

3. Concludes that there is an optimum level of frequent or daily consumption that best yields such health benefits

To understand this "communication conflict," compare the treatment of similar findings in two unrelated studies reported in the early 1990s, both sponsored by the American Heart Association (AHA). In a rare move, association officials broke into an ongoing, decade-old study of male medical professionals to announce that, among this large population, an aspirin every other day reduced the risk of a heart attack by 47 percent. The finding related to America's gravest medical challenge — cardiovascular disease. The news was trumpeted across all media. It is advertised heavily by aspirin producers and is widely supported in medicine today.

Two months earlier at an AHA meeting in California, similar findings were presented by the lead researcher for both studies,

Charles Hennekens, M.D. of Harvard University Medical
School. This earlier study reported that individuals who consumed the equivalence of "two beers or wines or one cocktail
daily" had a 49 percent lower risk of a heart attack. That's two
percent better risk odds from drinks which are a whole lot more
pleasant to consume than aspirin. AHA officials and virtually
everyone in medicine and public health continue to ignore the
drink findings because they challenge conventional medical
wisdom that all drinking is "risk taking." When the AHA supported only the aspirin results, I called and was informed by an
AHA official that the association couldn't publicize the alcohol
benefits for fear of stimulating alcohol abuse. If this benefit was
anecdotal or a rarity, public health caution might have been
warranted. It wasn't and it isn't.

These studies are part of a very large and accumulating cardiovascular literature in which daily, moderate drinkers enjoy
preferential statistics. Coverage in the popular media has made
many Americans at least vaguely aware of heart health benefits
in drinks, particularly with red wines. A miniscule number of
Americans are aware of the voluminous findings in this book
which suggest benefits for several dozen other illnesses from the
consumption of all types of licensed beverages. The "communication gap" deprives at least 130 million American consumers
of health data on which to make informed lifestyle choices.

The epidemiology needs to be correlated also with the volume
of work in other disciplines concerning abuse risk. Over the past
forty years, anthropologist Dwight Heath, Ph.D. has researched
patterns of alcohol use and abuse in many cultures. In a recent
text, *Drinking Occasions: Comparative Perspectives on Alcohol and
Culture*, Heath addresses this failure to adequately inform the
public: *It matters much when people drink, because the risks that tend
to be associated with alcohol depend almost entirely on the pace of
drinking. . . . Excessive drinking by a small percentage of those who
drink is linked with most of the damages to health, property, public
safety, and other risks that are, in varying degrees, associated with
ethanol . . . Only on rare occasions does a normally moderate drinker
drink in a way that results in any such problem* (Heath 2000).

Most European medical authorities do not suffer ambivalence
about drinking. The second edition of a British medical refer-

ence, *Health Issues Related to Alcohol Consumption* (Blackwell Science, Oxford, U.K., 1999), concludes: *The idea of an optimal level of alcohol intake is based on epidemiological evidence that overall mortality in a population, or mortality or morbidity due to specific causes, is lower among those who drink lightly than among abstainers or heavier drinkers* (Macdonald 1999). This British scientific survey presumes less illness and less premature death among moderate drinkers. This presumption is affirmed in the science many times over in the chapters that follow.

However, in no way does drinking *guarantee* good health. Moderate-living, well-exercised, daily drinkers can and do succumb to every disease considered in this book. But, the evidence attests that these folks have better risk odds. Epidemiology identifies the synergy between a moderate lifestyle and moderate drinking. Fit people who drink moderately emerge as the healthiest segment in many societies. From a layman's point of view, it matters little whether this status derives more from the healthy lifestyles than from the drinking. This is for scientists to sort out. This book's primary message is that wine, beer and spirits, moderately taken, are healthy, nutritious *foods*. Foods, properly taken, that are no threat to good health. Indeed, they emerge as the world's most versatile health foods.

A distinction between use and abuse

America's visceral fear of drinking is based in a complex of cultural myths (See Chapter 31). Public health organizations insist that everyone who drinks is at risk of abuse, that all drinking is "risk taking."

Federal and state health authorities do have important responsibilities in abuse prevention and treatment fields. The first major thrust of the federal government into prevention and treatment came when Congress formed the National Institute on Alcohol Abuse and Alcoholism (NIAAA) in the early 1970s. The agency's first director, psychiatrist Morris Chafetz, M.D., introduced a classical, European alcohol control policy: *Provide support for those people who choose to take alcohol in moderation or to abstain. Reduce the guilt feelings surrounding alcohol taking when it is in moderation* (Second Special Report to Congress 1974). There was nothing punitive or derisive in this early approach.

However, it didn't take long for prohibitionary forces to introduce an alternative, drinking-hostile approach into the NIAAA. The agency's second director, Ernest Noble, M.D., championed a neoprohibition agenda which has dominated the health bureaucracies ever since. Noble is quoted in one interview as saying: *Alcohol is the dirtiest drug we have* (Gross 1983). Noble cooperated in an international public health campaign to reduce per capita consumption as the best way to reduce abuse. American medicine – heavily dependent upon government funding – followed suit by incorporating many prohibitionary protocols into medical education and practice.

In real life, most American drinkers consume moderately. Doing so, they are at no greater risk from this practice than from dozens of other inescapable, random risks involved in daily life. Alcoholism professionals around the globe report that only about three percent of an average drinking population is composed of alcohol-addicted drinkers (*Alcohol Beverage Taxation and Control Policies*, Ninth Edition, 1997). Another five to ten percent abuse periodically but are not addicted in a strictly clinical sense. U.S. health agencies established a target goal of reducing U.S. per capita consumption 25 percent in their 1990 policy book, *Healthy People 2000*. This goal was reaffirmed recently in *Healthy People 2010*. While their reduction goal was not met, government propaganda influenced a downward trend in per capita consumption.

Most drinkers – yesterday, today and into the foreseeable future – have been, are and will be moderates who are in no essential danger from their consumption. The "risk taking" theme is fear propaganda designed to discourage drinking. It's akin to a government policy declaring automobile driving and high school football as "risk-taking" employments which should be avoided. Yes, there are real risks in driving and amateur sports, but not at a level that would justify major reductions among the entire population of motorists or quarterbacks.

Distinguishing relative risks

In December 2002, the Harvard Center for Risk Analysis released a study of relative risks of driving while talking on portable phones. The conclusion was that driver/phoners are responsible for " . . . *about 6 percent of U.S. vehicle accidents each year, killing about 2,600 people and injuring 330,000 others* (Study considered benefits to drivers and accident costs 2002). The report states: *Joshua Cohen, lead author of the study, said an individual has a small risk of being in an accident caused by a driver who is talking on the phone. . . People place a value on these calls, so just wiping out the phone calls should not be taken lightly.* The author reasoned that we routinely accept low risk activities because we value the benefits derived from some action. The risks in drinking and in drinking before driving are real, but not imperative risks. Neither are the risks in moderate drinking.

Relative Risk of CHD for Moderate Drinkers, versus Non-Drinkers

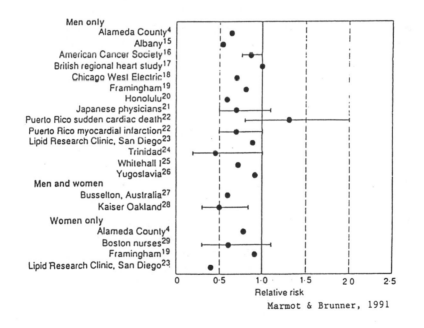

Marmot & Brunner, 1991

Reprinted with permission of the BMJ Publishing Group from British Medical Journal, Alcohol and cardiovascular disease: the status of the U-shaped curve, Marmot & Brunner, 303:565-568, 1991

Sorting out relative risks is what medicine does routinely, except when it comes to drinking. A glance at the graph above published thirteen years ago graphically shows the lowered relative risks of coronary heart disease in moderate drinkers. Studies in the above six nations and several U. S. States demonstrate fewer relative risks for heart disease among moderate drinkers.

Note that the Marmot and Brunner report came along shortly after Health and Human Services published its goal book *Healthy People 2000* which set a national target of reducing per capita drinking by twenty-five percent by the turn of the century. In November of that year, CBS *60 Minutes* aired the first of three television programs exploring the French paradox. It took an independent television news show to reveal to the mass public what medical research had known for decades. That moderate drinkers had lower heart disease risks.

The disconnect between scientific data supporting responsible drinking and American medical policy might well be termed the "American Paradox." The underlying medical mischief dates to the national prohibition campaign early in the last century. As outlined by Sinclair in *Era of Excess*, on June 6, 1917 the American Medical Association took an intemperate action which has muddied drinking issues in the medical profession ever since. A year earlier, federal health authorities had removed alcohol from the *United States Pharmacopoeia*, the roster of approved therapeutic drugs. The AMA's House of Delegates passed the following resolution:

> *WHEREAS, We believe that the use of alcohol as a beverage is detrimental to the human economy, and WHEREAS, Its use in therapeutics, as a tonic or a stimulant or as a food has no scientific basis, therefore, be it*
> *RESOLVED, That the American Medical Association opposes the use of alcohol as a beverage; and be it further*
> *RESOLVED, That the use of alcohol as a therapeutic agent should be discouraged.*

Sinclair, A., Era of Excess: A Social History of the Prohibition Movement, Harper & Row, Publishers, New York, 1964

To my knowledge, this impassioned resolution was never rescinded over the 20th century but its philosophical thrust remains in force in today. Consider just two evidences. Along with the Department of Health and Human Services, the AMA co-sponsorsed the most recent Alcohol Policy Conference, the biennial planning conclave of the dry movement in the U.S. In 2001, the AMA published a "Policy briefing paper" titled *Partner or Foe? The Alcohol Industry, Youth Alcohol Problems and Alcohol Policy Strategies*. The primary goal of this policy statement is to reject beverage industry participation in and funding of abuse prevention programs. In effect, demonizing the producers as well as the product. J. Edward Hill, M.D. chair of the AMA board of trustees justified this stand because of: . . . *recent evidence that alcohol damages the brains of young people*.

No recognition of the increasing *scientific evidence* that responsible drinking contributes to the nation's well-being. That drinks, taken moderately by most users, essentially are wholesome, health-enhancing foods. The AMA should enunciate any policies it chooses. But the association's systemic alcohol ambivalence supports the argument in this book that ambivalence reform must arise *within* medicine, from the clinical troops who deliver health care, if it is to come about at all.

Sinclair outlines how far afield the AMA resolution was from clinical medical practice in June 1917: *If the American Medical Association had really believed that alcohol was detrimental to the human economy, its condemnation would have been just. But alcohol was still being widely prescribed as a medicine in 1917. It was recommended by many doctors in cases of fainting, shock, heart failure, exposure and exhaustion. It was believed to be an antidote to snake bite, pneumonia, influenza, diphtheria, and anemia. It was used as a method of feeding carbohydrates to sufferers from diabetes. It was given to cheer and build up the aged. Insufficient research had been done to state definitely that alcoholic drinks possessed no food value. Nothing was said in the resolution about the fact that small quantities of alcohol taken with meals might aid the digestion and relax the mind* (Sinclair 1964). Alcohol had yet to be propaganized from common, clinical therapy to demon rum.

While this is history, it is prologue to the indifference and ambivalence which is manifest in medicine today. What is needed today is a public airing of the *relative risks* and *relative benefits* in responsible drinking. That being done, the majority of American physicians will come to recognize drinks (as do their European counterparts), not as lethal street drugs but as health enhancing foods (see Chapter 14) that should be taken only in moderation, especially when driving or operating dangerous machinery. This is the common sense approach. Recognize the danger and exercise appropriate cautions.

John Juergens, Ph.D., chair of the American Wine Alliance for Research and Education (AWARE), outlined the extent of the communication bias in medicine: . . . *of the more than 2,000 scientific articles published annually about alcohol, less than 15% address the effects of moderate alcohol consumption. Therefore, even if a physician sees a research article, it is most likely to focus on abusive consumption. This selective reporting of research substantially stifles the flow of new information from valid clinical research studies* (Juergens 1998). AWARE is an advocacy committed to bringing healthy drinking research to the attention of American physicians.

Popular media commentator and author Dean Edell, M.D. discusses the consequence of this communication failure in *Eat, Drink and Be Merry*. He observes: *Slightly more than one-third of American adults abstain completely from alcohol and there has been a steady decline in drinking overall . . . science is finding alcohol to be a marvelous medical preventive . . . the official response in medicine and public health has been nil* (Edell 1999).

Fortunately there exists a splendid legacy of medical leadership supporting a responsible drinking culture (See Epilogue). Fifty years ago, the pioneer patron saint of healthy drinking science Salvatore P. Lucia, M.D. wrote a series of five scholarly books and conducted numerous seminars and presentations which explored the role of drinking in medical history.

Lucia believed that epidemiology would some day exonerate responsible drinking. An educator in preventive medicine himself, Lucia propounded the theme that drinks are excellent *adjuvants* to a medical regimen. In medicine, an adjuvant is a pharmacological agent which is added to or consumed with a medicine to increase the desired effect. (For example, alcohol is the base or menstruum for most traditional patent medicines.) In *Wine as Food and Medicine*, Lucia proposes that Americans emulate European drinkers and look to wines as good, healthy foods that complement and enhance good medical practice:

> *In the wild scramble for therapeutic specificity, little thought has been given to the psychotherapeutic effects of the simple adjuvants to living that make life worthwhile . . . . On the other hand, no remedy for an organic illness can be successful if it produces only a psychologic effect . . . . This text deals with wine as a food and medicine.*

Lucia, S., Wine as Food and Medicine, The Blakiston Company, Inc., New York, 1954

In like temperament, this book does not seek to medicalize drinks. Quite the opposite. Along with Lucia, it features drinks in cuisine where the natural toxicity of ethanol in all drinks is tempered by the consumption of other foods and by the socializing and mentoring faculties of kith and kin. If a reader chooses to invest in but a single chapter, I strongly recommend Chapter 14, *Diet and Nutrition.* It's critical that open-minded physicians, the media and the public begin to question the absence of drinks in our nutritional literature. When drinks once again are foods, alcohol ambivalence will become irrelevant.

Finally, to distinguish this writer's personal opinions from the scientific reporting, each new chapter opens with an "Author's abstract." In these summaries, I provide personal analyses — editorials if you will — based upon nearly three decades of reviewing and writing about drinking issues. It bears repeating again that this book is journalism about published findings, not scientific authority concerning those findings. This book is medical *journalism*, not medical advice. It should not be employed as a medical primer.

Scientists have very different responsibilities and obligations than do journalists. I spend little time distinguishing causation from correlation. These pages confirm only that many beneficial drink findings do exist, largely unreported to practicing physicians and the public alike. That's the de facto communication gap. Physicians and researchers routinely discuss speculative findings about many drugs and diseases while prospective studies are ongoing. Medical authorities should report and debate drinking benefits as they do other developing therapies. The public needs to be participate in this debate since well-over one hundred and twenty million Americans drink.

The goal of this book is to bring to the fore critical health findings from studies which frequently have been funded by government (our taxes) and private philanthropy. In equity, these data belong also to the public, not simply to medical managers. The research depicts drinks as basic foods which contribute to health in the very same manner as other common foods. This being so, Ellison raises a critical clinical question in "Should doctors prescribe wine?" He concludes this challenging speech with a vexing statement: *By failing to give such patients [those not at risk] scientifically sound, balanced advice about the potential health benefits of moderate use, as well as the adverse effects of excessive or inappropriate use, physicians may be doing their patients a disservice* (Ellison 1994). A daunting challenge to the entire medical system, a profession pledged to do no harm.

If sufficient numbers of physicians and parents come to understand these factors, they will demand better coverage of responsible drinking research. If we can achieve a thorough airing of all the research as it develops – without bias or blinders – common sense eventually will prevail.

One factor favoring the goal of better reportage of healthy drinking science lies in the movement in medicine known as Complementary and Alternative Medicine (CAM). The cover story in the December 2, 2002 issue of *Newsweek* explains why mainline medicine is now staging a rapprochement with various avenues of alternative medicine. Here's why: *Nearly half of all U.S. adults now go outside the health system for some of their care. We make more visits to non conventional healers (some 600 million a year) than we do to M.D.s and we spend more of our own money for the privilege – about $30 billion a year by recent estimates. Complementary and alternative medicine, or CAM, is not a single unified tradition. The term covers practices ranging from the credible (acupuncture, chiropractic) to the laughable (coffee enemas)* (Health for Life 2002). Simply put, traditional American medicine is recognizing an economic imperative to follow its customer base!

In *Nature Cures: The History of Alternative Medicine in America*, medical educator James Whorton, Ph.D. suggests: *What world medicine requires, in essence, is that ancient healing methods, and ancient healing philosophy, be recognized as amenable to modern science, and that will require a more liberal interpretation of science* (Whorton 2002). Whorton then quotes Rene Dubos: *Modern medicine will become really scientific only when physicians and their patients have learned to manage the forces of the body and the mind that operate vis medicatrix naturae.* With the "healing power of nature."

Consider healthy drinking in this "natural" context. There is no more widely used "ancient" or "natural" healer than alcohol. It's been in constant use for health since the dawn of hieroglyphics. And a good bit of unrecorded history before then.

Alcohol ambivalence is not the most important medical issue of our day. Far from it. Medical care costs, liability insurance for doctors, managed delivery systems, insurance coverage for the public, cloning and other really serious issues cloud the health care horizon. Even the massive promotion of pharmaceuticals in the media vexes medicine today. The top fifty drugs (Vioxx, Lipitor, Prevacid, Delebrex, Glucophage, etc.) account for thirty percent of all prescriptions. Advertising and promotion of these select labels leaped 18.8 percent in 2000 to a gross of almost $132 billion. A recent skit by satirist Garrison Keillor on "The Prairie Home Companion" ended with a prophetic and worrisome line, "Drugs are not just for sick people anymore." There is nothing illegal in these promotions but they do exacerbate the costs of clinical care by downgrading other effective lower cost alternatives. The trend certainly is a reflection of our opulent, media-focused, health culture.

But, compared to other medical issues, drinking ambivalence does impact the health of over 130 million American drinkers as well as many moderate abstainers who remain dry because of unwarranted fears. Yet this alcohol ambivalence could be so easily resolved. No additional legislation or bureaucracies needed. No health czars or sophisticated agency rulemaking required. Alcohol ambivalence would diminish gradually through unbiased reporting of what the scientists are finding. Open communication of the findings to clinical physicians and to the public without bias or overblown, anti-drinking rhetoric would do the trick. Communication's the thing.

One final caveat deserves brief mention. Guilt by association has strong roots in American society. We're a suspicious lot. I am frequently challenged, as example, of being a spokesperson for alcohol producers because of my abiding advocacy for responsible drinking. Similarly, the medical research enterprise is suspect by some because of dubious associations. Bekelman reported on potential financial conflicts in the funding of biomedical research in the *Journal of the American Medical Association*. The study notes with alarm that about one-fourth of researchers have: . . . *industry affiliations and roughly two-thirds of academic institutions hold equity in start-ups that sponsor research performed at those institutions* (Bekelman 2003). Medical authorities are justifiably concerned that some research outcomes could be tainted because of dependence upon industry funding.

However, no one, including the American Medical Association, raises similar cautions about the prohibitionary, *anti-drinking* influences of *government funding* on research outcomes. Which is quite enormous. Caution is warranted but professional journal standards – peer scrutiny and the requirement of replication before acceptance – provides rudimentary confidence in the research process. Business interests may share the dispassionate and noble aspirations of science in supporting biomedical research. Caution is warranted. Exclusion isn't.

With these few critical reservations stated, American medicine enjoyed a marvelous twentieth century. Despite its current care delivery issues, the U.S. is one of the best places on earth to seek relief from illness. Swartzberg cites the ultimate proof: *In the year 2000 the average life expectancy in the U.S. reached record levels: 74.1 years for men, 79.5 years for women. Just one hundred years ago, American men lived to age 46, on average, and women, 48* (Swartzberg 2002).

This book amply evidences Lucia's predictions – that, over the last century, epidemiology has substantiated a legitimate but cautious presence for responsible drinking in family life, in public health and in clinical medical practice.

Have a good read.

Gene Ford 2003

Chapter I

Angina Pectoris

Relief from upper body pain

■**Author's abstract.** Alcohol and other components in drinks perform several remarkable functions which temper the piercing pains of angina and lessen the risks for heart attacks. These contributions have been recognized for centuries by medical writers. Only recently have these benefits become common knowledge. Still, very little has been done to incorporate drinks into clinical therapy. This chapter identifies the following benefits in moderate drinking:

■➡ Reduces vascular disease by one-third
➡ Drinks reduce both angina pain and heart attacks
➡ Significantly reduces total mortality
➡ Lowers dangerous LDL cholesterol
➡ Produces serenity and tranquilizes

When California's noted disease prevention specialist S. P. Lucia, M.D. wrote the book *Wine as Food and Medicine* in 1954, this nation was expanding vastly its commitment to research in the health sciences. From his own extensive research, Lucia expected that over time biomedicine would categorize drinks containing alcohol as among nature's healthiest foods. Indeed, science has. In 1997, a half century later, Sir Richard Doll, M.D., one of Britain's leading cardiologists, asserted with confidence that:

> *The evidence for a beneficial effect is now massive. It includes not only a reduction of about a third in the risk for vascular diseases but also . . . a reduction in total mortality . . . People should be treated as adults and told the facts . . .*

Doll, R., One for the Heart, British Medical Journal, 315:1664-1668, 1997

In many books, articles and presentations, Lucia argued that drinks are good foods which serve as adjuvants to medicines – as agents that embellish the work of conventional medicines. The tempering of heart diseases, stroke and cancer over the last century shows how medicine has confronted infectious diseases and extended life span. As the life span increased, diseases of aging began to dominate. Cancer and heart disease are the great levelers today, as seen in this recent *U.S.A. Today* comparison of mortality causes in 1900 and 1994:

1900	1994
Pneumonia 11.7%	Heart Diseases 32.1%
Tuberculosis 11.3%	Cancer 23.5%
Diarrhea/Enteritis 8.3%	Stroke 6.9%
Heart Diseases 8.0%	Bronchitis/Empha. 4.5%
Stroke 6.2%	Injuries 3.9%
Liver Disease 5.1%	Pneumonia/Influ. 3.6%
Injuries 4.1%	Diabetes 2.4%
Cancer 3.7%	AIDS 1.8%
Senility 2.9%	Suicide 1.4%
Diphtheria 2.3%	Liver Diseases 1.1%

One factor should be absolutely clear to readers in this opening chapter. This book constitutes a survey of *favorable* drinking science concerning vascular diseases and twenty-three other health conditions. The goal is to balance one hundred years of anti-drinking propaganda with some good news. It is the good news that remains largely unknown. Hundreds of books and advisories stress the health problems related to abuse. In the Prologue and in many chapters there are examples of the failure of general medical publications to report favorable findings about drinking. This criticism is necessary to establish a prevailing pattern of neglect. But, happily, a trend developed around 2001 for medical newsletters to insert more positive drinking effects. Here are excerpts from two such articles. "Preventing Brain Attack" in the June 2001 issue of *Harvard Health Letter* discusses strokes with this concluding paragraph:

> *Alcohol: Moderate drinking, defined as up to two drinks per day, seems to offer protection against ischemic stroke. In small amounts, alcohol increases "good" HDL cholesterol and tissue plasminogen activator, a part of the blood that keeps clots from forming. High alcohol intake may, however, increase the risk for hemorrhagic stroke.*

Preventing Brain Attack, Harvard Health Letter, Vol. 26, No. 8, June, 2001

A sidebar in the June, 2001 issue of *Harvard Men's Health Watch* presents responsible drinking benefits for several health conditions found in the Netherlands Zutphen study:

> *Among the men with diabetes or heart disease, those who drank at low to moderate levels scored better than teetotalers . . . and showed no link with cognitive decline . . . the new Dutch study suggests that low-dose alcohol won't impair — and even may help —cognitive function, even in older men. Think twice before you drink up . . . . But if you have none of these worries, you can enjoy a drink or two without worrying about your ability to think straight. Bottoms up.*

Smoking, Drinking, and Thinking, Harvard Men's Health Watch, Vol. 5, No. 11, June, 2001

These discussions demonstrate an even-handed, dispassionate communication of both benefits and risks in drinking. If that was the prevailing approach in medicine today, there would be no need for this book. The reality is that alcohol drinks can be helpful or harmful in the etiology of a variety of diseases. Over the last four decades, epidemiology has confirmed many positive facets of moderate drinking. These data now constitute an impressive and distinct category of scientific literature. Yet outside of a smattering of books – most written by practicing physicians – there is little cohesive treatment of alcohol benefits in American popular literature. Even though this research, in Doll's words, is now "massive in scope."

Heart problems are the great levelers

Heart disease leads this parade because heart problems are universal, irrespective of age, social position, gender, geography, or educational status. Clogged arteries, hypertension, strokes and heart attacks impact a significant percentage of American families. The American Heart Association (AHA) estimates that in 1998 there were 12,400,000 citizens with coronary heart disease (CHD) (Heart and Stroke Statistical Update 2001). The report estimates: *Cardiovascular diseases account for about 950,000 deaths annually (about 41 percent of total mortality from all causes)*. In addition to mortality, strokes are America's leading cause of long-term disability. As will be seen, alcoholic drinks can help to reduce many of these risks.

Cardiologists have long recognized drinking's contributions to better heart health. In 1931, in the midst of Prohibition, Leary provided a lengthy analysis in *The New England Journal of Medicine* which argued the case for therapeutic drinking, specifically for patients suffering from vascular diseases:

> *The question before us is whether alcohol . . . would have a proper place in the Pharmacopoeia . . . . Only 6 percent of 283 cases of chronic and excessive alcoholism under 50 years of age showed any evidence of arteriosclerosis. . . . Alcohol has been used in medicine, as a food and as a drug . . . . From the food standpoint, alcohol has the advantage that it is, perhaps, the most readily oxidizable food substance we know. Sugar is its only rival. It is an efficient producer of energy, which can save fats and proteids (proteins). It may supply up to 30 or 40% of the caloric requirements of the body.*

Leary, T., The Therapeutic Value of Alcohol, New England Journal of Medicine 205: 231-242, 1931

Seventy years ago, Leary characterized drinks as inexpensive foods that could help control cardiovascular disease. He denounced the removal of alcohol from the *American Pharmacopoeia* of approved drugs during Prohibition. This needless action by federal authorities removed a long-established nostrum from the physician's armamentarium. Ironically, during the thirteen years of Prohibition, the only legal dispensation of drinks came through a doctor's prescription. In *Wine as Food and Medicine,* Lucia cites a long stream of historical medical research which buttressed Leary's heart-health premise:

> *Pons and Broeckaert (1909) state that the alcohol in wine can render incontestable service as a heart stimulant. Charcot (1899), Llagnet (1931), and Guillermin (1939) agree that generous wines in fractioned doses act as stimulants in serious diseases of the heart . . . . The eminent 18th century English physician, William Heberden (1768), was the first to recognize and advocate the beneficial effects of wine, cordials and cognac for the relief of the pain of angina pectoris.*

Lucia, S., Wine as Food and Medicine, The Blakiston Company, Inc. New York, 1954

In 1966, Leake and Silverman in *Alcoholic Beverages in Clinical Medicine* reiterated this theme: *We feel therefore that the use of whiskey or other spirituous liquors is indicated in the treatment of organic occlusive peripheral vascular diseases, among the most important of which is atherosclerosis. There is widespread agreement on this* (Leake 1966). If there was widespread agreement on "whiskey's" contributions to reducing atherosclerosis, why wasn't the public notified? These few historical references demonstrate that scientists have long recognized what is only now becoming known to the public one hundred years later — that drinks can reduce heart disease risk.

Angina — the heart's early warning system

Millions of adults have experienced the terror and agony of angina pain. It often occurs following a spate of intense physical strain — running to catch a bus, shoveling snow, skiing or playing a spirited game of tennis. The American Heart Association's *Heart and Stroke Facts* notes the following:

*Angina pectoris can be treated with drugs that affect
1) the supply of blood to the heart muscle or 2) the
heart's demand for oxygen . . . drugs called coronary
vasodilators cause blood vessels to relax . . . the
opening inside the vessels (the lumen) gets bigger.
Then blood flow improves, letting more oxygen and
nutrients to reach the heart.*

Heart and Stroke Facts, American Heart Association, Dallas, 1999

Angina pain signals evolving problems for the entire cardiovascular system — the heart, the arteries and the organs sustained by the bloodstream. Angina complaints are among the
most common in hospital emergency rooms. It is estimated that
over five million emergency visits originate in angina pains.
Heart and Stroke Facts explains atherosclerosis — the reason for
most angina discomfort:

*Atherosclerosis affects large and medium-sized
arteries . . . (it) is a slow, progressive disease that
may start in childhood. In some people, it progresses
rapidly in their third decade. In others, it doesn't
become threatening until they're in their fifties or
sixties.*

Heart and Stroke Facts, American Heart Association, Dallas, 1999

Two conclusions can be taken from these data. First, by the
time angina strikes, a damaging plaque build-up and arterial
narrowing has already occurred in the blood vessels. Second,
dietary practices, including the consumption of alcohol, can
help prevent the build-up of plaque over an entire lifetime. The
French, Italians, Germans and other daily-drinking populations
enjoy lower rates of heart disease partially because alcohol helps
to keep the blood vessel walls clean and supple.

The dry lobby insists that drinking is an adult function. The
fact that drinks affect arteries in all age categories presents a
major hurdle to acceptance of drinks as foods by the dry lobby.
Unfortunately, drink producers and retailers have failed to challenge this campaign to deny access to supervised youth consumption. Yielding to dry lobby pressure, Congress voted to
withhold highway funding from states which refused to legislate

twenty-one as the age for legal purchase. Wyoming fought this mandate to the Supreme Court but lost because the Court ruled that Congress could allocate public health funding for the common good. The decision did not contravene Repeal's constitutional amendment noting that Wyoming could retain eighteen for drinking, but it would have to suffer the loss of critical highway funding as a consequence. No state could long suffer loss in highway funding. This was Congressional extortion.

A recent issue of *Harvard Men's Health Watch* carried an article titled "Coronary Artery Disease: A Lifelong Process." An illustration in the article demonstrates how the clogging of arteries begins between the ages of ten and twenty. Lesions are already forming in arteries of teen-agers that will presage heart problems at ages forty and above.

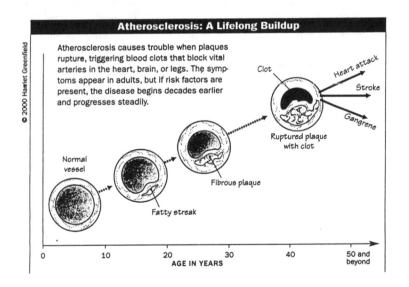

Permission to reprint granted by Harvard Health Publications from Coronary Artery Disease: A Lifelong Building in the February 2000 issue of Harvard Men's Health Watch.

By the age of twenty, fatty streaks can be found in healthy young arteries. By age thirty, fibrous plaques are common and, by the fourth decade, the plaque frequently ruptures into life-threatening blood clots. The article's text notes: *The symptoms appear in adults, but if risk factors are present, the disease begins decades earlier and progresses steadily . . . . Children don't get heart attacks, but they can begin to develop the early stages of atherosclerosis. Over the years the disease grows silently . . . atherosclerosis itself is slow, developing over years – and it often begins in childhood* (Coronary Artery Disease: A Life Long Process 2000). Tuzcu confirmed these findings in a study of 262 heart transplants at the Cleveland Clinic: *This study demonstrates that coronary atherosclerosis begins at a young age and that lesions are present in 1 of 6 teen-agers. These findings suggest the need for intensive efforts at coronary disease prevention in young adults* (Tuzcu 2001). These findings do not imply, nor does this book, that youth drinking is the one and only antidote to youth onset of atherosclerosis. But the findings in this and several chapters do suggest that moderate drinking could help resist its onset through life. Shouldn't physicians and mothers in alcohol consuming families be made aware of this positive factor? When used as a food with meals, wine may be the reason why the French have less heart disease than we do.

The article closes with a quote from William Wordsworth, *"The child is father of the man." Atherosclerosis often begins early in life, but it can also be prevented in childhood.* Is this one answer to the puzzling French Paradox? French youth drink at very early ages. It's certainly part of the answer. Should we re-examine our rigid adherence to discouraging drinking until twenty-one for the very same reason it is being denied – public health? Does delayed drinking establish a lethal proclivity that could be tempered by a balanced diet including judicious use of wine, beer and spirits? These are not idle questions. These are reasonable health issues.

The cholesterol factor

Most Americans today understand the need to moderate consumption of cholesterol-loaded fats. Cholesterol is discussed in greater detail in the following chapter on atherosclerosis. In relation to angina, recognize that two major cholesterols are critical to arterial health – high density lipoprotein (HDL) and low density lipoprotein (LDL). LDL cholesterol routinely transports the chemicals required for body cell building. Following cell replenishment duties, LDL cholesterol discards excess materials directly into the bloodstream. That dumping is the problem.

However, LDL's counterpart, HDL cholesterol, circulates through the vascular system performing as a vascular vacuum cleaner. HDL gathers up much of the insoluble detritus cast aside by LDL and transports it to the liver and other organs for elimination. This is why physicians strive to lower concentrations of LDL to a healthy level while looking to elevate the HDL. Remarkably, alcohol helps the body to achieve both goals. Drinks also contribute to heart health by reducing plaque formation and enhancing blood flow. These contributions combine to help reduce angina pain.

Harvard Medical School scientists have conducted many informative studies from data derived from the famous Physician's Health Study which involved thousands of male medical professionals from across the nation. Camargo compared nondrinking doctors with other physicians who consumed alcoholic drinks at various levels up to two drinks daily.

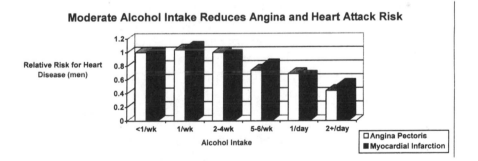

Illustration reprinted with permissions of the Wine Institute based on original source material from the Annals of Internal Medicine, Table 2, Camargo et al., Moderate Alcohol Consumption on the Risk for Angina Pectoris and Myocardial Infarction, 126:372, 1997. The American College of Physicians/American Society of Internal Medicine is not responsible for the translation of data.

Myocardial infarction is a medical term for a heart attack. In all research, an "inverse relationship" means less incidence of the problem. Camargo found that imbibing physicians enjoyed a decline in both angina pain and heart attacks as the number of drinks increased up to two-plus daily. These data link significant reductions of risk for two major heart conditions directly to alcohol consumption. His analysis concluded: *In this large, prospective study of U.S. male physicians, alcohol consumption had strong, independent, inverse associations with the risk of angina pectoris and myocardial infarction.*

Alcohol is not the only food contributor to vascular health. Many foods combine with physical exercise to moderate angina pain and to lower the incidence of heart attacks. Nor is alcohol a unique contributor to good cholesterol management. "Diet and Cholesterol: Foods that Help" in the August 1998 issue of *Harvard Men's Health Watch* notes: . . . *the result of 38 independent trials involving 730 subjects found that eating soy protein lowers blood cholesterol . . . fiber is not absorbed by humans, but . . . it has plenty of health value, reducing the risk of heart disease, diabetes, colon cancer, diverticulitis, hemorrhoids, hernias and other common ailments . . . Alcohol is not for everyone. but if you can use it properly − and if you enjoy it − you can improve your cholesterol with 1-2 drinks a day* (Diet and cholesterol 1998). Soy protein contributes. So do drinks. This research confirms drinks as good foods.

Other contributions of alcohol to the circulatory system include the reduction of arterial spasm from stress, an increase in blood flow as alcohol dilates or expands arterial walls, a reduction in blood pressure, a reduction in plasma insulin and an increase in plasma estrogen in females. Quite a combination of benefits from a byproduct of fermented fruit and grain!

The feel-good factor

Lucia stresses the unique role of drinks in uplifting the spirits of an ill person. Not only do drinks taste better than pills, but they initiate a sense of well-being, a precursor for recovery and rehabilitation. Doctors know that patients often neglect to take prescribed drugs. Avorn studied 7,287 patients in New Jersey's Medicaid program and found: *In both populations, patients failed to fill prescriptions for lipid-lowering drugs for about 40 percent of the study year* (Avorn 1998). If a daily brace of beer, scotch or wine can "fill-in" to some degree for those oft-forgotten cholesterol pills, the patient will benefit in two ways − in reduced pain and better spirits.

How a patient *feels* about any medicine (and perhaps how much he or she fears its after-effects) plays a part in both usage and effect. Placebo studies have demonstrated this. Modern medicine's concentration on drug therapy slights the efficacy of measures that uplift a patient's emotions. Feel-good products – coffee, drinks, candy and truffles – have supporting roles to play in good health. Lucia notes: *As a preventive agent, the main function of alcohol is to induce serenity by producing tranquilization* (Lucia 1971). Alcohol's benign role as a natural tranquilizer was stricken from American medical practice during the Prohibition epoch. Of course, many physicians continue to utilize drinks in therapy, but it is not a formally approved clinical practice.

Gender differences in angina pain

Sarah Speck, M.D., chief of cardiology at Seattle's Swedish Hospital, cautions against the assumption found in many early studies that men and women experience the same symptoms. Early studies had exclusively male participants. Speck notes in a hospital bulletin: *One of the most common symptoms of heart disease in men is angina – a heavy pressure in the chest when they physically exert themselves. But women with heart disease often experience other symptoms, including chest pain not associated with exercise, a rapid or irregular heartbeat, and persistent shortness of breath* (Speck 1998).

Because women have less challenging symptoms, they often arrive at emergency care facilities several hours later on average than men – critical hours for treatment of acute heart conditions. Contemporary cardiovascular studies include both men and women and the statistics and analyses are gender specific. It is important to distinguish, as Lucia did, between dietary and medicinal effects of drinks. British medical writer Stuttaford illustrates drinking's history as an angina adjuvant:

> *The famous eighteenth-century physician, Dr. Heberden, noticed in 1772 that a "nightcap" prevented nocturnal angina, but it was two hundred years before the effect of alcohol on this condition was scientifically investigated. In 1956, the Journal of the American Medical Association carried an account by Dr. Russek of experiments in which a*

couple of double whiskeys were compared with
nitroglycerin as preventers of angina.

Stuttaford, T., To Your Good Health! The Wise Drinker's Guide, Faber & Faber, London, 1997

Stuttaford noted that whiskey helped dilate constrained arteries thereby relieving some pain, but the prescribed nitro was more effective medically since it both relieved pain and helped restore normal electrocardiogram tracings. Drinks are best considered as foods that complement medicines.

Which drinks work best

All types of drinks can be effective for angina pectoris. However, anyone on a drug regimen should check with a doctor or a pharmacist before mixing alcohol with any prescribed or over-the-counter angina drugs.

The same issue of *Epidemiology* which revealed that aspirin helped to reduce the risk of heart attacks carried an editorial by Ellison suggesting that, tongue-in-cheek: . . . *a person might want to consider the advantage of washing down his aspirin with a glass of cabernet* (Ellison 1991). However, some support for Ellison's wry advice is found in Camargo's angina study: . . . *additive effects in reducing coronary heart disease when both alcohol and aspirin are taken regularly* (Camargo 1997).

The British medical text cited in the Prologue concludes: *The protective effect appears to be due to alcohol itself, and there is little basis to expect one particular beverage to be more effective than another* (Macdonald 1999). Varied findings about specific beverages and ideal numbers of drinks are found in the following chapters. Keep in mind that each study characterizes a specific population of individuals. The bottom line is that there is support in cardiovascular research for a wide range of daily drink (See Chapter 31).

Next we look to the root cause of angina and other unhealthy cardiovascular conditions – clogged arteries.

Chapter 2

Atherosclerosis

Fewer arterial problems

■ **Author's abstract:** We see compelling evidence in this chapter that moderate drinking can significantly lessen the incidence of clogged arteries. This health contribution was well-known fifty years ago. Despite this worthwhile advantage in fighting America's greatest health problem, only about sixty-five percent of Americans drink compared to more than ninety percent in France. This per capita disparity illustrates a serious medical communication problem.

■ ➥ Atherosclerotic build-up starts in childhood
   ➥ Daily alcohol intake reduces plaque build-up through life
   ➥ Moderate intake lowers the bad (LDL) cholesterol
   ➥ More antioxidants than in vitamins C, E and beta-carotene
   ➥ Some wines contain aspirin-like compounds
   ➥ Beer provides folates and B complex vitamins
   ➥ All types of drinks fight atherosclerosis

From a consideration of angina pains we move to an evaluation of "hardened" arteries. Arteries stiffen in two ways. First, as a natural process in aging called *arteriosclerosis*. As we age, arterial walls become less resilient. A second cause of "hardened" arteries is the accumulation of plaque deposits which form inside blood vessel walls, narrowing the opening, much as rust does in water pipes. These accumulations gradually narrow the inside diameter of the artery through which blood flows. The accumulation of plaque – often caused by dietary excess – is called *atherosclerosis.*

Harvard Men's Health Watch provides this concise definition:

Atherosclerosis is the disease that damages coronary arteries, causing heart attacks. It's the same disease that can affect arteries carrying blood to the brain or the legs, causing strokes or leg pain and gangrene. Usually explained as "hardening of the arteries," it's actually much more. The doctors who named the disease many years ago knew that sclerosis comes from the Greek for "hardening," but "athere" is derived from the word for "porridge." In fact, arteries with the disease accumulate a mushy, gruel-like material in their walls before they become stiff and hard.

Harvard Men's Health Watch, Vol. 2, No. 7, February, 1998

So atherosclerosis constitutes "porridge-clogged" arteries formed largely from the detritus of LDL – low density lipoproteins. In "The Good, the Bad and What's Healthy," *Harvard Health Letter* explains the contribution of HDL, often called the "good" cholesterol: *Cholesterol is a lipid, a form of fat. In the bloodstream, it comes packaged with proteins to form lipoproteins . . . this slippery, macro-molecular bundle . . . HDL earned the "good" moniker because it seems to scoop up excess cholesterol from blood vessels and deposits it in the liver. HDL eventually ends up in feces* (The Good, the Bad 1999).

In addition to narrowing the arteries and restricting blood flow, accumulating plaque tends to expand and work its way into the arterial inner walls. *Heart and Stroke Statistical Update* notes: *These cells accumulate and many of them divide . . . The endothelium becomes markedly thickened by these accumulating cells and the surrounding materials* (Heart and Stroke 1999). As the arterial walls narrow, the heart becomes less efficient.

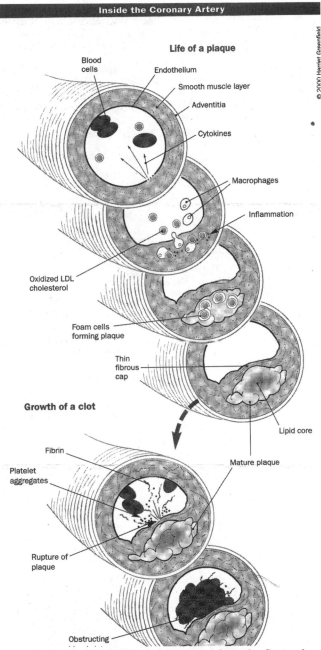

Inside the Coronary Artery

Life of a plaque

Blood cells
Endothelium
Smooth muscle layer
Adventitia
Cytokines
Macrophages
Inflammation
Oxidized LDL cholesterol
Foam cells forming plaque
Thin fibrous cap
Lipid core

© 2000 Harriet Greenfield

Growth of a clot

Fibrin
Platelet aggregates
Mature plaque
Rupture of plaque
Obstructing

Reprinted with permission and excerpted from the September 2000 issue of Harvard Men's Health Watch, Copyright 2000, President and Fellows of Harvard College

Think of the heart as the body's most efficient muscle. This central organ of existence is a tireless, faithful workhorse. It contracts over 100,000 times each and every day pumping nearly 2,000 gallons of blood. In a span of seventy years, the heart will beat over 2.5 billion times sending the very stuff of life coursing through the arterial system.

Drinking reduces atherosclerosis

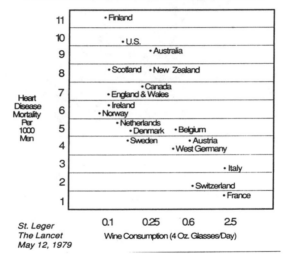

Heart Disease Rates in 18 Western Countries

This table is reprinted with permission of the Wine Institute and by The Lancet. Taken from St. Leger, et al., Factors Associated with Cardiac Mortality in Developed Countries with Particular Reference to the Consumption of Wine, The Lancet, Vol. 1:1016-1017,1979

Two benchmark studies released in the late 1970s show how nations with food-integrated drinking practices experience less cardiovascular disease. If governments and medicine are interested in lowering atherosclerosis, three decades of international studies should be accorded more serious consideration. The first of these major studies by St. Leger gathered data from eighteen nations. Finland, the U.S. and Australia — all alcohol ambivalent cultures — had the lowest consumption rates and the highest heart mortality rates. The best heart death rates were in France, Switzerland and Italy, all alcohol-integrated nations.

A mortality advantage for the drinking-integrated cultures can be seen in St. Leger's table. In this pioneer study, the authors were testing the hypothesis that wine drinking had a benevolent impact on heart disease. The study was among the first to recognize the U- and J-shaped curves which portray less coronary illness among moderate drinkers than both abstainers and abusers: *The analysis showed a J-shaped curve relationship between total mortality and alcohol drinking and a U-shaped curve for coronary heart mortality* (St. Leger 1979).

Many researchers utilize J- or U- shaped curves in their studies to demonstrate the preferential health status of moderate drinkers compared to heavy users and abstainers. De Lorimier explains: . . . *those who consume varying amounts of alcohol are compared to teetotalers or abstainers, who are assigned a relative risk of 1. Those who consume beverage alcohol in moderation have a 30-50% lower risk of overall mortality than abstainers, but those who drink excessively develop a mortality risk greater than abstainers* (de Lorimier 2000).

The findings in St. Leger's eighteen nation study were confirmed in La Porte's multi-nation survey which found that nations with daily drinking populations experienced less heart disease. La Porte evaluated also the daily levels of consumption to determine which levels of intake provided the greatest protection against heart disease: . . . *because alcohol may have a very different physiological effect at a daily intake of .02 oz as compared with 1 or 2 oz* (La Porte 1980). Both of these international surveys confirmed that nations which incorporated drinking into daily dietary customs had notably less cardiovascular disease. The next step was to explore the underlying biochemical mechanisms through which drinks might contribute to healthier hearts. Dozens of major studies have addressed that premise since 1980.

Cholesterol

Alcohol was identified as both raising the beneficial HDL and lowering destructive levels of LDL which deposit plaque. Maserei found: *Mean levels of triglyceride, HDL cholesterol . . . were higher at the end of the normal range (of alcohol consumption) compared with low alcohol periods, and levels of LDL cholesterol were lower*

(Maserei 1986). Suh was even more confident after studying 11,688 men who consumed drinks at various levels: *This finding provides strong evidence that HDL is a causal mechanism in explaining moderate alcohol's protection against coronary heart disease* (Suh 1992). High levels of HDL were found to be a positive factor in many studies.

These studies do not single out drinks as the only, or even the best, foods for the control of cholesterol levels. An article in the May 2000 issue of *HealthNews,* for example, reports that walnuts and pecans help to lower bad cholesterol: *Long considered a high-fat indulgence, nuts may deserve a bigger role in the diet* (Lower Your LDL 2000). Many other foods contribute to good cholesterol balance. Even candy? The Mars candy company notes that some of its bars are specially handled to "preserve their natural goodness." The company's web site notes the presence of polyphenols among the bar's natural goodness (Chocolate: The Next Health Food 2000).

A ten year study in the *Journal of the American Medical Association* reports that women who consumed twenty-two grams of fiber a day had a forty-seven percent lower risk of a heart attack. Many food labels now cite levels of fiber, polyphenols (antioxidants) and folate for consumer attention. Be aware that natural foods consumed in a varied diet seem to provide better protection than do these same elements taken as food supplements.

Be aware also that reports such as a recent study by Brown which occasioned the following misleading headline in the *Seattle Post Intelligencer* "Anti-oxidants may hinder some drugs." The article summarized research by Brown in the *New England Journal of Medicine* which concluded that the use of supplemental vitamins: . . . *may blunt the benefits of statins and niacin, which are used to lower LDL, the bad form of cholesterol, and raise HDL, the good kind of cholesterol that keeps the arteries flowing smoothly* (Brown 2001). There was nothing wrong with the research, aside from a relatively small base of participants. The headline and article failed to distinguish between supplemental antioxidants and naturally occurring dietary antioxidants. Alcoholic drinks definitely qualify among the better natural food sources of antioxidants and there was no evidence of beer, wine, leafy vegetable and tea antioxidants blunting the effects of Zocor, Pravachol or

Lipitor. No one is suggesting that Zocor takers lay off vegetables and fruits rich in antioxidants. In "Can antioxidants save your life?" *UC Berkeley Wellness Letter* notes: *Antioxidants are part of the chemistry of life, not something in a bottle that can miraculously prevent or cure disease. The best place to find them is in food, and in the two vitamin supplements we recommend − C and E* (Can antioxidants 1998). Look for a direct comparison of the impact of drinks and vitamin E later.

An article in *HealthNews* reports that: *Eating foods rich in folic acid and vitamins B6 and B12 (such as green leafy vegetables, oranges, and bananas can also lower homocysteine . . . . Despite mounting evidence, we don't yet have enough data to support the theory that folic acid, in the diet or in supplements, prevents cardiovascular disease* (Homocysteine 2000). While the antioxidant research horizon is still relatively new, no one contests the idea that foods are excellent sources of many antioxidants even though there is uncertainty about whether and how they are adapted. For this reason, the author concludes: *It is reasonable, however, to eat a low-fat diet rich in fruits and vegetables* (Homocysteine 2000).

Typically, this and similar articles routinely fail to mention drinks while discussing food sources of antioxidants. This is a major part of the communication problem. In most nutrition publications, drinks are non-factors. Still, the research literature abounds in presumptive evidence favoring drinks. In Italy, Ghiselli reports that: *These findings indicate that beer, which has a moderate antioxidant capacity combined with low alcohol content, improves plasma antioxidant capacity without negative effects* (Ghiselli 2000). In a decade long series of studies in Denmark, Gronbaek identified chemical contributions in wines apart from the alcohol: *Wine intake may have beneficial effects on all-cause mortality that is additive to that of alcohol . . . attributable to a reduction in death from both coronary heart disease and cancer* (Gronbaek 2000). These favorable commentaries seen routinely in the professional literature seldom appear in medical articles on various diseases which target the public. That's why it's necessary in this book to provide so many examples of omission. Not only is the public unaware of most healthy drinking findings but practicing physicians are similarly uninformed. There has been improvement in recent years in the medical newsletters but the information gulf remains wide and deep.

McConnell shows how regular daily drinking markedly raises HDL: *We tested the effects of a single, daily alcohol beverage . . . Our data indicated that the consumption of a single, daily alcoholic beverage for 6 weeks is associated with a significant increase in HDL and HDL₂* (McConnell 1997). Gaziano concurs: *. . . moderate alcohol consumption cuts heart attack risk by half by increasing both HDL₃ and HDL₂* (Gaziano 1993). While the studies clearly support daily drinking, an article printed as late as August 1999 in *Harvard Women's Health Watch* titled "Coronary Heart Disease: New Guidelines for Prevention" warned against drinking more than an arbitrary daily limit but mentioned none of drinking's benefits: *Limit daily alcohol intake to 4 ounces of wine, 12 ounces of beer, or 1 1/2 ounces of 80 proof spirits* (Coronary Heart Disease 1999). This bare, spare statement illustrates a disingenuous indifference about benefits in daily moderate intake coupled with a strong interest in limiting consumption.

The defining line in cholesterol science is stated by Rimm: *Alcohol intake is causally related to lower risk of coronary heart disease through changes in lipids and haemostatic factors* (Rimm 1999). Rimm concludes that alcohol consumption is a *causal* factor influencing better heart health. Popular medical articles should identify this factor, not just for heart disease but for the other diseases reported in this book.

Other biomedical constituents in drinks

While medical jargon is kept to a minimum in these pages, the prevalence of heart disease has familiarized the public with many important heart disease terms. Here are comments on some of the most important of these descriptors. In addition to the effects of ethanol (ethyl alcohol), researchers evaluate the impact of many other constituents in drinks that could explain their contributions to heart health. The problem in biochemical research lies not in identifying the presence of these chemicals but in sorting out which sources contribute which specific benefits. Remember that many other foods in a balanced diet provide similar constituents. An article in the November 23, 1998 *Time* magazine makes the point that many medicinal drugs are, or were originally, herb-borne:

> *An estimated 25 percent of all modern pharmaceutical drugs are derived from herbs, including aspirin (from white willow bark); the heart medication digitalis (foxglove); and the cancer treatment Taxol (Pacific yew tree). There might have been no sexual revolution without the birth-control pill, derived from a Mexican yam.*

The Herbal Medicine Boom, Time, November 23, 1998

Since drinks are among the most chemically complex of potable foods, the notion of residual health benefits makes perfect sense. A *Harvard Health Letter* article comments on the role of flavonoids: *Some researchers refer not to flavonoids but to polyphenols, which include compounds that are, in effect, several flavonoids strung together. Tannin, often discussed as a key health-conferring ingredient of red wine, is an example of a polyphenol. . . . How good is the evidence? In a word, lukewarm. Most of the research comes from cell cultures or animal experiments. It's always a leap to apply such findings to people . . . . In the absence of clear harm, you might as well bet on the chance that flavonoids are good for you* (Flavonoids 2000). It is important for science to keep an open – but firmly skeptical – mind. Here are brief explanations of terms that will be helpful.

The platelet factor: An article in *Practical Winery & Vineyard* describes platelets: *Heart attacks occur when platelets adhere to the roughened lining of a damaged blood vessel, forming an obstructive plug which then becomes solidified into a blood clot . . . Ethanol has a suppressing effect on local tissue factors that cause this clotting* (Wine and the heart 1994). Langer studied men of Japanese descent in the Honolulu Heart Program and concluded: *. . . about half of the protection against CHD by moderate alcohol consumption is mediated by an increase in high density lipoprotein (HDL). An additional 18% of this protection is attributable to a decrease in low density lipoprotein (LDL) cholesterol . . . The explanation for the residual 5% benefit attributable to alcohol is unknown but may include interference with thrombosis (blood clot) (Langer 1992).*

Fruit and Wine, Total Phenolics

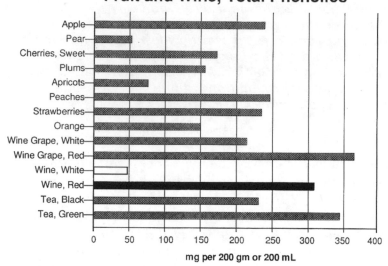

mg per 200 gm or 200 mL

Juices and Wine, Total Phenolics

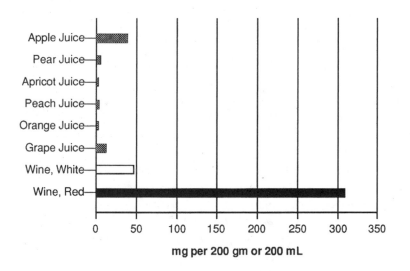

mg per 200 gm or 200 mL

Graphs reprinted with permission of Andrew L. Waterhouse, Ph.D., University of California, Davis

The antioxidant factor: As seen in the phenolic charts, antioxidants originate in many fruits, also in nuts and vegetables. At the University of California, Davis, Waterhouse isolated various levels of phenolic compounds (antioxidants). He found apples, peaches, strawberries and red and white grapes excellent phenolic sources, along with red wine.

Antioxidants flourish also in green and black teas. However, note in the second graph that when the raw fruits are processed into commercial juices, many lose much of their polyphenol potency. Red wine is one of the most potent final product sources of these important phenolics on the grocery shelf. In "How a Tonic Keeps the Parts Well Oiled," Zuger notes: *The antioxidant activity in a glass of red wine equals that in 7 glasses of orange juice or 20 of apple juice . . . Some white wines and dark beers have the same antioxidant activity* (How a Tonic 2002).

None of the medical newsletters followed by this author have referenced a comparison of wine's rich source of phenolics and antioxidants with other processed fruits and vegetables. Waterhouse cautiously notes that more research is needed to determine their physiological impact of these components: . . . *no one has yet confirmed that the consumption of these phenolic antioxidants, whether they are in wine, apples or strawberries, will affect your health. However, it is our hypothesis that the consumption of these compounds will explain the "French Paradox"* (Waterhouse 1994). However, every medical and nutrition source touts the consumption of fruits and leafy vegetables for good health. Why omit grape wine, one of the best sources?

Questions are raised frequently in the popular media about the efficacy of taking *antioxidant supplements* (pills) compared to consuming antioxidants in natural foods. In the April 2000 issue of *Harvard Men's Health Watch* a piece titled "Antioxidant Supplements and the Heart: What Went Wrong" comments on the results of thirteen studies. The author addresses a range of negative findings for heart disease prevention: *Just a few years ago, antioxidant pills were the rising stars in the fight against heart disease, but now they appear headed for the dustbin of history* (Antioxidant Supplements and the Heart: What Went Wrong? 2001). The author speculates on the many sources of antioxidants: . . . *the apparent protection in the observational studies may have depended*

*on subtle lifestyle factors rather than the antioxidants. Or the apparent
benefit may have depended on a combination of nutrients in fruits and
vegetables* (Homocysteine 2000).

Scientists do not yet know for certain how, or how many,
antioxidants impact the heart and other organs. There is speculation but no consensus. For this reason, authorities continue to
recommend diets which include fruits and vegetables, along
with wines, beers, tea, and fitness lifestyle practices. All of these
foods work together to effect the lowered health risks.

A 2001 report in *Nature* finds that polyphenols inhibit the
production of a peptide which contributes to atherosclerosis.
The study included measurements of twenty-three red wines,
four white wines and one red grape juice. The homogeneity of
the food properties in drinks is lost when disease commentaries
fail to include these tangible contributions. Many articles encourage consumption of fruits and vegetables but avoid mention
of wines, beers and tea. Yet, Gorinstein notes: *Red wine is richer
in total polyphenols than both white wine and beer, and beer has higher
levels of procyanidins, epicatechin and ferulic acid than white wine*
(Gorinstein 2000). Agewall finds: *These results support the hypothesis that it is the antioxidant properties of red wine that protect against
cardiovascular disease* (Agewall 2000). Comparing wine's antioxidants to other fruits, Bagchi writes: *Our studies show that activin
is a more potent antioxidant than vitamins C, E and betacarotene – up
to seven times more potent* (Bagchi 1997). Plant and alcohol antioxidants are not uniform crop to crop, year to year. Each bottle
of wine and each head of broccoli depend upon unique contributions derived from specific harvests. The thing to remember
is that a balanced diet including many fruits, vegetables – and
moderate drinking, if that is a proper choice – will provide a
diverse variety of health enhancing antioxidants.

Frankel in 1993 conducted a laboratory study concerning the
effect of wine phenols compared to vitamin E. The graph below
compares the impact of three common wine antioxidants– quercetin, epicatechin and resveratrol – with vitamin E. This is
fascinating data since Frankel found that wine's antioxidant
properties were up to seven times more potent than the popular
and fairly expensive E vitamin supplements. In this laboratory
test, where the Vitamin E levels off, quercetin, epicatechin and

resveratrol from wine continue to show impact up to four and
five times that of the E vitamin.

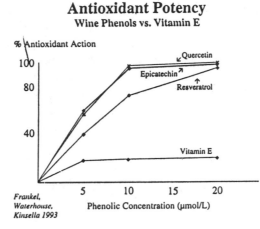

Reprinted with permission by The Lancet, Ltd. , Frankel, Waterhouse and Kindles,
The Lancet, Inhibition of Human Oxidation by Resveratrol, 341, April 24, 1993

It is very difficult to assess the degree of favorable response
occurring within the human body. But certainly this kind of
comparative evidence is worthy of mention in articles that speak
to the role of antioxidants in human nutrition.

Over 120 million Americans drink and many thousands relig-
iously ingest vitamin E. But there is little recognition of the fact
that there can be higher antioxidant concentrations in fermented wines than in the original grapes. Demrow found that
both red wine and grape juice were rich in antioxidants: *However, it took three times as much grape juice by volume to achieve the
same protective effect* (Demrow 1995). A 2001 study compared
polyphenols from 23 red wines, four white wines and a pink
wine as well as grape juice. The authors found that red wine
extract can suppress synthesis of a vasoconstrictor peptide (ET-
1) which indicates that: . . . *moderate consumption of red wine can
prevent CHD* (coronary heart disease) (Corder 2001). The
authors find this activity independent of any potential antioxidant impacts. The red wine was markedly more effective than

grape juice indicating a positive contribution in the fermentation process.

Yet, Keevil finds: *Purple grape juice may prevent the development and progression of coronary artery disease* (Keevil 2000). The question is not either/or but that some support should be shown for grapes and wine. Antioxidants have become so important in food processing that Canandaigua Winery formed a subsidiary called Polyphenolics, Inc. which produces and sells antioxidants from grape seeds. These additives go into many everyday products including nutritional supplements. While the research may question the impact of additives, there remains a large market for them.

In a paper on the role of polyphenols in beer oxidation, Pengelly notes: *An increasingly health conscious public is looking for foods and food supplements that provide antioxidants . . . In beer, there has been particular interest in prenyl-flavonoids, such as xanthohumol, a polyphenol from hops that has been shown in vitro to have many potential benefits* (Pengelly 2002).

Some studies even question the emphasis on vitamin E in over-the-counter vitamin regimens. "Vitamins under attack" in the *UC Berkeley Wellness Letter* recommends: *Take 200 to 400 IUs of vitamin supplements per day . . . It is possible that antioxidant supplements, unlike the nutrients in foods, may impact the antioxidant balance in the body* (Vitamins under attack 1998). The newsletter recommends daily consumption even though some upset might occur. "Vitamin E: E for Exaggerated?" appeared in the March 2000 issue of *Harvard Health Letter*. It notes: *Moreover, several such randomized studies have shown vitamin E wanting in terms of preventing heart disease . . . vitamin E needs to be taken with other vitamins to be effective* (Vitamin E 2000). In contrast, Bertelli found that: *. . . even an average drinker of wine can, particularly in the long term, absorb a sufficient quantity of resveratrol to explain the beneficial effect of red wine on health* (Bertelli 1998). "Antioxidant Overhaul" in *HealthNews* reports on side effects of overuse of supplements, noting: *The Institute says the best sources of these nutrients are foods such as citrus fruits, potatoes, and leafy green vegetables for vitamin D; nuts, seeds, and leafy greens for vitamin E; and seafood, meats, and grains for selenium* (Antioxidant Overhaul 2000). No mention of drinks.

Alcohol by itself is a pro-oxidant but the various phenols and nutrients contained in many drinks definitely qualify as antioxidants. The above article fails to mention drinks among good food sources of antioxidants. It does stress the importance of good dietary practices. Why not inform the moderate drinking public— about two-thirds of American adults— of these positive contributions to their well-being? That's a core issue of this book. Finally, while most of the above research concentrates on wine and beer polyphenols, *UC Berkeley Wellness Letter* reports on a Canadian study which found: . . . *martinis have much more antioxidant capacity than either gin or vermouth alone* (Shaken, not stirred? 2000). Surprised? In their processing, gin and vermouth are steeped in many herbals rich in natural antioxidants.

The free radical factor: A position paper by the Distilled Spirits Council defines the potential mischief of free radicals: *Chemicals that can accept an electron are known as oxidants (or free radicals). . . . produced normally in biologic processes and, because they are highly reactive, are thought to be involved in cellular injury and aging. Antioxidants are chemical compounds that can modify the effects of oxidants, possibly protecting the body from their effects. . . . Examples of flavonoids include quercetin, kaempferol, myricetin, apigenin and luteolin* (Distilled Spirits Council 1995). Oxidants are destructive chemicals which occur naturally in human biology. Natural foods, vitamins, drinks and health supplements all provide antioxidants that act to neutralize the destructive impacts of free radicals.

This is hardly a revelation. As early as 1968, Cambon attributed the elimination of free radicals in the body to wine. He noted: . . . *wine seems to be a most useful adjunct to treatment since it is a vasodilator, a diuretic and a tranquilizer . . . Moreover, the anthocyanins are closely related to flavonoids which have enjoyed some reputation in the treatment of Meniere's disease. A glass or two with the evening meal and again before retiring seems sufficient* (Cambon 1968). The antioxidative benefits of drinks were recognized in research a half century ago.

The aspirin (acetylsalicylic acid) factor: Few readers would associate wine with aspirin but a relationship is strong and persuasive in research. The public health establishment and medicine now promote an aspirin every-other-day for heart health. This practice grew from data gathered in the Physician's Health Study. Muller suggests that cardiac wellness is attributable in some degree to synergistic effects of ethanol and drink antioxidants including salicylic acid: . . . *significant concentration of salicylic acid is found in several California wines* (Muller 1994). Salicylic acid is a primary component of aspirin. One more healthy component resident in some wines.

The triglyceride factor: Blood analyses often include a reading of the level of triglycerides (TG). These are lipids similar to cholesterol. TGs are the most abundant fats in food. Some are manufactured in the liver and stored in the body as usable energy. However, an excess of TG is a marker for heart trouble. "Understanding Your Triglyceride Levels" in *Johns Hopkins Health After 50* notes: *One of the most recent efforts, the Copenhagen Male Study, divided 2,906 older men with no history of heart disease into three groups based on their TG levels. After eight years, there was a clear, direct relationship between high TG and incidence of heart disease* (Understanding Your Triglycerides 1999). These lipid levels rise and fall normally in the body and are best controlled by moderating fat intake and maintaining good exercise patterns.

While alcohol is thought to increase triglyceride levels, in Great Britain, Razay studied 1,048 women aged twenty-five to sixty and reported: *Compared with non-drinkers, women consuming a moderate amount of alcohol (1-29 g/day) had lower plasma concentrations of triglycerides, cholesterol, and insulin and a lower body mass index. They also had higher concentrations of high density lipoprotein cholesterol* (Razay 1992). Reduced triglyceride levels could be yet another drinking benefit for some individuals.

The fibrinogen factor: Mennen writes: *Fibrinogen is another risk indicator for cardiovascular disease (CVD), . . . stroke and peripheral artery disease . . . Some studies have found an inverse association between fibrinogen and alcohol use, but others did not find such an association. Alcohol seems to be related to CVD in a U-shaped fashion, and fibrinogen may be a mediator for its effect* (Mennen 1999). The authors speculate that moderate drinking may lower fibrinogen levels. Also in 1999, a study by Wang reports: *These findings demonstrate that moderate levels of alcohol reversibly reduce fibrinogen production in vivo and in vitro and therefore may contribute,* *in part, to the cardioprotective function exhibited by moderate alcohol consumption* (Wang 1999). The authors discovered the effect both in the laboratory and in humans. Abou-Agag looked to see whether phenolics affected fibrinolytic proteins and declared: *Wine phenolics increase fibrinolytic activity, independent of ethanol, and it is likely that the overall cardioprotective benefits associated with moderate red wine consumption are attributable to the combined, additive, or perhaps synergistic effects of alcohol and other wine components* (Abou-Agag 2001). Sierksma studied the effect of consumption of red wine and red grape juice taken with the evening meal on fibrinolysis and found: . . . *fibrinolytic activity in post-menopausal women . . . appears similar to the response described earlier for middle-aged men* (Sierksma 2001). Sierksma determined in a study with male volunteers who consumed 4 whiskey drinks with dinner that: . . . *the reduced risk for CHD in male, middle-aged moderate drinkers is not attributable to changes in hormone levels* (Sierksma 2002).

The folate and homocysteine factors: Folate offers consideration of an interesting, uniquely American saga which illustrates both unwarranted governmental intrusion and general indifference of medicine for a very important source of folate. The incidence concerns an effort of a small Washington brewery to pass on to its consumers the chemical constitution of their Grant's Scottish Ale. As with triglycerides, high levels of homocysteine in the bloodstream are linked with an increase in atherosclerosis. "Busy B's: Good for Your Heart?" in the *UC Berkeley Wellness Letter* notes: *In the normal course of events, the homocysteine that healthy people manufacture is converted into amino acids that do them no harm. This is accomplished by three B vitamins – B6, B12 and, probably most important, folacin (also called folate)* (Busy B's 2001). This commentary establishes sources of the B vitamins that are helpful in moderating levels of homocysteine.

Folate supplements have become the newest passion in heart disease prevention. As are many antioxidants, folate (folic acid) is found mainly in fruits and green, leafy vegetables– beans, asparagus, citrus fruits and juices. Willett comments on the American source of homocysteine: *Meat is a major source of methionine, and high intakes tend to elevate blood homocysteine levels, particularly when diets are sub-optimal in folate* (Willett 1996). Of course, contrary findings exist. A study by Bleich determined higher homocysteine among even moderate drinkers: *We postulate that elevated levels of homocysteine in social drinkers with regular moderate alcohol intake are at risk of developing cardiovascular diseases* (Bleich 2001). This study involved only sixty individuals, yet it produced a negative finding. Once again, the study composition is vital in all epidemiology.

The *Cleveland Clinic Heart Advisor* agrees with the importance of folate in the diet to counteract red meat intake: *The two main factors . . . are your genes and whether or not you're getting enough B vitamins, especially folic acid (folate) . . . Research has shown that supplementing the diet with folic acid can lower homocysteine* (Update on Homocysteine 1998). Rimm confirms the speculation: *These results suggest that intake of folate with vitamin B6 above the current recommended dietary allowance may be important in the primary prevention of CHD among women* (Rimm 1998). Federal agencies are so impressed with folate research that flour makers are now directed to include folate additives in all their products. Folates are deemed particularly important in a pregnancy diet yet it is widely known that few women take folate supplements. "Homocysteine" in the *Mayo Clinic Health Letter* reports: *The encouraging news about homocysteine is that certain vitamins may help . . . B complex vitamins − B6, B12 and folic acid (folate) − have been shown to work together* (Homocysteine 1997).

Hendriks followed two small groups of middle-aged men and found: *Moderate alcohol consumption changed plasma total cholesterol, total triglycerides and HDL composition in the postprandial period (following eating)* (Hendriks 2001). Koehler studied folate intake among 278 men and women aged sixty-six and ninety-four and determined: *The inverse association between folate intake and tHcy (total homocysteine concentration) was strongest among non users of supplements and among alcohol drinkers* (Koehler 2001). This older group of drinkers were advantaged over those using supplements alone. This targeted study provides some rationale for specific positive impacts among moderate drinkers.

Folate and folic acid are essentially the same substances. They are forms of a B vitamin which contribute to the formation of red blood cells. Despite the many references and support for folate supplements in medical and popular media, one will never find reference to what may be the most provident single natural source of the B complex vitamins and folate – beer.

A uniquely American saga

Several years ago, Bert Grant of Washington State's Yakima Beverages submitted his popular Scottish Ale for analysis by a professional laboratory. The printout shown below of this analysis was then affixed as an informational sticker on the brewery's cardboard six-pack containers. The Bureau of Alcohol, Tobacco and Firearms (BATF) threatened to rescind Grant's brewing license if he didn't remove the informational stickers which employ the same language mandated for hundreds of other common foods on a grocery shelf. Obviously, BATF does not look upon beer as a common food. According to BATF, free speech rights do not extend to brewers, vintners and distillers as they do to other other commercial food products.

GRANT'S SCOTTISH ALE

NUTRITIONAL INFORMATION PER SERVING (12oz.)		PERCENTAGE OF U.S. RECOMMENDED DAILY ALLOWANCE (U.S. RDA)	
SERVING SIZE	12 OUNCES (355 ML)	SERVING SIZE	12 OUNCES (355 ML)
Calories	145	Calories	5.4%
Protein	2.24 grams	Protein	4.0%
Carbohydrate	12.7 grams	Riboflavin (B2)	4.6%
Fat	0 grams	Niacin	14.6%
Cholesterol	0 grams	Folacin	62.5%
Sodium	8 milligrams	Pyroxin (B6)	13.9%
Potassium	195 milligrams	Vitamin B12	170.0%

Ingredients: Refiltered pure water, barley malt, Yakima Valley hops and pure culture yeast.

The BATF has never questioned the accuracy of the beer's chemical analysis, only its presence on the beer's six-pack cartons. The reproduction of Grant's sticker shows that a single bottle of Grant's Scottish Ale contains up to 62.5 percent of the recommended daily allowance (RDA) of folate and 170 percent of the RDA for vitamin B_{12}, two substances that medicine and public health highly recommend today. Shouldn't the general public be informed of these impressive beer contributions of folate and B vitamins? Women who drink beer should know about this rich source of folate. Does the BATF have the right to expunge this knowledge from the public view? Vexing questions.

The BATF's authority for this intrusion rests on their own narrow interpretation of the post-Repeal, Federal Alcohol Act. That legislation forbids licensees from claiming therapeutic values for their drinks in public *advertising*. The question is whether informing purchasers of chemical composition of their beer is a form of advertising or an exercise of legitimate communication. The irony is that drinks are the only foods in the U.S. which are now authorized and protected by a constitutional amendment.

This is a uniquely American saga. In the BATF's wisdom, we mustn't tell Americans about a rich source of vitamins and folate found in the nation's most frequently consumed alcohol drink. If we knew, we might all become alcoholics. But there are no legislative prohibitions justifying the deafening silence of every single piece of medical or public health literature about this source of folate and B complex vitamins. The government's crackdown on Scottish Ale's RDA sticker illustrates the atmosphere facing producers of drinks in the U. S. Lingering fears, punitive mechanisms of government and reservations in medicine militate against any serious consideration of potential health factors in responsible drinking − a majority American practice. The industries are leery of challenging government and medicine, as well as the virulent, anti-drinking lobby.

Recall the earlier *Harvard Health Letter* article which omitted drinks from a list of food sources for flavonoids. A 1998 *Harvard Men's Health Watch* newsletter replicated the omission by publishing a list of 15 foods in "B Vitamins and the Heart: What Men Can Learn from Women" It should come as no surprise that Scottish Ale (and no other drink source) is found on this important list. Drinks don't merit mention despite the developing science.

The December 2001 *Harvard Health Letter* carries an article titled "B Vitamins" touting the consumption of B_6, B_{12}, and folate. The article notes: *Folate is the key B vitamin for cancer protection. High intake is associated with lower cancer risk. It also seems to offset the increased cancer risk that comes with drinking alcohol. Women who consume even just one alcoholic drink per day have a slightly higher risk for breast cancer, for example. But data from several studies suggest that folate pushes down the breast-cancer risk that alcohol elevates* (B Vitamins 2001). Chapter 9 presents a variety of study findings on the alcohol/breast cancer risk but note here that there is no mention of the potential intake of B complex vitamins in beer, a rich source identified decades ago as attested below in Grant's autobiography. The article does conclude: *Needless to say, eating a well-rounded diet of healthful foods is always the best approach to nutrition.* Agreed, especially when drinks are included!

Operating under this ambivalence blockade, it is no wonder that physicians and other caregivers are generally unaware of the presence of folate and B vitamins in beer. In his autobiography, *Ale Master*, Grant recalls: *I remember when vitamin B12 was discovered in beer, back in the late 1940s. At the time, I was at Canadian Breweries' labs, and the more we analyzed beers, the more B vitamins we found – B5, B6 and B12. They come from the yeast and by-products of yeast fermentation* (Grant 1998). A recent Dutch study by van der Gaag confirmed that male beer drinkers had a thirty percent increase in vitamin B6 in their blood plasma, a level that was more protective than wine or spirits (van der Gaag 1999). As reported in the January, 2002 issue of *All About Beer*, a report in the *European Journal of Clinical Nutrition* relates: *The study measured blood levels of folate, vitamin B6 (pyridoxine) and vitamin B12 in 543 residents of Pilsen . . . The B vitamins they measured are linked to lower levels of homocysteine, a compound in the blood associated with increased risk of heart disease* (Beer is Good for Your Heart 2002).

It wouldn't take much digging to find these evidences of vital contributions in drinks.

All drinks are artery friendly

Most researchers report that all drinks provide some easing of atherosclerosis. A panel of French researchers concludes: *Wine polyphenolic compounds induce a vaso-relaxing effect of the vessels . . . Polyphenolic compounds reduce the oxidation of LDL . . . Wine consumption reduced fibrinogen and Factor VIIa which are two risks for CVD* (Wine, Nutrition and Health 1997). Duthie reports: *After an intake of 100 ml of whiskey or wine, the content of phenolic compounds in plasma as well as the antioxidant activity of plasma is increased similarly with both types of alcoholic beverages* (Duthie 1998). Buhner notes in *Sacred and Herbal Healing Beers* that: . . . *hops are high in estrogen. They're very good for women going through menopause* (Buhner 1999).

Klatsky reports on the cumulative data in dozens of studies: *Total alcohol consumption is inversely related to coronary heart disease risk for each sex, with wine being the most protective for women and beer the most protective for men* (Klatsky 1997). Rimm notes: *Results from observational studies . . . provide strong evidence that a substantial portion of the benefits of wine, beer or spirits are attributable to the alcohol content rather than to other components of each drink* (Rimm 1996). Zhang sums up these various reports: *Alcohol, at physiologically relevant doses, has a dose-dependent inhibitory effect on platelet aggregation. This could contribute to the beneficial effects of moderate drinking on the risk for coronary artery disease* (Zhang 2000).

Recall the *UC Berkeley Wellness Letter* comment: *Antioxidants are part of the chemistry of life, not something in a bottle than can miraculously prevent or cure disease. The best place to find them is in food* (Can antioxidants save your life? 1998). In an article "Think Twice About Nutritional Supplements and Medications," *Harvard Men's Health Watch* notes: *Americans spent $5.7 billion on vitamin and mineral supplements in 1997, up from $3.0 billion in 1990. Many of these dollars are spent to prevent cancer, but there is currently no scientific proof that the investment will be rewarded by better health* (Think Twice 1998). Implicitly – but not explicitly – the newsletter supports drinks which are excellent sources of antioxidants.

Many studies cited in this chapter and throughout the book are based on experiments conducted in laboratories, often with mice or other animals. Obviously what happens in animals studies or in a test tube can be postulated as no more than a *potentiality* in humans. But the progression of disease or wellness in these controlled studies helps researchers in constructing appropriate human studies. As example, Emeson, in a twenty-four week project, fed mice an atherogenic diet to develop atherogenic lesions similar to those in humans and then fed the same mice a moderate alcohol-containing diet to test the results.

This experiment found: . . . *that alcohol not only inhibits the initial development of atherosclerotic lesions but also inhibits the progression of existing lesions* (Emeson 2000).

To tie together these many reports, here are two contributions from a chemistry research text titled *Wine: Nutritional and Therapeutic Benefits* (Watkins, 1997). The significance of this source stems from its participating scientists – a 1995 symposium conducted by members of the American Chemical Society. One has to position chemists at the forefront of antioxidant research. The book's editor and symposium leader, Watkins, set the tone: *The toxic oxygen radical, unfettered and unchecked in the body, has been recognized as an important risk factor in the etiology of chronic, killer disease. The hazard of the oxygen radical can be countered by various antioxidants. Wine, rich in reducing substances, certainly offers therapeutic potential for many chronic diseases . . . which account for about 75% of the deaths in America* (Watkins 1997). Maxwell extends the speculation: *Although some recent epidemiological reviews have been less than enthusiastic . . . It is certainly true that red wine is the most potent antioxidant solution in clinical nutrition. What remains to be discovered is to what extent this activity is translated into meaningful effects in vivo* (Maxwell 1997).

These comments do not constitute an exclusive sales pitch for the consumption of red wines. This particular symposium was devoted to wine's effects. Skovenborg reports on a study at Guys Hospital in London on the TAA (total antioxidant activity) of 21 beers: *The lagers had a TAA in the range of 1.00-1.50 mm while the stouts and dark ales– due to a higher content of polyphenols– led the antioxidant contest with TAAs in the range of 1.50-2.00 mm* (Skovenborg 2002). Skovenborg also reported that a liter of beer supplies the following daily vitamin requirements: B^6 17%, Niacin 13%, Biotin 17%, Pantothenic acid 8%, and Folate 10-45%. Readers should not over-value the data from any of these reports, or any other group of studies, particularly those limited to animal models.

Skovenborg raises the question, "Is red wine better than beer?" He concludes, ". . . beer drinkers in some countries tend to make more unhealthy lifestyle choices than wine drinkers. Therefore the apparent good health of wine drinkers compared to beer drinkers in some studies seem to be a lifestyle effect and not a beverage effect." Skovenborg notes that in Germany, where beer is the common alcoholic beverage, all research shows that moderate consumption of beer protects against CHD.

Brenner in "Coronary Heart Disease Risk Reduction in a Predominantly Beer-Drinking Population" reports in *Epidemiology* in 2001 that: *Compared to abstainers, beer-only drinkers cut their risk of CHD in half . . . But wine-only drinkers reduce their risk by only 5% compared to abstainers* (Brenner 2001). In an editorial in the same issue, Rimm noted: *The results in Germany are similar to those reported in China, Japan, France, the United States and the United Kingdom, to name a few . . . Conversely, in a large cohort study in Denmark by Gronbaek, et al., very different associations were reported: drinkers of wine had substantially lower risk of coronary disease than drinkers of beer and spirits . . . Some might attribute the difference to chance — if not due to chance, must be due to factors not measured or accounted for in these analyses* (Rimm 2001).

Zuger quotes Rimm in "Evidence Mounting that Moderate Drinking is Healthful:" *If you step back, the data shows that alcohol is beneficial in all three beverages. If there is any differential, it is very small* (Zuger 2002).

While the jury may still be out on drink antioxidants for humans, there is compelling evidence of positive effects with animal models. Obviously, additional studies are needed to resolve if and how drinks provide bio-adaptable antioxidants. One 2000 *in vivo* study with the quite small base of twelve human subjects found none — van der Gaag traced the impact of red wine, beer and spirits in three week intervals and concluded: . . . *no significant effect on antioxidant status* (van der Gaag 2000). Nakahashi conducted a study of 1,580 male Japanese office workers, aged thirty-five to fifty-nine and reported: . . . *a prudent lifestyle, characterized by moderate alcohol use, watching nutritional balance and regular physical exercise may have an anti-atherogenic effect* (Nakahashi 1999). Let's hear the findings for both sides.

But, remember the caution. When reading new epidemiological findings, it is prudent to recall the cautions suggested by Finkel and Feinstein in the opening essay on epidemiology. Determine who made up the study population and where it was conducted. Gronbaek's work in Denmark favors wine while

Brenner's work in Germany demonstrate similar benefits in beer consumption. In another Danish study, Osler found significant changing drinking habits in recent years: *Both among men and women, alcohol use decreased during the study period (1982-1992), but changes were only significant among those with the highest education. Among the highest-educated men, the prevalence of moderate drinking increased from 77% to 82%, while the prevalence of heavy drinking decreased . . . Among the highest-educated women, the prevalence of abstinence increased from 15% to 22%, while the prevalence of moderate drinking decreased from 78% to 68%* (Osler 2001). Almost the reverse is true in the U.S. where the highest educated are more apt to be regular drinkers.

The predominance of studies in this book suggests that moderate intake and moderate lifestyle are the keys to benefits, more than specific beverage types. Another study by van der Weil emphasizes moderation in terms of atherosclerosis risk: *Drinking much alcohol in the evening results in an acute inhibition of fibrinolysis, which persists the morning after. This may predispose drinkers to accelerated atherosclerosis* (van der Weil 2001). But the author notes: *After 2 glasses of wine no marked disturbance of the circadian rhythm was found.* Moderation is the key to releasing any health benefit and avoiding harm from drinks.

Drinks as healthy foods

From the hundreds of studies cited in this book, it can be concluded that drinks are pleasant foods which provide nourishment, tranquillity, relief from stress and an abundance of antioxidants. Drinks also help to lower low density lipoprotein and to raise protective high density lipoprotein. As with green leafy vegetables, alcohol-containing beverages taken in moderation can provide tangible, measurable health benefits. However, as will be seen in the remaining chapters, the medical and nutrition communities rarely, if ever, consider drinks as foods.

An article in the *Journal of the American Medical Association* associates excess consumption of vitamin D with hip fractures among post menopausal women. A banner headline "Research links vitamin A to hip problems" initiated a half page article devoted to this study by the *Seattle Post Intelligencer*. In this study, Feskanich provides an analysis of data from the Nurses' Health

Study. This project included 72,227 North American nurses aged thirty-four to seventy-seven. The study sought to determine any relationship between intake of vitamin A and the risk of hip fracture among post menopausal women.

Feskanich speculates that too much vitamin A inhibits the ability of vitamin D to assist the body to absorb calcium. Feskanich held: *Our findings provide further evidence that chronic intake of excessive vitamin A, particularly from retinol, may contribute to the development of osteoporotic hip fractures in women. The amounts of retinol in fortified foods and vitamin supplements may need to be reassessed since these add significantly to total retinol consumption in the United States* (Feskanich 2002). In the study, the risk of fracture doubled with intakes above 2,000 micrograms of vitamin A daily, nearly triple the now recommended 700 microgram intake. Daily multi-vitamins typically contain over 1,500 micrograms which mixes with the beta carotine consumed in leafy vegetables which often converts to additional vitamin A.

Two things should be noted about this article. First, the study bolsters the argument expressed several times in this chapter and elsewhere that natural foods in a balanced diet – including drinks – are the best source of vitamins and minerals. Second,, there is no mention in the study or its references that drinks have been found to *lower* the risk of fractures by increasing bone density. Chapter 23 reports several of these studies – Holbrook, Felson, Rapuri, May, the Framingham Heart Study, Takada and Naves-Diaz. An earlier study by Feskanich evaluated drinking and bone density among post menopausal women holding that: *Women who consumed 75 g or more of alcohol per week had significantly higher bone densities at the lumbar spine compared with nondrinking women* (Feskanich 1999).

The reading public would be better served by including the favorable drinking data in fracture articles. While alerting to the danger of too much vitamin A, Feskanich did not advise readers to abandon multivitamins, vitamin enriched foods or supplements. His advice was to keep the intake of retinol and vitamin A supplements within reasonable limits.

Good advice, but it is seldom seen in the medical newsletters. Many senior citizens would welcome information that could lessen the impact of osteoporosis.

Research Addendum

✔ Khanna confirms a positive role for wine antioxidants. "Apparently wine procyanidins are active in the prevention of lipid oxidation of foods while in the digestive tract . . . Drinking wine at meals provides this kind of protection, and the final results are realized by the prevention of the development of atheromatous lesions" (Khanna 2002).

✔ Dale criticizes the fat-engrossed American diet: ". . . a 4 foot 6 inch woman who has gained 25 pounds since high school has twice the risk of diabetes and breast cancer and more than twice the risk of a heart attack" (Dale 1998).

✔ Stamler remarks on this progress: "Since the late 1960s, death rates in the United States from coronary heart disease have fallen steadily and markedly. This decline has involved all sectors of the adult population . . . the rate of mortality from coronary heart disease has fallen by over 30 percent, resulting in more than 800,000 lives saved since 1968 . . . These data lend strong support to the conclusions that improvements in lifestyle and lifestyle risk factors have contributed substantially to the decline" (Stamler 1997).

✔ Klatsky showed in 1981 the lowest mortality (6.3 percent in 1,000 deaths) among those who consumed 1-2 drinks daily (Klatsky 1981).

✔ Amarasuriya confirmed the ability of HDL to clean up the bloodstream: "The major protein of high density lipoprotein (HDL) takes up cellular cholesterol, thus initiating reverse cholesterol transport whereby excess tissue cholesterol is eliminated" (Amarasuriya 1992).

✔ Whitten and Lipp compare alcohol to aspirin: "Aspirin is one of the most important pharmacological tools that doctors have in treating patients at risk for coronary artery blockage, (it) works its magic through platelets. It reduces the adhesion of platelets . . . But aspirin is not alone in this regard. Wine appears to have a similar effect on platelets. In addition, it has a beneficial impact on blood lipids . . . giving it a far broader cardiovascular usefulness than aspirin" (Whitten 1994).

✔ Serge Renaud, the French scientist who appeared on the French Paradox telecast with Curt Ellison, notes: "At the moderate intake associated with the prevention of CHD, the mechanism of protection seems to be, at least partly, a haemostatic effect, possibly a decrease in platelet activity" (Renaud 1992).

✔ Fuhrman compared results with several groups of men who drank red or white wines and concluded: . . ."a daily consumption of red wine with meals brings about a decrease in oxidation of plasma and LDL. This decrease is linked not to a change in the vitamin content of the plasma, but to an increase in the content of polyphenols in plasma and LDL" (Fuhrman 1995). But Furhman's findings also concluded that processing white wines on their skins– as is common with reds– "leads to extraction of grape skin polyphenols and produces polyphenol-rich white wine with antioxidant characteristics similar to those of red wine."

✔ Dixon found a U-shaped relation between moderate drinking and lowered homocystein levels. "Red wine consumption is associated with lower fasting homocystein levels in severely obese individuals." (Dixon 2002)

✔ While its presence was associated as an aging factor, Nascetti discovered that, "Alcohol use was inversely associated with fibrinogen in a Mediterranean population. (Nascetti 2002)

Expect many new findings on the role of antioxidants and other factors outlined in this chapter in the years to come. The research pot is boiling over. As example, at press time for this book, *Alcohol Research* published an original article titled "The role of a hydroxide ion in alcohol oxidation." In it, Meijers notes:

> *Removal of alcohol from the body is mainly mediated by enzymes that belong to the alcohol dehydrogenase family. A prominent member of this family is zinc-dependent liver alcohol dehydrogenase (LADH,1) . . . The data provide strong evidence for the role of LADH and NAD in the neutralization of free radicals. . . Liver alcohol dehydrogenase has been identified as a free radical scavenger and the action mechanism presented here supports the view that the enzyme may be capable of neutralizing such radicals.*

Meijers, R., Lamzin, V., and Cedergren-Zeppezauer, E., The role of a hydroxide ion in alcohol oxidation, Alcohol Research, Vol. 7, No. 3, June, 2002

Let's open up some new lines of communication!

Chapter 3

Blood Clots

Drinks help reduce blood clotting

Author's abstract: Drinking lowers the incidence of blood clots. Since clots lead to heart attacks and strokes, one should expect to see and hear this message in the health media. One doesn't achieve a healthy heart simply by taking a pill, or a drink for that matter. Heart health, like every other facet of human health, depends on a combination of factors—lifestyle, exercise, diet and attitude. Drinks can help with blood clotting. Here's how:

- ➡ Fibrinolysis reduces the formation of blood clots
- ➡ The enzyme t-PA helps to regulate fibrinolysis
- ➡ Alcohol increases the body's production of t-PA
- ➡ In addition, ethanol inhibits platelet growth

The booklet *Heart and Stroke Facts* reveals: *Thrombus – a blood clot that forms inside a blood vessel or chamber of the heart* (Heart and Stroke 1999). The *American Medical Association Encyclopedia of Medicines* provides this definition: *Thrombosis (i.e., the formation of undesirable, persistent blood clots) occurs only if there is a disturbance in the balance between mechanisms that encourage clot formation, such as sluggish blood flow and fibrinolysis that restrain clot formation or dissolve clots.*

This book minimizes technical terminology. But fibrin is another of those terms that needs some definition. It is a protein which develops the fiber-like web that gathers in and holds together a forming blood clot. Alcohol in the blood facilitates a process called *fibrinolysis* which deters clot formation. Since alcohol dissipates rapidly from the blood system, daily drinking abets continuing fibrinolysis. In an analysis of data from 631 physicians in the Physician's Health Study, Ridker determined that a favorable association exists between moderate alcohol consumption and blood clots. He found that the body's production of an enzyme called tissue type plasminogen activator (t-PA) helped to regulate fibrinolysis. His study notes:

> The highest level of endogenous [created within the body] t-PA antigen were found among daily consumers of alcohol and the lowest levels of t-PA were found among rare or never consumers of alcohol . . . Our finding that the association of t-PA antigen and alcohol consumption is independent of HDL-C is particularly important since the HDL-mediated effects of alcohol intake have been estimated to explain less than half of the cardiovascular risk reduction attributable to moderate alcohol use . . . This study . . . strongly supports the hypothesis that improved antithrombotic and fibrinolytic profiles derived from alcohol intake may explain part of the cardioprotective effect of moderate alcohol consumption.

Ridker et al., News Release, Moderate Alcohol Intake May Reduce Risk of Thrombosis, American Medical Association, September 22, 1994

Daily drinking has been identified in many studies thus far as a contributor to balancing cholesterol levels and, in doing so, to lessening atherosclerosis. Thrombotic research associates drinks with a lower risk of blood clotting. Moderate drinking manifests a series of inter-related heart benefits.

The graph above reproduced from Ridker's study demonstrates increasing levels of t-PA at four levels of consumption. The best protection was derived from daily drinking. This study strongly postulates a positive role for alcohol in reducing blood clotting and, thereby, protecting vascular health. In the later coverage of strokes, we learn that t-PA is administered by doctors in emergency rooms when stroke or heart attack is imminent. By improving the level of t-PA, regular drinking abets cardiovascular health.

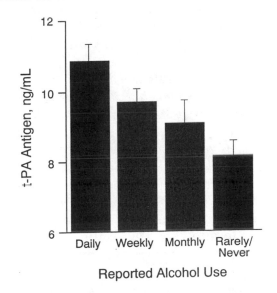

Reported Alcohol Use

Reprinted with permission of the Journal of the American Medical Association, Ridker et al., Association of moderate alcohol consumption and plasma concentration of endogenous tissue-type plasminogen activator, JAMA, 272(12): p929, 1994

Commenting on the Ridker study, Mitchell notes: *The net result is that not only is there less likelihood of developing atherosclerosis (a rather lengthy process) but there is also a greater likelihood that any clot formation would be resolved through the endogenous [within the body] thrombolytic pathways. These findings together help to explain why recent alcohol consumption (within the last few months) is as important as consumption over one's lifetime* (Mitchell 1994). Blood clot management is another specific benefit of moderate alcohol consumption particularly in mid-life and the senior-years.

In a concurring French study, Renaud found that: *The respon-siveness to thrombin was slightly increased at all levels of alcohol consumption* (Renaud 1997). Folts in the Coronary Thrombosis Laboratory at the University of Wisconsin tested components in red wine and other food sources looking for disease prevention properties and found: *Some of them (flavonoids) are both good platelet inhibitors and good antioxidants* (Folts 1996). Langer in 1992 found that drinks helped cholesterol management and speculated it might also help to avoid blood clots: *The explanation for the residual 50 percent benefit attributable to alcohol is unknown but may include interference with thrombosis* (Langer 1992).

Rubin confirmed earlier findings on both platelet and throm-bus activity: *Platelet deficits have been noted in alcoholics and in human experimental studies . . . ethanol diminishes thrombus formation on damaged arterial walls. Ethanol inhibits platelet activation* (Rubin 1994). Johansen studied red wine consumption by comparing subjects at rest and after acute exercise and reported: *Acute physical exercise leads to an immediate increase in t-PA as well as significant decrease of fibrinolysis time* (Johansen 1998).

Another study by Folts involving five men and five women compared the various impacts of alcohol, fruit juices and aspirin. The subjects consumed grapefruit, orange and grape juices over extended periods to allow for aggregation measurements. The purple grape juice – but not the other two juices – showed a significant anti-platelet effect: *The purple juice platelet inhibitory effect was stronger than a published standard for aspirin* (Folts 1998).

In a small study, Lacoste found two specific advantages of drinks: *Moderate alcohol use inhibits, in men and women alike, platelet thrombus deposition . . . This antithrombotic effect of a single alcohol drink, persisting for 6 h [hours] and even after the BAC has returned to baseline, may be clinically relevant to the cardioprotective effects of alcohol* (Lacoste 2001). Even after the alcohol is gone, the protection continues. Blood clotting research confirms the notion that constituents in drinks produced from fruits and grains have similar, and even greater, effects on body chemistry than the fresh fruits and grains from which they were produced. Alcohol may be the most important cardiovascular component in drinks. It certainly is not the only important one.

In the chemical society symposium mentioned last chapter, Maalej is quite specific about the consumption of alcoholic beverages and wine in relation to blood clotting:

Moderate daily consumption of alcoholic beverages is a negative risk factor for the development of atherosclerosis and coronary artery disease . . . We found that red wine and grape juice, but not white wine, inhibited platelet activity. Red wine and grape juice contain a wide variety of anthocyanins, and phenolic flavonoids including fungicides, tannins, anthocyanins and phenolic flavonoids . . . The antithrombotic effect of red wine and grape juice may be due to the flavonoids common in some vegetables, fruits and herbs such as tea.

Maalej, N., Demrow, H., Slane, P., and Folts, J., Antithrombotic Effect of Flavonoids in Red Wine, Wine: Nutritional and Therapeutic Benefits, American Chemical Society, Washington, D.C., 1997

One doesn't need a chemistry degree to pick out the essential findings from the above wine-specific studies. Moderate daily consumption of red wine is negative to the development of blood clots. Red wine and red grape juice both supply chemicals negative to the formation of blood clots, as do other fruits and vegetables, not excluding other types of drinks. The important observation is that relief from blood clotting may occur in moderate drinking. This factor should enjoy much wider comprehension among physicians, cardiovascular patients and the general public.

The information clot needs dissolution.

Chapter 4

High Blood Pressure

Less risk for hypertension

■ **Author's abstract**: A very high percentage of middle-aged adults and senior citizens experience hypertension. Research identifies benefits from drinks but it also stresses the contributions of life-style factors and diet. When dealing with hypertension, it is absolutely essential that drinkers stay within moderate consumption levels. The findings in this chapter include:

■ ➥ Regular light drinkers have less pressure induced strokes
  ➥ Light drinkers show favorable pressure profiles
  ➥ Risk advisories exclusively target heavy drinkers

High blood pressure is the most universal of all adverse heart conditions. *Heart and Stroke Facts* (1993) from American Heart Association reports on this stealthy killer:

> *High blood pressure (usually hypertension) has no specific symptoms and no early warning signs. High blood pressure increases the heart's workload, causing the heart to enlarge and weaken over time. It*

also increases the risk of stroke, heart attack, kidney
failure and congestive heart failure.

Heart and Stroke Facts, American Heart Association, Dallas, 1993

A 1997 Johns Hopkins Medical School White Paper titled
Hypertension describes the incidence of this disease:

Hypertension is the most prevalent condition in the
U.S. Nearly 50 million adults —28% of the population
—have blood pressure levels above normal or are
using lifestyle measures or medication to control
blood pressure . . . . Hypertension can easily go
undetected. It has been called the "silent killer"
because it usually produces no symptoms until it
seriously damages the heart, kidneys, brain or some
other site. Patients with sustained hypertension have
an increased overall death rate, especially from
stroke, heart attack, and kidney disease.

Hypertension, The Johns Hopkins White Papers, Johns Hopkins Medical Institutions,
Baltimore, 1997

In the above "Hypertension" pamphlet, there are three allu-
sions to drinking. The first , under "Reduced alcohol consumption," notes: . . . *hypertension is related to consumption of three or*
more alcoholic drinks a day in about 7% of those with blood pressures
of 150/95 (Hypertension 1997). The other two are: *Try non-alco-*
holic beer and wine and *The keys to preventing hypertension are weight*
loss, regular exercise, improved diet with plenty of vegetables, lower
sodium intake, and moderation of alcohol consumption. As in the
Johns Hopkins White Paper on aging and nutrition cited in the
Prologue, comments about drinking are predominantly cautious
or even negative in tone. "It may be good but . . . "

However, in the research journals, one seldom finds negative
treatment. The studies simply set for both the positive aspects
of moderate intake and the negative aspects of abuse. Moderate
drinking is viewed in many studies as a positive influence on
hypertension. Beilin in Western Australia reported in 1996: *An*
association between alcohol consumption and blood pressure levels has
been observed in over 60 population studies worldwide. The relation-
ship is generally linear with some studies showing a threshold effect at

around 2-3 standard drinks a day . . . Despite predisposing to hypertension, regular light to moderate drinking (1-4 standard drinks a day) appears to protect against coronary deaths and ischaemic strokes while heavier drinking increases the risk of haemorrhagic stroke and heart disease (Beilin 1996). It is one thing to say, as the Johns Hopkins paper does, that three or more drinks are causal to hypertension and quite another to state, as Beilin does, that many studies find that up to four drinks daily are associated with a drop in blood pressure along with cholesterol improvement and a drop in heart attacks. Because of the unique populations involved, different studies may elicit quite different findings. But a definite problem exists in the variable definitions of "light to moderate" and "heavy" drinking in the professional literature. Often the classification depends often on the researcher's degree of alcohol ambivalence.

With drinks, it's always the dose

In most of these studies, true drinking risks are associated almost exclusively with excessive or abusive intake. However, the side effects of moderate drinking, and there are some, are generally less daunting than those associated with hypertension medicines. As early as 1979, Ramsey in Glasgow reported on a study of 1,505 men with hypertension: *. . . finding a significant trend away from heart attacks in each age level among moderate drinkers* (Ramsey 1979). In 1985, a study by Jackson in New Zealand looked at the relationships between systolic and diastolic blood pressure among 1,429 men and women aged thirty-five to sixty-four and reported:

> *These findings suggest that in men and in women aged 50 years and older, there is a nonlinear relationship between blood pressure and alcohol consumption, and that there is a level of alcohol consumption, of approximately four drinks per day, below which drinkers have either similar or lower blood pressure levels compared to nondrinkers.*

Jackson, R., Stewart, A., Beaglehole, R., and Scragg, R., Alcohol consumption and blood pressure, American Journal on Epidemiology, 122:1037-1044, 1985

Many studies in the 1970s and 1980s developed positive data for light to moderate drinking and hypertension. Friedman in 1988 warned of the dangers of abusive drinking, the role of heredity and the problems in adult weight gain: *This large study confirms longitudinally the importance of obesity, weight gain during adulthood, alcohol, family history and, to some extent, salt as predictive and possible causal factors for essential hypertension* (Friedman 1988). It is very important to discuss these proclivities with patients who have family histories of alcohol or drug abuse. In 1992, Ekpo studied a variety of correlates of blood pressure among 5,200 men and women in northeast Nigeria and found a dose-dependent variation: *The prevalence of hypertension was higher in medium and heavy drinkers than in non-drinkers and light drinkers. Non-drinkers had a prevalence of 8.2% compared to 4.4% for the lightest drinking group and 16% for the 2-3 pints/day consumers* (Ekpo 1992). With hypertension, there is a moderate middle ground. Abuse and abstention are both problems.

That same year a study was released in Japan by Ueshima. It involved 4,759 randomly chosen men and women: *The authors conclude that the impact of alcohol drinking on blood pressure in men should be taken into account in the primary prevention of blood pressure related diseases and in the treatment of hypertension in both younger and older people. . . the prevalence of hypertension adjusted for body mass index was significantly higher in everyday male drinkers than in male non-drinkers* (Ueshima 1992). The following year in the U.S., Polomaki reported that: *Light to moderate alcohol intake appears to have an inverse association with the risk of ischemic stroke. The beneficial effect appears to be most prominent if the consumption of alcohol is regular and evenly distributed throughout the week whereas a sporadic and occasional pattern of drinking seems to weaken the association* (Polomaki 1993). In this study, regular, moderate drinking had an "inverse" or positive effect on ischemic stroke and the blood clotting which causes it. The health benefits may depend upon both dose and the ethnic populations involved. That's why physicians need timely, complete, and unbiased reporting of the entire research spectrum.

Researchers still doubt that light-to-moderate drinking *alone* lowers blood pressure. Many are persuaded that the positive effects result from a combination of life traits such as exercise and diet which are cited in the Johns Hopkins paper. This is a valid point of view. Concerned individuals should consult a cardiologist because of these many variables. Obviously, no one should medicate themselves based on a casual reading of a book or a magazine article. Conflicts in research findings are all too common. Biomedical studies involve widely disparate study populations. That's why it is dangerous to universalize findings from isolated studies. However, when drinks are treated as foods, incorporated into the daily diet and consumed at moderate levels, there is considerable evidence of health benefits for hypertension. The positive data may well rest upon a combination of dietary and lifestyle factors, but the epidemiology says the benefits are real.

In terms of diet, a 2000 article in *HealthNews* notes: *Olive oil contributes to the Mediterranean diet's benefits by lowering cholesterol (LDL) without affecting good cholesterol (HDL) . . . When the participants used olive oil, their systolic [top number] BP [blood pressure] fell by about 7 points, but sunflower oil had no effect on BP* (Olive Oil Lowers Blood Pressure 2000). The Mediterranean diet features wine, fruits, vegetables and unsaturated fats. It is virtually impossible to attach specific health benefits solely to any single factor. A symphony of chemical interactions is induced from the many foods consumed at a relaxed. Mediterranean meal, along with the warmth of social interchange and the equanimity of shared lives. This approach to eating is a lifestyle, not simply acquisition of energy. But it is also folly to discuss the Mediterranean diet excluding wine, beer and spirituous drinks, as many nutritionists do. This cuisine sans drinks constitutes a healthy regimen but it is a European diet, not *the* Mediterranean diet.

In *Hypertension,* Gillman attributes blood pressure benefits to young adults aged eighteen to twenty-six though, unfortunately,, it remains illegal for Americans under twenty-one to drink in public facilities. Gillman notes: *These results suggest a J-shaped association of alcohol intake with blood pressure levels in young adults (aged 18 to 26) with the lowest levels in consumers of 1 to 3 drinks per day* (Gillman 1995). This exceeds the two drink limit recommended by federal authorities. While this book sought out positive drinking research, it does not deny studies which find no benefits. Fuchs reviewed data from 8,334 participants in the

Atherosclerosis Risk in Communities studies and concluded: *Drinking in excess of 210 grams of alcohol weekly is an independent risk factor for hypertension* (Fuchs 2001). This study counted 210 grams per week (14 drinks) as "heavy drinking" and noted that: *. . . for black men only, light-to-moderate drinking is a risk.* There is no attempt to hide the problems in excessive drinking. Through all these chapters, readers should keep in mind that individual studies vary. Only when a sufficient mass of data confirms a benefit does a health consensus emerge.

Leppala studied male smoker/drinkers in Finland and classified a light drinking as under twenty-five grams a day, moderate drinking from twenty-five to sixty grams (four drinks) and heavy hitting at anything above sixty grams a day. In the U.S., twenty-five grams is just under two drinks. In Leppala's rationale, moderates could consume up to five drinks a day. The author concluded: *Alcohol use may have a distinct dose-response relationship with each stroke sub-type — linear for subarachnoid haemorrhage, U-shaped for intercerebral haemorrhage and J-shaped for cerebral infarction — but further studies are warranted* (Leppala 1999). One aspect of the failure to report the positive examples in medical magazines and newsletters is that practicing physicians have predominantly negative data at hand. What they need is a balanced perspective gained from unbiased reporting of the extant data.

Recall also the evidence that atherosclerosis begins in the teen years. So do problems with high blood pressure. Every researcher finds elevated risk for hypertension in high levels of consumption. Puddey reviewed the blood pressure literature and noted that: *Higher levels of alcohol consumption increased ischaemic and haemorrhagic stroke, left ventricular hypertrophy, congestive cardiomyopathy and cardiac arrhythmia* (Puddey 1997). In another review, Klatsky reported: *Epidemiological studies in the past two decades have firmly established a relationship between regular, heavier alcohol consumption and hypertension* (Klatsky 1996). Ishimitsu found: *These data suggest that habitual alcohol use in excess of 29 ml/day facilitates the development of left ventricular hypertrophy . . . light drinkers consuming 11-29 m. alcohol daily showed favorable profiles* (Ishimitsu 1997). Science never condones heavy or abusive drinking but neither does it foster abstinence.

Diet and stress in hypertension

In the Johns Hopkins White Paper *Hypertension,* Margolis notes that even small dietary adjustments can change blood pressure: *A low fat, high-fiber diet rich in fresh fruits and vegetables (is) the type of diet recommended to reduce the risk of heart disease – also appears to lower blood pressure* (Margolis 1998). Piendle found that the high potassium and low sodium balance in beer to be particularly advantageous for hypertension (Piendle 1986). Svetkey studied three dietary patterns and concluded: *The DASH diet significantly lowered systolic blood pressure in all subgroups and significantly lowered diastolic blood pressure in all but 2 subgroups* (Svetkey 1999). This study illustrates the positive relationship of diet to control hypertension.

Bulpitt made the appropriate comment in analyzing a study in Great Britain: *Whilst all drinkers should be made aware of increased risk of non-cardiovascular death associated with alcohol, advice on the increased risk of coronary death should be aimed at heavy drinkers alone* (Bulpitt 1994). The author clearly distinguishes between heavy and moderate drinkers . Whether your physician favors the DASH diet or some other dietary regimen for blood pressure management, it is appropriate to inquire about what research says about light to moderate drinking with the diet. Another promising study by Foppa reported: *Ingestion of 250 ml of red wine with lunch resulted in a lowered post-prandial blood pressure in centrally obese, hypertensive subjects. The effect lasted throughout most of the remaining daytime hours* (Foppa 2002). This small Italian study deserves wider evaluation and replication.

Hypertension can be managed. There is little mystery anymore about treating high blood pressure. Whelton assures us: *Treatment of hypertension is one of the most cost-effective means available . . . . Lifestyle alterations leading to weight loss, a decreased intake of dietary sodium, moderation of alcohol intake, and increased physical activity provide effective means to treat hypertension and to modify favorably other risk factors for cardiovascular disease* (Whelton 1996). Smith in *Time* magazine's September 11, 2000 issue does not condemn all drinking, but he fails to report the known benefits of light drinking. His column closes with: *Doing it naturally – with simple lifestyle changes such as losing weight, exercising more, reducing salt intake and drinking less alcohol – can be just as effective and lead to a lot fewer complications* (Smith 2000). The impulse to discourage drinking is common. "Doing it naturally" could also involve discreet, healthy alcohol consumption.

Recently the Chicago Heart Association Detection Project issued a report by Katsuyuki which involved 10,874 men aged eighteen to thirty-nine. The study's conclusion warns that average blood pressures in young men were: . . . *above normal significantly related to increased long-term mortality due to CHD, CVD and all causes* (Katsuyuki 2001). The author also cited earlier findings that: *Advanced coronary atherosclerosis was seen in most young American men undergoing autopsy during the Korean and Vietnam wars.*

We are discovering that the carefree, indulgent American way of life promotes heart and vascular problems. Recent studies have even brought into question the risks for stroke in what have been considered high-normal blood pressures – ranging from 130-139 systolic and 85-89 diastolic. To counter these risks, adoption of the Mediterranean and other low fat diets, daily exercise, social and religious communion and responsible drinking can combine to effect a moderation of blood pressure and cardiovascular problems.

Through this fourth chapter, it has been shown that moderate drinking can lessen angina pain, elevate the good cholesterol and lower the bad, help to eliminate atherosclerosis, to reduce blood clotting and to ameliorate the silent peril of hypertension. The majority of Americans who consume wisely deserve something more than the desultory medical reporting about these benefits. The American public deserves unbiased reporting on drinking impacts.

We turn now to an examination of a range of complications within the vascular system. The science quoted to date clearly shows that drinking benefits for heart health are not limited to red wine nor do they pertain exclusively to senior citizens. We've learned also that any benefits from drinking depend on moderating the "dose."

The dose shall set you free.

Chapter 5

Coronary Artery Disease

Fewer ischemic problems

■ **Author's abstract:** This section introduces ischemia, a term for problems of the vascular system. Studies from around the globe have found fewer premature ischemic deaths among moderate drinkers. Researchers reviewed international studies dating back to 1900 confirming these results. Blood clots are lessened and blood flow is enhanced among moderate consumers. Some key facts:

■ ➻ Moderate drinkers have less ischemic disease
   ➻ Higher per capita drinking nations have less ischemia

Ischemia is the clinical term for an impairment of blood flow to the body's organs or the obstruction of an artery. Ischemia of the heart muscle describes coronary artery disease (CAD). Several other acronyms are used. Some studies concern IHD (ischemic heart disease). At times, the term is CHD, (coronary heart disease) or CAD (coronary artery disease) when the problem involves the specific small arteries which surround the heart muscle. Each term implies a restricted blood flow.

Considerable progress was achieved in lowering CAD in the U.S. in the last half of the twentieth century. As early as 1986, a survey study of 356,222 individuals aged thirty-five to fifty-seven was conducted by Stamler with the following insights:

> *It is a reasonable inference that the steady and marked decline in CHD mortality in the United States since the late 1960s —greater than for any other country in the world (many countries have been steady in their rates, and others have registered rising rates —is related to the improvements in nutrition, and serum cholesterol distribution, as well as in other major risk factors (e.g., cigarette use, blood pressure).*

Stamler, J., Wentworth, D., and Neaton, J., Is the Relationship Between Serum Cholesterol and Risk of Premature Death from Coronary Heart Disease Continuous and Graded? JAMA, Vol. 236, No. 20, November 28, 1986

Over the second half of the twentieth century, the U.S. experienced a modest but steady rise in per capita alcohol consumption. During the 1980s, reports began to accumulate from many nations and diverse cultures that drinkers experienced lower rates of ischemic disease. Marmot studied alcohol consumption among 1,422 civil servants over a ten year period and concluded: *A multivariate analysis showed this U-shaped relationship between reported alcohol consumption and subsequent mortality to be largely independent of differences in smoking, blood pressure, plasma cholesterol and grade of employment* (Marmot 1981). In this study, alcohol consumption was one of those positive factors.

Cullen in the Busselton Study in Western Australia analyzed data from a twenty-three year prospective study and reported: *Compared with nondrinkers, moderate drinkers had an adjusted relative risk of death due to all causes of 0.76 . . . The adjusted relative risk for cardiovascular disease death among moderate drinkers was 0.68 and that of coronary heart disease death was 0.66* (Cullen 1993). Moderate drinkers (at a relative risk of 0.68) had thirty-two percent less risk for cardiovascular death than nondrinkers. On the European continent, Artalejo reported that: *Maintenance of the traditional Mediterranean life-style, involving a diet rich in fruit and vegetables and a moderate consumption of wine, preferably during meals, may contribute to sustaining the decline in CVD mortality in Spain* (Artalejo 1993). Alcohol is positively associated with the Mediterranean diet though the contribution of alcohol is frequently ignored by nutritionists (see Chapter 14). By the 1990s, studies across the globe identified moderate drinking with lower rates of CVD.

In 1986, Moore and Pearson at the Johns Hopkins Medical School undertook a massive review of alcohol and heart studies published around the world dating to the beginning of the century. They chronicled autopsy studies, ecological studies, case-control studies, cohort studies and ethnic group projects such as Japanese men living in Hawaii and the largely white suburban population in Framingham, Massachusetts. After analyzing over 160 separate projects, the authors declared: *A rich and diverse literature documents the association between alcohol consumption and coronary artery disease using a variety of methods. . . . The consistency, strength, specificity, dose-response and independence of association between moderate consumption and CAD implies a causal relationship* (Moore 1986). Little doubt left here. Drinking is found *causal* to better heart health. That was 1986.

Scientists mean something very specific when they employ the word *causal*. In viewing this large aggregation of studies, Moore and Pearson concluded that drinking lowered coronary artery disease. Drinking *caused* healthier hearts. Many other foods also contribute to heart health. The case was building for a scientific consensus for benefits deriving from the biochemical properties in drinks. Despite the abundance of confirming studies, *Dietary Guidelines for Americans* published by Health and Human Services and the Department of Agriculture in 1990 maintained the dry era mythology: *Alcoholic beverages supply calories but little or no nutrients. Drinking them has no net health benefit, (and) is linked with many health problems, is the cause of many accidents, and can lead to addiction. Their consumption is not recommended* (Dietary Guidelines 1990). By 1990, science had identified numerous health and nutritional benefits. These data conflicted with the 1917 AMA resolution stating that alcohol has no therapeutic values. The blinders were still firmly in place in medicine and the federal health establishment up to the mid-1990s. Both still discourage drinking for health.

As the 1990s drew to a close, reports of benefits accelerated as undoubtedly they will continue to flow into and through the new century. Recall that in 1998, Sir Richard Doll – Great Britain's famed researcher – concluded that alcohol's main contributions were with heart diseases: *The reduction in mortality is mainly attributable to ischaemic heart disease and cerebral thrombosis* (Doll 1998). A consensus was building.

Counterpoint from critics

Few conclusions in research transpire without heated conflict – especially when the findings challenge long-held precepts, such as Temperance suppositions. Shaper in 1990 held that the "non drinker" category in many studies was compromised because members in this category often were in ill health from previous abusive drinking: *A review of major prospective studies reveals an inadequate exploration of the nature of nondrinkers* (Shaper 1990). Criticisms were directed also at the validity of the U- and J-shaped curves. These and other doubts were reviewed by Anderson, a consultant to the World Health Association, as: *1) nondrinkers include unwell people who have given up drinking, 2) abstainers have more illness, 3) abstaining groups have a larger proportion of older, sicker people, and 4) relations of this category to smoking often were not well-enough defined* (Anderson 1994). Anderson argued against each of these objections stating: *Although there needs to be caution in the interpretation of the association, light drinking may well confer a benefit on certain population subgroups* (Anderson 1994). Better said as a majority of the drinking population.

In 1991, Marmot even questioned the assumption of higher heart mortality among *heavy* drinkers: *The studies examined did not show uniformly that heavy drinkers have a higher risk of cardiovascular disease than moderate drinkers* (Marmot 1991). To Shaper's claim that the abstinent group was corrupted by the presence of unwell former drinkers, Klatsky in a study of 121,840 subjects noted: . . . *the U-shaped alcohol-CAD relation is not due to selective abstinence by persons at higher risk. Findings support a protective effect of lighter drinking against CAD* (Klatsky 1990). In the study,

Klatsky separated data generated by lifelong abstainers from the data of ex-drinkers. As to the level of intake, data gathered from the Physicians Health Study by Sesso found: *These prospective data suggest that, among men with initially low drinking levels (1 drink per week or less), a subsequent moderate increase in drinking level may lower their CVD risk* (Sesso, 2000). Men with high original drinking levels had no reduction of CVD risk.

Stenosis describes the constriction within an artery. Liu studied drinking and coronary stenosis among men and women in Japan following coronary arteriography. The research reported: *Among men, the odds ratio of severe stenosis . . . was substantially lower than in nondrinkers for all categories of drinkers . . . Among women, current drinkers showed a small, non-significant reduction in risk for severe stenosis* (Liu 2001). The report continued: *The results demonstrate than alcohol use lowers the risk of coronary artery disease, especially severe coronary stenosis in men.*

Djousse studied the incidence of intermittent claudication (IC) (calf muscle fatigue) in peripheral arterial disease from data in the Framingham Heart Study and concluded: *These data are consistent with a protective effect of moderate drinking on IC risk* (Djousse 2000). Power found that: *Men drinking between 11-35 units of alcohol and women between 6-20 units of alcohol per week experienced fewer health-related problems than both nondrinkers and heavy drinkers* (Power 1998). This data confirmed the J- and U-curves which favor moderate drinkers. By the end of the 1990s, it was apparent that moderate consumers enjoy better health statistics, not only for heart disease but across an amazingly wide health spectrum of illnesses.

The few reports cited here verify many previous findings that moderate daily drinkers are able to maintain better health in every decade of adult living. Mainline, highly publicized studies such as Moore and Pearson and the two American Cancer Society projects lend credence to Doll's confident statement that ischemia is lessened by moderate drinking. Nowhere does this book claim that drinking alone is responsible for those favorable health statistics. Quite the opposite, these pages argue the obvious. Drinking helps.

Public health and medical authorities should – in recognition of this abundant research – acknowledge that moderate drinking is no *impairment* to good health and is a favorable *dietary* choice. In doing so, they would have to relinquish commitments to the control of availability agenda which seeks to reduce per capita consumption. That's the real medical anomaly. For many reasons– many of them economic, not medical – organized medicine is reluctant to do so.

Regional incidence of ischemia

In 1994, the U.S. Centers for Disease Control (CDC) published data on the rates of ischemic heart disease in the fifty states (Trends in Ischemic Heart Disease Deaths 1997). Each state's per capita consumption was rated against the average alcohol consumption for the entire nation. State alcohol consumption and rates of ischemia paralleled the global findings of St. Leger and La Porte in which heavier drinking nations had less CHD. For the most part, high per capita consuming states reported less ischemia.

SELECTED STATES	DEATHS PER 100,000	+/- AVERAGE DRINKING
Maryland	296.6	-3.7 under average
Minnesota	293.0	+7.4 over average
Washington	282.7	+0..9 over average
Colorado	266.2	+13.6 over average
Arkansas	263.9	+33.2 over average
Montana	249.9	+12.6 over average
Utah	251.5	-41.6 under average
Dist. Columbia	243.8	+72.9 over average
Hawaii	236.8	+10.7 over average
New Mexico	218.3	+4.7 over average

The data above includes selected states excerpted from the CDC study. The second column shows ischemic deaths per 100,000 people. The third column shows the percentage that this particular exceeds or or under the national per capita consumption level. Utah is interesting because it bucks the trend by having both less drinking and a low level of ischemia. This disparity obviously reflects the state's clean-living Mormon population. Utah demonstrates – as does the French paradox research – that other many lifestyle factors are important, along with drinking, for lower heart disease risk. Drinking alone does not guarantee better heart health. Individuals who eat poorly and have debilitating lifestyle habits – no matter where they live – will not be disease-protected by their drinking habits alone.

In the foreword to this book, University of Texas cardiologist Kaplan says that over-emphasis on the dangers of drinking can discourage individuals who could benefit from moderate use: *We should be very careful not to frighten the majority of the population who drink moderately so that they will deny themselves and everyone else the major protection against premature heart disease from regular, moderate alcohol intake* (Kaplan 1991).

As early as 1989, a news release issued by the American Heart Association directed attention to the importance of research on cardiovascular problems: *In the United States, CVD leads to more deaths each year – nearly 1 million – than all other causes combined* (AHA's Scientific Sessions Grow 1989).

Eleven years later, Rimm reviewed the literature and determined: *On the basis of published associations . . . 30 g of alcohol (about two drinks) a day would cause an estimated reduction of 24.7% in the risk of coronary heart disease* (Rimm 2000). In 2001, de Lorimier commented on the greatly expanded body of favorable literature: *There are now over 60 publications showing that moderate alcohol consumption (i.e. 1-4 drinks per day) reduces the incidence of myocardial infarctions as well as coronary disease mortality by a factor of 20-50% less than abstainers or very light drinkers in both men and women* (de Lorimier 2000). This accumulating evidence of the favorable relationship of responsible drinking to CVD problems deserves greater respect and attention from the American Heart Association spokespeople.

Still, the (heart) beat goes on.

Chapter 6

Heart Attacks

Fewer heart attacks than abstainers

Author's abstract: The focus of public concern is on the prevention of heart attacks. Ironically this chapter concerning heart attacks is one of the shortest. The obvious observation is that drinkers have lower risks for heart attacks than abstainers or abusers. In this respect, drinks are classed among the most important of heart health foods. Here are some findings:

➻ Long term drinkers suffer fewer damaging heart attacks
➻ Protection is found even among an overweight population
➻ Up to forty-nine percent lower risk found among daily drinkers

Research for this section is so copious as to be commonplace. Indeed, for every paper quoted in the first seven chapters, several dozen additional, confirming studies are available. This chapter contains but a smattering of findings which attribute special heart attack protection to moderate drinking. *Heart and Stroke Facts* describes a heart attack:

The medical term for heart attack is myocardial infarction. A heart attack occurs when the blood supply to part of the heart muscle (the myocardium) is severely reduced or stopped. This occurs when one of the arteries that supply blood to the heart muscle is blocked. The blockage is usually from a build-up of plaque (deposits of fat-like substances) due to atherosclerosis. A heart attack is often caused by a blood clot forming in a coronary artery . . . Such an event is sometimes called a coronary thrombosis or coronary occlusion.

Heart and Stroke Facts, American Heart Association, Dallas, 1999

As with ischemia, several terms are used to designate heart attacks – a cerebrovascular event, a myocardial infarction, a coronary thrombosis, and a coronary occlusion. In Chapter 3, blood clots were cited as atherosclerotic adhesions on the inner walls of arteries which separated to form blood clots. Clots can restrict the flow of blood to and from, as well as within the heart muscle itself.

Following a heart attack, an injured or dying portion of the heart muscle may trigger electrical activity called ventricular fibrillation, an uncoordinated heart throbbing which interferes with the measured flow of blood. It is vital in the early stages of a heart attack to keep the heart muscle pumping so that it can recover as much as possible on its own, often by rerouting oxygen-rich blood around the blocked artery.

Over the past two decades, dozens of studies conducted in many nations have reported fewer heart attacks among moderate drinkers. Yano in 1984 reported on a 10-year study of 7,705 Japanese men living in Hawaii in which alcohol consumption had a strong protective effect on myocardial infarction (heart attack). Stampfer in 1991 found similar results. In 1992, Razay studied 1,048 British women and found reduced risk among those who consumed up to the equivalent of two drinks a day. In 1993, Gaziano found that moderate drinking cut heart attack risk in half. Marques-Vidal in 1996 compared the impact of French wine drinking with distilled spirit consumption in Northern Ireland and found that both exerted protective effects. These are but a miniscule scattering of such studies.

One fascinating study in Germany by Keil involved overweight male and female beer consumers. It reported: *Lower to moderate alcohol consumption has a protective effect against CHD and total mortality in an overweight population* (Keil 1998). Miyame concludes that a prior drinking history is beneficial for those who suffer heart attacks: *Findings indicate that long-term alcohol consumption preconditions the heart and results in a reduction in damage following a heart attack and that adenosine A_1 receptors are required for this protective effect to occur. This may be a new mechanism whereby moderate drinking has a beneficial effect on cardiac health* (Miyame 1997).

An earlier study by Keil in *Epidemiology* established reduced coronary heart disease risk for beer drinkers in southern Germany remarkably similar to those of Renaud in southern France. Keil reported: *Among drinkers, men had an average alcohol intake of 42 gm per day, of which 33 gm per day come from beer. Women who drank had an average alcohol intake of 16 gm per day and derived about half of it from beer and the other half from wine. . . Intake of small to moderate amounts of alcohol is also associated with a lower total mortality risk in men and women* (Keil 1997). Two observations evolve from the Keil and Renaud studies. The first is that in Germany and France, both relatively heavy drinking nations, the average consumption is moderate. Keil's men averaged about three drinks daily and his women averaged only a single drink. Cultures which integrate drinking into the food regimen do not drink intemperately, as so many American medical warnings seem to imply. These findings refute the logic of the mantra "if you don't drink now, don't start for heart health reasons." Drinking daily around meals and in good fellowship promotes moderation, not abuse. The second factor found also in numerous other studies is that most individuals consume several types of beverages, though one type may predominate.

Another German study involving predominantly beer drinkers by Brenner offers some interesting insights about epidemiology and coronary artery disease risk. Its primary finding echoed others around the globe: *Our results support suggestions that the protective effect of moderate alcohol consumption against coronary artery disease is mediated in part by beneficial effects of ethanol on lipids and hemostatic factors* (Brenner 2001). These findings mesh with many others but the item of particular interest here is that the advantage favors beer drinkers: . . . *results of both German studies are remarkably consistent and support the suggestion that the beneficial effects of alcohol consumption also apply to subjects who exclusively or predominantly drink beer. Compared to abstainers, beer drinkers' risks were cut 50 percent while wine imbibers benefited only 5 percent* (Brenner 2001). Spirit drinker results weren't reported. Also noted: *Risk reductions were approximately the same (44-45%) for those who drank over 10 drinks per week and those who drank under 10 drinks per week* (Brenner 2001). The author noted that there were few "heavy drinkers" in the study in a nation where daily drinking is the norm! Interesting.

These findings provide an interesting contrast with Gronbaek's studies in Denmark which favor wine drinkers with little health impact for beer and spirit drinkers. An editorial by Rimm in *Epidemiology* discussed this disparity. First, the author posited alcohol as the most important causal agent for the benefits: *The evidence indicates that the association between moderate alcohol consumption and lower risk of CHD is causal and that abstaining from alcohol could be considered a risk factor for CHD* (Rimm 2001). Rimm further conjectured: *Diet and related lifestyle factors may confound the association between beverage choice and CHD to include these factors in future research.* Gronbaek made similar recommendations.

Rimm noted: *The results in Germany are similar to those reported in China, Japan, France, the United States and the United Kingdom, to name a few.* Many comments through the book taken from prominent medical publications discourage seniors, women, and the middle-aged from taking up drinking for health reasons. Yet, these commentators advise taking vegetables and fruits because of their potential impact on health. The rationale for ignoring alcohol benefits is the presumed and elevated risk of abuse or addiction. A growing number of physicians and researchers now suggest, along with Rimm, that *abstinence* may be the *real* risk.

This is the background battle simmering within medicine and public health. Should the people know — as Rimm notes above — that population studies around the world find responsible drinking *causal* to lowered heart risk (not to speak of the other benefits outlined in the following chapters)? This conflict is very real but very lopsided since conservatives hold nearly all of the positions of medical authority. Medical conservatism is buttressed by federal funding and private foundations sympathetic to the control of availability agenda. Many promote less per capita drinking. The only hope for a break in this stalemate is for a clinical revolt. But first, physicians must be better informed of these findings. Current resistance in medicine and public health to responsible drinking seems set in concrete.

Selective communication

Here are examples of the vein of rigid conservatism within the global medical community. In Western Australia, Holman suggests that wide dissemination of these favorable data would be medically unethical: *We conclude that in the absence of more adequate scientific knowledge and informed community debate it is unethical to promote low alcohol intake as a preventive health measure* (Holman 1996). Without wider communication of the findings, how can an "informed community debate" transpire? With well over 100 confirming studies on heart attack benefits, there is no "absence of scientific knowledge." Medical publications routinely report on much more speculative avenues of biomedical research. Alcohol findings are not entered into "informed community discussion." The premise that publicizing valid medical data can be unethical is truly puzzling. This concept presumes that we — the general public — are incapable of distinguishing healthy from abusive drinking or of benefiting from knowledge.

An alarming trend was reported in 2001 by the Centers for Disease Control. In a story reprinted in the *Seattle Post Intelligencer,* the agency reported that the death rate from cardiac arrest had risen dramatically among young American adults (Alarming news on cardiac arrest 2001). This study covered ages fifteen to thirty-four, relating the increased death rates to smoking, obesity and drug abuse. The growth in cardiac disease in younger age levels also may be another sad reflection of America's fat-saturated diet sans the moderating impact of drinks on vascular disease enjoyed by the French.

The American Heart Association enthusiastically backs mild aspirin use every-other-day to prevent heart attacks. This enthusiasm arises from analyses of the Physician's Health Study which determined a forty-five percent lower risk for heart attacks among doctors who took aspirin regularly. Several months earlier than the release of the aspirin data, the same lead researcher – Hennekens of Harvard – reported to another heart association meeting on the results of another long-range study funded by the association: *Analysis showed that compared with nondrinkers, people who drink moderate amounts of alcohol every day– defined as two beers or wines or one mixed drink– had a 49 percent lower risk of a heart attack* (Hennekens 1987).

Compare these two studies. The alcohol consuming group enjoyed a two percent *better* health risk than aspirin users (though the studies may have involved different methods). Not to mention that drinks constitutes a considerably more tasty and satisfying alternative. At the time, this writer called the AHA to inquire why the drinking data did not merit similar enthusiasm since over sixty percent of Americans drink. The response, remarkably similar to the one Jonathan Rauch experienced (see Epidemiology section), was that the heart association could not promote drinking because of the dangers of abuse. How about the dangers of infarctions? Why not support drinking if it lessens the disease the association is committed to remedy? Positive data about the nation's most serious health problem is downplayed to the 120 million-plus moderates, the ones most likely to benefit from the knowledge.

Contretemps

The majority of discussions in this book involve the biomedical sciences, as if all health wisdom resides in a test tube. It doesn't. The social science commentary interspersed in these pages demonstrates the many valuable contributions of other disciplines on drinking affairs. Social scientists discover and evaluate drinking deportment and tendencies, factors that are rarely noted in biomedical commentary. Anthropologist Heath notes: *In most nations the rationale that state authorities give for trying to restrict the availability of alcohol, even though it is a legal substance, is public health. . . . By contrast, until the twentieth century, alcohol held a fundamental place in the pharmacopoeia of most cultures, and it is still credited with a variety of preventive and curative effects* (Heath 1995). In contrast to most modern nations, our federal health authorities ejected alcohol from the nation's roster of approved therapeutic drugs. The AMA followed suit by banishing alcohol therapy from medical education and clinical practice. The restoration of drinking to some level of clinical favor is a medical imperative. American medicine has fostered an unseemly condition that actually deprives the public of reasonable and fair communication of vital health data.

Alcohol historian Rorabaugh notes: *Research cannot escape the social and political atmosphere with which it is conducted. This is perhaps particularly true for alcohol research, because so much of it has been government funded* (Rorabaugh 1996). Sociologist Levine writes: *The alcohol problem or alcohol abuse as it is commonly understood and talked about today, this medical, scientific and popular way of viewing alcohol is nearly 200 years old – but no older . . . drinking became an all purpose explanation for social problems – it became the scapegoat* (Levine 1983). Science writer Roueche' finds: *The popular mythology of alcohol is a vast and vehement book. . . . As a compendium of ageless error, of phantom fears and ghostlier reassurances, it probably has no equal* (Roueche' 1960). Sociologist Hanson notes: *Beverage alcohol has always played a valuable role in enhancing the quality of human life. Alcohol causes few problems in the majority of societies throughout the world . . . drinking abuse is least likely to occur in a society in which moderate drinking is encouraged* (Hanson 1995). Alternative academic disciplines have pertinent data to contribute to this debate. They should be accorded seats at the health policy table.

The role of platelets in heart attacks

Two studies released in 2000 associate the role of platelet activity and the utility of many alcohol beverages in heart attack protection. Serebruany concentrated on the role of platelet activity in a small group of patients who had experienced AMI (acute myocardial infarction). Platelet activity was assayed by a variety of methods among twenty-three patients leading to this conclusion: *These results confirm that moderate drinking is associated with diminished platelet activity in patients presenting with AMI. The ability of moderate alcohol use to favourably modulate the pre-reperfusion platelet status in such patients is of clinical relevance* (Serebruany 2000). This author urges a large-scale clinical test of this premise. In an eight year study at Kaiser Permanente hospitals involving 128,934 individuals, Klatsky found: *Our major conclusions from these data are that all types of alcoholic beverages protect against CAD and that additional protection by specific beverages is minor* (Klatsky 1991).

Another study conducted in the Czech Republic, a predominantly beer-drinking nation, concentrates on beer and spirits drinkers. Bobak outlines the primary goal of his study:

Many studies have shown an inverse association between alcohol use and CHD, with a possible flattening of the curve at higher drinking levels. It remains unclear whether this protective effect is confined to specific beverage types (such as red wine) or is attributable to alcohol per se. This question is complicated because wine drinkers may differ from people preferring other beverages or having a different drinking pattern . . . and by confining the analyses to people who do not drink wine or spirits.

Bobak, M., Skodova, A. and Marmot, M., Effect of beer drinking on risk of myocardial infarction: population based case-control study, British Medical Journal 320:1378-1379, 2000

Bobak identifies the importance of each study population. Wine drinkers tend to have attained more education, have higher incomes and maintain generally healthier lifestyles. These factors influence the results as do unique cultural and lifestyle practices of all study groups. Bobak's Czech beer drinkers are a vastly different group than Klatsky's northern California citizenry. While the cultural distinctions are many, the findings of better health among both groupings of moderate drinkers are nearly identical. Bobak concludes: *The lowest risk of myocardial infarction was found for men drinking almost daily or daily and for those who drank 4-9 litres of beer a per week. The protective effect of beer may be lost for drinking twice a day or more often. These results support the view that the protective effect of alcoholic beverages is attributable to alcohol per se rather than to specific substances in different beverages.*

New ways of looking at old problems

Cross-disciplinary studies support and broaden the limitations of biomedical research. This is why findings in the social sciences should be incorporated routinely into medical studies. In clinical practice, physicians routinely consider lifestyle influences in treating patients apart from blood workups and biochemical analyses. Clinical practice often is a by-guess and by-golly world. In *The Save Your Heart Guide,* Jones quotes one practicing physician: *You see a patient with only a 20 percent build-up one day and he'll have a 100 percent blockage the next. Other people with 50 to 60 percent blockage will live out their lives without anything happening. I can say that out of one hundred people like you, ten will die. But, I can't tell you if you will be one of the ten* (Jones 1996). Any data that can expand a understanding of lifestyle influences should be in the black bag of the practicing physician, including findings on drink therapy for those not at risk.

Zuger reports in "How a Drink a Day Helps the Heart:" *A drink or two a day provides the equivalent of a potent cholesterol medicine and a weak blood thinner, as well as a variety of other substances that may keep the body's metabolism tuned and its cells in good repair. . . . Moderate drinking can raise the levels (HDL) more than 10 percent . . . By comparison, running a few miles a week increases HDL a fraction of that, while the B vitamin niacin, probably the most effective medication for raising HDL levels, has to be taken at high doses that entail many side effects for similar results. The statin low-cholesterol drugs, which work by reducing LDL or bad cholesterol, seldom raise HDL levels substantially* (Zuger 2002).

Moreover, recent studies have found favorable impacts of sustained drinking patterns among heart attack survivors. *Johns Hopkins' Health After 50* reported that heart attack survivors are particularly vulnerable to continuing high cholesterol and elevated blood pressure levels (Prescription for heart attack survivors 2001). Mukamal conducted a cohort study among forty-five U.S. community hospitals involving 1,913 adults hospitalized with a heart attack. He concluded: *Self-reported moderate alcohol consumption in the year prior to AMI [acute myocardial infarction] is associated with reduced mortality following infarction* (Mukamal 2001). Drinking benefits – before and after infarction – were gathered from nearly 2,000 hospitals. These remarkable findings should be incorporated in all heart attack update articles. They seldom are. A companion study by Abramson involved 2,235 non-institutionalized elderly persons with a mean age of seventy-two. It reported: *Increasing levels of moderate alcohol consumption are associated with decreasing risk of heart failure among older persons* (Abramson 2001). Shouldn't senior citizens – and those who care for them – have access to such encouraging findings?

Another 2002 study in France by de Longeril found that heart attack survivors who consumed 2-4 drinks of wine per day reduced the risk of further cardiovascular disease by 50-60 percent; those who drank 2/day, reduced complications 59 percent; heavier drinkers (4-5/day) enjoyed a 53 percent advantage. The study held a 4 year follow up and noted: . . . *drinkers did not have a healthier diet than abstainers* (de Longeril 2002). One begins to wonder how much proof we need? Note also their drinking levels were in excess of federal standards.

Once again, we find no lack of support for drinking before and after heart attacks in the original professional journals. In "Should Patients With Heart disease Drink Alcohol?," Klatsky cites 24 studies in concluding: *The reports in this issue, plus other studies directly or indirectly supporting lower risk of heart failure or death after MI association with moderate drinking, seem to support a "yes" response. Importantly, these studies provide no evidence suggesting harm to these persons by moderate drinking* (Klatsky 2001). A recent article in the *Seattle Post-Intelligencer* reprinted from the *New York Times* carried this headline, "Aspirin after bypass surgery cuts death risk." The article suggested that prompt use of aspirin could save 8,000 lives a year following bypass surgery in the U.S. If medical authorities were as enthusiastic about Klatsky, Mukamal and Abramson's findings and communicated them to the popular media, many lives might be saved or extended.

The above *Health After 50* article fails to mention any of these sources. It simply ignores a solid line of research harking back to Dock who in 1968 echoed Lucia's theme that drinks provide a plus factor, particularly for seniors: *Alcohol is not needed for nutrition in most cases of stroke and heart disease, but it is invaluable in reducing dread and discomfort and permitting the patient to accept the blow which fate has dealt him. Alcohol is unequaled in its power to confer equanimity* (Dock 1968).

A recent study by Sierksma of a relatively small group of 19 men and women found a 35% drop in plasma C-reactive protein levels after three weeks in which men consumed up to 4 beers and women 3 during meals. In addition, fibrinogen levels predictive of blood clots dropped 12.4%. Of this study of C-reactive proteins, Ridker noted: *The implications of this are enormous. It means we have an entire other way of treating, targeting and preventing heart disease that was essentially missed because of our focus solely on cholesterol* (Sierksma 2002). More discoveries in this avenue of research will undoubtedly take place in the near future. The findings complement other heart-health benefits from drinks. Note that the level of consumption in the project exceeds the government's recommendations of no more than two standard drinks for men and one for women daily (See Chapter 31).

Once again, recall that the correlation between drinking and heart health is not new science. The statistics in the table below are taken from a study conducted by Brummer in *Acta Medica* (1969) thirty-two years ago. The study surveyed coronary mortality in relation to the consumption of coffee, cocoa, tea and alcohol in twenty countries. Here are figures from five of those nations – two with temperance leanings, Finland and the U.S., and three, France, Italy and West Germany, in which consumption is up to four times that of the U.S. The second column shows heart attacks per 100,000 people. The third column shows comparative alcohol intake in kg perperson.

Country	Men 55-65 yrs	Alcohol Intake
Finland	910.5	5.1
France	200.8	40.8
Italy	387.1	25.9
U.S.	923.7	11.1
W. Germany	500.2	20.2

This 1969 study and many confirming projects since, including the new findings of Mukamal and Abramson, clearly dem-

onstrate a statistical risk advantage for drink-integrated nations
– and drinking-integrated individuals. This manifestly apparent
advantage prompted Serge Renaud to declare on the CBS
French Paradox telecast: *It's well documented that a moderate intake
of alcohol prevents heart disease by as much as 50 percent . . . I mean
there is no other drug that is being so efficient as the moderate intake
of alcohol* (The French Paradox on CBS 1991).

In "Low-Dose Aspirin for Everyone," *Health After 50* provides
an excellent review of the role of aspirin in prevention of heart
attacks and stroke. The editor notes that: *. . . people with less than
1% risk of having a heart attack over the next 5 years probably would
not benefit from preventative aspirin and might experience needless side
effects* (Low Dose 2002). Those at low risk of abusive drinking
might want to look into moderate consumption for heart risk
reduction, as well as for positive impacts on other illnesses that
attend across the span of life.

Another analysis of the long standing Framingham study also
published in 2002 concerns alcohol's impact on congestive heart
failure. Reviewing data for 26,035 person-years for men and
35,563 person-years for women, Walsh reported that: *In the
community (Framingham), alcohol use is not associated with an increased risk of congestive heart failure, even among heavy drinkers (>15
drinks/week for men, >8 drinks/week for women). When used in
moderation, alcohol appears to protect against the development of
congestive heart failure* (Walsh 2002).

Old and contemporary studies confirm Renaud's conclusion
above about the extraordinary efficacy of moderate drinking for
heart disease. In a nation which purchases every manner of
insurance policy that can be devised by clever underwriters,
the knowledge that a moderate drink or two a day can lessen
heart attack risk, and perhaps prevent a recurrence of another
such event, presents an inviting and pleasurable insurance gam-
ble. A tasty one at that.

It's time to check out those risk odds.

Chapter 7

Strokes

Drinks can lessen the risk of stroke

■ **Author's abstract**: This final chapter on cardiovascular diseases contains more support for moderate drinking. Drinking helps to reduce ischemic or vascular stroke, the predominant stroke. But only when the consumption is limited to small, daily amounts of alcohol in place of heavy use or binge drinking episodes.

■ ⇢ Rates of stroke differ greatly among ethnic groups
   ⇢ Light alcohol consumption lowers risk
   ⇢ Lifelong abstention increases risk
   ⇢ A diet including fruits, vegetables, fiber, mono-unsaturated
      fats and moderate alcohol consumption lessens risk

Our final cardiovascular category is stroke. *Stroke*, the 1998 White Paper from Johns Hopkins Medical School, describes the conditions which constitute strokes:

A stroke is a medical emergency that arises when an artery supplying blood to a portion of the brain

*ruptures or becomes blocked, so that the brain cells
(neurons) in the affected area are starved of the
oxygen and nutrients normally provided by the blood.
One reason a stroke is so dangerous is that the brain
—unlike muscle or other kinds of tissue —has little
or no reserve stores of energy . . . some degree of
brain function may be lost in as little as four minutes:
after a few hours, cells cannot survive.*

Margolis, S., and Wityk, R., Stroke, Johns Hopkins White Paper, Baltimore, 1998

Stroke is a serious killer and disabler. According to the American Heart Association's *Heart and Stroke Facts*:

*On average, someone in the United States suffers a
stroke every 53 seconds; every 3.3 minutes someone
dies of one. . . . stroke ranks as the third leading
cause of death (1 of every 14.8 deaths) . . . Stroke is
a leading cause of serious, long-term disability in the
U.S. . . 457,000 males and 553,000 females were
discharged from hospitals in 1998 after having a
stroke.*

Heart and Stroke Statistical Update, American Heart Association, Dallas, 2001

A *Health After 50* article in May 2001 notes: *Each year, more than 600,000 Americans experience a stroke or "brain attack" . . . In addition to being the third-leading killer of American adults . . . About 450,000 people survive a stroke each year* (Your Stroke Survival 2001). That means that about forty-five of every sixty stroke victims survive, most with major disabilities. Under "Action Steps," the *Health After 50* article notes: *Drink only in moderation. Although 1 to 2 alcoholic drinks daily is associated with a modest decline in stroke risk, drinking larger amounts has the opposite effect.* It is good to be able to report that many articles in 2001 take a more enlightened stance about drinking. Let's hope it becomes trendy to include the benefits as well as the warnings.

In "Silent and Deadly," Smith, on *Time's* Health page, notes: *In 1999 alone, there were 750,000 full-fledged strokes in the U.S. and a half a million transient ischemic attacks (TIAs), or mini-strokes. . . Mini-strokes result from temporary interruptions of blood flow to the brain* (Smith 2000). *Time* estimates about 150 thousand more strokes than *Health After 50.* Both estimates represent a very large number of individuals and their families.

A stroke study conducted at the University of Cincinnati found American Heart Association stroke estimates skewed from over-dependence on data gathered among white, middle-class populations such as the residents of Framingham, Massachusetts (Pancioli 1998). Utilizing a mixed urban Cincinnati population, Pancioli's study elevated the national estimate to be as high as 800,000 per year. In addition, the authors estimated another half million transient ischemic attacks (TIAs or mini-strokes), a phenomenon seldom accounted for in stroke statistics.

Standard warning signs for stroke are:

✔ *Sudden weakness or numbness of the face, arm or leg*
✔ *Sudden dimness or loss of vision, particularly, one eye*
✔ *Sudden difficulty speaking or understanding speech*
✔ *Sudden severe headache with no known cause*
✔ *Unexplained dizziness, unsteadiness or sudden falls*

While each of these signs is individually distinctive, they can easily be attributed to other minor irritations common to the aging. Unlike angina pectoris, none are piercing or intensely painful. Those who care for women should be extra-alert for mild stroke symptoms. Administration of t-PA within three hours from the inception of an episode can arrest serious stroke damage. Readers will recall that daily drinkers are advantaged by higher natural production of t-PA. However, recent studies have identified as many as 1,500 deaths annually are caused by incorrect dosages of t-PA. From this, we see how critical timing, proper medication and skilled medical care can be in treating stroke.

Harvard Men's Health Watch distinguishes between the two types of stroke:

There are two major kinds of stroke, hemorrhagic and ischemic. Hemorrhagic strokes are less common but more cataclysmic; they occur when a blood vessel in

the brain bursts, spilling blood into the brain or the
fluid that surrounds it. Ischemic strokes, on the other
hand, result from a blockage of a blood vessel in the
brain.

Cholesterol and Stroke, Harvard Men's Health Watch, November, 1998

Cooper cites important ethnic differences in stroke occurrence: *The highest incidence of strokes in the world is in Chinese living in Taiwan. The second highest incidence is in Japanese living in Japan, and the third highest is in American blacks who have an incidence twice as high as U.S. whites* (Cooper 1988).

Again, it's the dose

The drinking level determines whether there is an advantage or an increased risk of stroke. Gill notes: *These results show an excess of heavy consumers of alcohol among patients with stroke. Among men, light alcohol intake (10 to 90 g per week) was associated with a reduction in relative risk, but there was a fourfold increase in the risk of stroke in those who reported heavy alcohol intake (>300 g per week). In conclusion, our data suggest that heavy current alcohol intake is an independent, under-emphasized and potentially reversible risk factor for stroke in men* (Gill 1986). The grams noted above show a benefit up to about two drinks a day and a disadvantage for over three drinks. In a large study including 128,934 participants, Klatsky found: *These results indicate that only heavy drinking is moderately associated with risk of hemorrhagic stroke. Light-to-moderate drinking does not appear to be associated* (Klatsky 2002).

But some studies show a very fine line between advantage and increased risk. In Israel, Ben-Shlomo found: *Alcohol may increase the risk of stroke 30-90%. The variations in risk found in this study with different comparative groups favor a hypothesis that alcohol consumption may modestly increase the risk of stroke, despite the lack of statistically significant findings* (Ben-Shlomo 1992). Rodgers set up a case-controlled study in 1993 at the University of Newcastle, U.K. Past drinking habits of 364 stroke victims were established: *Lifelong abstention from alcohol is associated with an increased risk of stroke. Moderate alcohol consumption may protect against cerebrovascular disease* (Rodgers 1993). When all factors were brought to bear, lifelong drinkers had an advantage over lifelong abstainers for stroke.

Truelsen and a Danish team discovered: *The results show that a daily wine consumption is associated with the lowest risk of stroke compared with nondrinkers* (Truelsen 1998). This study isolated daily drinking as a key positive factor. When daily drinking ceased, the alcohol-associated benefits also disappeared. None of these studies by itself is definitive. Once again, you need to know where the study took place and who were the participants. However, with benefits showing up among so many diverse cultures, moderate drinking is a good bet to lessen stroke risk.

As usual, there are two points of view about this assumption. Some studies question the existence of any drinking benefits. Wannamethee studied a group of middle-aged British men and found: *The relationship between the pattern of alcohol intake and the risk of stroke is unclear, in particular the increased risk observed in abstainers and the possible protective effect of light to moderate drinking. There is no convincing evidence that light or moderate drinking is beneficial for stroke risk compared with occasional drinking* (Wannamethee 1996). When the author stops splitting hairs, both light and occasional drinking appear to correlate with less stroke risk.

Most studies attribute benefits from each alcohol type. Kiechl reports: *The association between regular alcohol intake and the incidence of carotid stenosis was U-shaped . . . . We failed to find any differential effects of alcohol from various sources* (Kiechl 1998). Kitamura also found reductions in risk for all alcoholic beverages: *Only 0.5 percent of the beverage alcohol consumed by participants was from grape wine. The remainder was from distilled spirits, beer and rice wine* (Kitamura 1998). Whatever the beverages of choice, the benefits apparently are available.

Diet and stroke

As with other cardiovascular problems, diet plays a critical role in the development or the avoidance of stroke. Gillman discusses the diet and increased risk: *First, the origin of stroke is multifactorial, and a single recommendation about dietary fat may not apply to all persons. Second, the roles of dietary fat and type of fat in the genesis of all cardiovascular diseases . . . are unclear . . . for the present, primary prevention of stroke should include adequate intake of fruits and vegetables* (Gillman 1997). Lardinois feels that a low-risk, hypertension diet (such as the DASH diet) will affect the risk for stroke: *Weight reduction, sodium chloride restriction, and avoidance of excessive alcohol consumption appear to be the best nutritional approaches to the treatment of hypertension. The role of dietary alterations of fiber, calcium, magnesium, potassium, dietary fats, carbohydrates, and protein is less convincing* (Lardinois 1995). Willett includes drinking in an agenda for stroke risk reduction: *Available evidence generally supports a reduced risk of MI with increased consumption of fruit and vegetables, fiber, mono-unsaturated fatty acids, and moderate amounts of alcohol* (Willett 1996).

The American Heart Association campaign favoring aspirin to reduce the risk of stroke has had good results. An article in the May, 2000 *HealthNews* estimates that: . . . *20 percent of Americans over age 65 take aspirin regularly for pain relief or to reduce the risk of heart attacks and stroke* (Aspirin to Prevent Strokes 2000). The article notes that: *While finding that heart attack risk was reduced among aspirin takers, the meta-analysis found a 35 percent increase in the risk of hemorrhagic stroke. . . . The benefits of taking aspirin at low doses — less than 325 mg daily — to reduce heart attack risk probably outweighs the possible increase in the risk of hemorrhagic stroke.* Hemorrhagic strokes account for only about ten per cent of all strokes. This is balanced reporting on risks and benefits.

By contrast, the AHA and public health literature discourages drinking or fails to acknowledge the positive alcohol research on stroke. This is unbalanced reporting on risks and benefits. Pearson, author of the American Heart Association's guidelines on drinking, commented: *We know that there are substantial diseases related to alcohol. We have this cardiovascular benefit, but this should not prompt us to be putting up billboards on the interstate* (Just one drink 1999). As a spokesperson for the AHA, Pearson's comments are interesting. The association billboards aspirin while it downplays drinks. Medical diffidence disdains alcohol therapy.

In each of the thirty drinking conditions discussed in this book, moderate dosage is recommended as the key to initiating a benefit threshold. Calcoya notes: *Moderate drinking is a protective factor for all stroke types combined, but heavy drinking is a strong risk factor* (Calcoya 1999). Gill writes: *Moderate alcohol consumption (100-390 grams per week) was associated with a 30 to 50% reduction in risk of all three kinds of strokes: ischemic, subarachnoid and cerebral but there was a fourfold increase in the risk of stroke in those who reported heavy alcohol intake* (Gill 1991). This comment demonstrates balanced, unbiased reporting that often is missing in institutional publications.

The recent study by Mukamal in *Stroke* found that moderate drinkers among a group of 3,660 adults aged sixty-five and over had a fifty percent reduction in brain blockages but a slightly higher risk for brain shrinkage. Commenting on this finding in an editorial in the same issue, Bereczki noted: *Probably most people would choose to drink at least 15 drinks a week rather than be abstinent to get the benefit of a marked reduction of infarcts (blockages) for the price of a small increase in atrophy, especially if we consider that another report from the same study found that the atrophy group performed better than expected on cognitive and motor tasks* (Bereczki 2001). Many individuals might choose alcohol therapy to avoid stroke, if given the chance to choose. If medical communicators take the easy way out and simply ignore these findings in the professional literature, unbalanced perceptions are the inevitable consequence.

Brenner determined in a study of 22,000 male doctors that men who consumed from one drink per week to one per day had a seventeen to twenty-five per cent lower risk of stroke (Brenner 1999). In another review of the Nurses' Health Study involving over 84,000 nurses between the ages of thirty-four to fifty-nine, Hu suggests that a healthy lifestyle for women consisting of the following lifestyle habits could reduce heart disease for women a startling eighty-two percent:

✔ *Don't smoke*
✔ *Avoid being overweight*
✔ *Get at least half an hour of moderate exercise each day*
✔ *Drink alcohol in moderation — an average of one-half of a drink or a little more per day*
✔ *Eat healthy food, avoiding saturated fats and getting*

relatively large amounts of such foods as fish oil,
fiber, vegetable oils and whole-grain products

Hu., et al., How to reduce heart disease by 82%, Seattle Post Intelligencer, November 9, 1999

Cardiovascular Summing Up

The evidence presented in these first seven chapters defines drinks – as Lucia suggested they eventually would – as the most versatile of health foods, at least in relation to cardiovascular diseases. According to a variety of studies cited in this section, cardiovascular benefits include:

Lowering of LDL — Raising of HDL — Reducing
arterial stress spasms — Artery dilation increasing
blood flow — Reducing plasma insulin — Reducing
angina pain — Reducing risk of heart attacks —
Lowering of fibrinogen levels — Reducing adherence
of clot-forming platelets — Protection against
ischemia — Increasing levels of endogenous t-PA —
Lowering of blood pressure — Lessening the
incidence of stroke — Lowering of all cause mortality
— Raising a sense of well-being — Inducing
tranquillity

All these benefits derive from commonly available, inexpensive and delectable food products. Despite these findings many individuals, government spokesmen and social agencies in the field of medicine remain committed to reducing per capita drinking. This dominant American medical philosophy is seen in an editorial published in the July 1999 issue of *The Cleveland Clinic Heart Advisor*. In "Alcohol and Stroke: Too Much of a Good Thing?," the editors find little compelling in drink research and advise nondrinkers to eschew the practice. This advice comes from a cardiology clinic:

Does this mean that alcohol is a treatment for
coronary artery blockages or that people with heart
disease should start drinking to lower their risks of
stroke? Absolutely not. The message here, as
endorsed by the American Heart Association, is that
moderate alcohol consumption may decrease your

> *risk of stroke. If you choose to drink, keep it to less than two drinks a day. But if you don't drink, don't start. People with certain medical conditions or a family history of alcoholism should not drink at all, and there can be dangerous side effects of even a small amount of alcohol taken with certain medications.*

Alcohol and Stroke: Too Much of a Good Thing? The Cleveland Clinic Heart Advisor, Vol. 1, No. 7, July, 1998

Why "absolutely not." Why not at least consider moderate drinking's relationship to stroke risk? It is hoped that readers are coming to understand that repeated warnings of high risk of addiction is Temperance bunkum. Most Americans who drink enjoy the practice over a lifetime without serious risk. This "absolutely not" attitude in medicine discourages informed choice. Fear of the drinking is so deeply entrenched in medical practice that millions of moderate living individuals are needlessly exposed to greater risks for cardiovascular disease.

Real living risks are unavoidable. There is no absolutely risk-free drinking, as there is no absolutely risk-free automobile driving, skiing, bicycling, snow-boarding or jogging — or risk-free pharmaceutical drugs, for that matter. Living itself is risky business. What is missing in the "if you don't drink now, don't start" advisories is perspective and relativity.

Consider the risks Americans face in taking prescription drugs. On Thursday, April 5, 2001 a full page advertisement in the *Seattle Post Intelligencer* invited the attention of type-2 diabetes patients. It urged Glucophage users to consider new Glucophage XR. Noted under "Important Information" was the following: *Glucophage XR is not for everyone. In rare cases, Glucophage XR may cause lactic acidosis (build-up of lactic acid in the blood) which is serious and can be fatal in half the cases . . . The most common side effect is diarrhea* (Attention Glucophage Users 2001). The side effects of this drug range from diarrhea to death. In any medical regimen, risks must be evaluated against benefits. The attending physician calmly discusses the options and involves the patient in the decision. Not so with drinking. The benefits are ignored by medical authority and the advice is "don't start."

Five days later, the *Seattle Post Intelligencer* carried another full page ad devoted to the merchandising of Allegra-D, an allergy medicine. But, cautioned the ad: *Allegra-D must not be taken if you are also taking MAO inhibitors (medicines that treat depression) or if you retain urine or have glaucoma, severe high blood pressure, or severe heart disease . . . diabetes, heart disease, glaucoma, thyroid disease, impaired kidney function, or symptoms of an enlarged prostate* (Major Congestion in Seattle 2001). How is the average person to appreciate the symptoms or risks for all of these exotic illnesses? The reality is that modern medicine presents a thicket of risks which require patients to exercise caution, discretion and adherence to safe levels of a variety of prescriptions. Only with drinking does the profession perceive that the same trustworthy patients are incapable of following prescribed levels.

A case in point

A report delivered to an American Heart Association convention in 1997 concerned results of the Manhattan Stroke Study. Over 1,200 inner-city men and women participated. Over half of the subjects were Hispanic. About thirty percent were African American. Sacco reported: *Light or occasional alcohol consumption lowered stroke risk by up to 62 percent compared to non-drinkers* (Sacco 1997). Knowing that blacks are at the greatest stroke risk, lowering stroke levels among inner city residents by such a significant margin could lower total stroke incidence in society. Withholding these findings from the general public (and black patients in particular) borders on raising civil rights considerations. Sacco offered a rationale for caregivers to convey information about the protection that moderate drinking could have:

> *Moderate alcohol consumption, up to 2 drinks per day, was significantly protective for ischaemic stroke after adjustment for cardiac disease, hypertension, diabetes, current smoking, body mass index and education . . . Moderate alcohol consumption was independently associated with a decreased risk of ischaemic stroke in our elderly, multi-ethnic urban*

*subjects, while heavy alcohol consumption had
deleterious effects.*

Sacco, R., Elkind, M., Boden-Albala, B., Lin, I., Kargman, D., Hauser, W., Shea, S., and Paik, M., The protective effect of moderate alcohol consumption on ischaemic stroke, Journal of the American Medical Association, Vol. 281, Vol. 1, pp53-60, 1999

The positive findings continue to pile up. Berger notes: *Light-to-moderate alcohol consumption reduced the overall risk of stroke and the risk of ischemic stroke in men* (Berger 1999). *Harvard Health Letter* reports: *But in low-to-moderate amounts, alcohol is almost a health food because of its beneficial effects on arteries and cholesterol levels . . . having just one drink a week was protective against stroke* (Pre-emptive Strikes 2000). *UC Berkeley Wellness Letter* advises: *A daily drink or two (wine, beer, or liquor) may reduce by half the risk of ischemic stroke* (Wellness facts 1999). Almost a health food!

Li concludes in a study of basilar arteries taken from male and female dogs that: *. . . The findings, when viewed in the light of other recent results, suggest that antioxidants may prove useful in the amelioration and treatment of alcohol-induced brain damage and stroke* (Li 2001). Positive antioxidant commentary is found in many of the following chapters. In a study of 166 hospitalized patients in India, Zodpey found: *The results of this study indicate that heavy drinking in general increases the risk of haemorrhagic stroke . . . The current study did not find a significant association between mild or moderate drinking and haemorrhagic stroke. In fact, earlier studies suggested that alcohol use at low levels may have some protective effect on the cerebral vasculature* (Zodpey 2001).

The good news accumulates.

The reality is that America is gradually winning the heart disease battle. *UC Berkeley Wellness Letter* notes: *Since 1921, heart disease has been the major killer of American men and women. Death rates from all forms of heart disease peaked in 1950 and then began an overall decline . . . and have dropped 60 percent from their peak* (Progress against heart disease 1999). Beginning in 1950, per capita drinking in the U.S. increased until the neoprohibition era was introduced by the government (with tacit support of medicine), which, in the latter three decades, influenced a gentle decline in consumption. Did the increases in moderate drinking contribute to the heart disease decline? The research in the first seven chapters would say so. Is there risk in drinking? Of course. As there is in prescription drugs and recreational pursuits.

Risk is fundamental to human existence. Most contemporary drugs have serious side effects; some, like Glucophage and Allegra-D, may even be lethal when used by truly at-risk people. As it does with medicinal drugs, American medicine should distinguish between the majority who are at little or no risk and the minority at certain risk, between use and abuse. To impose unwarranted fears for all drinkers is to deprive the majority of critical health information. This is a clinical absurdity. Yet it is the way American medicine treats drinking today.

In his introduction to *Alcohol and Pleasure: A Health Perspective*, Peele argues:

> *After a long-standing period of public health attention to alcohol, one primarily concerned with the problematic aspects of drinking, alcohol consumption remains both a major public health concern and a popular, widespread, and irreducible activity. Even the sternest public health advocates cannot reasonably expect to eliminate or indefinitely reduce drinking worldwide, nor do the data clearly show that such a goal would produce public health. Pleasure in drinking is an understated phenomenon.*

Peele, S., and Grant, M., Alcohol and Pleasure, Brunner/Mazel, Philadelphia, 1999

The remainder of this book will flesh out the argument that a large, diverse and substantive agglomeration of positive research is being neglected because of prevailing cultural and medical assumptions about drinking. It will be difficult for some readers to accept this premise. Here is a repetition of a significant conclusion from Rorabaugh writing in the *Social History of Alcohol Review*:

> *Research cannot escape the social and political atmosphere within which it is conducted. This is perhaps particularly true for alcohol research, because so much of it has been government funded. Alcohol history has followed trends in alcohol research. In the sober, financially restrained nineties, alcohol history has moved away from both the large*

> *generalizations that occupied the seventies and the*
> *more detailed studies of the eighties. Instead, there*
> *is pressure to make alcohol history "relevant" by*
> *stressing studies that might "pay off" in terms of*
> *eventual declines in drinking . . .*

Rorabaugh, W., Alcohol History: Personal Reflections, History of Alcohol Review, 32-33, 1996

This from an historian with an alcohol studies specialty writing for other historians in a small, professional review. It amounts to history shop talk. It demonstrates the reality that the government exerts significant pressures on the research community to produce studies which exemplify its theme that reducing drinking promotes public health.

Another frequent dissimulation lies in the attempt to narrow any drinking benefits to older age levels. The government's *Dietary Guidelines for Americans* concludes that: . . . *moderate consumption provides little, if any, health benefit for younger people* (Dietary Guidelines 1995). The authors of this phrase could hardly be unaware of the copious positive research on drinking for many illnesses across the span of life. Malarcher published in *Stroke* the results of a study of over 600 women fifteen to forty-four years of age reporting that: . . . *light to moderate drinkers had 40% to 60% lower risk of ischemic stroke than never drinkers* (Malarcher 2000). Age-conservatism is nothing more than damage control for those in government, public health and medicine who want to lessen per capita drinking. It is a medical disservice to both youth and young adults.

Readers should grasp why it is necessary for this book to present so many instances of alcohol ambivalence in medical literature. It is essential to drive home the point that medical indifference (or outright opposition) to drinking is a serious and unremitting medical problem itself. It is necessary to present multiple examples of benign neglect in conventional medical publications to demonstrate the problem. The real debate on drinking and health has yet to begin. A critical mass of practicing doctors and caregivers need to grapple with this problem before a serious debate and remedies can ensue.

In closing this section, recognize once again the progressive and ever-evolving process called epidemiology. In a report in a December 2002 issue of *Journal of the American Medical Association,* Ka He sorted through data from 51,529 participants in the Health Professionals Follow Up and deduced that men who eat seafood — even as seldom as once a month — may cut their risk of stroke by more than 40 percent. In a Februry issue of the same journal, Reynolds reported on a meta-analysis of 122 reports and 35 studies world-wide seeking the relative risks involved with drinking and stroke. The study concluded that heavy drinking increases the risk while moderate consumption may lower it. Could both fish consumption and drinking be involved in the same risk reduction? Of course. How much relative influence could be attributed to fish or to the drinks? Who knows? Since we are dealing with complex dietary inputs, can one ever know?

An interesting aspect of the fish study was that *any* fish source — not specifically the high omega-3 fish types formerly identified as beneficial — provided benefits. Apparently also, the more fish consumed, the greater the advantage. The same escalation in consumption is definitely not true for alcohol. Heavier drinking increases risks. These projects offer a few lessons about epidemiology. They demonstrate how little we really know about how nutrition works inside the body. We are continually surprised by such findings. They also demonstrate how daily food choices — such as the intake of fish or drinks — can make significant impacts on human health. That is why healthy drinking science deserves more attention and respect in medical journalism.

These many findings suggests that readers need to keep an open mind about other odd findings in the following chapters. Epidemiology keeps probing. We should pay attention to — but not bow down to — its revelations. Caution and common sense are the bywords. We move from the cardiovascular cluster to a focused, two-chapter discussion of drinking and cancer, a medical platform full of more surprises and more odd inconsistencies.

Keep an open mind. The data gets even more provocative.

Chapter 8

Alcohol and Cancer

Surprising alcohol benefits

■ **Author's abstract**: Cancer involves a very complex series of diseases which share common biochemical processes. Unfortunately, everything about cancer has a political dimension because of the enormous budgets allocated to its research and treatment. The critical message for drinkers is that many surveys show moderate drinkers have lower, not increased, risks of developing certain cancers. Here are some notes from these studies:

■ ➽ Alcohol appears unrelated to cancers of the lung
    bladder, prostate, stomach, ovary and endometrium
  ➽ Antioxidants in beer appear to be toxic to cancer cells
    in the breast, colon and ovaries
  ➽ Wine's phenolic compounds protect against some cancer
  ➽ Two to three drinks a day reduce cancer rates

The Medical Advisor published by Time/Life Books sets forth the basics of cancer:

The four major types are: carcinoma, sarcoma, lymphoma, and leukemia. Carcinomas —the most commonly diagnosed cancers —originate in the skin, lungs, breasts, pancreas, and other organs and glands. Lymphomas are cancers of the lymphatic system. Leukemias are cancers of the blood and do not form solid tumors. Sarcomas arise in bone, muscle, or cartilage, and are relatively rare.

The Medical Advisor, Time/Life Books, Alexandria, 1997

Comparative causes of cancer

Smoking and tobacco use 30%	Women's reproductive factors 3%
Obesity and diet 30%	Excessive alcohol consumption 3%
Lack of exercise 5%	Poverty (aside from diet) 3%
Carcinogens in work place 5%	Environmental pollution 2%
Viruses 5%	Excessive sun exposure 2%
Family history 5%	Medical procedures & drugs 1%
Body size 5%	Salt & food additives 1%

The above data is excerpted from a *Harvard Men's Health Watch* list of the factors thought to be responsible for various cancers. The percentages represent each factor's portion of all cancers. In this roster, alcohol is the ninth overall cause, and it is linked only with "excessive consumption." It ranks down there with poverty and female reproduction problems.

Hendriks quotes from a series of papers on cancer risk presented at the 30th International Medical Advisory Board Conference conference in Brussels in October 2002: *P. van den Brandt provided an overview on the relation between alcohol use and cancer. Of all lifestyle factors relevant to cancer, alcohol plays a modest role: the attributable risk for alcohol is 4-6% (for comparison, the attributable risk of 30% for smoking and 20-50% for diet)* (Hendriks 2003).

Drinking is the only one of these factors which also is *preventive* of certain cancers. Its risks are further qualified by the realization that excessive drinkers generally have poor dietary and health habits, making them extra vulnerable to many diseases. In the worst case scenario, alcohol is a minor cancer factor and the risk is limited to abusive drinkers. This does not mean that moderate drinkers are free from the risk of various cancers. It means only that drinking itself is a low risk factor.

The good news about cancer is that rates for most types have been static or declining over the past two decades. Through the 1990s, breast cancer rates remained roughly constant but death rates from this disease declined 2.2 percent, colon and rectal cancer rates dropped 1.8 percent and lung cancer rates among men fell 1.7 percent. These statistics attest to the efficacy of early identification and improving treatment techniques, along with the decline in smoking.

Upper digestive tract cancers

Digestive tract cancers are the ones most closely associated with drinking. In 1994, Longnecker published a review of the literature titled "Alcohol Consumption and Risk of Cancer in Humans: An Overview." He declared that: *Recent epidemiologic data continue to support alcoholic beverage consumption as a cause of cancer of the mouth, pharynx, larynx, esophagus and liver* (Longnecker 1995). Two years later, Longnecker published another review which reported: *Alcohol intake appears not to increase risk of cancer of the lung, bladder, prostate, stomach, ovary, endometrium, or of melanoma* (Longnecker 1996). In these reviews, alcohol is positively associated with five airway cancers but excluded from 7 others. Whether alcohol is truly "causal" or whether it acts as a co-carcinogen in some way is subject to continuing debate.

Zeegers comments on bladder risk: . . . *a clear association between alcohol use and bladder cancer among men, if any, is probably modest. No association between alcohol use and bladder cancer risk was found in women* (Zeegers 2001). Michaud similarly finds no association with pancreatic cancer: *Data from these two large cohorts do not support any overall association between coffee intake or alcohol intake and risk of pancreatic cancer* (Michaud 2001). Even the pronounced association for oral cancer is somewhat mitigated by Zavras because of moderate drinking: *The moderate drinking levels in Greece may explain in part the low rates of oral cancer mortality among Greek men. The aetiology of oral cancer in Greek women needs to be further investigated* (Zavras 2001).

The point to remember is that hundreds of studies are underway on cancer at any one time around the world and many report either positive effects or neutrality with responsible drinking. With the above patterns already established, many new affirmations can be expected in future years. The problem is that federal health authorities and the major cancer societies infrequently mention or consider these positive alcohol findings in their communications to the public. In fact, cancer association literature infers a subtle association of drinking with cancer that is seldom challenged in public health literature.

Some studies even question the assumption that drinking is the key promoter for esophageal cancer. Tuyns comments: *There are, however, several regions in the world where alcohol and tobacco use is far less widespread . . . the incidence of esophageal cancer is nonetheless very high. In some of these regions, it is suspected that the population suffers various dietary insufficiencies: this would suggest that food factors are of importance in the causation of the disease* (Tuyns 1987). Dietary deficiencies among heavy drinkers may be a larger contributor to these cancers than drinking.

Castellsague studied populations in Brazil, Argentina, Paraguay and Uruguay and found: *Simultaneous moderate drinking and moderate smoking, but not moderate drinking alone, is associated with risk for oesophageal cancer* (Castellsague 1999). Populations which lack ready access to fruits and leafy vegetables are at increased risk for this cancer, lending some credence to the role of antioxidants in cancer prevention. In some regions of China, where there is heavy consumption of red skin onions which are high in antioxidants, little cancer is found.

Flavonoids and free radical research

Those red onion skins in China contain high concentrations of antioxidants similar to those in red wines, green tea and leafy vegetables that were discussed in the cardiovascular chapters. The *UC Berkeley Wellness Letter* explains the role of free radicals and their threat to human physiology: *They're unstable molecules that develop under various physical conditions. . . The theory is that free radicals may work their way toward the center of cells where they cause fundamental changes in the genetic material and damage the cell's cancer-prevention apparatus. Free radicals may also damage cells in artery walls, facilitating plaque build-up. . . . The damage free radicals due to our cellular or genetic material may be responsible for the effects of aging* (Do free radicals 1998).

Antioxidants that apparently fight free radicals are found in abundance in many drinks. In 1998, Buhler delivered a paper including this opinion: *That some flavonoids in hops inhibit activity of the cytochrome 450 enzymes system. . . . Some of the hop flavonoids were observed to be toxic to cancer cells from the human breast, colonic and ovarian tissue, at concentrations which did not harm normal cells* (Buhler 1998). Hops in beers may help fight breast, colon and ovarian cancers. The role of beer and wine in providing these flavonoids is seldom, if ever, mentioned in the literature published by various cancer societies and the federal government.

Watkins reported to an American Chemical Society symposium: *The toxic oxygen radical, unfettered and unchecked in the body, has been recognized as an important risk factor in the etiology of chronic, killer disease . . . . Wine, rich in reducing substances, certainly offers therapeutic potential for many chronic diseases, such as cardiovascular disease and cancer, which account for about 75% of deaths in America* (Watkins 1997).

Again, recognition of this positive therapeutic potential in drinks is notably lacking in government and American Cancer Society literature. A communication curtain prevails.

Progressive antioxidant research

On the subject of antioxidants, a *UC Berkeley Wellness Letter* notes: *The chemicals in tea . . . may have anti-cancer effects as well as heart benefits. Though green tea was once thought to have the most polyphenols, it turns out that black tea has a similar amount* (Green, black and red 2000).

Ebeler constructed an animal model to demonstrate that diets rich in fruits and vegetables and wine consumption may delay the growth of tumors: *Consumption of fruit and vegetable rich diets is protective against cancer, however, the actual dietary factors that may be involved are not known. Recent epidemiologic evidence also indicates that wine may contain non-alcoholic constituents which protect against cancer* (Ebeler 1997). As they do against heart disease.

Few, if any, nutrition texts discuss the above conclusion about wine antioxidants. A Johns Hopkins *Health After 50* article notes that: *Eating plenty of vegetables – especially broccoli, cauliflower, cabbage and other cruciferous vegetables may lower the risk of prostate cancer* (Longevity Facts 2000). No mention of drink antioxidants.

And *HealthNews* in early 2000 notes that: *A dietary supplement called quercetin (a substance found in red wine, onions and green tea) can offer some relief for prostatitis* (Follow Up 2000). Quercetin is found abundantly in red wines.

From these citations, it is apparent that there are health enhancing antioxidants in many foods, including wines, beers and spirits. Even chocolate has been found to harbor protective flavonoids and antioxidants. To compete with these natural foods, pharmaceutical companies are currently underwriting studies for over 300 bio-technological medicines, over half of which are designed to fight cancer. This type of research investment develops effective new drugs but the public also should be made aware of the rich resources found in natural foods which come to our dining tables at relatively modest costs.

Leighton and colleagues at Georgetown University Medical Center have experimented for many years with quercetin, a common wine compound: *Studies begun in our laboratory a number of years ago suggest that the anti-carcinogen factor which is present in red wine . . . . Quercetin is found in the outer layers of several edible plants . . . Quercetin is one of the most potent anti-carcinogens naturally occurring in the human diet* (Leighton 1990). Leighton reports that the fermentation process frees quercetin from its sugar bonds, allowing it to provide special protection to the upper segments of the digestive tract: *Although the concentration of quercetin is greater in onions, it is not available until it reaches the colon, the end of the alimentary canal.* Surh notes that: *Resveratrol reduced the survival potential of tumourous cells* (Surh 1999). Apparently, during fermentation of grape juice, wine flavonoids are concentrated and become more effective. These data should increase medical interest in all fermented beverages. Unfortunately, alcohol research is of scant interest to most cancer specialists. It's a politically incorrect vein.

Pezzuto discovered that: *. . . resveratrol is naturally present in blackberries, peanuts as well as in grape skins, all of which have been found to be cancer-preventative in vitro* (Pezzuto 1997). A team of researchers in Illinois, New York and Japan with Subbaramaiah concluded that resveratrol may inhibit cancer growth: *These inhibitory effects could be explained, in part, by the antioxidant properties of resveratrol* (Subbaramaiah 1998). In France, Renaud found resveratrol a factor inhibiting carcinogenesis: *Cancer mortality was significantly reduced 20 percent among those who drink 2 to 3 drinks a day compared to non-drinkers* (Renaud 1998).

Antioxidants are of particular benefit in problems in the aging. In "Green, black and red: the tea-total evidence," the *UC Berkeley Wellness Letter* notes: *The chemicals that make tea a potential protector of health . . . may have anti-cancer effects as well as heart benefits. . . . In fact, exactly what these tea antioxidants do in the human body is still to be determined . . . . Tea may have benefits . . . Stomach cancer remains a major killer in China and Japan, where the highest amounts of green tea are consumed* (Green, black and red 2000). So the potential is real but the specific impacts of these antioxidants remain unclear since the bulk of the research has occurred in animal models.

Drink antioxidant contributions to some cancer reduction seems undeniable. Naturally, scientists are conservative about these contributions in view of the variables in this very complex field of research. But shouldn't cancer literature recognize the potential of alcohol constituents in the same way that contributions from tea and leafy green vegetables are suggested? Clifford summarizes this research: *If ethanol is known to favour the development of certain cancers, it seems, in view of this study, that wine and particularly its phenolic compounds has a protective effect towards the onset of certain cancers . . . . Catechin is the main phenolic compound along with gallic acid, epicatechin and caffeic acid and the other polyphenolic compounds which enter into the composition of wine* (Clifford 1996). The irony is that the ACS's own studies confirm a beneficial relationship which goes unrecognized in the association's literature.

The American Cancer Society surveys

In the first of two landmark studies, Boffetta found: *. . . a 20% relative risk reduction for those consuming one-two drinks and a 17% for those consuming three-four drinks per day. Furthermore, moderate consumption of alcohol was associated with a decreased incidence in overall mortality including cancer* (Boffetta 1990). These conclusions echo those revealed in cardiovascular studies. Up to four drinks daily provided significant reductions in premature mortality *including cancer!* The second ACS study by Thun was released in 1997 involving approximately 490,000 men and women: *While overall mortality was reduced, alcohol consumption was associated with increased rates of death from cirrhosis and alcoholism and from cancers of the mouth, esophagus, pharynx, larynx and liver combined* (Thun 1997).

However, the Thun report identified heavy drinking with those cancers. Light drinkers had the fewest cancers: *In most subgroups, the rates of death from all causes were lowest among people who reported one drink of alcohol daily.* Commenting on the Boffetta study in the same issue of *Epidemiology*, Ellison notes: *Consumers of less than two drinks per day also showed slight decreases in their risk of death from other leading cases of death: accidents, cerebrovascular disease, and all cancers combined.* (Ellison 1990). These ACS studies vindicate a positive role for moderate drinking. That fact is hard to find in ACS or government literature.

"Political" science and cancer research

The science presented here shows moderate drinkers having less cancer, whatever the underlying reasons. At a minimum, one can assume that moderate intake does not appear to be a direct cause of cancer. At this juncture, it will be helpful to consider the politics surrounding cancer research. Pressures are placed on researchers and project managers to conform to certain political pre-suppositions about drinking. Major funding sources including federal agencies and foundations support some very shaky scientific positions. Researchers who look for project funding are mindful of the policy assumptions promulgated by cancer associations and government agencies.

Here is a quote from American Cancer Society literature which reflects the heavy hand of government: *Limit consumption of alcoholic beverages, if you drink at all. Alcoholic beverages, along with cigarette smoking and use of snuff and chewing tobacco, cause cancers of the oral cavity, esophagus, and larynx.* (Cancer Facts 1998). Drinks are linked routinely with tobacco products. There is nothing objectionable about reporting the negative consequences of *heavy* drinking, as long as the favorable research for *moderate consumption* is accorded similar space. That distinction is almost never made. It is ironic in view of the positive findings in the cancer society's own surveys.

The conflict originates in a three decade-old consortium of
mutual interests organized by the World Health Organization
(WHO), the progenitor of the the "control of availability"
agenda. WHO alcohol abuse control programs advise limitations on product availability and a lowering of consumption in
all member nations. There is nothing subtle or secretive in this
advocacy. Further, the agency promotes a linkage of drinking
with smoking. Tobacco, of course, is a recognized carcinogen.
These efforts constitutes a brand of "political" science, not
biochemical research. The linkage of alcohol and tobacco was
unveiled at a 1988 World Health Organization sponsored conference in Australia:

> *Governments should commit themselves to the
> development of Healthy Public Policy by setting
> nationally determined targets to reduce tobacco
> growing and alcohol production, marketing and
> consumption significantly by the year 2000.*

The Adelaide Recommendations: Healthy Public Policy, Second International Conference
on Health and Public Policy, Adelaide, South Australia, April 5-9, 1988

There is only one way to interpret this policy. The association
of alcohol with a recognized carcinogen is done to discourage
drinking. It is a purely political strategem. It is also crude guilt
by association. Public health officials from dozens of nations
attended the conference and concurred in this goal, including
those representing the United States. The policy was embraced
by federal health agencies in the early 1990s. Carrying the
linkage one step further, a WHO affiliate in 1988 came to the
controversial conclusion that: *Alcoholic beverages are carcinogenic
to humans.* This declaration by the International Agency for
Research on Cancer (IARC) has been disputed by independent
cancer specialists. But it stands as U.S. policy.

Regarding the declaration, Hellman notes: *All that one can
conclude at the present time seems to be that the direct carcinogenicity
of alcohol, if it exists, is only manifest under the most complex circumstances . . . there is in my judgment insufficient evidence to unqualifiedly
label ethyl alcohol or alcoholic beverages per se as direct carcinogens to
humans* (Hellman 1989). In his book *To Your Good Health*, Stuttaford reports the reaction of a meeting of cancer specialists held

at the University of Louisville in 1993: *The American figures showing that 75 percent of oral cavity cancers are associated with drinking have to be viewed in the light of the fact that no experimental studies have shown that alcohol by itself is carcinogenic* (Stuttaford 1997). Though it lacks any scientific credibility, the IARC declaration of alcohol carcinogenicity was – and is – the position of the U.S. government.

In *The Reports on Carcinogens, 9th Edition,* the National Institutes of Health supported the IARC statement declaring that: . . . *alcohol beverages are carcinogenic to humans* (The Reports on Carcinogens 2000). If researchers do someday determine with clinical certainty that alcohol is either a mutagen or a cell division promoter, the government and ACS cancer "causation" warnings will be merited. At this time, however, they verge on purposeful, political deception.

To date in animal experiments, alcohol has failed to cause cancer under any conditions. Government officials are cautious about the role of antioxidants because of a lack of *in vivo* proof of their impact. Yet our government has no hesitancy in declaring alcohol a carcinogen without a single animal model experiment as proof. The is cancer politics. Despite these declarations, even some researchers at the National Institute on Alcohol Abuse and Alcoholism recognize the tenuous rationale that links alcohol with tobacco: *Finally, society has attempted to minimize the consequences of using both alcohol and tobacco through public policy actions, including health warning labels, restrictions on advertising, and age restrictions on use. Unlike tobacco, however, moderate use of alcohol has certain health benefits* (Alcohol and Tobacco 1995).

While government is cautious about drink antioxidants, one enterprising firm needs no proof. A new French product has hit the market: *Arkopharma has begun to sell a red wine extract pill called French Paradox . . . but a far greater demand in the United States* (May I recommend the pill de Roussillon, sir 2001).

The reservations about governmental findings of alcohol carcinogenicity are serious and well-founded. One vocal critic of the ruling, Emanuel Rubin, has specialized in research into the pathological and metabolic consequences of alcohol consumption. He has published over 150 papers and near 100 book chapters and reviews (as reported in papers at the Health Effects of Moderate Alcohol Consumption Symposium, University of Toronto Medical School, 1994). Rubin's presentation at the Toronto symposium concluded with this point: *In summary, ethanol does not appear to be a carcinogen, either as an initiator or as a promoter. The epidemiologic data are inconsistent and do not adequately account for possible confounding variables* (Rubin 1994). In a 1990 editorial in *Epidemiology*, Ellison says that alcohol's impact is not limited to heart disease: *While this "protective" effect of alcohol was due primarily to an approximately 20 % reduction in deaths from coronary heart disease, the data indicate that consumers of less than two drinks per day also showed slight decreases in their risk of death from the other leading cases of death: accidents, cerebrovascular disease, and all cancers combined* (Ellison 1990). Rubin and Ellison may be scientifically correct, but they are in a political minority in the current climate.

In closing, consider Zang's 2001 study titled "Revaluation of the confounding effect of cigarette smoking on the relationship between alcohol use and lung cancer risk, with larynx cancer used as a positive control." Zang and associates studied 2,953 male and 1,622 female hospitalized lung cancer cases. Zang reported: *. . . alcohol had no effect on lung cancer following this adjustment (for smoking). . . By contrast, the effects of alcohol on larynx cancer remain high . . . the often-reported association between alcohol and lung cancer risk can be fully explained by the confounding effect of cigarette use* (Zang 2001). This single finding does not put to rest the issues of whether alcohol is a stimulator or co-carcinogen, but it strongly suggests that the linkage commonly presented for lung cancer is less than solid.

Among many in the research community, the issue of alcohol carcinogenicity remains in doubt. The public health stance on drinking and cancer today is reminiscent of the blinders-on reasoning which led the American Medical Association down the Temperance path in 1917. The flat assertion that alcohol is a carcinogen is simple-minded and without credible scientific grounding. That drinking is associated with some cancers is not in question. But the accumulating science suggests that public health's unrelenting enmity to drinking is short-sighted and, hopefully, will be short-lived.

Research Addendum to Chapter 8

Here are more references from a very large and profuse cancer literature. These few items portray a more complex relationship of drinks to cancer than the American Cancer Society's statement. "Limit consumption of alcoholic beverages, if you drink at all." Since over 130 million Americans choose to drink, the relationships between drinking and various cancers deserves more than this equivocal dismissal.

✔ In a large New York State study including 27,544 men and 20,456 women: "This large cohort study offered little support for an association between lung cancer and alcohol use" (Bandera 1997).

✔ A survey of non-Hodgkin's lymphoma victims reported that: "The use of beer or wine was not associated with NHL risk. Among women, use of spirits was associated with a reduced risk in a dose dependent manner" (Nelson 1997).

✔ A review of American blacks and whites concluded: "The results indicate that drinking at the levels typically seen in the U.S. general population is probably not a risk factor for pancreatic cancer. However, heavy drinking may be" (Silverman 1995).

✔ In the area of colorectal cancers: "For colon cancer, no association with either total alcohol use or consumption of beer or wine could be demonstrated; for spirits, an inverse association was found" (Goldbohm 1994).

✔ Cancer of the tongue was explored and reported: "Overall, alcohol drinking was not found to be significantly associated with the risk of tongue cancer in this study" (Zheng 1997).

✔ A study of Wisconsin women found: "This study suggests that, unlike breast cancer, endometrial cancer is not positively associated with alcohol intake" (Newcomb 1997).

✔ A study of 400 cases along with 297 controls reported: "The protective effect of alcohol could not be attributed to one particular type of alcohol-containing beverage, but beer appeared to have the most pronounced effect. These results suggest an inverse association between moderate alcohol consumption and endometrial cancer risk among young women" (Swanson 1993).

✔ Confusion is found in studies of drinking and prostate cancer. Hayes studied subjects aged 40 to 79, including blacks and whites, and reported: "The results show that a consumption of less than 24 drinks per week barely increases the average risk of prostate cancer in comparison to nondrinkers" (Hayes 1996).

✔ Sesso studied 7612 Harvard University alumni and recorded: "Men initiating alcohol consumption between 1977 and 1988 had a twofold increased risk of prostate cancer compared to men with almost no alcohol consumption at both times" (Sesso 2001).

✔ A study of male drinkers reported: "We found compelling evidence for no association between low-to-moderate alcohol consumption and prostate cancer" (Breslow 1998). Miranda also found beer protective against prostate cancer (Miranda 1999).

✔ While Miranda found beer protective in relation to prostate cancer, another Canadian study by Sharpe conducted in Montreal among 4,000 men aged 45-70 concluded: "Beer was the most prevalent type of alcohol consumed in this population and showed the strongest association with prostate cancer (Sharpe 2001). Conflicting findings suggest the existence of other contributing factors for prostate cancer.

✔ Three more prostate studies found: "No noteworthy relationship was found for alcohol and tobacco consumption" (Tavani 1994). "There was no statistically or clinically significant association between alcohol consumption and prostate cancer" (Lumey 1998). In three Canadian provinces it was observed: "Our results do not support a positive association between total alcohol, coffee and prostate cancer" (Jain 1998).

✔ An article on benign prostatic hyperplasia notes: "Those who drank moderately . . . were about 40% less likely to develop BPH" (Exercise and the Prostate 2001).

✔ A suggested link is made for cancer with a chemical produced as the body breaks down alcohol: "These findings suggest a role for acetaldehyde, a recognized animal carcinogen, in the development of human cancers" (Yokoyama 1998).

✔ An article suggests that there is no single causation in cancer: . . . when it comes to cancer, the quest for a single ingredient is folly. Fruit and most especially vegetables probably have an anti-carcinogenic cocktail" (Beta carotene 1999).

✔ Alcohol is non-carcinogenic by itself: "Although the exact mechanisms by which chronic alcohol ingestion stimulates carcinogenesis are not known, experimental studies in animals support the concept that ethanol is not a carcinogenic, but under certain experimental conditions is a cocarcinogen" (Seitz 1998).

✔ Papillary thyroid cancer in women was studied in relation to smoking and drinking: "Like for smoking, the risk reduction was most prominent for current drinkers. The risk reduction was greater for women over 45 years of age than for younger women" (Rossing 2000).

✔ Beer may protect against effects of carcinogens in foods. "Japanese researchers tested 24 different beers and found that nearly all of them had a potent inhibitory effect against heterocyclic amine mutagens, particularly the stouts. They also reported some inhibitory effect with sake, red and white wine and brandy, but not whisky" (Arimoto-Koboyashi 1999).

✔ Resveratrol in grapes and other plants has striking antioxidant and anti-inflammatory activities. ". . . that resveratrol reduced both the survival potential of tumorous cells and the ADN synthesis capacity of these cells" (Surh 1999)

✔ With colon cancer in Japan, the role of alcohol is unclear. "These findings indicate that smoking is a risk factor for adenoma in Japanese men and women. The role of alcohol, however, is less clear. The finding of a possible association of alcohol use with rectal but not colonic adenomas is consistent with earlier site-specific studies" (Nagata 1999).

✔ A study of 28,265 men and women in Denmark found antioxidants in wine may provide protection. "The authors concluded that in men, a high consumption of beer and spirits is associated with an increased risk of lung cancer, whereas wine intake may protect against the development of lung cancer" (Prescott 1999).

✔ A Chicago team discovered that resveratrol may be considered as a phytoestrogen. "The effects observed with resveratrol occur . . . similar with those needed for the obtention of anti-inflammatory, anti-platelet, anti-carcinogenic effects" (Gehm 1997).

✔ In a study of smoking and alcohol consumption relating to endometrial cancer risk, Weiderpasse notes: "Alcohol use appears not be be associated with risk for endometrial cancer in postmenopausal women (Weiderpasse 2001).

✔ In a review of the two major medical profession studies– doctors and nurses– Michaud determined that: "Results from two large US cohorts confirm that neither coffee nor alcohol is a risk for pancreatic cancer (Michaud 2001).

✔ A case controlled study in French hospitals concluded: "These results do not support an association between total fluid consumption and risk for bladder cancer. Alcohol use may be a protective factor for men but not for women." (Geoffroy-Perez 2001).

✔ Sharpe found that, "Daily drinking of any alcoholic beverage was associated with elevated risks of cancer of the . . . colon and the rectum" (Sharpe 2002).

✔ As part of a breast cancer detection survey, Flood isolated data on colorectal cancer and reported. "Alcohol use appears not to correlate with risk of coloractal cancer in American women. (Flood 2002).

✔ From data gathered in a twenty year study in Copenhagen, Denmark including 12,989 men, Albertsen reveals, "Neither drinking level nor beverage type appears to be a risk factor for the development of prostate cancer."
(Albertsen 2002).

These and many other reports from many nations explore the positive and negative effects associated with ethanol, antioxidants, and other constituents in drinks. The fact that the American Cancer Society and agencies of the federal government virtually ignore the positive findings is unsettling. Another example is found in the pamphlet "The New American Plate," a diet for preventing cancer published by the American Institute for Cancer Research. The AICR is the third largest cancer charity in the nation.

AICR estimates that: . . . *30-40 percent of all cancers could be prevented by changing the way we eat and exercise* (The New American 2001). The sole mention of drinking in the AICR booklet on a cancer favorable diet is: "Drink alcohol only in moderation, if at all." The party line in American public health and cancer agencies is "if at all," with no referencing of health benefits.

It's a classic case of political "corruption."

Chapter 9

Breast Cancer

Drinking risks exaggerated

■**Author's abstract**: The relationship between alcohol consumption and breast cancer is unsettled and unsettling. One line of studies finds a definite but generally weak relationship. Other studies find no tangible linkages. Alcohol is thought to be involved in only about three percent of breast cancers. Women need to evaluate many factors, including family history of breast cancer. They should also check the comparative risks for heart disease and breast cancer:

■ ⇢ More misinformation than facts appear in the media
 ⇢ Breast cancer risk increases as a woman ages
 ⇢ Light alcohol consumption is not related to breast cancer
 ⇢ A true causality link has not been established
 ⇢ Heart deaths far exceed those of breast cancer

Confusion on risk statistics

Breast cancer commentary abounds in print and electronic journalism. Unfortunately, too much of this voluminous reporting is misleading or sensationalized. Consider the following

really outlandish quote from a book released by Arnot, a popular physician commentator:

*Alcohol is fast emerging as a major risk. The risk of
breast cancer is increased 11 percent per drink per
day. Four drinks a day and your risk increases 44
percent . . . . If you're going to drink for your health,
wait until you need it — that's well into your fifties
— then drink sparingly.*

Arnot, B., The Breast Cancer Prevention Diet, Little Brown and Company, Boston, 1998

The foregoing chapters on cardiovascular disease and cancer
cast doubt on everything Arnot says above. The only place that
alcohol is "fast emerging as a major risk" is in Dr. Arnot's fertile
mind. If all the women in America took his advice and waited
until their "fifties" before drinking moderately, female
atherosclerosis and cardiovascular deaths could balloon. Marton in *To Your Health* clarifies some realities about breast cancer
research: *Since the 1970s, there have been more than 40 epidemiological studies that have examined the role of moderate alcohol consumption
. . . the worst case scenario indicates that a woman who drinks more
than two drinks per day may have a 1.25 percent increase in cancer
risk. For a 30 year-old woman of average cancer risk, this translates
into going from a lifetime risk of getting cancer at about nine percent
to one of just above eleven percent* (Marton 1996). An increase of
from nine to eleven percent risk – the worst case estimate
– hardly calls for a lifetime of premenopausal abstention as
apparently suggested by Arnot.

Breast cancer risks pertain *over the lifetime of each woman,* not
independently and totally at all stages of life as the above quote
implies. Using this long range perspective, a thirty year-old
woman does not face the full nine to eleven percent risk. The
UC Berkeley Wellness Letter spoke to this distinction: *The one-in-
eleven figure applies to all American women indiscriminately, from age
1 to 85. . . The incidence of breast cancer in the population rises with
age. A 40-year-old woman has about a 3.3% chance of developing
breast cancer by the age of 60* (Alcohol and Breast Cancer 1988).
The risk escalates rapidly as women enter their senior years. An
article in the *Mayo Clinic Health Letter* puts it this way: *At age 30,*

the risk is one out of 2,525 women. At age 80, it is 1 out of 10 (What are your chances 2001).

The following figures from "How Age Affects Breast Cancer" appeared in the February 1999 issue of *HealthNews*.

Decade of life	Per cent who get breast cancer	Per cent who die of the cancer
30s	4%	0%
40s	13%	3%
50s	23%	6%
60s	26%	7%
70s	24%	11%
80s	14%	13%

Arnot was right about one thing – the risk of breast cancer escalates in the fifth decade. Arnot neglected to mention the many findings of drinking's potential benefits to heart health and many other physical conditions. Anyone choosing to defer "health" drinking until their fifth decade should evaluate these other benefits before making the abstention decision. This is why American medical practice should develop a cohesive, cross-disease exposition of all relevant drinking science.

One study involved a cohort of 36,856 women diagnosed with alcoholism in Sweden. Even among this heavy drinking population, Kuper found: . . . *contrary to expectation, that alcoholism does not increase breast cancer risk in proportion to presumed ethanol intake* (Kuper 2000). Even alcoholic levels of drinking did not increase risk! A 1997 survey of women in the *Archives of Family Medicine* reveals widespread public confusion about breast cancer risk. Thirty-four percent of female respondents rated breast cancer as their greatest threat. Only seven percent chose cardiovascular disease, by far the leading cause of premature female mortality. A Canadian study by Rohan notes: . . . *alcohol consumption might be associated with increased risk of breast cancer at relatively high levels of intake* (Rohan 2000). As demonstrated in previous chapters, public health and medical agencies discourage the reporting of such positive findings. This diminishment yields a negative harvest. Public confusion about drinking exists with all thirty diseases covered in this book.

Keep in mind the reality that breast cancer risk rises as women age, as do the risks for many diseases. Breast cancer can strike at any age but, in general, it's a disease of advancing age.

Genetics and other factors

Some researchers believe that the most significant risk for breast cancer is genetic – a family history of the disease. In 1991, Rubin expressed this concern in a commentary to the Bureau of Alcohol, Tobacco and Firearms:

Breast cancer is a disease for which there are many risk factors, such as age, genetics, diet, and hormonal status. These risk factors confound studies of the alleged association between alcohol consumption and breast cancer in such a way that the causative role of any single environmental factor has not been elucidated.

Rubin, E., Letter to Bureau of Alcohol, Tobacco and Firearms, Jefferson Medical College, Department of Pathology, Philadelphia, 1991

Many studies emphasize environmental factors. *HealthNews* reported on a study of 45,000 twins in Northern Europe which found that: . . . *genes play a relatively minor role in most cancers.* The study attributed from fifty-eight to eighty-two percent of cancer causality to environmental factors. In "A Scientific Perspective on the Latest Wine and Breast Cancer Research" published by the Wine Institute, a monograph from International Life Sciences Institute (ILSI Press, Summer 1993) says this: . . . *any recommendation that women should limit their alcohol consumption specifically in order to reduce their risk of breast cancer cannot be supported or justified by the existing epidemiological evidence* (A Scientific Perspective 1993). Huang points to possible influences from hormone replacement therapy and excessive weight: . . . *as much as one third (34 percent) of new cases of post menopausal breast cancer are caused by hormone replacement therapy, adult weight gain or both* (Huang 1997). Genetic predispositions, age, hormones, body weight and dietary habits all apparently can contribute to breast cancer. As with general cancers, breast cancer research findings constitute a mixed bag. To demonstrate this point, here are examples from opposing lines of research – some that connect drinking with breast cancer and other studies that find no identifiable connection between the two.

Research associating drinking with breast cancer

A widely publicized breast cancer review was released in February 1998 by Smith-Warner and sixteen associates. It evaluated six prospective studies conducted in Canada, the Netherlands, Sweden and the United States. A total of 322,647 females were evaluated in the projects, some of which extended for as long as eleven years. The survey report stated:

Alcohol consumption is associated with a linear increase in breast cancer incidence in women over the range of consumption . . . . Among women who consume alcohol regularly, reducing consumption is a potential means to reduce breast cancer.

Smith-Warner, S., Spiegelman, D., Yuan, S, van den Brandt, P., Folsom, A., Goldbohm, A., Graham, S., Holmberg, L., Howe, G., Marshall, J., Miller, A., Potter, J., Speizer, F., Willett, W., Wolk, A., and Hunter D., Alcohol and Breast Cancer in Women, JAMA, 279:535-540, 1998

Kelsey made two interesting observations about this survey: *First, the authors find an increased risk for breast cancer in heavy post menopausal women only among those who have never used hormone replacement therapy . . . Second . . . this large cohort study provides perhaps the strongest evidence to date that weight gain from early adulthood is important in the etiology of post menopausal breast cancer* (Kelsey 1997).

The research is a mixed lot. A 1997 study by Swanson added another twist by associating alcohol only with late stages of breast cancer: *Our data support the accumulating evidence that alcohol consumption is associated with increased risk of breast cancer and further indicate that alcohol acts at a late stage in breast carcinogenesis* (Swanson 1997). Vaeth agrees but identifies other contributing factors: *The stage at which breast cancer is diagnosed is an important determination of prognosis . . . the association between alcohol consumption and disease stage may be due to the relationship between heavy consumption and other unhealthy behaviours* (Vaeth 1998). These studies suggest a linkage between alcohol and breast cancer.

Research finding no breast cancer connection

Other studies dispute the linkage theory. One survey on breast cancer was based in the records of the half-century Framingham study reported by Zhang. The group analyzed data on 2,700 women who were followed for forty years along with more than 2,200 of their daughters who were followed for up to twenty-four years. The study concludes: *Light consumption of alcohol or any type of alcoholic beverage is not associated with breast cancer risk* (Zhang 1999) – at least in this middle-class, largely white, Boston suburb. An associate on this study, Ellison, who appeared on the CBS French paradox telecast, noted: *The results from this prospective cohort study, based on two generations of women, suggest that neither a light-to-moderate level of alcohol consumption nor consumption of any particular type of alcoholic beverages increases the risk of breast cancer* (Zhang 1999).

Survival rates for black females with breast cancer is considerably lower than for white females. A study of breast cancer among black women was carried out for five years at Howard University. McDonald reports: *Breast cancer survival rates among postmenopausal African American women may be lower for drinkers than for non-drinkers* (McDonald 2002). The study found advantage among women who reported as little as one alcoholic drink per week. These positive data generate practically no coverage in the medical media.

As a consequence, many articles in the popular media simply assume an existing link between drinking and breast cancer. As with general cancers, the drinking link is far from consensus in the research literature. One can see in breast cancer coverage the depth of the communication problem about drinking benefits. Alcohol-positive findings are seldom found in popular literature as are the widely publicized negative presumptions.

A case-control study in Toronto that compared 400 breast cancer cases to 800 control subjects. About it, Miller wrote: *Reported drinking of wine, beer or liquor combined was not associated with cancer risk . . . . These results do not support the hypothesis that alcohol consumption increases cancer risk* (Miller 1987). Lindegard in a letter to the editors of the *New England Journal of Medicine* reported on a ten year study in an isolated Swedish community: *Thus, within the study design of general white population that was both ethnically and socio-economically homogeneous, among the 1,123 cases of breast cancer seen at the only general hospital serving this population during a 10-year follow-up, we were unable to confirm the suggested association between breast cancer and alcohol consumption* (Lindegard 1987).

In 1994, Schatzkin noted: *The alcohol-breast cancer hypothesis remains intriguing, but causality has not been established* (Schatzkin 1994). In Italy, a high wine-consuming nation, Ferrarone notes: *There is too little evidence to conclude that alcohol causes breast cancer . . . alcohol related health outcomes, which may include a protective effect of moderate drinking against heart disease, should be at the base of broader public health recommendations* (Ferrarone 1998). Similarly, Reichman reported: *It is not clear whether the association between alcohol and breast cancer is causal* (Reichman 1995). Macdonald notes: *Even a causal link at higher drinking levels is most likely to be seriously compromised by unknown confounders* (Macdonald 1999).

Gapstur studied estrogen use and the increase in breast cancer in post-menopausal women and observed: *Significant multiplicative interaction between alcohol intake and non-contraceptive estrogen use . . . . No association between alcohol use and breast cancer has been observed among never-users of estrogen* (Gapstur 1992). Harris followed 1,467 breast cancer cases contrasted with 10,178 control subjects studying education, occupation, race and marital status, cigarette smoking, body mass and age: *This investigation provides no compelling evidence that alcohol has a role in the genesis of breast cancer . . . neither do they provide a compelling evidence that alcohol has a role in the genesis of this malignancy* (Harris 1988).

Study reports conducted separately in five European countries among post-menopausal women (Germany, Switzerland, Northern Ireland, the Netherlands and Spain) found: *These results do not support a dose-response effect of alcohol on breast cancer risk, although consumption levels were too low to exclude increased risk with high regular intake* (Royo-Bordonada 1997). Over and over in this book, dose distinctions are stressed. The positive aspects of drinking are specifically and frequently associated with light and moderate drinking. In 1993, Rosenberg analyzed twenty-seven case-control studies conducted in the U.S. and thirteen other countries and concluded: *Based on what is known or suspected, there is no compelling biologic reason to believe that alcohol consumption might influence the risk of breast cancer* (Rosenberg 1993).

Concerned women should wonder why they haven't been informed of these positive results.

Breast cancer and cardiovascular risks

The most important breast cancer factor neglected in medicine today is the comparison of the risks for heart disease and breast cancer among women. The problem emerges when the breast cancer risk is compared to cardiovascular risks. An editorial in the May 1987 issue of *The New England Journal of Medicine* suggests that breast cancer warnings should concentrate on high risk women: *One needs to consider the fact that alcohol in moderate quantities appears to increase levels of high-density lipoprotein cholesterol and may reduce the risk of coronary heart disease. One might recommend, then, that women at especially high risk for breast cancer such as those who are obese, who have had few children, who were first pregnant when they were older than 25, or whose mothers had breast cancer, should curtail their alcohol ingestion* (*The New England Journal of Medicine* 1987). This suggests that the prevention focus should be on those deemed at known risks in preference to the Arnot's scare tactics aimed at the entire female population.

In a 1996 symposium, Ellison had these observations:

Among women, death rates from CHD (coronary heart disease) far exceed those from breast cancer, especially after menopause. Further, in epidemiologic studies, women who consume moderate alcohol tend to show striking reductions in the risk of CHD, even women who suffer a myocardial infarction before the age of 50. Nevertheless, we must individualize the message on alcohol to individuals based on a number of factors, including the age and sex of the person. For an individual woman, we must also consider whether or not she has a family history or other risk factors for CHD and for breast cancer.

Ellison, R., Alcohol Consumption: Beneficial to Your Health?, Wine in Context Symposium, American Society of Enology and Viticulture, Reno, June, 1996

Whitten in *To Your Health* provides a global perspective on cancer: . . . *cancer causes 20 percent of all deaths in North America and Europe, yet no more than 3 percent of that total is possibly due to heavy alcohol consumption. . . By contrast, cardiovascular disease causes about 50 percent of total deaths, with light, regular wine drinkers enjoying about a 40 percent reduction in their risk of this disease. If alcohol were eliminated entirely, the possible small decreases in total deaths because of reduced cancer risk would be accompanied by an enormous, if not easily calculated, increase in deaths due to cardio-vascular disease* (Whitten 1994). These comparative risk statistics are seldom seen in medical journalism because drinks remain forbidden fruits.

Two studies released in 2000 report on the Carolina Breast Cancer Study. This project included a population-based, case-control study of black and white women in North Carolina. The area encompassed was predominantly suburban, small-town and rural. The women, age twenty to seventy-four, had 890 cases of confirmed invasive breast cancer compared to 841 controls. From this study, Kinney reported: *Little evidence was found for an association between recent or lifetime alcohol use and breast cancer risk among either black or white women* (Kinney 2000). Another similar finding by Marcus negates the influence of youth drinking: *These results are consistent with previous evidence that specific adolescent exposures (e.g. early onset of smoking) may influence later breast cancer risk. Early initiation of alcohol use and adolescent exposure to environ-mental cigarette smoke apparently are not risk factors for breast cancer* (Marcus 2000).

Many physicians will be surprised at the abundance of find-ings concerning moderate drinking. It is seldom mentioned in literature produced by health associations such as the American Cancer Society. A search of ACA's www.cancer.org page dem-onstrates this problem. The web site warns of a possible connec-tion between moderate drinking and breast cancer: *. . . even at levels of moderate drinking – not exceeding one drink of alcohol daily – the current evidence suggests that there is some increase in breast cancer risk.* This is, at best, misleading in view of the many studies cited above that find no relationship with light drinking.

To justify their dire predictions, the American Cancer Society web page references a study by Dorgan in the the *Journal of the National Cancer Institute* concerning serum hormones. Dorgan studied fifty-one women who consumed fifteen to thirty grams of alcohol a day for eight week periods and determined: *Results suggest a possible mechanism by which consumption of one or two alcohol drinks per day by postmenopausal women could increase their risk of breast cancer* (Dorgan 2001). A study involving fifty-one women is deemed more important than the dozens of much larger study finding of no linkage.

It is perfectly appropriate for the cancer society to cite the Dorgan and other negative studies. It is questionable medical ethics to ignore the positive line of research. Major studies such as Rohan found risk only at high levels of intake. Huang found a relationship only with hormone replacement therapy. or Zhang found no evidence of a linkage in the forty years of Framingham mothers' data and another twenty-four years of data for their daughters. Lindegaard in Sweden recounted ten years and 1,123 cases of breast cancer at the same hospital with no connection to drinking. The South Carolina study found no relationship of drinking and breast cancer among black or white women. . This is not happenchance. It's selective reporting for political purposes.

Michael Thun, M.D., vice president of epidemiology for ACS and lead researcher on the second major ACS survey, did recognize in the same article that one drink per day may reduce the risk of heart disease. However, Thun failed to bring up the importance of relative risks for female heart attacks as compared to breast cancer risks. About fifty percent of all female mortality is due to heart disease. Moderate drinking can reduce this risk by as much as forty percent. A low three percent of all cancers are attributed to drinking, and then only with excessive intake. Also missing is cross-referencing of alcohol-mitigated risks for diabetes, kidney and gall stones, ulcers, osteoporosis, cognition and Alzheimer's, acute hospitalization, gastro-intestinal upset, strokes and all cause mortality. Sadly, cancer specialists inhabit a very small ballpark and they control the game.

Oncologist Finkel in *In Vino Sanitas* sums up the comparative data concerning drinking and breast cancer: *What is one to do while waiting for the truth? Consider the bottom line. In general, although breast cancer is a risk for all women. . . The risk of death for coronary disease, for which the data is clearly more conclusive, considerably exceeds that from breast cancer, so the net effect of wine in particular is likely beneficial* (Finkel 1998). Clinical medicine routinely balances risks and benefits for most treatment regimens. Physicians should not only balance the risks of breast cancer with cardiovascular disease for their patients, but also include analyses of how responsible drinking relates to other problems endured by particular patients such as diabetes, gallstones, stress, osteoporosis and weight control. As the following pages demonstrate, each is favored by responsible intake.

More evidence of antioxidant benefits

As found in cardiovascular research, many studies suggest beneficial impacts of dietary polyphenols, particularly on breast cancer tumors. While there is promise in animal model research, years may pass before antioxidant pathways can be resolved for humans. But what is known to date is too important and too far-reaching to be hidden from public discussion. Women should be made aware of antioxidants in drinks in the same manner as those found in leafy vegetables and tea. These findings should be discussed with patients. Recently in France, Delmas reported that: *The proliferation of cancer cell lines in human and rat livers . . . indicate that the different cell types are inhibited in a dose-dependent manner by resveratrol* (Delmas 2000). Similarly, Damianaki found: *. . . low concentrations of polyphenols can have a beneficial effect, particularly by limiting the proliferation of breast cancer cell lines* (Damianaki 2000). These are drink antioxidants.

Positive polyphenol findings have been reported in studies from Framingham, Massachusetts, Italy, Australia, Toronto, Switzerland, Northern Ireland, Spain, France and the Netherlands. Similar research findings involving disparate cultures cannot be relegated to chance. Add to these data the mere three percent of all cancers being alcohol related and the alcohol-breast cancer threat is greatly qualified. For a more detailed discussion on antioxidants refer to Chapter 2.

The politics of cancer and drinking

As discussed in the previous chapter, the politics surrounding the research and treatment of cancer is nearly as complex and controversial as the diseases. As with other controversial social issues, government funding sources and private philanthropy favors politically correct projects. In cancer research, temperance policies matter.

Both positive and negative findings concerning drinking are cited in this book. In reading the lot, there is both lingering uncertainty and hopeful findings. The resurgence of Temperance movement in the 1970s brought into play control of availability programs, all of which discourage drinking. The bureaucratic thrust since the 1970s has been to reduce the number of drinkers and the amount consumed. This commitment to lessen per capita drinking ignores the needs and interests, and the health benefits enjoyed by the moderate drinking majority. This federal campaign constitutes a serious public health deficit.

The confusion in cancer politics is not limited to drinking policies. All cancer risks are frequently magnified in the popular media. An example is the perceived danger of pesticides in foods. In *Killer Tomatoes,* Lynch notes: *If you're worried about pesticides causing cancer, you'd better not eat broccoli, bananas, peaches, peas, pineapples, potatoes, or even tomatoes. Going organic is futile. Each of these fruits and vegetables – and scores more – produces natural pesticides that have been shown to cause cancer by the same tests that condemn many synthetic pesticides* (Lynch 2000). Fear of pesticides on fruits and vegetables has generated a massive new organic agriculture.

This book's focus is drinking and good health. The positive reports about drinking and cancer wallow in an staged atmosphere of fear and doubt. This political spin inevitably impacts legislative and administrative action. Lynch quotes from a paper prepared by Ames and Gold, cancer researchers at the University of California at Berkeley: *Of all dietary pesticides that humans eat, 99.99 percent are natural. They are chemicals produced by plants to defend themselves against fungi, insects, and other animal predators. . . . Publicity about hundreds of minor hypothetical risks, such as pesticide residues, can result in loss of perspective on what is important* (Lynch 2000). Antioxidants which protect the maturing fruits and vegetables quite likely are responsible for some of the health benefits attributed to drinks.

A survey of studies conducted around the world is cited in a *Health After 50* article: *The risks for many types of cancer can be*

reduced (but not eliminated) by healthy lifestyle measures (The Truth
About Diet and Cancer 1999). In a sidebar of "healthy practices," the article includes desultory advice: *Avoid alcohol: If you
do drink, limit consumption to two drinks or less per day.* Since
American medicine now promotes an upper limit of two drinks
daily for men and one for women, this seems appropriate advice.
But how is it "The Truth About Diet and Cancer" to omit any
mention of the drink-positive cancer findings provided in this
and the previous chapter?

It is important for readers to understand how the Temperance
legacy persists in alcohol research. In *Era of Excess*, Sinclair
explains the precedents:

> After the Civil War, the prohibitionists found new
> weapons. . . . The temperance societies set out to
> diffuse the results of medical research through
> pamphlet and pulpit. But they were careful to diffuse
> only that scientific data which was in line with their
> beliefs. . . Widespread use was made of medical
> statistics to win over the intelligent. The dry
> propagandists were among the first to discover the
> modern device of bemusing the opposition with facts
> and figures, while forgetting to mention any contrary
> evidence.

Sinclair, A., Era of Excess, Harper Colophon Books, 1964

Such negative casting is not unusual today. In the cancer
disciplines, the prevailing unease about any drinking (drink
moderately, if at all) originates from the very highest levels of
power and influence in medicine, in private health associations
and in government. Justification for this hostility to drinking
rests on the shaky international declaration that alcohol is a
carcinogen (see previous chapter). Despite the noble goals
which motivate their work, cancer associations, public agencies
and individual researchers are under enormous pressures to
conform to these negative protocols. Every aspect of cancer
research is clouded with limiting caveats, doubts and partisan
reservations concerning drinks.

Yet, there are promising research horizons. Here are some
closing risk perspectives on breast cancer that deserve airing.

Tseng: . . . *the generally moderate level of alcohol intake among U.S. women, the breast cancer attributable to alcohol intake is small. Widespread efforts to reduce alcohol consumption would not have substantial impact* (Tseng 1999). Garland: . . . *there is unlikely to be a large effect of moderate alcohol consumption on breast cancer risk among young women* (Garland 1999). Tavani: *Like for older women, alcohol use seems to be no strong risk factor for breast cancer for women under 40* (Tavani 1999).

Ferrarone: *There is still too little evidence to conclude that alcohol causes breast cancer . . . in the absence of a clear biological mechanism and in view of the moderate extent of the association, any cause-effect inference remains open to discussion . . . Critical consideration of all alcohol related health outcomes, which may include a protective effect of moderate drinking against heart disease, should be at the base of broader public health recommendations* (Ferrarone 1998). La Vecchia: *The putative biologic mechanisms by which alcoholic beverages could exert a carcinogenic effect on breast epithelium . . . (is) . . . far from established* (La Vecchia 1985).

A similar conclusion is reached in *Health Issues Related to Alcohol Consumption* published by International Life Sciences Institute. McPherson in "Alcohol and Breast Cancer" concludes: . . . *in spite of very intensive investigation, evidence for a causal relationship between moderate or "social drinking" and breast cancer in women is lacking. . . It is inappropriate at this time to make any recommendations to reduce moderate alcohol use simply on the basis of its alleged effect on the incidence of breast cancer* (McPherson 1999).

This completes seven chapters concerning cardiovascular disease and cancer, the dominant illness clusters. This book now moves to evaluations of healthy drinking beyond these high mortality diseases. The following twenty-one chapters discuss potential benefits for other diseases or conditions in responsible drinking. They create a mosaic of drinking benefits virtually unrecognized in American medical practice.

It's fascinating reading.

Research Addendum to Chapter 9

✔ Human stress now is considered a breast cancer risk. *The Medical Advisor* cautions: "All of these factors may contribute to cancer causation, yet cancer is not caused by any single factor. Cancer results from a "multifactorial hit" of age, inherited predisposition, general health, and carcinogenic exposure. For example, some people exposed to particular carcinogens will develop cancer, while others, exposed just as intensely to the same carcinogens, will not . . . . Thus everyone's cancer risk profile is complex and unique" (The Medical Advisor 1996).

✔ The *UC Berkeley Wellness Letter* notes that: "Scientists are beginning to unravel the physiological pathways between the brain and body. Through these pathways, stress can have measurable effects on such systems as the immune, cardiovascular, and endocrine systems, as well as the brain itself . . . . When stressful events persist or recur frequently, this can be expressed in a variety of physical illness symptoms" (Demystifying stress 1998).

✔ A bulletin issued by the Wine Institute about breast cancer contains these qualifications: "There is a clear difference between case control and cohort studies. Case control studies . . . rely on retrospective data where subjects who have developed breast cancer provide past consumption data statistics based on memory which may be limited by what researchers call recall bias. Researchers stress that cohort studies provide much more reliable results since data is collected prospectively (on an ongoing basis for years). Then the data is analyzed to find differences between subjects who developed breast cancer and those who didn't. Most cohort studies find an association to breast cancer with higher alcohol consumption levels" (A Scientific Perspective 1993).

✔ Vachon looked to a family history among breast cancer patients and concluded: "An increased risk of breast cancer due to an increased frequency of alcohol consumption may be limited to women with a family history of breast cancer" (Vachon 2001).

✔ Three recent studies evaluated the link between drinking and breast cancer. "The authors conducted a meta-analysis of epidemiologic studies carried out through 1999 . . . Overall there was a monotonic increase in the relative risk of breast cancer with alcohol consumption, but the magnitude of the effect was small" (Ellison

2001). From the Nurses' Health Study, more data yielded: "Compared with never drinking alcohol, one drink per day from age 18 years increases risk to age 70 by 7%" (Colditz 2000). A German study found that: "These data suggest that low-level consumption of alcohol does not increase breast cancer risk in premenopausal women" (Kropp 2001).

✔ de Lorimier surveyed the data and reported: "For post menopausal women, the protective effect of alcohol consumption in reducing the risk of atherosclerotic disease outweighs the weak evidence for an increased risk of breast cancer." (de Lorimier 2000).

✔ An interesting speculation is introduced by a recent study by Vachon. The Minnesota Breast Cancer Family Study carried out from 1944 to 1990 provided data that led to the conclusion that: "An elevated risk of breast cancer due to a high drinking frequency may be confined to women with a family history of breast cancer." (Vachon 2001).

As reported in *AIM-Digest* (Vol. 11, No. 4, February 2003), two new British studies extend the uncertainty. In the first, a survey of 50 studies involving 150,000 women in many nations, Reeves notes in the *British Medical Journal*, : *The balance between harmful effects on breast cancer and its beneficial effects on heart disease depend on a woman's age. Before about 60, breast cancer is a more important cause of death than heart disease. After the age of 65 or so, when the risk of heart disease becomes much greater . . . the benefits of moderate drinking are more apparent* (Breast Cancer 2003). The other study, seen in *Annals of Internal Medicine,* quotes Doll that alcohol account for only a small portion of breast cancer in developed countries: . . . *its lifetime cardioprotective effects probably outweigh its hazards* (Breast Cancer 2003).

Because of these many mixed reports, scientists and physicians are prudently cautious about alcohol and other other potential triggers for breast cancer. Human stress, as example, may be a critical element not factored into many studies (see Chapter 25). What can be said with certainty is that wine, beer and spirits offer some threat, as well as some beneficial promise, for the avoidance of breast cancer, and many other diseases.

A second look at the data and clinical monitoring of the research is suggested.

Chapter 10

Aging and Alzheimer's Disease

Many benefits for the aging

■ **Author's abstract:** As the senior citizen roster continues to swell in America, it is inevitable that problems with cognition, memory and Alzheimer's disease will also expand. It is important to keep in mind that the percentage of seniors who suffer from Alzheimer's is still quite low. Many active seniors retain mental faculties into and through their ninth decades. Some research indicates that light drinking may delay dementia, loss of cognition and even the dread Alzheimer's. Seniors and those who care for them should be more aware of these points:

■ ↝ Alcohol protects against cerebral lesions
  ↝ Alcohol may delay Alzheimer's onset up to three years
  ↝ Drinkers retain slightly better cognitive skills
  ↝ An 80 percent decrease is found in the rate of dementia

With the 65-and-older population projected to increase 15 percent (to more than 39 million) by 2010, their offspring, the Baby Boom generation, can expect to become the most "sandwiched" in history. For the first time, a married couple will likely spend more years caring for a parent than for a child.

Brothers, Joyce, Are You Caught in the Middle?, Parade Magazine, June 28, 1998

Americans over the age of sixty-five numbered 33.5 million in 1995. By 2030, it is estimated that one of every five people in the U.S. will be older than sixty-five – the current age of retirement. Life expectancy actually increases as we age. A female of seventy years is expected to survive to eighty-five. A male at seventy enjoys life expectancy of 12.5 more years. If a woman reaches eighty-five, her life expectancy increases 6.4 years (Monthly Vital Statistics Report 1998). Should seniors drink? If so, how much? These are important decisions, not only for seniors but for the middle-aged caregivers who are "sandwiched" between caring for children and parents (according to Brothers 1998).

With the self-interest of the aging and family members who must care for them, one would think that any positive health data would be rapidly transmitted through the profusion of articles on aging, if not the senior grapevine. If readers were puzzled by medical disinterest in drinking benefits for heart disease and cancer, they will be astounded by the wholesale neglect of similar research about the aging. Very few American physicians are aware of the favorable evidence about drinking despite the fact that aging citizens dominate their patient rolls.

Since family members play a major role in senior care, these health care amateurs need to become familiar with healthy drinking research. "Helping the Patient by Helping the Caregiver" in *The Johns Hopkins Medical Letter* notes: *Twenty-two million Americans – one in four households – provide assistance for older relatives, friends or neighbors. Nearly half receive absolutely no help with their care giving responsibilities. Twenty-five percent of all care givers are 65 to 75 years old; another 10 percent are 75 or older. Adding to this burden, many care givers have health needs of their own* (Helping 2000). As the numbers of seniors rise, extra burdens fall primarily on the immediate family.

Through this chapter, a number of research projects are cited which support responsible drinking among the aging. In one recent study, Bond studied 1,836 Japanese Americans aged sixty-five to one hundred and reported: *Light to moderate alcohol consumption for men and women (up to 1 drink per day) is associated with better cognitive performance compared with abstainers or heavy drinkers . . . These results are consistent with other studies which found that abstainers and heavy drinkers are at higher risk for developing cognitive problems than light to moderate drinkers* (Bond 2001). The important factor here is that, as we will see in the pages to come, a considerable body of supportive evidence already exists. It is indefensible that the medical system fails to pass on drinking research to clinical physicians in the same manner as it speculates openly on other disease research.

The physicians who make the decisions and the non-professionals who deliver service to the elderly need to know more about healthy drinking science. This is not to say that all old folks need to, want to, or should drink. But for many, drinks may relieve stress, stimulate appetite and even delay some illnesses of aging.

Cognition loss a natural process

Science finds that some loss of cognition– the ability to reason– and memory is expected as we age. "Aging, Memory and the Brain," in *Harvard Women's Health Watch* predicts that two-thirds of seniors will suffer some normal memory loss: *Fortunately, the field of neuroscience has made tremendous progress in differentiating between age-related memory changes and more serious conditions caused by disease processes and brain injury* (Aging 2000). Caregivers need to understand and accommodate this loss.

Many HMOs and insurance groups promote regular exercise regimens, sensible dietary habits and regular social activities for senior members. This writer's HMO, Group Health Cooperative of Seattle, picks up fees for seniors who exercise at local health clubs. They know that active, sociable seniors have fewer acute medical needs. A May 1988 article in *The Lancet* tells of two London surveys which confirm this premise: *. . . the reduction in mortality risk was most dramatic for those who engaged in moderate regimens: those included walking, gardening, or light housework done several times a week or cycling, running, or swimming at least once a week* (Lancet 1998).

Another study of over 9,200 seniors discovered less hospitalization and nursing home occupancy in the early 1990s. This advance was attributed to healthier lifestyles and programs that keep seniors active. Be mindful that these health gains have correlative risks. Exercising is universally encouraged of seniors but there are problems, as identified in a *UC Berkeley Wellness Letter: Percentage increases in reported sports-related injuries among those 65 and over: +54%. Percentage of these injured seniors who were women: 40%. Sports with the greatest increase in injuries among older people: bicycling (+75%), followed by exercise classes, weight training and skiing* (UC Berkeley 1998). These negatives should not dissuade seniors from exercising. The gains clearly outweigh the risks. This logic applies also for moderate drinking – some benefits and some risks. The goal is moderation in all things.

Cognition and drinking

The number of studies that attribute special benefits for the elderly in drinking is remarkable, both in its volume and in its relative obscurity. In a study of the psychological benefits of moderate alcohol use, Peele notes: *Moderate drinking may, however, confer even more cardiovascular and overall health benefits for the elderly than for other age groups* (Peele 2000).

A Netherlands study suggests that elderly people who drink moderate amounts of alcohol may reason better than those who do not drink. Every senior wants to reason better. Launer in the Zutphen Elderly Study concluded: *Alcohol may provide short-term protection against cerebral lesions and consequently cognitive impairment . . . . In conclusion, moderate alcohol intake appears to be inversely associated with poor cognitive function* (Launer 1996). In science, inverse association always means less incidence of the problem. This Zutphen study found that moderate drinking increased cognitive functioning among seniors. This finding ought to be of considerable interest to clinical physicians but few will ever see the data in senior care literature.

However, U.S. senior health is generally good. In a 1997 report in the *Journal of the American Medical Association*, Wetle found substantial progress over the past two decades in senior care: *Now, nearly 25 years later, the science base has grown in depth, breadth, and detail. Less than two decades ago, for example, loss of cognitive function was called senile dementia and was considered part of normal aging or was attributed to "hardening of the arteries." Today, we understand that dementia in people of all ages, including the very old, comes from disease and that for people aged 65 years of age and older most dementia is caused by Alzheimer's disease* (Wetle 1997). Wetle noted that there are 1.4 million fewer disabled elders than there would have been in 1982, had disease rates remained constant. So, in general, American medicine deserves a corporate pat-on-the-back by its senior clients.

The September 1998 issue of *Health After 50* reports: *The most common cause of cognitive decline or dementia in the United States, AD (Alzheimer's Disease) affects 3 to 4 million older adults, 6 to 8% of people over the age of 65* (Health After 50 1998). Three years later, the same newsletter clarified who suffers the malady: *One in 10 people over age 65 and nearly half of everyone over age 85 — develop Alzheimer disease* (New Tools 2001). Whether the actual number is six or ten percent, a very large number of U.S. seniors require extensive care. Every advanced Alzheimer's patient requires a number of professional and domestic caregivers. Hawkes reported in the *London Times* on a multi-national study of 829 Alzheimer's patients in the U.S., Canada and Germany: *Non smokers who drink and have the gene (susceptibility to Alzheimer's) can delay the onset of the disease by more than 3 years if they consume more than 3 drinks a day* (Hawkes 1996). This line of research needs to be fully explored since it could affect so many elderly and millions more who care for them.

At the World Alzheimer's Congress in 2000, Farrer reported: *Those who consume one or two glasses of beer or wine per day have a 30 percent lower risk for Alzheimer's* (Farrer 2000). Another study in the Boston area by Cupples concluded:

Alcohol consumption within nationally recommended limits may protect against AD. However, it would be premature to recommend alcohol use as a prophylaxis until the protective mechanism is understood and until the minimum level and duration needed to realize a benefit have been defined more precisely.

Cupples, L., Weinberg, J., Beiser, A., et al., Effects of smoking, alcohol and APO genotype on Alzheimer's disease: the MIRAGE study, Alzheimer Report, 3:105-114, 2000

However, if these reports were developed for any other common food, one would find major coverage in medical publications and copious advertising of its merits in the media. Barring individual patient medical contraindications, why shouldn't seniors consider the potential of limited alcohol prophylaxis. It isn't as if the seniors would be taking NSAIDs which have serious medical side effects in extended or excessive use. Drinks have been employed as prophylaxis agents in the diet of humans since before recorded history!

Consider, by comparison, the raging controversy over hormone replacement treatment (HRT). Numerous medical publications and many radio and TV programs report on potential benefits of HRT, though its "protective mechanisms" and side effects are not fully understood. If the potential health benefits of drinking for seniors were treated in a similar educational manner as is HRT, many conditions affecting seniors – heart disease, cancer, diabetes, tremors of the hand, gallstones, ulcers and acute hospitalization – would be openly discussed. For example, the potential of alcohol to delay the onset of Alzheimer's disease would be widely debated.

Such drinking benefits are almost never cross-referenced over a spectrum of common senior illnesses. Instead, medical articles for this segment of the population display a "don't ask, don't tell" mentality. Here are two more examples of this reticence. The American Medical Association publication "Alcoholism in the Elderly: Diagnosis, Treatment, Prevention: Guidelines for Primary Care Physicians" is mum on *any* benefits in responsible drinking for the elderly. Only alcohol abuse is considered. An article in *Harvard Women's Health Watch* recommends a range of dietary supplements potentially helpful in warding off Alzheimer's including vitamin E, ginkgo biloba and estrogen replacement. No mention is made of the exploratory findings on drinks (Alzheimer's Disease 1999).

A 250 page report geared for senior citizens with the lugubrious title *Successful Aging: The MacArthur Foundation Study shows you how the lifestyle choices you make now – more than heredity – determine your health and vitality* completely ignores positive values in drinking for the elderly. Its index contains eight alcohol references, all dealing with abuse. The study is devoid of positive drinking commentary.

One would presume that editors at Harvard Medical School publications and the MacArthur Foundation as well as the geriatric specialists at the AMA would want to alert clinical physicians about the intriguing findings about moderate drinking among the elderly. They all know that drinking declines markedly in the senior years meaning that crucial benefits might be lost in gradual abstention. Instead, unless asked, they don't tell. Similar reticence is seen in *Health After 50*'s "Health After 100: Secrets of the Centenarians:" . . . *a modest reduction in the risk of heart disease and stroke. Doctors generally do not recommend that people who abstain from drinking take it up to gain these benefits* (Health After 100 2001). What's wrong with a modest reduction in heart disease and stroke? What's unimportant about benefits for cancer, diabetes, angina, ulcers, osteoporosis, kidney stones, cognition, etc? Abstainers shouldn't want these benefits?

If doctors don't pass on these data to their patients, it may be because they are so poorly informed themselves. For more about medical reticence see Chapter 32 which discusses the reluctance of physicians to speak out about drinking benefits. It suggests that the time has arrived to do just that.

Antioxidants and cognition

Antioxidant findings crop up once again. In "Can Taking Vitamins Protect Your Brain?" the *Harvard Health Letter* suggests a possible contribution of antioxidants to senior health: *There are two principal ways that vitamins, or lack thereof, affect brain cells. Some vitamins are antioxidants, which means they react with, and therefore blunt the deleterious effects, of oxygen free radicals* (Can Taking Vitamins 2000). Virgili reports on red wine polyphenols: *Resveratrol and other antioxidants contained in red wine may play a role in protection against excitotoxic brain damage* (Virgili 2000). How can these important findings be summarily set aside?

At the University of Milan, Bertelli and colleagues found that resveratrol (a polyphenol common in the skins and seeds of red grapes) plays a positive role in delaying aging. Is this a reason why so many winemakers are still active and hearty in their eighth and ninth decades? These same antioxidative chemicals are thought to reduce the incidence of cancer and cardiovascular diseases. Bertelli suggests that resveratrol triggers a sevenfold increase in the effectiveness of an enzyme called Mapkinase which stimulates and regenerates neural cells (Bertelli 1998). These cells involve the brain's communication system and could be involved in improved cognition. This research needs much more communication and consideration.

Radford reports: *The findings come in light of studies reporting various health benefits of wine drinking, in particular a study from Bordeaux last year which found that moderate wine drinkers were less prone to senile dementia than non-drinkers* (Radford 1999). In "Alcohol and the Aging Brain," Finkel finds that alcohol abuse is often initiated by unrelated mental problems: *Psychiatric disorders, especially depression, are much more likely to cause alcohol abuse than [for it] to result from heavy drinking. However, moderate drinking has been reported in a number of studies to improve the function of the brain* (Finkel 1998). Though hearing benefits are not considered in this book, Popelka recently found: *There is evidence for a modest protective association between moderate alcohol use and hearing loss* (Popelka 2000). The research clearly distinguishes use from abuse. Apparently the editors of *Health After 50* (see above) do not feel that senior citizens are capable of such distinctions.

Eckardt suggests: *Recent studies have also noted some positive effects of moderate ethanol consumption on cognitive performance in the aging human* (Eckardt 1998). Another study by the INSERM research group in France, the institute which developed many of the French paradox heart studies, considered dementia and Alzheimer's in "Epidemiology of Vascular Aging." Dufouil reports: *A lower risk . . . in both men and women, and other studies have found moderate alcohol consumption to be associated with improved cognitive function in elderly populations* (Dufouil 1997). Findings of lower risk for cognitive loss in both sexes is ignored in medical publications which target seniors.

Some aging studies do not find benefits in drinking. But the number of findings for better cognition among light drinking senior citizens continues to amass. So distorted is our fear that seniors will over-consume that we fail to communicate benefits in a food that most elders have used moderately throughout their lives.

Long term impacts

Galanis undertook an eighteen-year study of 3,556 Japanese-American men living in Hawaii. His paper notes: *Men who consumed up to one drink per day during middle age were later found to have significantly better cognitive test results than nondrinkers . . . These results are consistent with those of most previous studies* (Galanis 2000). In this study, one drink a day produced a forty percent lower risk for diminished cognition in aging. The study shows a cumulative benefit in daily drinking from middle age through senior years. Over twenty million households face the problems of their elders with failing cognition. Would the caregivers in these homes be interested in this research? They might.

One elderly cognition study in France gained wide notoriety in the media in 1997. Orgogozo directed studies of dementia with 3,777 subjects age sixty-five and older who lived in south France and consumed wine regularly. The authors found: *Results show an 80% decrease in the frequency of dementia and a 75% decrease in the frequency of Alzheimer's disease after a 3-year follow up* (Orgogozo 1997). Orgogozo noted: *Wine consumption remains one of the last pleasures of this stage of life; our findings argue against prohibiting mild or moderate wine consumption in the elderly.*

Holmgren reported on a twenty year study of World War II veterans conducted at the Indiana University School of Medicine which opined: *We know that the intake of alcohol affects the central nervous system, but what we found instead showed that moderate drinkers retained slightly stronger cognitive skills than the non drinker or heavy drinker* (Holmgren 1993). Invariably, the moderate drinking, moderate living, moderate eating, moderate exercising group demonstrates the best health data.

Many nursing home studies conducted over the past forty years show favorable behavioral data for residents given small amounts of alcohol daily. Drinking residents are better behaved, happier and require fewer medicines for sleeping. Yet extended-care protocols do not encourage drink regiments. A drink a day could save money for long-term care facilities in lowering the need for drugs and occasioning fewer disciplinary problems among a restless, bored population. Drinking reservations are based in our ambivalent culture and in the reluctance of medicine to associate any benefits with drinking.

The following graph on cognitive performance is informative
in several respects. Christian reported on a survey of reasoning
skills in a retrospective study of 4,729 twins. Those who consumed from eight to sixteen drinks per week exhibited the
highest cognitive scores. Nondrinking twins scored well but
slightly lower than the eight to sixteen drinks per week group.
Obviously, good cognition is not dependent upon drinks alone,
but neither is it harmed by drinks. Former but now abstaining
drinkers – undoubtedly including some with previous drinking
problems – recorded the lowest levels in these tests. The study
noted: *No evidence was found to indicate an association between
moderate long-term alcohol intake and lower cognitive scores in aging
individuals . . . Perhaps the most noteworthy is the lack of evidence that
moderate alcohol consumption impairs the cognitive function of individuals* (Christian 1993).

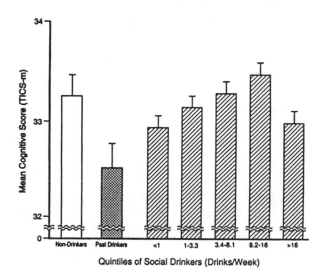

Quintiles of Social Drinkers (Drinks/Week)

Christian's graphic forms an upside-down, U-shaped curve.
As drinking increases so does cognition but it turns down when
intake reaches the 8-16 drink per week group. Note, however,

that the above 16 per week still registers higher than the 1 per week grouping. This graphic demonstrates that daily drinking among seniors is not an impairment to healthy cognitive functioning.

Cross-referencing the mortality aspects

When daily drinking is related to other health conditions, Christian's study gains added significance. Various chapters in this book associate moderate drinking with a number of healthful conditions — better bone density, less heart and vascular disease, less kidney and gallstones, fewer colds, reduced diabetes risk and lower premature death rates — compared with abstainers and abusers. This points to the desirability of cross-referencing of drinking research for all illnesses among senior patients. Drinks might benefit two or three conditions afflicting an aging patient. Such referencing was common in the nineteenth century. The current policy of excluding drink therapy instituted by the American Medical Association in 1917 needs revisiting!

In medical workups with the aging (or for any age), physicians should inventory a patient's drinking habits and consider the potential effects of light drinking on any acute condition. But, to render such informed care, clinical physicians need to be exposed to the entire body of healthy drinking research.

Though mortality research is detailed in a later chapter, here are some findings on death expectations in senior research. Scherr studied different regional populations — one among residents in East Boston, another in Iowa and a third in New Haven — and discovered: . . . *moderate alcohol consumption is associated with lower mortality in the elderly, as it is in middle-aged populations* (Scherr 1992). Pahor studied moderate drinking and the incidence of deep venous thrombosis and pulmonary embolisms among 7,958 persons over sixty-eight years of age: *Low to moderate alcohol consumption is associated with a decreased risk of deep venous thrombosis and pulmonary embolism in older persons* (Pahor 1996). Colditz studied coronary and all-cause deaths in 1,226 elderly male and female Massachusetts residents: *The inverse relationship between light alcohol consumption and CHD mortality was much stronger than that observed for death from all causes* (Colditz 1985).

De Labry used the same working premise in a twelve-year long elderly study and concluded: *These results lend support to the hypothesis of the beneficial effect of moderate drinking with respect to mortality* (De Labry 1992). Simons studied Australian seniors in New South Wales and reported: *Alcohol intake in the Dubbo elderly appears to be independently associated with a significant increase in life expectancy* (Simons 1996). Blow studied the elderly in primary care settings and determined: *Among older adults, light-to-moderate drinkers may have the best health and abstainers have the poorest health* (Blow 2000). These studies uniformly found better health and longer lives among moderate drinking seniors. One project demonstrated an important benefit that can occur with responsible drinking. Popelka found: *In general the prevalence of hearing loss decreased significantly with increasing alcohol consumption . . . those who consumed over 11 drinks per week had the least risk of any hearing loss, about 30% lower than those who did not drink* (Popelka 2000).

Consider again the frustration of journalist Jonathan Rauch (see page xvi in Epidemiology section). Rauch contacted his father's doctor, a famous Harvard researcher and an American Heart Association official trying to determine whether moderate drinking could help his father's mild hypertension. He concluded: *I think the message most people would get from (these) sources is: Drinking isn't all bad, but eschew it anyway . . . To continue today's policy of muttering and changing the subject verges perilously on saying not just that too much alcohol is bad for you but that ignorance is good for you* (Rauch 1998). Is this all medicine has to offer?

Hundreds of books, pamphlets and videotapes are published annually on the problems of alcohol abuse. The presentation of positive drinking research in no way discredits these efforts. Balancing the communication with a rationale for the responsible consumption provides no threat to rehabilitation and abuse prevention programs. It is a fair assumption that the elderly in society are not apt to become abusers en masse if they learn of new findings about moderate intake. Here is a summary of the positive findings reported in this chapter on aging:

*Reduction in mortality risk . . . Protection from
cerebral lesions . . . Delays onset of Alzheimer's . . .
Less prone to dementia . . . Stronger cognitive skills .
. . Less medicine needed . . . More alert and friendly .
. . More sociable . . . Relief of minor pain . . . Lower
mortality . . . Healthier minds and bodies . . .
Pleasurable and beneficial . . . Correlates with longer
life . . .Better hearing*

In view of these findings, the resistance in medicine to a responsible drinking ethic for the elderly is puzzling. When considered as a group, the thirty benefits listed in this book are much more than the "modest reduction in risks." Despite this impressive roster of benefits, resistance to their communication in medicine remains strong. Another *Health After 50* article on senior drinking states: *No matter what your age or gender, if you don't drink, experts do not recommend starting* (When Alcohol 1999). Why do experts not recommend against moderate alcohol therapy if it is found to be effective in research? Obviously, some "experts" have their heads in Temperance clouds. By now, readers should understand why it is necessary to repeat this theme in nearly every chapter. The final two chapters implore practicing physicians, alternative caregivers and mothers to work to remedy the communication problem. This important audience must understand how a whole body of research is being slighted by archaic professional protocols.

The reality is that many international studies demonstrate moderate drinking benefits for the elderly. Simons and others studied an aging population in Dubbo, a small, rural town in New South Wales, Australia. The group included 1,235 males and 1,570 females. Over the period, alcohol use was described as moderate. The study concluded:

*Moderate drinking appears to be associated with
longer survival in men aged 60-74 and in all elderly
women. In men, there was no evidence for a
differential effect between 1-2 drinks and 5 or more
drinks daily. It is premature to promote the use of*

alcohol for prevention of dementia, but this century
may witness a completely new role for alcohol.

Simons, L., McCallum, J., Friedlander, Y, Ortiz, M., and Simons, J., Moderate alcohol
intake is associated with survival in the elderly: the Dubbo Study, Medical Journal of
Australia, 173:121-124, 2000

The most important line in this chapter – or perhaps the whole book – is the last one in the above quote. Simons recognizes that healthy drinking science has grown to such an accumulation that it cries out "an entirely new role for alcohol" within the medical profession. That there is a difference between informing an interested public and "promoting alcohol." Senior citizens – and those who care for them – have to make hundreds of trying adjustments as they age themselves while caring for older relatives. Seniors deserve to be informed of these many studies. They aren't being told now.

A survey on the issues surrounding drinking among the aging was published in 1987 in *Drug and Alcohol Dependence.* Stall reports: *Probably the most interesting finding to have been replicated in the alcohol and aging literature is that decrease in prevalence of heavy and problematic drinking seems to occur as a concomitant of the aging process* (Stall 1987). This finding was published fourteen years ago. It shows that an aging audience is not one ripe for addiction, though there may always remain a serious level of addiction among the elderly. Stall's survey points to the fact that most older people don't drink as much as they used to. Elders rarely overdo anything. Most of those who drink do so moderately and enjoy longer, more comfortable lives partially as a consequence of the drinking. Why not let all seniors in on this secret?

An interesting study was released in the *New England Journal of Medicine* concerning the impact of NSAIDs in the delay of Alzheimer's. The study included 6,989 residents in a suburb of Rotterdam who were fifty-five and over and free of dementia at baseline. The group was followed for an average of 6.8 years. The study probed the effects of regular use of nonsteroidal, anti-inflammatory drugs – such as Ibuprofen or Naproxen – on the onset of dementia and Alzheimer's disease. Over this period, 394 developed dementia and 293 were afflicted with Alzheimer's. That's close to the percentage of Alzheimer patients among the aging in the U.S. The study came to this conclusion: *The long-term use of NSAIDs may protect against Alzheimer's disease but not against vascular dementia* (in't Veld 2001).

Another study on aging and dementia from the Netherlands was released in *The Lancet*. In "Alcohol consumption and risk of dementia: The Rotterdam Study," Ruitenberg reported: . . . *light to moderate alcohol consumption is associated with a reduced risk of dementia in individuals aged 55 years or older . . . The effect seems unchanged by the source of alcohol (Ruitenberg 2002)*. In this study, 5,395 individuals were followed over six years. Consumers of one to three drinks a day had a forty-two percent lower risk while somewhat more than one drink a week had a twenty-four percent lower risk. The Rotterdam findings replicate Orgogozo's work in Southern France that demonstrate that daily drinkers fare better than periodic drinkers. Another six year study of Americans by Ostermann concluded: . . . *moderate drinkers generally had less than half the odds of disability that abstainers had* (Ostermann 2001). How much proof is necessary to get American medicine to tell seniors the truth about drinking?

The controversy over mass advertising of pharmaceuticals is commented on by Gupta in the December 2001 issue of *Time* in "Rx: Not for the Elderly:" . . . *according to last week's Journal of the American Medical Association, nearly 7 million older Americans – about one-fifth of the population age 65 or older – are given medications that are rarely appropriate for people their age . . . nearly 1 million swallow pills that an expert panel has determined senior citizens should probably never take* (Gupta 2001). In addition to the well-known side effects of long-term NSAID use, Gupta identifies eleven other categories of drugs to "Keep away from." The message is to be alert about all drugs and supplements. Never take anything new without the counsel of a caregiver.

The popular media are fascinated by long life. Commentaries in the press frequently relate drinking habits of those reaching very old ages. It was widely reported that a recently deceased Frenchwoman Marie Bremont celebrated her 115th birthday with a glass of wine and chocolates. The medical challenge lies in recognizing many lifestyle habits and inherited genes contributed to Marie's long life. It's obvious that, for Marie, wine and chocolates were no problem and very pleasant life extenders.

Several months later, the media reported on the passing of the world's oldest man, Antonio Todde, a lifelong Italian shepherd. Todde died in the small village of Tiana, Sardinia just shy of his 113th birthday. He had left his native island just once to serve in World War I. His advice on aging was brief: *Just love your brother and drink a good glass of red wine every day.*

This is not to imply that all centenarians should drink. It is to say that drinking is common among many centenarians. An article in the January 2001 *Harvard Health Letter* titled "Living to 100: What's the Secret?" reports on the Harvard University project which was first undertaken as the New England Centenarian Study and now extends throughout the world. It reports that the number of centenarians in the U.S. in 2000 as around 72,000 but it projects their number by 2050 to be 834,000! The article stresses the importance of a good diet and the potential role of antioxidants in controlling the body's free radicals. In sum, the article advises the factor centenarians share is moderate habits: *They're simply following the standard health commandments: don't smoke, keep trim, get exercise, manage stress, and avoid social isolation* (Living to 100: What's the Secret 2002). In "Training Resource Guide" published for members of the Society of Wine Educators, Finkel notes: . . . *nearly 7,000 elderly residents of Massachusetts, Connecticut, and Iowa were studied . . . Like so many other studies, this one indicated that low or moderate alcohol consumption correlates with longer life, with better mental function* (Finkel 1998).

As we age, our smell faculties gradually wane. A study in the *Journal of the American Medical Association* indicates that about a quarter of individuals aged 53 to 97 years of age suffer "impaired olfaction." Participants between 50 and 60 lost an average of six percent of olfactory skills. Some in the 70 to 80 group lose up to thirty percent of odor perception. At age 80, the loss rises to as much as 63 percent. Since odors constitute about 70 percent of flavor, consider the fact that alcohol has the psychological ability to make foods taste better and to encourage social interchange. Discouraging drinking in elders robs them of a natural food which encourages appetites while easing aging's burdens.

The ice is breaking, but it's still mighty thick!

Research Addendum to Chapter 10

✔ Elderly use of hospital emergency rooms: "Regular drinkers were functionally and socially more independent than non-regular drinkers " (van der Pol 1996).

✔ The shrinking brain myth is noted in a Harvard Health Letter: "Although the brain does shrink by 5%-10% by age 70 or 75, researchers have recently discovered that people do not lose nearly as many cells as was previously thought . . . . the surface of the brain, appears to be healthy even in later years" (Preserving Memory 1998).

✔ Another brain shrinkage study involved employees of a Japanese company divided into light, moderate and heavy drinking categories. Moderate drinkers consumed up to 340 grams per week, approximately 25 drinks. Kubota found: "Heavy drinking, but not moderate drinking, seems to exaggerate the brain shrinkage that comes with aging" (Kubota 2001).

✔ In a 3-month study, a nursing home gave two ounces of wine with supper meals and found happier residents among drinkers: "As far as the preparation of food was concerned, 85 percent of those having wine were happy with the way the food was cooked, as opposed to only 43 percent of the non-wine patients. All of the patients who had wine with their meals felt that their food portions were large enough, but only 51 percent of the non-wine patients thought the portions were adequate" (Sarley 1969).

✔ A report at an AMA conference found: "Elevated homocysteine levels (are) a possible risk for Alzheimer's and lower blood levels of vitamin B_{12} and folate among Alzheimer's patients" (Clarke 1998). Both of these conditions are advantaged among regular drinkers.

✔ A study on the effects of beer on elderly psychiatric patients: "After about 12 ounces of beer each, the tippling group proved much more sociable than did the fruit-juice crowd who remained unchanged" (Becker 1974). Beer also is a good source of folate and vitamin B_{12}.

✔ A text on drinking among the elderly notes: "The data on alcohol use in old age suggest that a balanced perspective could be achieved if society were willing to abandon some of its assumptions and stereotypes. Alcohol use appears to be more moderate among the elderly when compared with other age groups" (Mishara 1980).

✔ An article published by NIAAA recommends for the elderly no more than a single daily drink: " . . . to relieve minor pain, to aid the appetite, and to improve bowel function" (Dufour 1992).

✔ A study of 9,704 community-dwelling white women aged 65 and above notes: "Compared with current moderate drinkers (average 3.5 drinks a week), nondrinkers had significantly poorer function (both self-reported and measured) on all of the performance measures except tandem walk" (Nelson 1994).

✔ A British study on Australian WW II veterans found: "While some scientists have argued that long-term alcohol intake could contribute to impaired brain function, especially in later years of life, this new study and others have provided evidence of either no effect or a beneficial effect of moderate alcohol consumption on cognitive abilities" (Dent 1996)

✔ A study of the effects of alcohol and tobacco on Alzheimer's revealed: ". . . moderate wine consumption was found to be associated with a fourfold diminishing of the risk of Alzheimer's disease" (Leibovici 1999).

✔ The medical conflict about drinking among the aging is focused in comments by Ticehurst at a Gerontology Conference in Wellington: "The paradox is that alcohol can be seen as beneficial for physical health while, on the other hand, it can cause misery and illness" (Elderly may benefit 1999).

✔ As early as 1969, Sarley observed that the nursing home was an ideal venue for judicious use of drinks with seniors. "For geriatric and convalescent patients, wines can be served to stimulate appetites and aid digestive processes. It has been recognized that wines can act as tranquilizing and relaxing agents in the treatment of all patients (Sarley 1969).

Chapter 11

All-Age Cognition

Drinks enhance brain functioning

■ **Author's abstract:** Good cognition or normal reasoning faculties are of concern throughout life. Many factors, mood being prominent among them, determine how well we respond to various stimuli. Readers will appreciate the following research which suggests a positive drinking contribution to everyday cognition. Moderate drinkers may enjoy enhanced performance of routine tasks. Since alcohol is a recognized mood leveler, this conclusion is warranted. Consider these findings:

■ ➽ One to four drinks a day favors cognitive functions
 ➽ Moderate doses increase happiness, euphoria, and carefree feelings
 ➽ Drinkers have a lower risk for poor cognitive performance

Cognition — the acquisition of knowledge through perception, reasoning and intuition — is not of concern just for the old folks. Healthy cognition is important to everyone throughout life.

Elias came to this conclusion studying middle-aged participants in the half-century-old Framingham, Massachusetts survey:

> *Light to moderate alcohol consumption among women (1-4 drinks per day) was positively related to many domains of cognitive performance . . . a smaller, more limited positive relation for men at relatively high drinking levels (4-8 per day).*

Elias, P., et al., Alcohol Consumption and Cognitive Performance in the Framingham Heart Study, American Journal of Epidemiology, Vol. 150, No. 6, pp550-589, 1999

These are truly remarkable conclusions. They imply that drinking facilitates the most distinctive attribute of humanity – the ability to reason and make informed choices. Elias notes: *. . . a positive association between alcohol consumption and cognition is strikingly reminiscent of a similar relation found between alcohol consumption and improvement in cardiovascular disease mortality rates, all-cause mortality and cardiovascular diseases* (Elias 1999).

This is illness cross-referencing at its best. These findings do not suggest that good cognition is dependent upon drinks. That's nonsense. But drinks may facilitate the process. None of the health benefits defined in this book are exclusive to drinking. The purpose here is to identify drinking's unique dietary contributions so convincingly that our nation will modify its anti-drinking policies. Good health does not depend upon consumption of alcohol beverages. But moderate drinking can benefit health.

Alcohol can be appropriately evaluated only when all its impacts are presented in such a comprehensive manner. Medicine's inhibitions about drinking were identified by researchers decades ago. In 1968, Dock presented the following commentary at a Wine Institute seminar. He saw a lingering malaise about drinking left over from Prohibition among both patients and physicians – 34 years ago! *An entire generation of physicians in the United States lost touch with the medical lore of wine during the period of National Prohibition . . . today, with increasing emphasis on nutrition and preventive medicine, research workers are finding renewed interest in the medical values of wine, broadening our understanding of it and sharpening those truths distilled from empirical data recorded by thoughtful physicians over the past centuries* (Dock 1968).

At mid-century, Dock noted that anti-drinking protocols prevailing within the medical profession were depriving physicians and patients of an appreciation of the health attributes of therapeutic drinking. Little has happened to alter medical ambivalence over the intervening thirty-four years. The care delivery systems in America, public and private, conventional and alternative, remain Temperance oriented. In the 1990s, government agencies and some medical associations gave grudging recognition of alcohol's contributions in lessening cardiovascular disease risk. But those benefits often are said to apply only to middle-aged and senior men and the recognition is always couched in pejorative mantras such as, "If you don't drink now, don't start."

No threat to brain functioning

To begin at the cognitive beginning, moderate drinking is no threat to mental health. As the previous chapter amply demonstrated, there exists a very respectable body of work crediting drinks with better cognition for all ages. In 1985, a professor at the University of Melbourne, South Australia debunked one of the most persistent canards of the dry lobby — that drinking kills brain cells. Elwood in the Caerphilly Study evaluated 1,879 men aged fifty-five to fifty-nine and determined: *Age and social class show strong associations with cognitive function . . . . Neither tobacco smoking nor the drinking of alcohol seem to be associated with cognitive functioning* (Elwood 1999). Elwood found no brain impairments among moderate drinkers. Bowden concurred in a 1985 study: *Unfortunately, the research on social drinking has given rise to some alarmist claims. On the available evidence these claims appear to be quite unjustified . . . It is important to distinguish the effects of moderate imbibing at levels generally regarded as safe (50-80 ml of ethanol daily). Nothing in the cognitive literature warrants a revision of the recognized safe limits* (Bowden 1985). That's three to five drinks daily.

A recent issue of *Harvard Health Letter* addressed the importance of developing and utilizing brain capacity: . . . *memory loss isn't an inevitable, anatomical withering away, and second, that it is worth striving to keep your brain cells busy. . . the theory is that the neurons of the intelligent and educated brain have more connections than a less intelligent, less educated brain. The dementia rates may reflect the fact that people with a larger brain-reserve capacity can perhaps afford to lose more neural connections before the loss shows up* (You Can Remember This 2000). Rigorous, continuous mental exercise facilitates brain cell activity and brain health. The trend today among the aging to keep busy physically and mentally may well contribute to reduction of dementia.

Excessive intake does threaten cognition

As is revealed in each succeeding chapter in this book, the good effects of drinking diminish with excessive levels of consumption. Intake must be moderate to obtain positive results. In a 1996 review of cognition research, Parsons provides a progressive scale of damage in excessive drinking:

> *Our conclusions support an alcohol-causal threshold hypothesis and suggests the following testable hypothesis: persons drinking five or six U.S. standard drinks per day over extended time periods manifest some cognitive inefficiencies; at seven to nine drinks per day, mild cognitive deficits are present; and at 10 or more drinks per day, moderate cognitive deficits equivalent to those found in diagnosed alcoholics are present.*

Parsons, O., and Nixon, S., Cognitive Functioning in Sober Social Drinkers: A Review of the Research since 1986, Journal of Studies on Alcohol, 59:180-190, 1998.

No researcher questions the damage involved in excessive drinking. But five or six drinks per day exceeds by more than double the average consumption levels of the majority of daily drinkers and the daily upper limits suggested by federal health authorities. Ten or more drinks per day is raging alcoholism. The authors found that cognitive inefficiencies did not kick in until participants reported heavy, daily drinking. Arbuckle conducted a test of moderate, social drinking on cognitive abilities and found: . . . *social drinking has relatively circumscribed effects on cognitive functions* (Arbuckle 1994).

While some cognition studies do not identify alcohol-related benefits, all agree that *no damage occurs* from moderate intake. Dufouil looked to gender differences and concluded a definite advantage for women: *The odds ratio for being a high cognitive performer . . . (are)+ for women who usually consumed two or more drinks per day in comparison with nondrinkers* (Dufouil 1997). Dent evaluated long term consumption with older men living in Australia: *No evidence was found that apparently persistent lifelong consumption of alcohol was related to cognitive function of these men in old age* (Dent 1997).

Schinka studied army veterans from the Vietnam war and determined: *Differences between groups defined by drinking level revealed no significant effect of alcohol use on cognitive function* (Schinka 2002). In the Honolulu Heart Study, Galanis gathered data from 3,556 Hawaiians of Japanese ancestry. His data suggests: *Moderate drinking among middle-aged men in this population was positively associated with cognitive performance at older age* (Galanis 2000). As with vascular health, drinking during the middle years correlates to better cognition in aging.

Institutional caution abounds

A review of thirteen cross-sectional studies conducted among elderly clients over a twenty-four year period at the Royal Edinburg Hospital was released in 1999. Chick found better mental health among moderate drinkers but cautioned: *There will be few, if any, patients whom doctors should advise to drink to improve mental health* (Chick 1999). The perfunctory medical reservations kick in. When research scientists fail to support their own findings, the buck gets passed on to practicing physicians who, because of anti-drinking protocols and little coverage in the literature, have scant familiarity with the research. As a consequence, there is little impetus to correlate healthy drinking findings for a range of diseases and conditions. Positive research on drinking and cognition, kidney stones, acute hospitalization, the common cold, comparative earnings and other lesser categories languish in dusty medical journals.

Mainline research has identified substantial cognitive benefits in responsible drinking. Baum-Baicker reviewed this growing literature as early as the mid-1980s and reported:

(1) Alcohol in moderate amounts is effective in reducing stress . . . (2) Low and moderate doses of alcohol have been reported to increase overall

*affective expression, happiness, euphoria,
conviviality and pleasant and carefree feelings.
Tension, depression and self-consciousness have
been reported to decrease with equal doses. (3) Low
alcohol doses have been found to improve certain
types of cognitive performance. Included here are
problem-solving and short-term memory.*

Baum-Baicker, C., The Psychological Benefits of Moderate Alcohol Consumption: A
Review of the Literature, Drug and Alcohol Dependence, 15, 1985

Baum-Baicker's positive review of the science was published
sixteen years ago. Every physician knows that happiness, euphoria and conviviality enhance disease prevention. Alcohol's
mood-elevating attribute complements biomedical status by
raising HDL cholesterol and reducing tumor growth. Mood
elevation is the primary motivation for drinking. But few private
citizens understand that normal alcohol euphoria can help to
ward off disease.

Launer studied a group of Dutch men over a three-year period
and found that moderate drinking individuals already suffering
chronic illnesses had maintained higher cognitive functioning
than abstainers: *After adjustments for age, education and smoking
status, men with cardiovascular disease/diabetes and low to moderate
alcohol intake had a significantly lower risk for poor cognitive function
than abstainers* (Launer 1996). Even after illness has struck, mental faculties benefit from drinks. Hendrie studied cognitive functioning among black American drinkers: *The scores of abstainers
were worse than those of subjects in the lightest drinking category. The
pattern of scores for cognitive performance and daily functioning was
similar between current and past drinkers* (Hendrie 1996).

A 1993 study speculates that memory is enhanced by drinking.
Tyson reports: *Compared to placebo subjects, alcohol significantly
facilitated the recall of 25 words whether administered immediately or
40 minutes after learning. In addition, alcohol significantly increased
the memory words associated with pictures when incidentally learned
before drinking and significantly decreased incidental learning after
drinking* (Tyson 1993).

Readers should recognize why this book reprints so many
quotes directly from the literature. These data are seldom found

in either popular or medical literature. Yet, the majority of mid-life, casual drinkers need to know of these findings which could initiate meaningful health advantages. For senior citizens, for those in their middle-years pledged to elderly care, for diabetics and for cardiovascular patients, and for individuals suffering some loss of memory, there is promise of protecting and extending reasoning faculties. All Americans deserve access to this encouraging body of research.

The relative risks of abuse

Public health factotums and the media-active dry lobby mistrust the self-control of the average American. That is why so much of their literature discourages even moderate consumption. "If you don't drink now, don't start." It is true that for some abusers, knowledge of health values in drinks could become one more rationale for drinking too much. But, should knowledge of benefits for the majority be set aside because of the proclivities of an abuse-prone minority?

Many references in anthropology and sociology report that heavier consuming nations like Italy, Germany, France and Spain have serious alcoholism and abuse problems but most have fewer per capita abusers than the United States. In *Society, Culture, and Drinking Patterns Re-examined*, Rooney notes that among Spanish consumers: . . . *even for heavy drinkers, sociability appears to be closely integrated with alcohol consumption* (Rooney 1991). In *Drinking Occasions*, Heath finds: . . . *empirical evidence from around the world has generally shown fewer problems in those cultures and countries where consumption was relatively high, disproportionately more problems where consumption was relatively low* (Heath 2000). Heath's exhaustive review concludes: *Alcoholism, alcohol abuse, and alcohol dependence, even in the general sense of acute or chronic problem drinking, are rare in societies through the world, and have been throughout history.*

A more revealing study of the fifty states by Linsky, "Drinking Norms and Alcohol-Related Problems in the United States," reveals that: *States that have the strongest cultural biases against beverage alcohol tend to be the same states that experience the most problems (i.e. the highest arrest rates associated with drinking)* (Linksy 1986). The study found Mississippi with the most problems per capita from drinking and Nevada with the fewest. A similar study by Dull of Tennessee cities of 10,000 population revealed: *The findings indicate that alcohol availability measures are almost uniformly negatively correlated with the dependent variables. The "forbidden fruit" concept was advanced to explain the findings* (Dull 1986). Governmental and medical overemphasis on the dangers may well be producing adverse consequences in our society which promote abusive drinking.

This issue needs wide discussion, debate and, hopefully, resolution within the medical community. Physicians will face more and more difficult questions as the public gradually becomes more aware of these positive health findings. How many seniors with prematurely diminished faculties could have delayed the darkening curtain by an innocent drink or two daily? How many young and middle-aged adults could handle the pressures of careers and marriage with a better understanding of the role of responsible drinking? What of the extra burdens placed upon the "sandwiched" family caregivers as a consequence of the veil of silence surrounding drinking and cognition research? These are highly speculative questions that have no simple answers. Yet they are practical questions which face physicians daily. "Why didn't I know?"

Current cognitive research clearly demonstrates better odds for moderate drinkers who remain both physically and mentally active throughout life. Isn't that what we all seek in medical advice – the best possible odds? As any practicing physician would attest, these kinds of positive drinking studies infrequently appear in medical publications. In reality, by suggesting a moderate drinking regimen for selected patients who give every evidence of moderate life habits, physicians would not be plunging them into radical, uncharted waters. Drinking therapy is common in European medicine where cardiovascular disease and aging statistics often are better than our own.

One final study on cognition from Denmark is worthy of note because many recent studies there have found a favorable relation between wine drinking and overall health. Mortensen concludes: . . . *wine consumption is a general indicator of optimal social, cognitive and personality development . . . the association between drinking patterns and social and psychosocial characteristics may largely explain the apparent health benefits of wine* (Mortensen 2001). Once again, epidemiological data is intimately related to regional demographics. Danish wine drinkers are a better educated, upper level strata. Always study the audience studied

When cognition research is combined with similarly favorable statistics for cardiovascular diseases and cancer, moderate drinking becomes a credible alternative to abstention based solely in fear. Peruse the first two lines of the NIAAA *Alcohol Alert* on "Alcohol and Cognition" to see the alcohol research communication problem: *Research shows that alcohol adversely affects the brain. When health professionals encounter patients who are having cognitive difficulties, such as impaired memory or reasoning ability, alcohol use may be the cause of the problem* (Alcohol and Cognition 1989). Shouldn't that have read "alcohol abuse" instead of "use?" In three pages of "science" about the problems of abusive drinking and thirty-one scientific references, this government paper has no mention of positive research on cognition and responsible drinking.

Our government does not want us to know much about health benefits in responsible drinking. For seniors or for the rest of us.

It's something to "reason" about.

Chapter 12

Common Cold

Eighty-five percent less risk

Author's abstract: Americans spend many millions annually fighting the miseries of the common cold. Two benchmark studies were conducted by the same scientist in the 1990s. Each involved cold viruses. In the first, moderate daily drinkers enjoyed astonishing risk protection compared to non-drinkers. But there has descended a curtain of silence in medical circles about how drinks may ward off a cold virus. Hot toddy anyone?

This chapter is textbook evidence for the failure of the medical system to communicate the good news about drinking. It reports on only two studies, both of which were conducted in the U.S. and Great Britain by the same researcher. In 1993, Sheldon Cohen and associates, in London and at Carnegie Mellon University in Pittsburgh, released a report of a year-long prospective study involving over 400 male and female, nonsmoking, adults. The researchers were looking for any relationship between drinking and the common cold. And they found one!

Volunteers for the first study agreed to be quarantined and exposed through nasal drops to one of five cold viruses. The subjects were followed through the ensuing week. What they found was that resistance to the administered viruses improved progressively with the increasing amounts of alcohol consumed. The results of the first study appeared in the *American Journal of Public Health*. Cohen wrote: *The benefits of alcohol consumption in relation to susceptibility were unexpected* (Cohen 1993). Of the 391 subjects inoculated, thirty-eight percent (148) developed colds. Of the 243 who avoided infection, 169 were nonsmoking drinkers. Surprisingly, there was also a definitive dose response. Consumers of two to three drinks daily had an eighty-five percent greater resistance. Those drinking one to two drinks daily had a sixty-five percent lower risk and those who drank less frequently than daily had a thirty percent lower risk. Remarkable.

Articles on the common cold were published in two recent Harvard Medical School publications. The first, "The Common Cold: An Update on Therapy," appeared in *Harvard Men's Health Watch* in 1997. The author rated the efficacy of various "cures" for the miseries of the common cold. Strategies ranged from the old stand-by chicken soup (it's the hot vapor above the bowl that stimulates mucous flow and alleviates congestion) to antihistamines (they dry out the nasal membranes providing relief from congestion but they thicken the mucous). Well, almost everything was covered except, of course, Cohen's findings about how drinks helped to prevent colds.

The second article "Relieving the Common Cold" appeared in *Harvard Health Letter* in 1998. The three page summary of cold prevention techniques covered the waterfront again from echinacea to chicken soup except, of course, Cohen's 1993 report. Or any other reference to one of the most ancient balms for the common cold – alcohol. The authors at Harvard could hardly have been unaware of Cohen's work which was published in the *American Journal of Public Health* five years earlier. We are the only major industrial nation which formally excludes alcohol as a therapeutic drug. It's obviously time to amend this indiscretion based in Temperance fervor. In addition, no doctor could be unaware of alcohol-based cold nostrums which are common in nearly all folk medicine. Cohen suggested that his findings warrant additional investigation, but follow-up has been sparse.

There was no rush to replicate or disprove the findings. They have been virtually ignored.

Apparently medical ambivalence has determined that what we don't know about drinking won't hurt us. In a prescient aside in his report, Cohen noted: *Up until now, the relationship between alcohol consumption and susceptibility to common upper respiratory infections in healthy, nonalcoholic humans has not been studied* (Cohen 1993). Why not? One might wonder why one of nature's most persistent discomforts does not deserve more research funding. This writer cannot claim universal knowledge of all publications on this subject, but no responses have been forthcoming in the dozen or so popular reporting journals reviewed regularly.

In 1997, four years after his first study, the results of another cold study by Cohen were published in the *Journal of the American Medical Association.* In this project, the authors widened the research horizon by evaluating a number of influences on cold infection. This project evaluated the impact of friends, family, work and community activities on cold sufferers. This study found:

> *Although smoking, poor sleep quality, alcohol abstinence, low dietary intake of vitamin C, elevated catecholamine levels, and being introverted were all associated with greater susceptibility to colds, they could only partially account for the relation between social network diversity and incidence of colds . . .*

Cohen, S., Doyle, W., Skoner, D., Rabin, B., and Gwatney, J., Social Ties and Susceptibility to the Common Cold, JAMA, Vol. 277, No. 24, June, 1997

Alcohol abstinence is posed as a risk factor! In Cohen's previous study, alcohol abstinence was a factor for higher rates of viral infection. In this project, 125 men and 151 women, ages ten to fifty-five, were enlisted from the Pittsburgh area. The researchers reported that resistance to cold infections is multifactorial: *Several health practices were associated . . . as well as benefits of moderate alcohol consumption . . .* That was the single scientific reference to the effects of drinking with no explanations as to dose response and other factors even though it could have been referenced in Cohen's earlier study. Why weren't the

favorable statistics from that study cited as corroborating
authority? What could prompt this institutionalized disinterest
in the research community about quite remarkable evidence of
resistance to the common cold? Was the Cohen 1993 project
poorly designed and executed or flawed in some manner?

A challenging newspaper article by Haney begins with "Scientists smell success with cold medicine" found in the *Seattle Post
Ingelligencer*. After several failed tests, a new drug produced this
result: *In these people, runny noses and other symptoms completely went
away in an average of six days, compared with seven days in the
rhinovirus sufferers getting placebos* (Haney 2001). The article also
notes: *Colds are the single most frequent reason why people go to the
doctor. Antibiotics are worthless against colds, though doctors often
prescribe them anyway.* If widely known, individuals might choose
to reduce the rate of infection rather than to take a drug which
might chop the final day in a week of misery!

In the spring of 2002, a new study was released on drinking
and colds among faculty and staff in five universities in Spain.
Takkouche reported that: *Total alcohol intake and beer and spirits
consumption were not related to the occurrence of common cold, whereas
consumption of wine was inversely associated with the risk of common
cold. When drinkers of >14 glasses of wine per week were compared
with teetotalers, the relative risk was 0.6 (95% confidence interval:
0.4, 0.8) after adjustment for age, sex, and faculty/staff status. The
association was stronger for red wine. . . Findings suggest that wine
intake, especially red wine, may have a protective effect against common
cold. Beer, spirits, and total alcohol intakes do not seem to affect the
incidence of common cold* (Takkouche 2002). The study had a
population of 4,272 spread among the staff of 5 universities.

It would be great to see similar studies in universities in Great
Britain, France, Germany, and the U.S. It would be interesting
to see if protection occurred with all types of beverages.

It will also be interesting to see whether this new finding from
the *American Journal of Epidemiology* will be accorded the scant
(scandalous) coverage of Cohen's findings.

Cold sufferers arise! You've nothing to lose but the sniffles.

Chapter 13

Diabetes Mellitus

Enhances dietary management

■ **Author's abstract:** Diabetes is a major disease. As with cancer and heart disease, advisories about disease management are read by millions of individuals, some of whom have had bad personal or family experiences with drinking. To avoid confusion, discussions of drinking benefits for diabetics should be strictly limited to responsible use with medical advice. With this caveat, the public should be informed that many studies find that moderate drinkers have less apparent risk of Type 2 diabetes.

■ ➡ Moderate alcohol use among male diabetics lowers future risk for poor cognition
➡ There is less diabetes incidence among moderate drinkers
➡ Diabetics can drink alcohol in moderation

In "Great news about avoiding diabetes," *UC Berkeley Wellness Letter* notes the alarming increase of Type 2 diabetes: *Industrialized nations, particularly the U.S., are in the midst of an obesity — and hence a diabetes – epidemic. More than 16 million people already have Type 2 diabetes* (Great News 2001).

Mixed messages from medicine

At present, the public receives either mixed or negative messages about drinking and diabetes. Here are quotes from three health newsletters which justify this assertion – the *Johns Hopkins Medical Letter*, the *Mayo Clinic Health Letter* and *Harvard Men's Health Watch* – all three excellent sources for health information aimed at a general readership.

These discouraging examples are followed by positive scientific citations about diabetes and drinking, one dating as early as 1954. The gulf between the typical newsletter treatment and the scientific literature demonstrates medical ambivalence. These are examples of the drinking communication bias. The first is from an eight page, diabetes supplement "Medical Essay," published by the *Mayo Clinic Health Letter:*

Diabetes is actually a group of diseases with one thing in common —a problem with insulin. The problem could be that your body doesn't make any insulin, it doesn't make enough insulin, or it doesn't use insulin properly.

Insulin is a hormone secreted by your pancreas. It's a key part of the way your body processes the food you eat because it helps maintain the proper level of a sugar (glucose) in your blood. Glucose is your body's fuel. Cells use it to produce energy to grow and function.

Diabetes, Supplement to Mayo Clinic Health Letter, February 1998.

This informative, well-written supplement from the famed Midwest medical clinic covers all essential aspects of the disease and lists actions to reduce its impact. A subhead titled "Alcohol," provides this brief warning: *Alcohol prevents the release of glucose from your liver and can increase the risk of your blood sugar falling too low. If you drink alcoholic beverages, do so only in moderation and eat food before you have a drink. Food helps moderate the effects of alcohol.* Quite good advice, but the authors fail to inform readers of any favorable relationship of drinking with the disease. The implication clearly is that none exists.

A similar article, "Do You Have Diabetes?" appeared in *Harvard Men's Health Watch*. The article outlines the characteristics of the two major types of diabetes. It defines the functions of blood sugar and discusses a new drug called Troglitazone. The article suggests that a diet: . . . *high in fiber, low in simple carbohydrates, regular exercise and weight loss can help prevent Type 2 diabetes from occurring in the first place* (Do You Have Diabetes 1997). Again, impeccable general advice with no mention of favorable drinking research despite the fact that: *As many as 8-10 million Americans have type 2 diabetes without knowing it.* A reasonable percentage of those ten million Americans with latent diabetes conditions undoubtedly are drinkers. Shouldn't they be informed about both the benefits of moderate intake and the dangers of excessive drinking for diabetics.

The third example is found in Johns Hopkins Medical School *Health After 50* newsletter. In "Five Keys to Diabetes Control" the author highlights the importance of mental attitude for newly diagnosed diabetics: *Not surprisingly, the gloom was most pronounced among those who needed medication, especially insulin . . . . . But there's no need to become discouraged just because you occasionally slack off or discover that your blood glucose levels are less than ideal* (Five Keys 1998). Moderate drinkers could be counseled that light drinking might help dispel the inevitable diabetic gloom.

Scientific support for diabetic drinking

None of these comprehensive articles mentions the long-standing therapeutic practice of using a daily drink (100-140 calories) in replacement of a carbohydrate. None mentions the findings of Launer with regard to mental acuity: *After adjustment for age, education, and smoking status, men with CVD/diabetes and low-to-moderate alcohol intake had significantly lower risk for poor cognitive function* (Launer 1996). However, another Johns Hopkins publication, the 1998 White Paper "Diabetes Mellitus," contains a more elaborate commentary about drinking for diabetics:

People who have diabetes can drink alcoholic beverages in moderation. In a recent study, 10 people

taking insulin for type 1 diabetes, and 16 people with
type 2 diabetes (most were treated with oral
hypoglycemics), were given 1.3 oz of vodka before
dinner, 13 oz of red wine during, and 1.3 oz of
cognac after the meal. Blood glucose tests showed
that none of the subjects experienced hypoglycemia
or a significant rise in blood glucose at any time.

Margolis, S., and Saudek, C., The Johns Hopkins White Papers, Diabetes Mellitus, Johns
Hopkins Medical Institutions, Baltimore, 1998

The 2002 version of the Johns Hopkins White Paper on diabetes adds: *The calories from alcohol should be exchanged for those*
that would normally be allotted for fat servings. Drinks that contain
smaller amounts of sugar, such as light beers and dry wines, are
preferable (Diabetes Mellitus 2002).

These references provide thoughtful, unbiased coverage of
responsible drinking science. However, many more civilians
come across the newsletter articles than see the White Papers
which target a clinical audience. Another article in the January,
2002 *Health After 50* titled "Cutting Your Diabetes Risk in Half"
reviews the latest research but, again, fails to report any of the
positive comments from the White Paper.

At a minimum, these examples demonstrate a pattern of
"mixed messages" concerning drinking and diabetes. Occasional positive statements can be found but more commonly
they are omitted. Of course, these publications utilize many
authors who bring to their commentaries a range of personal
experience, opinions and biases. However, any random perusal
of diabetes articles will reveal under-reporting of favorable
drinking science.

Alcohol therapy in diabetes has a long history. Lucia's 1954
book *Wine as Food and Medicine* devotes a chapter to "The Use of
Wine in Diabetes Mellitus." It begins with this statement:

Wine occupies a valuable position in the diet of the
diabetic under the present-day and pre-insulin
methods of treatment. Prior to the advent of insulin,
energy foods that could be utilized without burdening
the pancreas or exaggerating its deficiency were of
tremendous importance. Wine was then, as it is now,
preferred as a source of beverage alcohol because of

*its moderate concentration and because of the fact
that drinkers of wine are temperate.*

Lucia, S. Wine as Food and Medicine, The Blakiston Company, New York, 1954

However, Lucia did report a reticence even then among some physicians to utilize this positive data in clinical practice: *The limitation of the diet of the diabetic imposes a severe psychological restriction on the patient, but it also imposes a moral obligation on the physician . . . . Joslin states that in no disease would the use of alcohol appear to be more beneficial or justifiable, yet he does not prescribe it for personal reasons* (Lucia 1954). Then, as now, medical reticence reigns. In a 1981 symposium, Wine, Health and Society, Forsham's presentation was titled "Wine and Diabetes:"

*Wine in moderate amounts may be consumed safely
by most diabetics and offers moderate mood
elevation. The dangers —hypoglycemia, antabuse
reaction, polyneuritis and atherosclerosis —are
minimal with moderate consumption . . . . The
advantage results from moderate mood elevation in a
population many of whom may be depressed over
their disease.*

Forsham, P., Wine and Diabetes, presentation to Wine, Health and Society Symposium,
San Francisco, November 13, 1981

In Forsham's presentation, moderate drinking is depicted as a minimal risk and credited for mood elevation properties. Every article on diabetes could include these clean and clear distinctions. In another presentation to a meeting of the Society of Medical Friends of Wine on November 5, 1986, Forsham was specific as to dose: *The moderate intake of wine is perfectly acceptable for the diabetic provided that the intake is restricted to two glasses a day, and that the patient does not suffer from diabetic neuropathy . . . . When a diabetic is recovering from a severe illness or from surgery, the administration of wine or sherry before and during meals is most useful as an appetite stimulant apart from raising morale* (Forsham 1986). Mars also provided dosage information and found no relationship of moderate consumption with one diabetic fear, disease of the retina: *Alcohol consumption in moderate (<or = 1 oz/day) does not appear to affect the occurrence of diabetic retinopathy* (Mars 1994).

In 1994, Facchini tested the hypothesis that alcohol enhances insulin glucose adaptation: *Light-to-moderate alcohol consumption in healthy men and women is associated with enhanced insulin-mediated glucose uptake, lower plasma glucose and insulin concentrations in response to oral glucose, and a higher HDL cholesterol concentration. The changes in glucose and insulin metabolism may contribute to the lower risk of coronary heart disease* (Facchini 1994). Would not this discovery be of interest to the nearly eight million Americans with diabetes? Should it be included in diabetes articles?

The following year Rimm examined the association between smoking, alcohol consumption and the incidence of non-insulin dependent diabetes in middle age and older men: *Moderate alcohol consumption among healthy people may be associated with increased insulin sensitivity and a reduced risk of diabetes* (Rimm 1995). Rimm's study included all kinds of alcohol beverages. This finding was derived from an analysis of data collected in the Health Professional's Follow-Up Study. Subjects were 41,810 male doctors who were free of diabetes at the start of the study. It would be of interest for a general readership.

Another 1995 study involved 7,735 men aged forty to fifty-nine in Britain. Regarding this study, Shaper reported: *A nonlinear association between alcohol intake and diabetes was observed with the lowest risk among moderate drinkers (16-42 units/week) relative to a baseline group of occasional drinkers* (Shaper 1995). Male moderate drinkers in Britain had lower risk than nondrinkers. The following year, Bell reported that alcohol use by the diabetic has been controversial but concluded: *The mechanisms of the beneficial effects of alcohol include positive effects on insulin resistance, HDL cholesterol, platelet aggregation and fibrinolysis. Since the diabetic patient has an especially high risk of ischaemic heart disease because of these factors, the use of a moderate amount of alcohol should not be discouraged* (Bell 1996). Sage advice.

In the British Regional Heart Study including 7,734 men 40-59, Wannamethee discovered a nonlinear, inverse relationship between alcohol use and risk for Type II. He reported: *Serum insulin and HDL-cholesterol explained some (20%) of the risk reduction associated with moderate drinking (Wannamethee* 2002). In another study, Konrat reported: *Alcohol use correlates inversely with fasting insulin levels . . . Insulin may be one of the factors explaining the protective effect of moderate drinking on CHD risk* (Konrat 2002). Rounding out these recent studies, Davies reported: *Light-to-moderate drinking (1 or 2 drinks daily) is associated with a reduced risk of type 2 diabetes, reduced fasting insulin levels and/or improved insulin sensitivity . . . Consumption of 30 g/day of alcohol (two drinks daily) has beneficial effects on insulin and triacyl-glycerol levels and insulin sensitivity in non-diabetic postmenopausal women independent of BMI* (Davies 2002).

These are not lightweight, isolated anecdotal commentaries. They are taken from major studies involving thousands of subjects in numerous nations. Over and over, this book makes the point that this or any other line of study may shift or even reverse a particular line of findings in subsequent studies. A wide range of diverse studies have isolated favorable data on moderate drinking for diabetics. At the very minimum, this research deserves mention. Since diabetes tends to run in families, younger members of a family not yet afflicted by the disease could profit from this information.

Other positive research

In 1997 a study by Lazarus on drinking and insulin resistance revealed: *Subjects consuming moderate amounts of alcohol had the lowest fasting insulin and fasting insulin resistance index values . . . . These findings suggest the possibility that the coronary heart disease-protective effects of moderate alcohol use are at least partially mediated by insulin* (Lazarus 1997). A study by Mingardi on the impacts of drinking among diabetic men and women who had experienced peripheral vascular disease (blockages in leg arteries) found: *The prevalence of PVD was similar among men who drank regularly and among those who did not, whereas PVD was significantly lower in women with a moderate alcohol consumption* (Mingardi 1997). Valmadrid studied 983 late-onset diabetics over 68 years of age and notes: *These results suggest an overall beneficial effect of alcohol use in decreasing the risk of death from CHD (cardiovascular disease)* (Valmadrid 1999). Note how many of these studies cross-reference positive findings for heart, vascular problems and other disease pathologies.

Two recent studies, one with males taken over twelve years and another with females over sixteen years, confirm the greatest protection against Type 2 diabetes lies with moderate, frequent drinkers. Conigrave studied nearly 47,000 male health professionals and developed fascinating data that one/two days per week drinkers and three/four days drinkers had only marginally reduced risks. But: . . . *those drinking 5 or more days per week had the lowest risk, even when consuming less than 1 drink per day* (Conigrave 2001). The author continued: *Frequent low-to-moderate alcohol consumption appears to offer the greatest protection against Type 2 diabetes, regardless of the type of alcoholic beverage chosen or the total amount of alcohol consumed over a week.* Hu followed 85,000 female health care professionals for sixteen years and discovered that as little as a half-a-drink per day along with other healthy lifestyle factors: . . . *was associated with an incidence of Type 2 diabetes that was approximately 90% lower than that found among women without these factors* (Hu 2001). Hu classified "absence from alcohol" a risk on the same levels as smoking and poor diet. Similar findings continue to accumulate with little transfer of information to the affected public.

The healthy living, daily drinking segment of our society emerges as the healthiest segment in our society. The two studies above included over 130,000 men and women. Yet the November 2001 *UC Berkeley Wellness Letter* article "Great news about avoiding diabetes" that opens this chapter makes no mention of drinking impacts, positive or negative.

Another of the growing series of analyses of data involving U.S. physicians and other health professionals concerned 2419 participants who were first diagnosed with diabetes at age 30 or above. After adjustment for potential confounders, the authors concluded that: *Moderate drinking is associated with a lower risk for CHD in men with type 2 diabetes mellitus, for beer, wine and spirits alike* (Tanasescu 2001).

Continuing medical indifference to this growing body of healthy drinking science is a fact of life – an unfortunate fact for those who suffer this disease.

Social ambivalence

In August 2001, the National Institutes of Health released the results of a major study on Type 2 diabetes. The *Seattle Post Intelligencer,* reflecting on the University of Washington Medical

School's participation in the study, had this piece of editorial advice: *Eating less fat, exercising more, not smoking and reducing alcohol intake can go a long way toward curing the nation's health care ills* (Another disease affected by habits 2001). The popular media generally follows the conservative tack presented in medical journalism. In view of the studies cited here, the *Post Intelligencer* could have said "reducing excessive alcohol intake." That would presume that the reporter was sufficiently enlightened by the voluminous medical reporting system. Medical information is projected routinely through hundreds of news releases from government health agencies, private disease societies, medical schools and from an elaborate media program by the American Medical Association. There exists a large contingent of medical journalists and literally thousands of health web sites. The reality is that positive drinking data enjoys low priority in these systems.

As a consequence, the *Post Intelligencer* editorial does not urge readers *to reduce abusive drinking* or to drink *only moderately which may help to protect against Type 2 diabetes*, but simply to *reduce drinking*. This editorial exemplifies the communication problem. Americans harbor an irrational antipathy toward drinking because the media fails to broadcast the good news that the system doesn't deliver. Unless the media become better informed about healthy drinking science, they will continue innocently to compound the problem. Insufficient levels of communication have been shown for the thirteen diseases discussed to this point. And will be shown as well in those that follow.

However, recent medical newsletters promise a more balanced presentation. *HealthNews* in January 2002 reports on a study in the *American Journal of Epidemiology* by Kao which found: *However, more moderate levels of alcohol consumption do not increase risk of type 2 diabetes in either middle-aged men or women* (Kao 2001). An informative side-bar written by Holly Atkinson, M.D., the newsletter's editor, states: *But there's no need to stay away from alcohol completely. When consumed in moderation, alcohol appears to reduce the risk of heart disease, stroke and diabetes* (Atkinson in Follow Up 2002). Physicians need to be exposed to more of this kind of commentary. One hundred years of anti-drinking orthodoxy is difficult to overcome.

Restricting the ebb and flow of research data from physicians and caregivers and, in this case, from the millions of diabetics in the nation makes no *public health* sense. Pittman characterizes this cultural retrenchment as "social ambivalence:" *In cultures such as the United States and Ireland, marked by ambivalence toward alcohol usage, there is conflict between co-existing value structures toward the appropriate function of alcoholic beverages . . . Myerson has used the phrase "social ambivalence," in reference to American cultural attitudes toward drinking. It is his position that this ambivalence limits the development of stable attitudes toward drinking that are found in certain other cultures; moreover, it restricts the meaning of drinking to one of hedonism and insulates drinking practices from social controls. Thus, drinking becomes an extreme and uncontrolled form of behavior for many* (Pittman 1996).

The American Diabetes Association (ADA) web site provides timely advice for diabetics who choose to imbibe. The association clearly does not recommend drinking but, for those that do, it suggests choosing drinks on the dry side and the liberal use of spritzers or sparkling water to make those drinks last over a longer period. Unfortunately, this leading authority on diabetes mellitus remains silent about the benefits in prudent drinking.

Solitary drinking without the moderating impact of food and friends encourages solitary abuse, for diabetics and for other drinkers. Consuming moderately, with friends and family in convivial circumstances, contributes to a resistance to diabetes and other common illnesses. An alternative to the tongue-tied stalemate in American medicine would be the adaptation of European-style integration of drinking with foods and social interchange.

It's an alternative worthy of consideration.

Chapter 14

Diet and Nutrition

Abundant evidence of food values in drinks

Author's abstract: This chapter supports my core argument—that even if drinking benefits were to be attributed totally to other lifestyle habits or genetics, drinks still would remain, in the words of Brilliatt-Savarin, as "the king of potables," one of life's most exquisite and versatile foods. Here's why:

- Alcohol constitutes six percent of the entire U.S. diet
- Ancients who drank beer were better nourished
- Aqua vitae was considered the mistress of all medicines
- Drinks provide B-complex vitamins, riboflavin pantothenic acid, nicotinic acid and all thirteen minerals necessary for sustenance of human life
- Drinks provide a good substrate for energy production

Alcohol is the king of potables, and carries to the nth degree the excitation of our palates; its diverse preparations have opened up to us many new

sources of pleasure; it gives to certain medicaments
a strength they would not have without it.

Fisher, M., Translation of Brilliatt-Savarin's The Physiology of Taste, Harcourt Brace
Jovanovich, New York, 1978

This is, in the judgment of the author, the most important chapter in the book. It concerns food. As is American medicine, American nutrition is a highly accomplished field. Few nations enjoy the expertise and research of our nutritionists, skills which unfortunately are generally ignored by the majority of citizens. An ignorance which contributes to obesity, heart disease, diabetes and a range of consequent illnesses.

If there is a signal failure within American nutrition, it lies in the tendency to omit any substantive recognition of the nutritional contribution of drinks. Hundreds of books are published every year about nutrition and food preparation. Astonishingly few provide any serious treatment of the role of drinks as nutritious foods. If medical publications are ambivalent on the subject, nutrition books and magazines are downright tonguetied. For most nutritionists, drinking has little consequence or meaning for their discipline.

Alcohol ambivalence in nutritional circles exceeds that attributed to the medical profession, and for many of the same reasons. Healthy drinking science is rarely seen in food science curricula. It is true that most of the vitamins and minerals found in drinks exist at trace levels. But vitamins, minerals and antioxidants do exist in drinks and at sufficient levels to impact the health of millions of American drinkers. The scientific revelations in this book point to alcohol and other drink constituents as independent contributors to dietary health.

Drink calories alone constitute a major energy source for the daily or frequent drinker. Considered solely from an energy-viewpoint, ten to twenty percent of a moderate, daily drinker's calories are derived from drinks. We burn alcohol calories along with fat and carbohydrate calories when we walk, talk or think. Suter explains that: *Alcohol accounts for some 6% of total energy intake in adults in the U.S.A.* (Suter 1994). The contribution to human energy is substantial. It should be acknowledged. de Lorgeril reports that: . . . *an acid-rich Mediterranean diet seems to be more efficient than currently used diets in the secondary prevention of coronary events and death* (de Lorgeril 1994). Hendriks administered doses of beer, wine or spirits to healthy middle-aged men before and during a dinner meal and found: . . . *that moderate alcohol consumption with dinner affects plasma triglyceride concentration as well as HDL composition* (Hendriks 1998). Triglycerides and blood plasma may not be nutritional passwords but both are important elements on a doctor's chart.

Drinks in antiquity

Wine and beer were integral, staple foods in all ancient cuisines. McGovern tells of a pottery jar found in the northern Zagros mountains in Iran dating to 5,000 B.C. It establishes wine as an important dietary staple:

The new evidence belongs to the period when the first permanent human settlements, based on plant and animal domestication and minor crafts such as pottery-making, were being established. The new evidence has important implications for the origins of viticulture as well as for the development of our modern diet, medical practice and society in general.

McGovern, P., Earliest Evidence Dates Wine Back At Least 7000 Years, Wine Culture and Society Series, Wine Institute, Vol. 1, No. 1., San Francisco, June, 1996

Katz, an associate of McGovern at the University of Pennsylvania, has accomplished stellar work in defining the origins of wine and beer in the food chain:

In a broad historic sense, the domestication of the grape along with other fruits marked an important and interesting dividing line in human antiquity—as clear as the Neolithic revolution which led to the original domestication of cereal grains and animals. It also represents an important turning point in the further evolution of cuisine. With the incorporation of these new foods into the repertoire of foods available for regular consumption, new adaptations probably came into play relating to the nutritional balance and metabolism of the populations involved.

Katz, S., Wine and the Origins of Cuisine, A Symposium on Wine, Culture & Healthy Lifestyles, The Wine Institute, New York, May, 1987

Katz and Voight explain how "selective advantage" convinced early tribes to incorporate beer into their diets both as pleasurable beverages and as observable contributions to good health:

. . . individuals and groups who consumed beer were better nourished than those who consumed wheat and barley as gruel or who ignored these wild resources. Beer would have had sustaining powers well beyond any other food in their diet except animal proteins. In biological terms, beer drinkers would have had a "selective advantage" in the form of improved health for themselves and, eventually, for their offspring (Katz 1996).

Distilled spirits came along much later than wine and beer, both natural ferments. A sixteenth century physician, Hieronymous Braunschweig, was convinced that the first-released, steam vapors boiled from wine or beer would cure nearly anything that ailed a person:

Aqua vitae is commonly called the mistress of all medicines. It eases the disease of coming of cold. It comforts the heart. It heals all of old and new sores on the head. It causes good color in a person . . . . It also gives young courage in a person, and causes him to have a good memory and remembrance. It purifies the five wits of melancholy and of all uncleanness.

A sampling of nutritional findings

Positive scientific findings about drinks and dietary health exist in profusion. Here are examples:

✔ The conversion of ethanol into usable energy is significant: "The energy of alcohol was found to be about 75 percent as available for physiologic purposes as was the energy derived from a similar supplement of sucrose . . . . Having established the fact that most of the alcohol goes to acetate, and since acetate can be oxidized in all tissues of the body, it seems reasonable that a large part of the potential energy of alcohol can be tied up . . . which will then be available as needed for muscular work" (Moore 1951).

✔ In 1996, this energy transfer was confirmed: "The contribution of alcohol to energy intake in the U.S.A. is 4.4-5.6%. Among alcohol users, 10% of energy may be derived from alcohol, and among alcoholics as much as 50%" (Mattes 1996).

✔ Lucia wrote in 1971: "Recent analyses have shown that useful supplementary amounts of Vitamin-B complex are to be found in wines, including traces of B_1. Riboflavin is one . . . . Others are pyridoxine, pantothenic acid and nicotinic acid. All of these are essential to human nutrition . . . . Wine contains traces of nearly all of the thirteen major mineral elements necessary for survival" (Lucia 1971).

✔ Piendl analyzed beer: "Beer contains more than 30 minerals and trace elements which largely originate from malt. One litre of beer almost covers half the adult daily requirement (ADR) of magnesium, 40% ADR phosphorus, and 20% ADR potassium . . . The polyphenol content of beer at 154 mg/litre of beer is relatively high" (Piendl 1998).

✔ Buhler found that: "Xanthohumol, found exclusively in hops, is six times more effective than antioxidants found in citrus fruits and almost four times more effective than antioxidants found in soy products. . . Combined with vitamin E, xanthohumol has even greater antioxidant activity" (Buhler 2000).

✔ Dr. Amerine, Professor of Enology at the University of California, Davis, has referred to wine as: "A chemical symphony composed of ethyl alcohol, several other alcohols, sugar, other carbohydrates, polyphenals, aldehydes, ketones and pigments, with half a dozen vitamins, fifteen to twenty mincrals, more than twenty-two organic acids and other things that have not yet been identified" (McDonald 1986).

✔ McDonald identifies some wine constituents: "An analysis of wine a few years ago – 112 wineries involving 428 wines – revealed that the sodium value for all but eight of the wines was less than 40 milligrams per liter. The potassium value ranged from 500 to 1,300 milligrams per liter; this creates a very favorable potassium to sodium ratio. . . . In addition, while distilled spirits have virtually no sodium or potassium by themselves, certain mixes with which they are consumed can contribute significant amounts of either of these elements" (McDonald 1986).

✔ McDonald's comments in 1986 about the role of potassium were confirmed in 1998 in a study conducted at the Harvard University School of Public health: "Wine has contributed to the normal and the medically controlled diet at least since the eighth century, B.C., when the Greek physician-philosopher Hesiod accurately viewed wine both as a food and as a medicine. . . other ancient physicians already knew one may cure a malady by an artful and intelligent dietetic regimen, or induce it by an improper one. It can accurately be said that just as many medicines are foods, so are all foods medicines" (Acherio 1998).

✔ Drinking does not interfere with adaptation of other foods: "Many epidemiological studies indicate that alcohol-derived calories added to food intake of men and women in amounts of 0-25% of total energy do not appreciably alter the average daily intake of other macro nutrients (carbohydrate, fat, and protein)" (Leibel 1993).

✔ In a controlled study, Rumpler compared ethanol energy to other sources in men and women: "These data clearly show that on an energy basis, ethanol and carbohydrate are utilized in the diet with the same efficiency" (Rumpler 1999).

Research accepts the idea that foods are healthy in the sense that everything we eat supports human health. Drinks are presented in this book as foods, not as drugs or substitutes for medicines. These random reports portray alcohol, and the variety of vitamins, minerals and compounds in drinks, as foods which harmonize with and embellish all cuisines. In 1998, Forsander asked a rhetorical question which may startle many but which is the logical conclusion of the research:

> *Ethanol has such good properties as a substrate for energy production that we are faced with the problem of explaining, not why it is consumed, but why it is not consumed in still larger quantities by non-alcoholic humans or by animals.*

Forsander, O., Dietary Influences on Alcohol Intake: A Review, Journal of Studies on Alcohol, 59:26-31, 1998

A crack in the anti-drinking facade

Yet Forsander's logic would have rough sledding today at a typical medical or public health conclave. The fourth edition of *Dietary Guidelines for Americans* did a dramatic about-face by minimally recognizing alcohol's contributions to heart health, though the pamphlet remains dubious of any nutritional values. Kennedy comments about this grudging recognition of the research: *First, the tone is less negative and the discussion in the Dietary Guidelines Bulletin mentions that moderate alcohol intake may enhance enjoyment of meals. In addition, moderate alcohol consumption may offer some protection from coronary disease* (Kennedy 1996). Even so, the 1996 *Guidelines* marked a significant watershed in federal alcohol policy.

At the time, Whitten noted: *Despite its very tentative and almost apologetic tone, the publication of the updated Dietary Guidelines for Americans marks a momentous shift in our government's official posture*

*on the health effects of drinking. It may free conservative physicians and
scientists from the fear of public retaliation that so often inhibits their
comments regarding the health effects of wine drinking* (Whitten
1996). Unfortunately, the 2000 edition of *Guidelines* contains
little new information relating to health and nutrition despite
the flood of favorable epidemiology since the previous issue in
1995. The battle for balance is far from over at the federal level.

Another federal recognition of public health in drinking
originated in 1996 when the NIAAA announced a series of
program grants to study the health effects of moderate alcohol
consumption. The modest fifteen initial grants totaled
$2,740,577 for fiscal year 1996. Though the grants allocated to
benefits still represent a very small spit in a very large funding
bucket, the symbolic significance of these awards cannot be
overstated. Alcohol *health* research now has a place at the
NIAAA table. Topics included coronary heart disease,
osteoporosis, women's health issues, medications and overall
health, arenas which already hold promising research. When
this program was implemented, Wine Institute president De
Luca noted:

> *These NIAAA awards represent a truly historic step.
> Though modest in initial dollars, they are huge in the
> message given to our research and academic
> institutions that we are headed towards a broader
> national science policy on alcohol.*

De Luca, J., President's Report, The Wine Institute, San Francisco, October 16, 1996

Any historical perspective reveals that drinks have been recognized down through the ages as good, natural, nutritional
foods. The efforts of the government and alcohol-ambivalent
health interests to demonize wine, beer and spirits over the past
two centuries in America have been very effective. Trenchant
and long-lived fears of alcohol addiction yield ground very
slowly. What is needed now is sufficient recognition of the
research by health-interested citizens to create a political
counter force to the prevailing temperance ideology.

Recognition came with the introduction of the Mediterranean
Diet Pyramid in a 1993 conference sponsored jointly by the
Oldways Preservation & Exchange Trust and the Harvard Uni-

versity School of Public Health. The Oldways trust is a private foundation devoted to the promotion of foods which contribute to good health.

The dietary pyramids

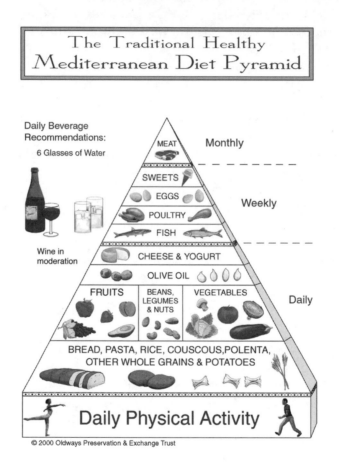

The Mediterranean Diet Pyramid, © 2001 is reprinted with permission of Oldways Preservation and Exchange Trust, Boston

This auspicious conference introduced a major renovation of the Department of Agriculture diet pyramid that appears widely in food and nutrition publications. It incorporates features of the Mediterranean cuisine.

This new approach broke from from the red meats and dairy products featured in the government's pyramid. The other notable innovation was the recommendation of wine with meals.

Walter Willett, chair of Harvard's Department of Nutrition, noted during the conference: *Wine is optional (on the pyramid), but can't be forgotten as an important part of the Mediterranean diet* (Willett 1993). Dimitrios Trichopoulos, chair of the Harvard School of Public Health added: *Wine drinking is a custom during meals in most Mediterranean countries. Drunk in moderation with meals it reduces the risk of coronary disease about as much as the regular taking of aspirin* (Trichopoulos 1993).

Despite its neoprohibitionary leanings, the World Health Organization endorsed the Mediterranean Diet Pyramid in 1994 including its reference to wine consumption. How could any agency located in Europe deny the obvious. The distinguishing attributes of the Mediterranean pyramid are a less saturated fat and wine consumption. Wine and other alcohol beverages are in common use throughout the Mediterranean basin. In 1993, Farchi reported on a twenty year study of mortality among rural Italians. This group reported: *The dietary pattern that corresponded to the lowest mortality rate (25% after 20 years) was: more than 2800 kcal/d . . . with more than 41% of the calories coming from unsaturated lipids, and between 13% and 19% from alcohol* (Farchi 1993). More than 50% from olive oil and wine. A very, very small percentage of Americans ingest nineteen percent of daily calories from drinks.

The Oldways Preservation and Exchange Trust and ENA, a private development corporation, have established a Center for Mediterranean Diet Studies on the idyllic island of Chios. Located in the Aegean archipelago off the eastern coast of Greece, the center is supported by private and government funding. More enticing revelations can be expected from this cooperative enterprise in years to come. K. Dun Gifford, president of the Oldways Preservation and Exchange Trust, has since staged dietary conferences around the U.S and in many other nations.

In the process, the Trust has produced a series of pyramids featuring many ethnic diets which now include a variety of alcohol beverages.

Ellison supports the European diet: *A Mediterranean diet, high in fruit, vegetables, and grains, also typically includes one or two glasses of wine per day. With the evidence currently available, they conclude that alcohol, when consumed responsibly in most populations, is an important component of the Mediterranean diet and a component of a healthy lifestyle* (Ellison 1995). Kushi writing in the same issue of the *American Journal of Clinical Nutrition*, concludes: *Although dietary factors alone may not fully explain the excellent health of Mediterranean populations, available evidence strongly suggests important contributions of high consumption of fruit, vegetables, and whole grains; moderate intake of alcohol; and low consumption of animal products, saturated and hydrogenated fats, and refined carbohydrates* (Kushi 1995).

Nearly fifty years ago in 1958, Lolli in *Alcohol in Italian Culture* defined normal drinking patterns for Italians that would qualify in America as raging alcohol abuse. Despite a traditionally heavy ingestion of wine through life, Italians have a relatively low incidence of alcoholism. The early exposure to wine in the diet takes away the thrill of a forbidden fruit so common in American youth: *No emphasis is placed by the Italians on any "psychological" or "escape providing" qualities of wine, and only a single person among the 1,453 subjects expressed fear that the use of wine might lead to alcoholism* (Lolli 1958).

Note that only one of the 1,453 Italians interviewed in this survey feared that their own level of drinking might lead to abuse or addiction. The European integration model for alcohol control establishes drinks as natural, universally available foods, not as fearful intoxicative drugs. While deluged with dietary advice, Americans are given very little understanding of the health benefits of drinks by the nutrition fraternity. Mediterranean cultures enjoy a range of wines, beers and spirits without guilt, health concerns or addiction fears.

Note also that as American per capita drinking has escalated gradually over the past half century, the rates of alcohol abuse have slowly declined, as has the incidence of abuse and drunken driving among youth. Increases in levels of drinking do not equate with a rising abuse patterns. In fact, a more enlightened, diet-oriented drinking pattern lessens abuse. Many Americans have assimilated the Mediterranean philosophy in recent decades by switching from a red meat-centered, snack food cuisine to meals featuring fruits, light meats, olive oil along with wine, brews and other drinks. Laudable progress.

Mediterranean diet sans wine?

The longest-lived Italians in the Farchi twenty-year study derived between thirteen and nineteen percent of their daily calories from alcohol drinks. It is preposterous to consider the impact of the Mediterranean diet – as many American medical publications and nutritionists still do – without crediting the mood elevating and nutritional values in drinks. Articles published in *Harvard Women's Health Watch, Time* and *The Cleveland Clinic Heart Advisor* about the Mediterranean diet irrationally ignore alcohol's substantial contributions to the diet.

In September, 1999, *Harvard Women's Health Watch* published "What Minerals Do We Need?" It contained a handy chart setting forth the "RDA's (Recommended Daily Allowances) for vitamins" along with the major food sources that supply them. The table ignores the more than twenty minerals and numerous vitamins provided in wines, spirits and beers. It ignores the Grant's Scottish Ale laboratory analysis which found in a single beer 62.5 percent of the RDA for folacin and 170 percent of the need for vitamin B_{12} (see Chapter 2). It's as if wine, beer or spirits have no consequence and no real impact on the American diet. Could the authors be oblivious of the nutritional constituents in these beverages? Highly unlikely.

The Harvard RDA chart follows the unwritten protocol by failing to inorporate the food dimensions of drinks. The November 11, 2001 *Parade Magazine* in a series on "The Year's Best Food News" stated: *Grapeseed extract fortifies food. Many studies have confirmed that grapeseed extract is rich in naturally occurring antioxidant compounds that may help protect the body from disease . . . Expect to see ActiVin brand grapeseed extract in energy bars, iced teas, fruit juices and cereals* (The Year's Best 2001). Ironically, *ActiVin* translated from French means *active wine*. Really good news would have been recognition of the contributions of wines, beers and spirits to a healthy diet. Not yet!

Another example is found in "Mediterranean Diet Reduces Risk of Second Heart Attack," in the *The Cleveland Clinic Heart Advisor*: . . . *the so-called Mediterranean diet – based on fish, fruits, vegetables, cereals, beans, grains and olive oil – can reduce the risk of a second heart attack or other cardiac "event" by as much as 50-70%* (Mediterranean Diet 1999). What? No mention of the wines and beers that grace every Mediterranean table? The article evaluates fat and caloric intake and concludes that the diet: . . . *not only lowered the the chances of cardiac death and heart attack but protected against heart-related complications such as unstable angina (severe, uncontrollable chest pain), stroke, heart failure, and blood clots in the lungs and elsewhere (pulmonary or peripheral emboli).* Each of these health benefits have been attributed in previous chapters to drinks. How is it medically or scientifically justifiable for the Mayo Clinic to omit any reference to drinks which are major components in the Mediterranean diet?

Similar neglect is found in "Eat Your Heart Out," from *Time's* July 19, 1999 issue which presents an elaborately illustrated discussion of "surprising new research" on heart health. In this very detailed coverage, a total of 46 words are allocated to drinking. Only red wine is identified as a qualified health contributor! The commentary notes: *We used to think alcohol is bad for you, no exceptions. What doctors say now: A substance called resveratrol, found in grape skins, may reduce bad levels of cholesterol* (Eat Your Heart Out 1999). No mention of other types of drinks, or of the multiple health impacts of alcohol and the numerous other constituents, aside from resveratrol, or the favorable association of drinks on many other illnesses – angina, blood clots, cancer tumors, kidney stones, diabetes, etc.

Engs has researched drinking proclivities of various cultures reaching into antiquity. In "Do Traditional Western European Drinking Practices Have Origins in Antiquity?" she contrasts traditions for heavy consumption in northern Europe from the moderate consuming patterns established in southern European cultures: *In contrast to these Mediterranean attitudes, patterns and norms, the northern attitude concerning alcohol consumption is one of ambivalence (extremes of heavy drinking vs. abstinence). . . They are often consumed on occasions other than meals. Heavy, often episodic drinking occurs on weekends or special occasions* (Engs 1995). America has inherited from northern European cultures patterns of solitary abuse.

Despite the widespread interest today in ethnic cuisines, most of which favor drinks, Temperance traditions still control the agenda in public health. Drinking is never recommended in public health literature. The Mediterranean approach makes better public health sense than the atherosclerotic entries featured in our government's pyramid shown below.

A perspective

The premise of this book is that drinks essentially are health giving *foods*. This is an appropriate place to reflect upon what's been revealed in the research as well as the negative attitudes revealed in medical publications. Two new books provide a backdrop for these ruminations: *Eat Drink and Be Healthy: The Harvard Medical School Guide to Healthy Eating*, Walter C. Willett, M.D., Simon & Schuster, New York, 2001 and *American Medical Association: Complete Guide to Men's Health*, Angela Perry, M.D., and Mark Schacht, M.D., eds., John Wiley & Sons, Inc., New York, 2001

Willett has made a sterling contribution toward the support of the Mediterranean diet. Willett's book also presents the praiseworthy new food pyramid shown on the following page. The text includes generous references to the benefits of responsible consumption. Surprisingly, the American Medical Association text also contains a few grudging admissions of drinking benefits: *Statistically moderate drinkers live longer than both nondrinkers and heavy drinkers, reflecting alcohol's ability to reduce some of the risks associated with heart attack, stroke and diabetes.* But, scattered through through the AMA text, the dangers of drinking dominate: *Alcohol is the most commonly used drug in the United States. Nearly 14 million Americans are dependent on it or have other problems associated with drinking. These problems cost the nation more than $100 billion annually in medical care and lost productivity.*

One must be cognizant of these dangers because alcohol abuse is a very serious problem in the U.S. For an analysis of the tendency to overstate the risk of abuse and other Temper-

ance myths, turn to Chapter 31. For comparison purposes, this
and the following page show Willett's and the federal food
pyramids.

Willett's Healthy Food Pyramid

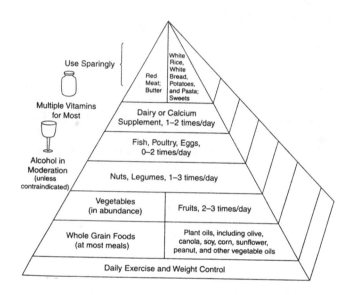

Reprinted with permission of Simon & Schuster, from Eat, Drink and Be Healthy, by
Walter C. Willett, Copyright 2001, Harvard University, President and Fellows of Harvard College

There is no question that Willett's Healthy Food Pyramid is
an innovating addition to the debate. It embraces the Mediterranean diet as compared to the government's pyramid shown
on the following page. But both Willett's book and the medical
association's text fail to elaborate drinks as staple foods with
multiple health benefits. In his commentary at the conference
which introduced the Mediterranean Diet Pyramid, Willett
noted: *Wine is optional (on the pyramid), but can't be forgotten as an
important part of the Mediterranean diet.*

The U.S. Government Food Pyramid

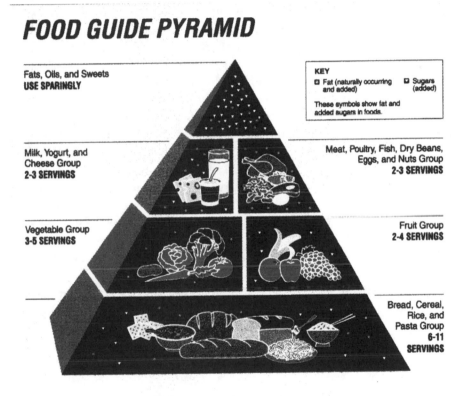

FOOD GUIDE PYRAMID

If Willett believes, as I am sure he does, that drinks are *important parts* of the Mediterranean diet, why not include them within the pyramid's food sections? Why not discuss drinks in the chemical dimensions accorded other foods? Willett establishes moderate drinking as a proper, optional component of his diet but nowhere does he discuss drinks as basic foods.

Wines and beers fall naturally into the fruit and grain groups. All drinks result from the natural fermentation of fruit and grains. Mezzano evaluated the complementary effects of the Mediterranean diet and spoke specifically to red wine intake: *Intervention and epidemiological studies have shown that some dietary factors and light-to-moderate drinking protect against cardiovascular disease. Foods of animal origin appear to correlate directly, and food of vegetable origin, fish and alcohol, inversely with CHD mortality* (Mezzano 2001). The author then says forthrightly: . . . *moderate use of red wine further improves the haemostatic profile of a Mediterranean diet. Such a diet and moderate use of red wine have complementary, mostly beneficial effects on haemostatic cardiovascular risk factors.* In this study, Mezzano discusses drinks as *foods* which are inversely related to heart disease mortality. The American nutrition profession needs to come to grips with its aberrant exclusion of an important food grouping in their deliberations.

Willett lost a stellar opportunity to identify the range of vitamins, minerals, antioxidants, and the interactions of alcohols, aldehydes, and congeners in drinks which temper so many disease pathologies. Lets hope he rectifies this omission in future work. Health and food writers and interested citizens who read Willett's book will miss valuable insights on drinks as healthy foods. The December 2001 issue of the *UC Berkeley Wellness Letter* provides thoughtful comparisons of the Willett and USDA pyramids in "Building a better pyramid," but it finishes with gratuitous remarks about drinking. This is the mischief caused by avoiding a recognition of drinks as foods:

> *The Willett pyramid recommends a daily multi-vitamin pill "for most people," as well as alcohol in moderation (unless contraindicated). These are good ideas; we also recommend a multi-vitamin/mineral for most people. It is true that alcohol in moderation helps protect the heart, but this does not mean that nondrinkers should necessarily start drinking for health reasons. Drinking may raise the risk of certain cancers —and does increase the risk of falls,*

*crashes, and other injuries. And some drinkers do
become alcoholics.*

Building a better pyramid, UC Berkeley Wellness Letter, Vol. 18, Issue 3, December 2001

Individuals become addicted to almost everything we eat and
to most of the "feel good" medicines we ingest to relieve our ills.
Everything from ice cream to aspirin is subject to abuse. Reasonable warnings are appropriate for all indulgence. Specious
warnings like the one above deflect from the reality that drinks,
ice cream and meat are all simply abuse-subject foods.

Ironically another article in the same *Wellness Letter*, "Consider
a drink a day," *recommends* drinks as one of five substances useful
for raising HDL cholesterol. Nutrition books recommend five
servings a day of fruits and vegetables for health reasons. Beer,
wine or a cocktail with meals should qualify as one of those five
servings. It is encouraging to see growing recognition of heart
health values in drinks in the medical newsletters but it is
discouraging to see their values diminished by obtuse warnings
of abuse and addiction.

The critical differences between Willett and USDA pyramids
lie in the region of fats and trans-fats. Willett writes: *But the
USDA Pyramid's recommendation to use fats "sparingly" ignores the
fact that the other kinds of fat – the monunsaturated and polyunsaturated fats found in olive oil and vegetable oils, nuts, whole grains, other
plant products and fish – are good for your heart* (Willett 2001).
Drinks contribute ten to twenty percent of daily calories for
millions of Americans. How can this large contributor to the diet
continue to be ignored? What kind of *science* is this?

The AMA and Willett books are hardly unique in ignoring
foods as drinks. *The Wellness Encyclopedia of Food and Nutrition*
assembled by the staff at the *Wellness Letter* at the University of
California, Berkeley is a 512 page compendium of nutritional
information which has no reference whatsoever to alcohol or
drinking in its index. To presume that drinks have no effects or
value in America's diet is a preposterous, but common assumption, in American nutritional science.

The science here has amply demonstrated that drinks provide
calories, B complex and other vitamins, minerals, folate, antioxidants in profusion, carbohydrates, polyphenols, aldehydes,

ketones, high potassium and low sodium concentrations, and so
on. Laboratory tests determine some drink constituents to be
more effective than popular vitamin supplements. Nutritional
authorities present them, in effect, as permissible, pleasant recreational drugs with no intrinsic dietary values.

Here is a convincing example of how this Berlin wall between
the science of healthy drinking and the public diverts attention
from really vital research. A study conducted in 1975 — at the
time that the federal government was initiating its neoprohibition campaign — was reported in the February 1975 *Bulletin of
the Society of Medical Friends of Wine* in "Wine in Nutrition Study."
Here are the first four paragraphs of the article:

> *The centuries-old belief that wine used with meals is
> an aid to nutrition has been confirmed by a research
> project at the University of California in Berkeley.*
>
> *In the first such study ever made, a liter of Zinfandel
> wine or a liter of an equivalent (11.5 percent)
> aqueous solution of ethanol were fed daily with a
> controlled isocaloric diet to six healthy young adult
> males while their feces, urine, and sweat were
> collected an analyzed.*
>
> *The results showed that all of the subjects had
> absorbed from their diet significantly more of such
> nutrients as calcium, phosphorus, magnesium, iron,
> and zinc after taking the wine than after taking the
> alcohol solution.*
>
> *Equally significant was that when dealcoholized wine
> and deionized water were substituted for the wine
> and for the alcohol solution during part of the 75-day
> study, the results were similar. Significantly greater
> absorption of nutrients was found after the
> dealcoholized wine than after the water.*

Wine in Nutrition Study, Bulletin of The Society of Medical Friends of Wine, Vol. 17, No.
1, February, 1975

These challenging results should have been replicated many
times over in the last quarter century employing a variety of
alcohol beverages and consumption conditions. The goal of
nutrition science is to stimulate more efficient absorption of
critical nutrients. Perhaps pursuit of this line of research would

have anticipated some of the mysteries surrounding the French paradox and other reported health benefits. The article recounts the pristine laboratory standards employed in this experiment: *. . . subjects of the experiments are isolated from visitors. They are given supervised exercise, their weight, temperature, pulse, respiration, and test performance are measured daily and blood samples are taken frequently.* The National Institutes of Health utilized this facility for other nutritional experiments. Contrast this remarkable (but inexplicably forgotten) experiment with the statement nearly 20 years later published in an NIAAA *Alcohol Alert* titled "Alcohol and Nutrition" edited by Gordis:

> Alcohol inhibits the breakdown of nutrients into usable molecules by decreasing secretion of digestive enzymes from the pancreas. Alcohol impairs nutrient absorption by damaging the cells lining the stomach and intestines and disabling transport of some nutrients into the blood. In addition, nutritional deficiencies themselves may lead to further absorption problems. . . . Even if nutrients are digested and absorbed, alcohol can prevent them from being fully utilized by altering their transport, storage, and excretion.

Alcohol and Nutrition, Alcohol Alert No. 22, PH 346, NIAAA, Washington, D.C., 1993

If Gordis had titled his paper "Alcohol *Abuse* and Nutrition" or "*Alcoholism* and Nutrition," his critical comments would have relevance. Every drug in the clinician's black bag can cause some collateral damage, even death, if consumed in excess. This 1975 study demonstrates that a moderate intake of wine can stimulate the absorption of more nutrients than the same diet without the wine. The NIAAA and American nutrition science has chosen to ignore this line of research.

A responsible drinking optimist has to applaud the recognition of drink benefits as even minimally reported in the Willett and AMA books. Such recognition presages a new era in nutrition science. But the continuing failure to treat drinks as foods and to discuss the range of relevant scientific findings for conditions other than heart disease and diabetes diverts important media coverage. The consequence of this neglect is seen in a review of Willett's book in the *Seattle Times* on Sunday, November 4, 2001. In a full page discussion of Willett's "Mediterranean style" diet, not one syllable appears on the "important part" that drinks play in the Mediterranean cuisine. In American nutrition, drinks have no relevance to healthful diet.

Amid these negative examples, it is encouraging to find in the January 2003 *UC Berkeley Wellness Letter* both red wines and red grapes as ideal sources for the flavonoid quercetin: *We do think you should get as much quercetin as you can – from foods. Apples, onions, raspberries, black and green tea, red wine, red grapes, citrus fruit, cherries, broccoli, and leafy greens are the way to go* (Quercetin: an apple a day 2003). We are closing in on open recognition of drinks as foods. Concerned physicians could open up the system to full disclosure.

While this book lauds the excellent work done by Oldways trust, Professor Willett and others in recognizing drinks as optional food items, we urge them and other nutritionists to initiate full treatment of drinks and their components in nutrition literature. That step will go a long way to shelving ambivalence and introducing the responsible drinking culture.

Of all the questions raised in this book, the failure of nutritionists and medical literature to credit the positive contributions of alcohol drinks is the most bothersome. Following a study of 100,000 women born between 1925 and 1950 who were covered by the French teachers insurance organization, Kesse concluded: *Part of the detrimental effects of alcohol on health may be attributable to poor dietary patterns of heavy drinkers. This points to a confounding role of eating pattern and nutrient intake in the relation between alcohol and health* (Kesse 2001). Heavy drinking and poor dietary choices create the health problems associated with drinking, not moderate intake. Moderate intake is health positive.

In many cultures drinks are highly valued, as seen in Brilliatt-Savarin's prescient assumption: *Alcohol is the king of potables, and carries to the nth degree the excitation of our palates.*

We can all drink (and eat) to that!

Chapter 15

Lumbar Disc Surgery

Improved recovery

■ **Author's abstract:** Dr. Lucia would probably have chalked up this entry to his "plus factor" —mood elevation. In this chapter, a German surgeon's findings add a new dimension to drinking — improvement in post-operation recovery. It would be interesting to explore this odd phenomenon following other surgical procedures.

Based upon a single study, this is the shortest of our thirty healthy drinking reports. However the author references twenty-seven other studies in reaching his conclusions. These other reports may be of interest to lumbar surgeons. Patients facing such surgery would appreciate reviewing this finding. Rasmussen reported in the *European Spine Journal* (Rasmussen 1998) about his investigation on whether smoking or the intake of different alcoholic beverages impacted the post-operation recovery period up to 2.5 years after first-time lumbar surgery.

A total of 148 former patients responded to the questionnaire. Of these, twenty-five percent were nondrinkers, thirty-one percent reported beer as their beverage, thirty-three percent preferred wine and ten percent consumed both beer and wine. This was a small but unique cohort. Each respondent had undergone lumbar disc herniation surgery performed by Rasmussen. Three factors were evaluated over the recovery period – pain, impairment, and self-assessment of recovery. The author reports:

> *Smoking could not be shown to be an independent risk factor for the outcome . . . . In conclusion, intake of wine was found to be strongly associated with a good prognosis after first-time lumbar disc surgery. Further research is needed to explain a biological or behavioural mechanism behind the suggested beneficial effect of wine on the results of back surgery.*

Rasmussen, C., Lumbar disc herniation: favourable outcome associated with intake of wine, European Spine Journal, Vol., 7, No. 1, pp24-28, 1998

The report continues: *Only two patients state spirits as their favourite beverage and were therefore excluded . . . Further analysis of the different type of alcohol consumption in relation to outcome showed that a favourable outcome was associated with either wine drinking alone or wine and beer.* The author conjectures that: *Wine may therefore, as a working hypothesis, contain such compounds which are able to reduce lumbar artery stenosis due to atherosclerosis . . .* If confirmed, this would provide yet another beneficial dimension to the chemical composition of wines and brews, quite likely involving their antioxidants. Rasmussen called for further research into this aspect. I have found none.

The author did not request the amounts consumed by respondents: *. . . because the reported alcohol consumption is known to vary with the type of alcohol . . .* but he undertook a regression analysis of the data in an attempt to rule out other lifestyle habits as possible confounders. His conclusions were that the wine or wine and beer in combination did the trick. Rasmussen continued: *Further research may find that lifestyle traits of wine consumers and the way wine is consumed may be responsible for the differences.*

Disc sufferers should ask their physicians to review this single study's findings and its twenty-seven references.

It couldn't hurt.

Chapter 16

Gallstones

Significantly reduced risk

■ **Author's abstract**: This chapter on gallstones and the one on kidney stones that follows share a trait with the chapter on diabetes. That common factor is woeful medical communication about the reduced risk among some drinkers. Moderate drinkers who are diabetic and who suffer gallstones or kidney stones would have to do a little digging to correlate research identifying some value in drinks for all of three conditions. Here are benefits reported in recent gallstone research:

■ ↦ Moderate drinking protects against both gallstones and vascular disease
↦ Female drinkers had a thirty percent lower risk of gallstones
↦ Drinkers were associated with lower incidence of gall bladder disease
↦ Frequent, not infrequent, drinking provides protection

There exists a small but impressive body of science which finds a reduced gallstone risk among moderate drinkers. Thornton in 1983 studied twelve healthy volunteers with moderate alcohol intake. During the study period, the subjects consumed thirty-nine grams of alcohol daily (the equivalent of three drinks) for six weeks and then abstained for another six weeks. Of particular interest to heart patients, Thornton observed that: *HDL cholesterol rose significantly when alcohol was being consumed and fell during abstention* (Thornton 1983). This finding supports the idea that daily moderate drinking raises high density cholesterol levels. Of particular interest to gallstone sufferers, the report continued: *These data provide further evidence of a biochemical link between cardiovascular disease and . . . gallstones and suggest that moderate alcohol intake has some protective effect against both diseases* (Thornton 1983). Daily moderate drinking was found protective against both diseases.

This finding buttresses the argument for routine cross-referencing of alcohol research findings among patients with multiple health problems. Physicians treating the above diseases separately should be aware of the patient's drinking patterns and of the possible beneficial effects or problems in light to moderate drinking. The right kind of drinking may favor several health conditions.

In 1989, Maclure looked at data gathered in the Nurses' Health Study involving over 88,000 nurses. The review included consideration of many dietary factors, obesity and alcohol consumption. It was found that obesity increased the incidence of symptomatic gallstones. The authors reported: *. . . consumption of moderate amounts of alcohol significantly lowers the risk of symptomatic gallstone disease . . . . In particular, women who consume more than five grams of alcohol a day (the equivalent of a third of a glass of wine) had about a 30% lower likelihood of developing symptomatic gallstones . . . consumption of beer lowered the risk by 20%* (Maclure 1989). The Thornton and Maclure studies were released in the 1980s. They demonstrated that light daily drinking can lower gallstone risk. This information should have wide visibility in clinical practice.

Of course, this does not infer that alcohol is the only recommended therapeutic application. It's but one option among many. But patients ought to be given options, including this therapy. Leitzmann reviewed responses to the Physicians Health Professionals Follow-Up Study which included 46,008 males in the medical fields and found: *Men who drank 2 to 3 cups of regular coffee per day had a 40 percent lower risk of developing gallstones* (Leitzmann 1999). Keep in mind that both alcohol and coffee are popular, inexpensive foods, not medical drugs. None of the references in this book are meant to disparage use of or to take the place of conventional drugs. Rather, the data argue that the many positive impacts of drinks, coffee and other foods should be considered "plus" elements, as adjuvants to medicines.

Drinking and gallstone findings

A 1994 medical survey of 58,462 Italian adults was reported in *Alcohol Issues Insights*. The article presented the following remarkable regression of gallstone risk with increasing alcohol consumption among this large study population:

17% lower at 2 drinks per day or less;
33% lower at 2-4 drinks per day, and;
42% lower at 4 or more drinks per day.

Moderate Drinking Associated with Lower Risk for Gallstone Disease, Alcohol Issues Insights, Vol. 11, No. 1, September, 1994

In wine drinking cultures such as Italy, four glasses daily could be routine consumption. That level would constitute rampant abuse in America's Bible Belt. Temperance adherents are unlikely to embrace even a modest level of daily drinking, despite these studies. But individuals with no inhibitions about drinking should not be deprived of this therapeutic choice because of constraints imposed by the dry minority. American medicine is faced with a thorny decision. Should positive drinking findings be incorporated into clinical practice. This would imply a rejection of the government's programs to reduce per capita consumption. Alcohol cannot remain the "dirtiest drug we have" (Noble 1986) and also perform healthy therapy. Many thousands of individuals who experience the pain of gallstones would concur — if they were informed.

A 1995 study released by La Vecchia discovered: . . . *a 20% risk reduction in gallstone disease among moderate alcohol beverage consumers, with wine being the preferred beverage* (La Vecchia 1995). Another 1998 study by Simon looked at the relation of ascorbic acid supplement for gallbladder disease. The author reported: *After adjustments for potential confounding variables, use of ascorbic*

188 The Science of Healthy Drinking

acid supplements among drinkers was associated with a decreased prevalence of gallbladder disease (Simon 1998). Of course, wines are highly acidic.

A 1998 paper by Attili reported: *Factors protecting against GS [gallstone] comprise: low carbohydrate (males and females) and protein (males) intakes, high fibre (females) and moderate alcohol intake (males) consumption, and a shorter overnight fasting period for both sexes* (Attili 1998). Sahi looked at predictors including body mass, smoking and other characteristics in a survey of 21,582 male alumni of Harvard University and reported: *Alcohol use appears to be inversely related to risk. Inconsistencies in previous findings may be due in part to small study samples and confounding by obesity* (Sahi 1998). Leitzmann found: . . .*frequent intake (5-7 days/week) of any given amount of alcohol was associated with a decreased risk, as compared with nondrinkers* (Leitzmann 1999). Caroli-Bosc studied individuals living in a small French village and determined: *Alcohol use at a level of 20-40 g/day was found to be protective* (Caroli-Bosc 1998). Okamoto found in a study of over 9000 Japanese men and women aged 30-69 that: *Alcohol use appears to correlated inversely with the prevalence of gallstones* (Okamoto 2002). There's a pattern in this research. A positive correlation that is neglected in medical communication. Kono looked at records of 14,500 Japanese military men and concluded: *Alcohol use seems to confer protection against the development of gallstones* (Kono 2002).

Federal efforts to lower per capita drinking contravene the benefits that are associated with moderate, regular drinking. To break this institutionalized reticence, clinical physicians will have to demand better reporting of all developing alcohol research from the publications that cross their desks.

A recent *UC Berkeley Wellness Letter* illustrates the poor communication status. The article reports on the positive impact of coffee on gallstone formation. The writer should have reported parallel findings for drinks. Open, unbiased communication of all pertinent health research should be the standard.

Americans are capable of making informed health decisions, if given all the options. A stimulating thought.

Chapter 17

Gastro-Intestinal Problems

Better than Pepto Bismol

■ **Author's abstract:** Does there exist a stomach untouched by gastric upset? Research demonstrates that moderate drinking can help calm the stomach in the same manner as Pepto Bismol. In addition, the acidity and high alcohol content of some drinks combine to ward off salmonella and shigella in contaminated foods. Those who suffer persistent stomach distress should not look to drinks as cures, but, once again, moderate intake can contribute to relief. Here's how:

■ ➥ Drinks promote the flow of saliva for good digestion
  ➥ Wine resembles gastric juices more than any other beverage
  ➥ Drinks induce better absorption of nutrients
  ➥ Some drinks tested better than Pepto Bismol

Time/Life's *The Medical Advisor* defines gastritis:
Gastritis is a general medical term for inflammation of the stomach lining. . . . Gastroenteritis is a general

*term that applies to many types of irritation and
infection of the digestive tract (The Medical Advisor
1996).*

To relieve stomach upset, *The Medical Advisor* recommends
preparations containing bismuth subsalicylate (Pepto Bismol
being the most famous brand). One study below finds drinks can
provide more powerful relief than bismuth! It is important to
understand that excessive drinking can seriously compromise
gastric functions. Bode identifies a range of problems caused by
excessive alcohol use: *Alcohol may interfere with the structure as
well as the function of the GI-tract segments* (Bode 1997). Heavy
drinking can lead to serious gastric dysfunctions, ulceration of
the stomach and the duodenum, impairment of the pancreas,
and damage to the liver. Moderation is the maxim.

Mendelson recognizes these problems but distinguishes between use and abuse: *The amount of alcohol usually consumed by
social drinkers can easily be broken down by the liver without any
permanent ill effects. In this cluster of organic illnesses or cellular
conditions which are alcohol-related, we are once again faced with
distinguishing use from abuse in order to adequately assess the role of
drinking in health* (Mendelson 1985). Dose does matter very
much. Whitten ascribes holistic values to wine that is taken with
food, a favorable state of mind and body undoubtedly experienced by beer and spirit aficionados as well:

> *The real effect of wine on our digestive tract occurs
> in the process of digestion itself. This begins even
> before we start to drink. The smell, sight, or even the
> very thought of any food or drink stimulates the flow
> of saliva and prepares the stomach and intestines for
> action. When wine actually enters the mouth, the flow
> of saliva increases at once, reaching its peak about
> ten minutes after drinking, and the increased
> salivation continues for at least an hour with or
> without additional food. This is an important part of
> the digestive process because saliva contains the
> enzyme salivary amylase, which begins the
> breakdown of starches and complex sugars and
> lubricates the esophagus for swallowing. Another*

*enzyme secreted in the mouth in response to the acid
stimulus of wine begins the breakdown of fatty acids.*

Whitten, D., and Lipp, M., To Your Health! Two Physicians Explore the Health Benefits of
Wine, HarperCollins West, New York, 1994

The author ascribes to wine an "initiator role" which triggers
emotions and intellect to the degree that the meal is not only
more enjoyable but the body is empowered to adapt more
vitamins and minerals as a consequence. Wow!

The very pits

We seldom think of our stomachs as acidic chambers, roiling,
churning cauldrons of toxic fluids with the power to leach from
raw foods the nutrients and minerals necessary for normal cell
growth. According to "Stirring Up Helpful Bacteria," *our tum-
mies are: Home to 10 times as many bacterial cells as human cells.
Indeed, about 100 trillion bacterial cells from 550 different species,
reside in the human gut* (Stirring Up Helpful Bacteria 2002). The
article continues to note that while some of these bacteria can
cause disease, most are beneficial in defending the body from
disease.

Lucia describes the harmonious contributions of wine in this
acrimonious atmosphere: *Wine, oddly enough, resembles the gastric
juice more closely than does any other natural beverage. In small
quantities, it increases salivation, gently stimulates gastric acidity and
digestion, and aids in normal evacuation* (Lucia 1971). Bellia reports
that: *Apparently beer is rich in silicon in the form of silicic acid which
is extracted from malted barley in the brewing process. It is readily
absorbed by the body, thereby preventing absorption of aluminum and
possibly aiding its removal via the kidneys* (Bellia 1994). The authors
also noted that an aluminum imbalance is often linked with
Alzheimer's disease, one more reason to favor moderate consumption.

Anecdotal examples of protection

Desenclos reports in *Epidemiology* about an incident in which
people became ill from eating oysters contaminated with
shigella or salmonella. He found that the individuals who were
drinking at the time avoided the toxic reaction: *After controlling*

THE PHYSIOLOGY OF ALCOHOL

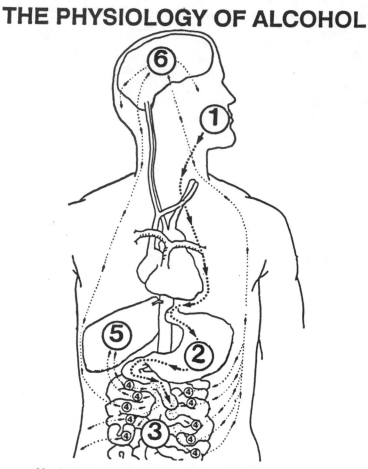

Alcohol passes from the mouth to the stomach (2) where small amounts are absorbed, depending upon the amount of food in the gut. More than 90 percent of the alcohol is passed by the small intestines (3) directly into the bloodstream (4). This occurs without digestion or any other chemical change of the alcohol. Oxidation or reduction of the alcohol into its constituents of water, carbon dioxide and energy occurs in the liver (5). Since this organ can oxidize slightly over one half ounce of absolute alcohol hourly, the remaining portions of alcohol continue to circulate in the bloodstream. The primary impact of the alcohol in the bloodstream occurs in the brain (6) and on the central nervous system.

for potential confounders, a protective effect for beverages that have an alcohol concentration of >10% was found, but no protective effect was found for beverages with an alcohol concentration of <10% (Desenclos 1994). This report reflects a common folk-belief that certain foods protect against an upset stomach. In a similar incident Perdue notes: *The outbreak of diarrhea, nausea and high fever affected more than one third of the 1,700 passengers aboard the cruise ship Viking Serenade and may have contributed to the death of one man already seriously ill with cancer and heart disease . . . medical experts and research indicate that alcohol and wine consumption may have prevented many passengers from getting ill* (Perdue 1994). Perdue quotes an official of the Centers for Disease Control as saying that the CDC is not interested in alcohol consumption and would not include it in the investigation: *Our agenda is primary prevention. If alcohol is protective, I don't know the answer to that* (Perdue 1994). This incident reflects the prevailing indifference in public health circles to another contribution of drinks to health. The CDC "agenda" is to seek a reduction of drinking by 2010, as stated in the *Healthy People 2010* goal book.

A laboratory study

More credible evidence of wine relief for gastric problems is found in a classic *in vitro* study by Weisse published in 1995.

The objective was: *To test whether red and white wines are as potent as bismuth salicylate against bacteria responsible for traveler's diarrhea to try to explain wine's legendary reputation as a digestive aid* (Weisse 1995). Weisse sampled red and white wine, diluted absolute ethanol and tequila against bismuth salicylate in two different solutions. The study references other conclusions including: *. . . red and white wine, straight and diluted, proved equally superior to all other solutions* (Weisse 1995).

Weisse tested the wines and tequila against salmonella, shigella and E-coli and concluded: *Red and white wine proved superior to all the other solutions against the three bacteria tested. Both samples of wine decreased the bacteria count . . . . Bismuth salicylate was substantially superior to the tequila solutions except against Sonnnei, in which it was only marginally superior. Diluted alcohol showed no significant reduction in the colony counts when compared with sterilized water. . . One explanation for wine's reputation as a digestive aid is that it may, like bismuth salicylate, prevent diarrhea and its efficacy is a least partly due to its antibacterial properties* (Weisse 1995).

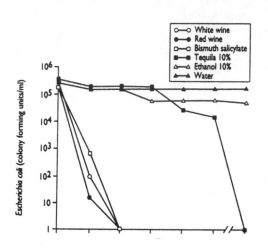

Reprinted with permission of the BMJ Medical Group from Weisse et al., Wine as a digestive aid: comparative antimicrobial effects of bismuth, British Medical Journal, 311: 1457-1460, 1995

The Weisse experiments demonstrate how white and red wines are equal to and are quicker in effecting relief than bismuth salicylate. Science proves the worth of some folk remedies, as Lucia predicted a half century ago.

Absorption and other attributes

McDonald reports: . . . *the ability of alcohol, especially as wine, to stimulate the appetite and accelerate digestion of food. There have been implications in the literature that, with improved appetite and digestion, there is also a beneficial effect on the absorption of nutrients* (McDonald 1976). This study supports the evidence of increased absorption found in the 1975 California study reported in the previous chapter. Protection against gastro-intestinal upset plus increased absorption of nutrients! McDonald's findings seem to validate the results of the 1975 experiment reported in Chapter 14. Nutrient absorption — a vital contribution!

Recall that in the cardiovascular chapters some wines were found to contain chemicals found in aspirin. The Weisse study was conducted in a laboratory. Impacts in humans could vary substantially from this controlled laboratory experiment. But the Weisse study provides a rationale for why drinks have garnered such esteem in folk medicine through the centuries. They work! Another important physiological aspect was reported by Probert in a study of whole gut transit time. He reported: *Alcohol use quickened transit in both sexes* (Probert 1995). So drinks can calm the stomach and as well as promote healthy and more comfortable clearing of the stomach.

The report on a recent Spanish study on an outbreak of acute salmonella gastric infection noted: *Very few studies have examined the effects of alcoholic beverages in case of a food-borne outbreak . . . These findings suggest that the use of alcohol during or immediately after consumption of contaminated food may be a protective factor for acute salmonella gastrointestinal infection in a dose-dependent fashion* (Bellido-Blasco 2002). The study covered 102 of 120 individuals who attended the event held in May 2000. The report noted: *The protective effect of alcohol was strongest for subjects who had drunk more than 40 grams of alcohol, with attack rates being 95% for those who had not drunk alcohol, 78% for those who had drunk less than 40 grams and 54% for those who had drunk more than 40 grams.*

Quite likely, the combination of the alcohol and wine's low pH medium are important to wine's efficacy in resisting gastro-intestinal bacteria. Some researchers conjecture that wine's polyphenols (antioxidants) may also play a role. Whatever the reasons, to the degree that wine and other drinks ease "traveler's stomach," the temperate drinker is truly blessed.

To this point, research citations have evidenced how drinks diminish the growth or incidence for some cancers, how they help to reduce cardiovascular disease, help to retain cognition, to delay the onset of Alzheimer's, to confound the cold virus, to increase a sense of well-being, to stimulate adaptation of vitamins and minerals, to relieve stomach distress, and to mitigate gallstones formation. And there are another thirteen chapters to go.

Something's missing twixt the glass and the lip — the missing element is public comprehension of the complex health contributions of responsible drinking. These benefits need to be balanced against the costs and the damage inflicted on society by alcohol abusers. A real collision of interests lies ahead as our nation becomes more informed of these many studies. More books favorable to responsible drinking are being published and more prominent physicians are speaking out (see Recommended Reading and Epilogue).

As the public begins to assimilate the fact that healthy drinking data is being withheld currently and often downplayed, tensions are bound to rise. An informed public will pressure medicine and government to review their entrenched aversions to drinking. See also Chapter 27 on ulcers for other gastro-intestinal findings.

Next we evaluate gender distinctions

Chapter 18

Gender Differences

Inequality between genders

◼ Author's abstract. In this chapter, I run the risk of losing half of my readership. Yet I must report the unfortunate reality that women are physiologically incapable of drinking as much as men. Early on in their drinking careers, most women recognize this fact and temper their intake. That's what this book is about —temperate drinking. Now, if we could only temper American male machismo . . . Here are some key differences found in the research.

◼ ◈ Less scientific data has been developed on female drinking
   ◈ The average female body is comprised of less water than the average male so it can support less water-soluble alcohol
   ◈ Consequently, women generate higher blood-alcohol levels
   ◈ Ironically, female drinking is on the rise; males consume less
   ◈ Women who drink moderately have fewer gallstones and coronary heart disease than abstaining women

The feminine factor

Through history, women have demonstrated more moderate drinking habits. This temperance benefits society in many ways. In a session of the Association of Gynecology and Obstetrics in March 1998, Doty explained that for many years the research community had failed to generate separate female research data: *It has been about 30 years since the medical profession began to recognize that women and men respond differently and show different symptoms to various diseases. But it's just in the past couple of years that people have said "women's health." It just didn't exist. We are at the ground-breaking in this* (Doty 1998). And for similar ground-breaking for female "healthy drinking."

It is necessary to review all drinking research findings from a female perspective. It is essential that mothers and fathers, husbands and wives, boyfriends and girlfriends accommodate a more conservative style of female drinking. Unfortunately, too often macho attitudes prevail in the research (and in the tavern), as reported in the *New York Times* in April 2000: *Medical researchers who receive federal money often flout a 1993 federal law that requires them to analyze effects of new drugs and treatments on women, three new studies have found* (Pear 2000). Here are some reports that emphasize the differences.

One important but still controversial gender distinction has to do with female biochemistry. Women can drink less and are at greater risk of serious organic damage from excessive drinking. Frezza explains the reason for higher blood-alcohol concentrations and why liver disease risk is greater for women:

After consuming comparable amounts of ethanol, women have higher blood ethanol concentrations than men, even with allowance for differences in size, and are more susceptible to alcoholic liver disease. Recently we documented significant "first pass metabolism" of ethanol due to its oxidation by gastric tissue . . . . We conclude that the increased bio-availability of ethanol resulting from decreased gastric oxidation of ethanol may contribute to the enhanced vulnerability of women to acute and chronic complications of alcoholism.

Frezza, M., Padova, C., Pozzato, G., Terpin, M., Baraona, E., and Leiber, C., The Role of Decreased Gastric Alcohol Dehydrogenase Activity and First Pass Metabolism, New England Journal of Medicine, 322:95-99, 1990

In "Alcohol and Special Populations: Biological Vulnerability," ICAP Report 10, the authors note: *By virtue of their physiology, women are more susceptible than men to the effects of alcohol. A smaller blood volume and higher proportion of body fat mean that the effects of alcohol are felt at lower doses in women than they are in men . Women and men also differ from each other in the way they metabolize alcohol. The activity of alcohol dehydrogenaze (ADH), the other key enzyme involved in the breakdown of ethanol, is roughly 70-80% greater in men than it is in women* (Alcohol and Special Populations 2001). The paper cites both Frezza and Leiber for its conclusions.

More research is needed in this field but Gilson adds this **practical advice:** *The underlying point is that, pound for pound, women do reach higher peak blood alcohol levels than men on equal quantities of alcohol* (Gilson 1993). If nothing else is retained from this consideration of gender differences, it should be understood that, for women, less is truly more. Beyond that first principle, here are some specific gender differences.

Some gender differences in the literature

✔ There are a few distinctions in moderate intake: "Alcohol in moderation appears not to be generally toxic. Acetaldehyde, the first breakdown product of alcohol, may be generated at higher levels in women" (Finkel 1998).

✔ Custom plays a tempering role: "Historically, women's and men's drinking patterns have always differed. Women consume at lower rates, develop fewer problems . . . and abstain from alcohol in greater numbers" (Knapik-Smith 1997). Unfortunately, the trend today shows that men are drinking less and women more. Hopefully, this trend will be reversed as women become more familiar with the science.

✔ In truly abusive drinking, there are few gender differences: "There is little evidence that the natural history of alcohol dependence in women is substantially different than in men" (Schuckit 1998).

✔ Some findings, of course, are unisex: "Total alcohol consumption was inversely related to coronary heart disease risk for each sex, with wine being the most protective for women and beer being the most protective for men" (Klatsky 1997).

✔ But the high consumption levels are more pronounced with women. "Women consuming 1-14 units/week had a reduction in coronary heart disease, but there was an increased prevalence of hypertension among those consuming >14 units/week" (Nanchahal 2000).

✔ Some studies confirm an unfortunate trend in female consumption: "Over the period, men increased their consumption by 8% while women upped their drinking by 37%. The two groups are converging toward a weekly consumption frequency" (Saelan 1992).

✔ Similarly from the Netherlands: "The proportion of heavy drinkers (>21 drinks weekly) among men had markedly decreased . . . but the proportion of heavily drinking women (>14 drinks weekly) had not. Among women the number of heavy drinkers over 40 even increased so that the sexes did not differ" (Lammers 1995).

✔ A warning from Virginia Mason Hospital in Seattle: "Women became intoxicated more quickly than men and face greater risk of eventual health damage. Liver and brain damage caused by alcohol progresses faster in women. The menstrual cycle intensifies the effects of alcohol just before a woman's period begins" (Regarding Women 1990).

✔ However, there appears no drinking challenge to the female cycle: "Alcohol use apparently is not a serious risk factor for menstrual cycle disorders in American women" (Kritz-Silverstein 1999).

✔ Even estrogen is affected: "Alcohol stimulated the production of estradiol, the same form of estrogen doctors prescribe to post-menopausal women to control bone loss and prevent heart disease" (Gavalier 1992).

✔ The need for cross-disease studies is noted: "Women who drink alcohol in moderation (2 to 6 drinks/week) have lower gallstones, coronary heart disease and total mortality compared to women of the same age who do not drink alcohol" (Colditz 1985).

✔ Heavy female drinking in mid-life appears to be related to dropping out of high school: "Going on to college is associated with lower levels of heavy drinking when individuals reach their late twenties and thirties" (Muthen 2000).

✔ Baron reviewed findings from twenty-four hospitals in Sweden over a two year period of women who sustained hip fracture after minor trauma and reported: "Alcohol use has a modest inverse association with risk for hip fracture, especially among taller women" (Baron 2001).

As contradictory as some of these findings now seem, they will be resolved as the research process continues. Female drinking studies undoubtedly will produce more conflicting findings. Recht provides a deserved *mea culpa* for male researchers' failure to gather and to distinguish female data: *Throughout the ages, women have often been the target of choice for groups that would impose harsh standards of morality on society. . . This is true now when a woman tends to be more concerned about her body and physical appearance than a man, and thus will listen more closely to information pertaining to her health, be it true or false* (Recht 1997).

A southern Sweden project illustrates the new trend for gender-sensitive studies. Bengtsson gathered information from a population of 92,962 females over 15 years and reported that drinking is a potentially protective factor in avoiding systemic lupus erthymatosus: *Smoking may be a risk factor while alcohol use appears to be associated with a lowered risk* (Bengtsson 2002).

The tendency for hyperbole in stating female drinking risks is seen in an editorial from the November 2000 *Harvard Women's Health Watch* which acknowledges: . . . *lower risk for — and mortality from heart disease . . . a reduced risk for Alzheimer's disease. But even moderate drinking can place you at increased risk for conditions such as breast cancer, hip fracture, and possibly colon cancer, and it can interfere with your reproductive ability* (Women and Moderate Drinking 2000). The article raises the specter of multiple risks in moderate drinking while ignoring positive research on kidney stones, cognition, diabetes, osteoporosis and so on. If the article had originated from Mothers Against Drunk Driving or some other dry advocacy, it would come as no surprise. It is unconscionable overstatement in a Harvard University Medical School publication. Since Roman times, medicine has imposed more severe limits on female drinking. *C'est la vie.*

A more balanced alternative is suggested by Engs: . . . *moderate drinking, in particular of wine, is associated with longevity and better health among women and men* (Engs 1996). If we are to move from antipathy and ambivalence to a family-oriented, European-style drinking culture, women need to learn a whole lot more about healthy drinking science. Indeed, if women fail to accept this educational challenge, our drinking future will quite likely mirror its desultory past. And more gender problems.

Anytime gender is the issue, I say *vive la difference*!

Chapter 19

Acute Hospitalization

Fewer acute visits for moderate drinkers

■ **Author's abstract:** Hospitalization is another instance where causal factors can be numerous and complex in nature. Yet it is striking that moderate drinkers have less acute care hospital visits. For whatever reasons, moderates don't show up in emergency rooms as frequently as abstainers. At a minimum, this supports the efficacy of a stable lifestyle that includes moderate drinking.

■ ➡ Both male and female drinkers have fewer acute hospital visits—up to thirty-three percent fewer
➡ Frequent drinkers in Canada make less use of health care systems

This chapter and the one that follows discuss general benefits that are unrelated to specific diseases. Their data have more to do with economics than medicine, but they constitute tangible benefits to one's economic health, as well as to the health care delivery system.

In 1983, Longnecker published an analysis of acute hospitalization — unscheduled visits to hospitals or emergency rooms. The findings imply that moderate drinkers enjoy some extra protection against medical emergencies. This study was based on data derived from the federal government's 1983 National Health Interview Survey, an analysis of data which included alcoholic beverage consumption and acute hospitalization.

In this study, moderate drinkers utilized emergency care facilities less than heavy drinkers or abstainers.

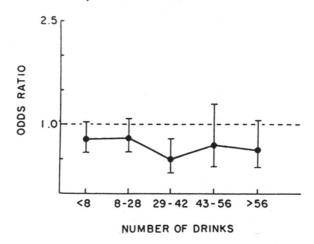

Reprinted with permission of American Journal of Public Health, Longnecker & MacMahon, 78:153,1983. Copyright by American Public Health Association.

Over 17,600 individuals responded to the survey. The data were adjusted for confounding variables including age, race, income, and smoking. The study concluded:

The adjusted odds ratio of having one or more hospitalizations for current drinkers relative to life-long abstainers in females was 0.67 and in males 0.74. U-shaped relationships between levels of current alcohol intake and odds of hospitalization were found. While some causes of hospitalization are clearly increased among drinkers, the overall acute

*care hospitalization experience of moderate drinkers
appears to be favorable.*

Longnecker, M., and MacMahon, B., Associations Between Alcoholic Beverage
Consumption and Hospitalization, 1983 National Health Interview Survey, American
Journal of Public Health, 78:153-156, 1983

The study produces another U-shaped curve, showing most
benefits for daily, moderate drinkers. The Longnecker data
reported an impressive thirty-three percent advantage in emergency hospitalizations for female moderate drinkers and twenty-
six percent for male moderate drinkers. The National Health
Survey is an ongoing federal project which inventories civilian
use of medical facilities.

The best result (the least acute hospitalization) occurred
among men who consumed between two and six drinks per day.
The authors found these results "striking" and compared them
to an earlier Klatsky study at Oakland's Kaiser Permanente
Medical Center which found: *There is consistency of less acute
hospitalization for those who consume from 8 to 56 drinks over a two
weeks period* (Klatsky 1981). Men who reported three drinks per
day had the least acute hospitalization. In another patient review in September 2000, Kaiser Permanente researchers found:
*Those who consumed 3 or more drinks per day had the lowest average
number of outpatient visits per year and were the least likely to be
hospitalized* (Drinkers Less Likely 2000). Three per day drinkers
experienced seventy-two hospitalizations per 1,000 compared
to 144.1 for nondrinkers, a remarkable difference.

A cautious researcher might attribute this condition to chance
or socio-economic status. But, combined with the many other
health advantages for drinkers outlined so far in this book, daily
drinking emerges, at a minimum, as no health encumbrance. In
addition, the authors speculated that it is likely that moderates
had *under-reported* their actual drinking levels. Other studies
have found that respondents often under-report drinking in such
surveys. To the degree that under-reporting exists, the subjects
in these studies had favorable hospitalization statistics while
drinking *even more* than they reported.

Richman found a similar pattern in the use of health care
facilities among moderate beer drinkers in a nationwide Cana-

dian Health Survey: *Thus the positive health levels of beer drinkers observed in this study may be simply mute testament to the success of mass advertising — with healthier individuals increasingly indicating beer as their beverage of choice* (Richman 1985). This kind of speculative commentary favoring drinking is a rarity in medical journals. The authors questioned governmental policies in the U.S. and Canada that associate alcohol advertising only as a corrupting factor for youth and adults. The authors conjectured that advertising images of moderate beer consumption depicting happy, convivial social conditions may actually encourage moderate use. That idea would be a hard sell to Canadian and U.S. public health authorities.

Another study released in 1997 by Kunz confirmed the Canadian and Longnecker findings. This report found that frequent drinkers were less likely to use *any* health care system.

Men who consumed 2 or less drinks every day averaged 7.8 visits, but men who drank 5+ every day averaged 6.2 visits, the lowest use of the health care system among these 35,246 Canadian adults age 18 and over.

Kunz, J., Alcohol Use and Reported Visits to Health Professionals, an Exploratory Study; Journal of Studies on Alcohol, 58:474-479, September, 1997

It would be a mistake to jump to the conclusion from the above commentary that five drinks a day is a healthier regimen than two drinks. But these various studies, based largely in government documentation, should engage the interests of those who worry about the costs of health care and the incidence of acute care. If daily moderate drinkers place a lower economic burden on health care, public health leadership ought to recognize drinking as a positive factor. Despite these strong evidences of less hospitalization and health care use by moderate drinkers, there is no evidence the public health professions has recognized, much less endorsed these findings. They run contrary to public health drink reduction goals in Canada and the U.S.

Costs are a critical variable

One can speculate that, to the degree that these nations do actually lower per capita consumption, some acute care expenditures will rise. Further burdening health care delivery. There is an Alice in Wonderland coloration to North America's ambivalent drinking policies. The U.S. government claims that alcohol abuse costs the nation up to $140 billion — a highly inflated figure at best (see Chapter 31). Savings in acute hospitalization and lower incidence of illnesses among moderates are never factored into programs which seek to rein in health care costs.

The Richman, Longnecker, Kunz and Klatsky studies in this chapter question prevailing temperance policies strictly on a cost/benefit rationale. These findings suggest that an individual's good health rests on multiple lifestyle factors. Drinking can be a positive contributor. Even if all of the identified drinking benefits were attributable to other factors, it is obvious that daily drinking does nothing to increase acute hospital visits. This assumption of neutrality challenges the federal control of availability agenda which seeks to reduce all consumption. As a society, we don't restrict or discourage skiing or night time driving, even though a very considerable number of individuals are injured in these specific activities. We accept certain inevitable risks and encourage safe practices. As we should for responsible alcohol consumption.

These few studies do not put the abuse-risk arguments to rest but they deserve much wider consideration and debate. One goal of this book is to generate interest in new perspectives to replace old drinking myths. This and the following chapter introduce fascinating economic factors which challenge the government's anti-drinking agenda. When economic and health benefits are wedded to moderate drinking, real questions are raised about about the prejudices in America's public health constabulary.

There's something to be said about fewer emergency hospital visits and a few more bucks in the billfold.

Chapter 20

Personal Income

Higher average earnings among drinkers

■ **Author's abstract:** Here's one of those, "Aw, come on!" chapters. Honest, I didn't make it up. Serious, well-designed and peer-reviewed studies of major corporate employees demonstrate a generally higher wage scale among moderate drinkers. Moderate drinking is part and parcel of a lifestyle that initiates many benefits. The proof lies here:

■ ➡ Alcohol consumption has a significant effect on income
　➡ Drinking may actually enhance job performance
　➡ Male alcohol users have higher wages than non-users
　➡ Moderate alcohol consumption leads to increased earnings

"You can't mean that drinkers make more money than abstainers." "Yep, 'it's true." Think of it this way. Individuals with moderate living habits quite likely miss less work, are tardy less often, and are more attentive to work requirements. Little wonder that, as reported in the following studies, these individuals are rewarded in the paycheck for due diligence.

In the following studies, financial health (income) is correlated with human health. That's understandable also. Healthy, cheerful, industrious individuals perform better and are rewarded for their deportment and production. Yet, the presumption that higher income could be a *healthy drinking benefit* borders on the bizarre. That is substantiated in professional surveys carried out in major corporations by qualified economists. Biomedical researchers are not likely to be exposed to this kind of data. Higher wages do not guarantee better health, but middle and upper income folks in this nation do enjoy better access to medical care – quite likely they always will. We've already established a variety of health benefits among moderate drinkers. The question raised in this chapter is what impact, if any, does *drinking* itself have on wage levels.

As always, it is important to know the make-up of each study group. For example, the half-century-old Framingham Study involves predominantly upper middle-class, white individuals living in a comfortable Boston suburb. Framingham residents constitute a dramatically different demographic than residents of Nome, Alaska or the Watts district of Los Angeles.

Add to this caveat, Ellison's conclusion of "causal unknowability." Despite a proliferation of study data, causality will never be absolutely certain as to why some groups enjoy better health than others. The myriad life influences in any reasonably-sized study group renders scientific certainty beyond reach. Ellison speculates on the degree of credit to accord an individual's life habits compared to drinking habits. Are wine drinkers more healthy because of their beverage choice or because of an array of living choices? Previous chapters have demonstrated that daily drinkers form the healthiest subset in most studies. Both moderate living and daily drinking contribute to these statistics. But there is little scientific certitude. In this debate, it really doesn't matter whether the chicken or the egg arrived first; both contribute to a healthy diet.

In this sense, drinks are net contributors to well-being. Ellison continues:

*And you can see that all types of alcohol had a
reduced risk in comparison to those who never drank.
On the other hand, you can see that those who
consumed wine had a much lower risk, of only 40% of
the non-drinkers, whereas there are less protections
from the other two types of alcohol. But we all know
that wine drinkers are different from beer drinkers or
from whiskey drinkers. There are certain differences
in the U.S. in who consumes wine. We know that wine
drinkers are better educated, they smoke less, they
have better health habits. We don't really know
whether healthier people drink wine or is it the wine
making them healthier.*

Ellison, C., Presentation to the National Wine Coalition at the National Press Club,
Washington, D.C., September 26, 1994

Keep in mind that no scientific study could ever represent the
total demographics of the U.S. population – an impossibly diverse aggregation of individuals and lifestyles. Yet many very
large surveys (as the American Cancer Society studies) demonstrate strikingly similar and definitely preferential health statistics for moderate drinkers of many persuasions living all over
the world. We cannot discount this synergism. These comparable statistics help to explain why moderate drinkers also are
preferred wage earners.

Drinking and income studies

Of course, scientists are skeptical of everything. It's in their
nature and training. Doubt is an ingrained, positive attribute.
Even viewed with healthy skepticism, these data on drinking
and income are compelling. Heien, in "The Relationship Between Alcohol Consumption and Earnings," concludes: *The results show that alcohol consumption has a significant effect on income*
(Heien 1996).

One would guess that this "net effect" was negative because
of the presumption of poor work habits and lost hours associated
with poor health among abusive drinkers. Not so. Heien reports
that moderate drinkers enjoyed better wage records than both
abstainers and abusers. A year earlier than Heien's survey, the
Triangle Group located at the University of North Carolina

reported similar evidence in a survey of 1,000 employees at four different corporations. Looking for a relationship between earnings and daily drinking, French and Zarkin commented:

In the midst of a unified effort by government and private officials to create a drug-free work place, our findings that moderate drinking may actually enhance job performance may be equally unsettling to some people, especially business leaders. Nevertheless, while alcohol use is certainly not beneficial for all individuals, it may not have nearly the negative consequences people imagine.

French, M., and Zarkin, G., Is moderate alcohol use related to wages? Evidence from four work sites, Journal of Health Economics, 14:319-344, 1995

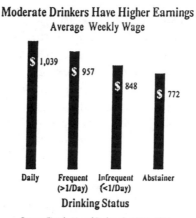

Moderate Drinkers Have Higher Earnings
Average Weekly Wage

Source: French, M. and Zarkin, G. APHA, 1993.

Graph reprinted with permission of the Wine Institute and from the Journal of Health Economics, French & Zarkin, Is moderate alcohol use related to wages?, Vol. 14, Vol. pp 319-334, 1995

These findings should have substantial impact on public policy. They don't. In the above graph, French and Zarkin demonstrate how moderate drinkers enjoy higher wages than abstainers, with a gradual escalation to the highest wages rewarded to daily drinkers. In 1998, Zarkin followed-up his earlier survey by comparing those findings with data gathered in the

National Household Survey on Drug Abuse (NHSDA), an on-going government survey. These data originate in households which include individuals twelve years of age and older. The survey asks questions on alcohol and illicit drug use, as well as information on the wages and hours worked. The authors noted: *Using a sample of employees at four work sites, they found that individuals who consume approximately 1.5 to 2.5 drinks per day have significantly higher wages than abstainers.* This study demonstrates a solid link between higher wages and moderate drinking.

In another report, Zarkin found:

Men who use alcohol have approximately 7% higher wages than men who do not drink . . . The emphasis on policing and monitoring alcohol use per se may be misplaced. Perhaps policy makers and employees should pay more attention to identifying negative consequences associated with alcohol abuse (such as performance problems and absenteeism) rather than focusing only on quantity and frequency measures of use.

Zarkin, G., et al., Alcohol use and wages: new results from the National Household Survey on Drug Abuse, Journal of Health Economics, 17:53-68, 1998

Slater studied drinking habits among 2,910 adults and found: *Moderate drinkers who reported an average of 2 drinks per occasion and who drank 3 or more times per week, had an average annual income of $71,400* (Slater 1999). Once again, daily drinkers earned the most in this grouping. Slater also reported that the second highest annual income in the group was awarded the heavy drinkers. Episodic drinkers came in at $27,600, a notch less than abstainers who averaged $35,950.

Many explanations could be devised for the fact that daily drinkers earn more. Probably, as Ellison has speculated, the precise reasons are unknowable. What should no longer be ignored in public health literature is the reality that daily, moderate drinking *does not impair* good work performance. From a different frame of reference, Mansson reported in a 1999 study that middle-age disability pensions were more numerous among heavy drinkers and nondrinkers than among moderate drinkers:

Heavy drinking as well as teetotalism appear to be positively correlated with disability pension, while light to moderate drinking was found to be beneficial with respect to the risk of future disability pension. Whether the favourable effect of moderate drinking is attributable to alcohol per se or to other life-style factors concomitant with moderate drinking is unknown.

Mansson, N., Rastam, L., Eriksson, K., and Israelsson, B., Alcohol consumption and disability pension among middle-aged men, Annals of Epidemiology, 9:341-348, 1999

Vahtera reviewed the medical records of more than 6,000 men and women in Finland in which there was absence from work for sickness based on a physician's examination. The study notes: *We found that lifelong abstainers, former drinkers and heavy drinkers had higher rates of sick leaves than moderate drinkers* (Vahtera, 2002). From these few studies, it can be induced that moderate drinkers constitute the best performing, long-term workers. They demonstrate that middle-of-the-road, reasonable-living, moderate drinkers constitute a healthy and productive segment of society. Once again, they challenge the government's commitment to reducing per capita drinking for *public health* reasons. That may be why you seldom (never?) find these studies in government or medical literature. These "facts" don't fit with the campaign to lower alcohol consumption. One wonders how much confirming data might be developed if government health agencies were as interested in the tangible benefits of moderate consumption as in lowering all alcohol consumption.

An interesting side-bar to these studies is that the data shows little penetration of the glass-ceiling for wages which favors male employees over females. Zarkin notes: *Our results suggest that male alcohol users have higher wages than non-users . . . . For women, the estimated alcohol use premium is approximately half as large as for men* (Zarkin 1998). Wage prejudice for the males remains intact.

Heien's study participants averaged age forty. Nearly all were white, married, in good to excellent health with earnings of $43,000 or more per year. This is not universal America but it's pretty close to a middle class profile. These findings confirm the common sense assumption that healthy, happy people are more productive during their working periods. The economic system rewards fidelity and superior production. That's the heart of the free enterprise system. These studies show how moderate drinkers are more successful in the most vital clinic of life — the workplace.

Bringing together the disciplines

The findings in this and the previous chapter are based in economics and sociology, disciplines suggested earlier as valuable cross-references for researchers in the biological and medical sciences. Medical writers could profit from greater familiarity with the parallel work done in other academic disciplines. You can study mortality from an exclusively pathogenic viewpoint and miss many of the factors that contribute to disease etiology. For instance, Fried surveyed a community aged over sixty-five years and determined that income directly affects life span: . . . *that men had a 2.3-fold higher risk for death compared to women; that people with income less than $50,000 per year had a higher risk for death compared with those making more money* (Fried 1998). Economics definitely impact health. Physicians aren't responsible for raising the income levels of patients, but they should be sensitive to this kind of economic data which impacts health. Of course, as incomes rise, better health care becomes available and more attention is paid to diet and other habits which yield greater longevity (Lantz 1998).

Each distinct body of learning brings special expertise, viewpoints and experiences. In *Alcohol in Its Cultural Context*, Marshall provides sixteen "generalizations" about drinking derived from global observations of dozens of anthropologists. His third generalization pertains to this discussion: *When members of a society have had sufficient time to develop a widely shared set of beliefs and values pertaining to drinking and drunkenness, the consequences of alcohol consumption are not usually disruptive for most persons in that society* (Marshall 1979). This may explain why alcohol-integrated societies in western Europe have fewer abuse problems and enjoy greater health benefits from their drinking. They avoid some drinking problems through a shared set of beliefs and standards which support responsible drinking and impugn drunkenness.

America's "shared set of beliefs and values" about drinking today are almost entirely negative. They do not accommodate responsible use as a healthy norm. Our culture shuns the integration of drinks as real foods in the manner of the French, Spanish, Italian and German populations. Alcohol control practices in this nation may actually contribute to solitary drinking, youthful abuse and carnage on the highways. Yes, German, Italian and French societies do have serious levels of abuse and drunk driving. A certain level of lawlessness and a core of mindless abusers is inevitable in any society. But America's current flawed "set of myths" about drinking militate *against* good public health.

The drink or the drinker

No specific type of drink or level of drinking has been identified with higher wages. The financial rewards apparently derive from a synergy of personal habits along with a set of beliefs and priorities that motivate a happy, relaxed, goal-oriented worker. Klatsky, Pittman, Ellison and others have isolated a set of lifestyle habits and routines that distinguish wine drinkers (Profile of the Wine Drinker 1991). In the 1980s and 1990s, many drinking studies featured wine's impacts. Many physicians are wine drinkers and a surprising number have interests in or own wineries. However, the majority of studies identify heart and other health benefits with numerous alcohol sources. Wine may continue to a primary focus because of its heavy concentrations of antioxidants. It may even be depicted as the first among equals, but beer and spirituous drinks are also healthgiving.

As the comparative studies of Gronbaek in Denmark, Brenner in Germany demonstrate, all drinks containing alcohol emerge as health beneficial to varying degrees. Individuals are advantaged in choosing a favorite beverage, or in favoring them all just as they choose to consume certain vegetables and fruits.

To round out the personal income issue, Heien asserts a strong economic relationship between moderate drinking and income: *The broad conclusion of these medical studies is that alcohol abuse and abstinence both have a negative effect on CAD (coronary artery disease) while moderate consumption has a positive effect. The economic hypothesis derived from this conclusion is that income will be negatively related to abstinence and abusive drinking and positively related to moderate drinking* (Heien 1995). This is the inevitable conclusion based upon a melding of economic and medical research.

Heien's opinion was buttressed in a 1997 survey by another economist, Hamilton, in a study of 1,750 Canadians: . . . *that moderate alcohol consumption leads to increased earnings relative to abstention ... moderate drinkers earned 7.4% more on average than abstainers* (Hamilton 1997). Hamilton's finding of a wage advantage for moderates is within a half of a percent of that isolated in Zarkin's studies. Moderate drinking pays off!

This chapter has established a novel scenario – that regular, responsible drinking is a contributor to personal income. In consideration of these findings and the many other findings of health benefits, medical leadership, federal health agencies and the political system should reassess public health antipathy to drinking.

In view of the profusion of favorable epidemiology, our alcohol ambivalences are no longer relevant. They are counter-productive. Unless health leadership moves toward proportional recognition of the positive aspects of European control practices, American workers will be subjected to another ambivalent, less healthful and less "profitable" century ahead.

Moderate drinking – a real pocketbook issue.

Chapter 21

Kidney Stones

Remarkable reductions in risk

■ **Author's abstract:** The research in this chapter parallels the one on gallstones. In both, excess chemicals in an organ produce crystals which occasion excruciating pain on passage. It would be nice to report widespread public communication of these findings. There isn't any. Kidney stone sufferers (men and women) should demand more open communication of these findings.

■ ⇢ Men are four times as likely to have kidney stones than women
⇢ Wine can reduce stone formation up to thirty-nine per cent
⇢ Increase in stone formation was seen with grapefruit juice consumption
⇢ Drinking beer lowers the risk of kidney stones

After reading the chapter on gallstones, it should come as no surprise that drinks can also reduce the incidence of bruising, painful kidney stones. A *UC Berkeley Wellness Letter* outlines the threat of kidney stone formation:

> *Most people will never form a kidney stone. But about 10 to 12% of those in industrialized societies will suffer from nephrolithiasis, better known as kidney stones, at least once in their lives. Men are four times more likely to have the disorder than women.*

Kidney stones: myths & facts, UC Berkeley Wellness Letter, p 5, March, 1998

The article describes the process:

> *All kinds of waste products are filtered out of blood by the kidneys and excreted in urine. All stones are mixtures of minerals, chiefly calcium, magnesium, and phosphate, plus oxalic acid (mostly produced in the body, but also found in some foods), uric acid (an end product of metabolism from meat), and rarely the amino acid systeine . . . . The most common stones are almost pure sodium oxilate (the salt of oxalic acid).*

The *Wellness Letter* article advises that heavy consumption of fluids reduces stone risk but warns: *Go easy on alcoholic and caffeinated beverages, which tend to dehydrate.* This advice was offered in 1998 by one of the most widely-read of the medical newsletters. Compare it with findings two years earlier by Curhan.

Curhan compared the impacts of twenty-one different beverages on the risk of symptomatic kidney stones. A cohort of 45,289 men ranging from forty to seventy-five years of age with no history of stones was followed for six years. In this large group, 753 stones were documented, considerably less than the estimated ten percent incidence. Despite the stern warning in *UC Berkeley Wellness Letter* to avoid alcohol and caffeine, the men who consumed caffeinated coffee, tea, beer and wine significantly *reduced* their risk of developing kidney stones: *Wine reduced the risk of stone formation by 39%, the strongest inverse association of all beverages* (Curhan 1996).

This comparison illustrates another failure to communicate favorable alcohol findings. How many physicians are aware of this study? Two years before the *Wellness Letter* warned stone sufferers against drinking alcohol, Curhan had reported: . . . *the risk of stone formation decreased by the following amount for each 240-ml (8 oz) serving consumed daily: caffeinated coffee, 10%; decaffeinated coffee, 10%, tea, 14%; beer, 21%; and wine, 39%.*

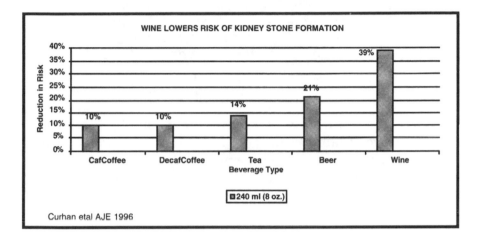

Reprinted with permission of Oxford University Press from Curhan et al., Prospective study of beverage use and the risk of kidney stones, American Journal of Epidemiology, 143(3):240-247, 1996

Curhan's report was published in the *American Journal of Epidemiology,* hardly an obscure publication, but the data was not picked up and broadcast in any of the medical newsletters subscribed taken by this journalist. Curhan noted an *increased* risk for stones in daily servings of apple juice (thirty-five per cent) and grapefruit juice (thirty-seven per cent). This data about two highly popular juices is also worthy of distribution. Though more research is warranted, these findings are pertinent contemporary data for chronic stone sufferers. At the very minimum, the findings should be verified or disputed and the results widely shared.

Curhan and associates continued their investigations and released more data in 1998 involving a cohort of women who participated in the Nurses' Health Study. Ages ranged from forty to sixty-five years. None in this grouping had a history of kidney stones. During 553,081 person-years of follow-up over an eight-year period, 719 cases of kidney stones were documented. The multivariate model adjusted for seventeen different beverages and other confounding risks:

> *Risk for stone formation decreased by the following amount for each 240 ml (8 oz) serving consumed daily: 10% for decaffeinated coffee, 8% for tea, and 59% for wine. In contrast, a 44% increase in risk was seen for each 240 ml serving of grapefruit juice.*

Curhan, G., Willett, W., Speizer, F., and Stampfer, M., Beverage use and risk for kidney stones in women, Annals of Internal Medicine, Vol. 128, No. 7, pp 534-540, 1998

Curhan's second study verified the first establishing similar advantages for moderate drinking women. In the Nurses' Health Study participants, wine again emerged as the most protective beverage for avoiding kidney stones. The authors noted: *An increase in total fluid can reduce the risk for kidney stones, and the choice of beverage may be meaningful.*

A study published in 1999 by Hirvonen compared the impact of various beverages on stone formation among male smokers. The authors referenced earlier cohort studies which had found both total fluid intake and coffee, tea and beer lowering the incidence. This study's questionnaire was answered by over 27,000 male Finnish smokers. Beer consumption in this group was found to be protective: *These data suggest that magnesium intake and beer consumption are inversely associated and fiber intake is positively associated with risk for kidney stones . . . Because beer, but not wine or spirits, seems to be protective against kidney stones, the physiological effects of beer components other than alcohol, especially hops, should be examined* (Hirvonen 1999). The remark raises again the presumed efficacy of antioxidants. This study also demonstrates that findings can vary substantially for different study populations. Finnish smokers differ from American middle-aged doctors and nurses.

The reticence of editors in the medical newsletters to report drink-favorable data presumably reflects an unwarranted fear of contributing to abusive drinking. This is puzzling obsession in view of the side effects dangers in many medicinal drugs. There is a small-print warning buried in a full page newspaper ad for

VIOXX, a newly-popular non-steroidal, anti-inflammatory drug (NSAID) which is recommended for "osteoarthritis and pain:"

Serious but rare side effects that have been reported in patients . . . have included: Serious stomach problems, such as stomach and intestinal bleeding . . . These problems, if severe could lead to hospitalization or death . . . Serious allergic reactions including swelling of the face, lips, tongue and/or throat . . . Serious kidney problems occur rarely, including acute kidney failure and worsening of chronic kidney failure . . . More common, but less serious side effects have included . . . Upper and/or lower respiratory infection, headache, dizziness, diarrhea, nausea and/or vomiting, heartburn, high blood pressure, back pain, tiredness, urinary tract infection . . . These side effects were reported in at least 2% of osteoarthritis patients receiving daily doses of VIOXX

Imagine if you could, advertisement in the Seattle Post Intelligencer, Wednesday, September 13, 2000

Are there genuine risks of developing a pattern of abusive drinking in establishing a therapeutic use? Of course. But with the worldwide incidence of alcohol addiction at somewhere around three percent of all drinkers, the risk is minimal. But there are similar risk rates for therapeutic drugs. Consider the stated side effects from VIOXX. As demonstrated frequently in this book, daily consumption of alcohol containing drinks can impact favorably on dozens of different health conditions while VIOXX is recommended primarily for arthritis and pain.

This book does not suggest that drinks should be substituted for therapeutic drugs. Nor does it deny the possibility that some moderates might overindulge using health as the rationale. It simply argues for a more balanced perspective about drinking risks. It does assert that the risk of alcohol addiction is egregiously overstated in medical literature.

All of the findings cited in this book could be reported in the medical and popular media with appropriate warnings in place of the current obligatory anti-drinking slogans. Here is an example of an appropriate warning in a *Health After 50* sidebar titled "Remedies." It reports the findings of the Finnish study and concludes with appropriate, non-inflammatory concern that any drinking remain within prudent limits.

> *Drinking beer lowers the risk of kidney stones, according to a Finnish study of 27,000 men between 50 and 69 years of age. Specifically, each bottle of beer consumed per day was correlated with a 40% reduction in risk. One possible explanation is that the water and alcohol in beer increase urinary output and thus dilute the urine, which may reduce the opportunity for stones to form. However, the same protective benefits did not occur with wine or spirits. Another hypothesis, therefore, is that certain compounds found in brewer's hops decrease the excretion of calcium, the prime constituent of kidney stones. Despite the benefit of reducing kidney stone risk, drinking more than two beers per day increases the risk of other health problems, including heart and liver disease.*

Remedies, Health After 50, Vol. 11, No. 9, November, 1999

This is fair, unbiased reporting that will elevate healthy drinking science to a much wider audience. If the commentary had also cross-referenced positive findings for other diseases, it would be exemplary medical journalism. However, another article on kidney stones in *Health After 50* as late as May 2002, "Revised Anti-Kidney Stone Recipe," failed to mention any of the favorable alcohol research.

The medical information floodgates are opening – but ever so cautiously.

Chapter 22

Mortality and Morbidity

Extended life and less illness

■ **Author's abstract:** Through life we strive nobly to avoid premature death—and as much illness as possible along the way. Despite the best of intentions, most of us stretch our safety envelopes by engorging on fats and sweets, over-doing caffeine and alcohol, driving too fast and playing too hard. Research suggests that drinks can help to ameliorate many excesses. Research finds that light drinkers live longer and have fewer health problems. Moderates are not invulnerable. They do also get sick and die prematurely for many reasons, but the favorable odds are on their side.

■ ➡ Reduced risk of premature death for drinkers vs
   abstainers varied from ten to forty per cent
   ➡ Protection appears less for women and Asians
   ➡ Moderate drinking increases longevity from all causes
   by about three per cent

Morbidity is the clinical term for disease, the forerunner of mortality, the termination of life. Aside from traumatic foreshortening — a woodsman's ax for a stately tree or a automobile crash for a human being — all living things on planet earth struggle daily to avoid debilitating disease. To stem the inevitable tide of injury and infectious diseases which lead ultimately to premature mortality, epidemiologists study the etiology (the pathway) of various pathogens (agents of disease) or lifestyle factors which cause or impact morbidity. That's life, and death.

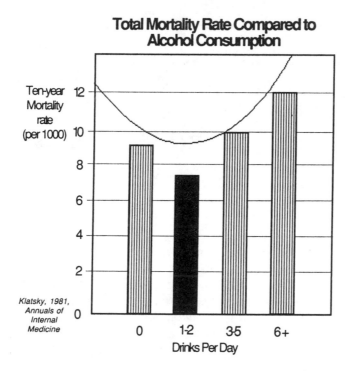

Graph reprinted with permission of Wine Institute and reproduction of data with permission of Annals of Internal Medicine, Alcohol and Mortality, Klatsky et al., 95:139–145, 1981 with the understanding that American College of Physicians/American Society of Internal Medicine is not responsible for the accuracy of the Wine Institute translation

The curve above from a ten year study forms the appearance of a flat J or a sweeping U. The U-shape curve depicts mortality related to rate of drinking. The best mortality rate is seen among participants who consumed up to two drinks daily. This is one of many similar studies conducted by Klatsky nd associates at the Kaiser Permanente Medical Center in Oakland, California. Credit American medicine with the improving mortality rates over the past century. Epidemiology demonstrates this accomplishment. As scientists gained skill in interpreting such data, they discovered that moderate drinkers experienced less illness and longer life.

Many U- and J-shaped curves are found in the literature. A thirteen-year study by Doll of physicians in Great Britain released in 1994 demonstrated similar U-shaped curves for heart disease, all cause deaths, and all cancers (Doll 1994). Doll's inclusion of other killer diseases favored by the consumption of between eight and twenty-eight units (drinks) per week clearly widened the benefit horizon.

Between Klatsky's pioneering study in 1981 and Doll's in 1994, dozens of global studies have developed similar risk statistics. A difficulty faced with epidemiological data lies in the uniqueness of each study group. Every population has singular characteristics. Individuals living in a certain time and place reflect both personal and cultural traits identified with their settings. However, when similar mortality curves and findings occur in many places and from diverse types of studies, a working scientific consensus is established. Most scientists today accept a consensus for cardiovascular benefits among responsible drinkers.

The scientific consensus

Here are examples of such regional studies. In the U.S., Sesso gathered data from the Physicians' Health Study for 18,455 men who had no history of heart disease or cancer. He concluded that, to avoid future cardiovascular problems, young men should increase average levels of alcohol consumption: *These prospective data suggest that, among men with initially low alcohol consumption, a subsequent moderate increase in alcohol consumption may lower their CVD* (cardiovascular disease) risk (Sesso 2000). How frequently does one find this kind of advice from medical sources? It challenges the contention that heart benefits from drinking apply only to upper middle-aged and senior citizens. Sesso found no distinctions for benefits in the types of alcohol drinks.

Observers must be careful not to generalize from a single set of figures. Italy, for example, is the first industrialized nation to have a larger population over sixty-five than under fifteen years of age. One could rationalize that wine drinking from crib to casket is the critical factor in this longevity. In reality, many other factors contribute to Italian longevity statistics. One can make a very good case for wine's influence, but the entirety of the Mediterranean diet, family genetics, lifestyle and cultural factors must be factored in. This book argues over and over that drinking can be a positive influence, not necessarily the only or the the critical influence.

Statistics developed in Denmark by Gronbaek originate in a nation with markedly different cuisine, drinking habits and a much more taciturn population than found in Italy. Gronbaek reports: *Wine consumption may have a protective effect on all-cause mortality that is additive to that of alcohol* (Gronbaek 2000). Gronbaek's work shows that wine drinkers, but not beer and spirit drinkers, have a lower risk of cardiovascular and other disease. One 2002 Danish study speculates that: *Wine drinkers appear to be at lower risk of becoming heavy drinkers or alcohol abusers than beer drinkers* (Jensen 2002). Compare these data with several studies in Germany (Brenner 1997 and Hoffmeister 1999) which report beer drinkers enjoying the more favorable mortality statistics. Keep always in mind that Denmark is not Rome, London, Paris, New York or Kankakee, Illinois. Place matters in all epidemiology.

Skovenborg perused data on heart attacks gathered in the MONICA surveys sponsored by the World Health Organization. Subjects included men and women ranging from thirty-five to sixty-four years of age in forty-two communities and several nations. The percentages of non-fatal heart attacks in these cities demonstrated a startling variation: . . . *907 per 100,000 for North Karelia, Finland to 73 per 100,000 for Beijing, China . . . from 241 per 100,000 in Glasgow, U.K., to 24 per 100,000 in Toulouse, France* (Skovenborg 1995). Maskarinec studied 40,000 people with Caucasian, Chinese, Filipino, Japanese and Native Hawaiian ethnicity and reported benefits for drinkers: *The protective effect was J-shaped . . . for all groups* (Maskarinec 1998). The range of 900 heart attacks per 100 thousand in Finland to under 100 in France demonstrates the need to ferret out unique, regional influences. That's why the research on the French paradox has been so important. It emphasizes that place really matters.

Some studies produce diametrically conflicting findings. In 1999, Hart reported little impact on heart disease among moderate drinkers in Scotland: . . . *this study of 5,776 male Scottish workers found little effect on either heart disease or mortality rates among moderate drinkers* (Hart 1999). Genetics, lifestyle and preference for spirituous drinks could be factors. In a 1999 article, the *Cleveland Heart Clinic Newsletter* commented on a U.S. finding: *A study conducted on 22,000 men over more than 10 years at Brigham and Women's Hospital and Harvard Medical School found that the risk of dying from all causes was 28% lower in men who consume five to six drinks a week, but 51% higher for heavy drinkers than for teetotalers* (The Great Cocktail Debate 1999). Scotland reports little impact but Boston finds lower incidence among moderates. Place matters.

Two very large American Cancer Society national surveys confirm that "occasional to moderate drinkers" enjoy advantages in all-cause mortality across our nation. But public health and cancer society commentators fail to emphasize this positive finding, preferring to remonstrate against the perils of excessive drinking. An editorial in *Alcohol Issues Insights* describes this tendency:

> *Doctors and reporters stressed that alcohol's benefits were "small," did not offset the risks . . . . But the evidence is mounting that moderate drinking reduces risk of death. . . The results of five recent mortality studies of over 625,000 adults from different nations (found). . . The reduced risks of death for drinkers vs abstainers varied considerably in these studies from a factor of 10% to nearly 40% lower, depending on the population and the consumption rate, but each of these major studies*

*found a significantly reduced risk of death for
light-to-moderate drinkers.*

Light, Moderate and Heavy Drinkers have Lower Death Rates than Abstainers: American
Cancer Society Study, Alcohol Issues Insights, Vol. 14, No. 12, December, 1997

This introduces another "local" influence – the politics of drinking in U.S. public health. In his review of a book written about American medical politics, *PC, M.D.: How Political Correctness is Corrupting Medicine*, Sullam notes: . . . *public health, (which) sits at the intersection between epidemiology and government. Politics cannot be eliminated from public health any more than it can be eliminated from public finance* (Sullum 2001). Public health authorities deliberately over-emphasize problem drinking. Drinking gets little respect or recognition in American medicine. Contrast American medical reticence with the findings of Renaud in France where medicine, public health, politics and commercial interests all favor responsible drinking.

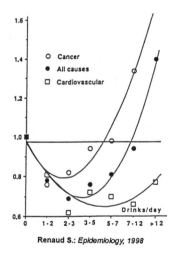

Renaud S.: *Epidemiology, 1998*

Reprinted with permission of Epidemiology, Renaud, S., et al., Alcohol and mortality in middle-aged men from Eastern France, 9:184-188, 1998

Renaud's graph dramatically illustrates benefits at least partially attributable to responsible drinking among residents of

Southern France. Over eighty per cent of the participants consumed wine as their primary alcohol beverage. The study involved over 34,000 middle-aged men over a period from ten to fifteen years. The report notes: *The results are intermediary between benefits observed on cardiovascular diseases – 30 (per cent) for consumption of 3 to 5 glasses a day – and those observed on cancers – 20 (per cent) for 2 to 3 glasses of wine a day. The results show a decrease in all-cause mortality by 30 (per cent) and 20 (per cent) among subjects which consume respectively 2 to 3 and 3 to 5 glasses of wine a day* (Renaud 1998). The French paradox wonders why these favorable findings exist in a population that indulges in all manner of dietary excesses.

These statistics reflect French citizens who share a vastly different drinking (and eating) ethic than our own. French research portrays none of the alcohol ambivalence found in the U.S. In France, a drinker may consume up to five glasses of wine on any one day, or over a lifetime with little concern from family, physician or institutions of public health. Why? Because wine is an integral element in the French diet. See our arguments in Chapter 14 that drinks should be accorded food status. Our medical institutions sternly advise no more than one drink for women and two for men on any one day (see Chapter 31). Renaud lives and conducts his studies in starkly different, alcohol-tolerant culture.

French drinkers are physically and mentally conditioned to high levels of consumption. This process develops extraordinary alcohol tolerance. It is appropriate to discourage undisciplined drinking for heart health, but why promote abstention (If you don't drink; don't start) as many U.S. medical articles do? There's a big difference in attitude. The first (NHANES) federal health survey reported: *Moderate drinking increases time until death from any cause by about 3 percent, whereas heavy drinking reduces time until death by about 2 percent.* U.S. officials could reveal these health advantages without encouraging abuse.

The trick in evaluating epidemiology is to always determine the time, place and any unique characteristics of the study's participants. Within this framework, a physician or individual can determine the comparative relevance of dozens of international studies which suggest health benefits. For brief, compre-

hensive abstracts from hundreds of longevity studies, call the
California Wine Institute which has archived drinking science
for the past half century. Their research department can be
reached at 415-512-0151.

A cavalcade of mortality findings

One could fill the remaining pages of this book with commentaries about favorable drinking and mortality. Alcohol impacts
most profoundly the cluster of cardiovascular diseases, the
world's most prolific killers. Slow the pace of heart and vascular
deaths and inevitably all-cause mortality lessens. Here are selected citations published in many nations which prove that
alcohol *abstinence* should be considered as the real "risk taking."

✔ In France, 34,014 middle-aged men were followed for 5 years and
found: "A moderate intake of wine (2-5 glasses per day) was associated with a 24-31% reduction in all-cause mortality . . . the intake
level associated with the highest protection for all-cause mortality
could have been as little as, or less than, 2-3 glasses per day" (Renaud
1998). Note that the report categorizes 2/5 drinks per day moderate
intake.

✔ A German 18-month study of 8,000 construction workers found
that: ". . . teetotalers were nearly three times more likely to die compared to men who consumed 1-49 grams of alcohol per day" (Brenner
1997). That's a little over three drinks daily. Brenner mentioned the
role of alcohol but also concluded: "Additional mechanisms may account for the strong protective effect of moderate beer consumption."
Two other German researchers (Keil 1997) and (Hoffmeister 1999)
found beer the most providential in that beer drinking nation. Hoffmeister speculated that if European beer drinkers suddenly abstained
that there would be significant increases in cardiovascular disease
and a two year drop in life expectancy.

✔ In the Russian Federation in 1995, it was reported: " . . . average
expectation of life at birth has fallen especially sharply for men: By
1993, it had slumped to 59 years . . . below the age at which a pension starts" (Ryan 1995). Another Russian study compared total mortality for men and women with U.S. statistics and reported:
"Age-adjusted mortality rates were higher for non-drinkers than
lower level drinkers in both genders and countries" (Deev 1998).
Even in that excessive drinking culture, moderate drinkers exhibit the
best longevity results.

✔ A 1996 project revealed: "Studies of total human mortality data have yielded a U-shaped curve with respect to mortality versus alcohol consumption" (Derr 1996).

✔ Another analysis of the Physicians Health Study in 1998 reported: "Although heavy alcohol consumption increases total mortality, light to moderate consumption decreases cardiovascular and all-cause mortality in apparently healthy people" (Muntwyler 1998).

✔ A Lung Health Study enrolled 5,887 cigarette smokers with airway obstructions aged 35-60 and reported: " A significant protective effect of moderate drinking was found among men, but not women. . . A baseline pattern of drinking eight or more drinks per occasion was associated with fewer hospitalizations and deaths" (Murray 1998). Even among smokers, drinking has more favorable mortality consequences.

All but one of these studies were published in the late 1990s. This is *contemporary* health data. Ironically, the 100,000 individuals who die annually in American hospitals from side effects of doctor-prescribed drugs corresponds to the number of deaths that federal agencies attribute to drinking (a death figure disputed in Chapter 31). Drugs with potentially lethal side effects are administered routinely because the adverse effects impact only a small minority. The negative effects from drinking impacts only a minority of drinkers.

Periodically recognition creeps into government research papers of the positive relationship between drinking and mortality. In a 1966 publication,"Alcohol and the Cardiovascular System," the NIAAA's Dufour notes a long history of medical recognition:

> *The idea that moderate alcohol consumption might be beneficial in the context of preventive medicine is not new. Raymond Pearl, one of the pioneers of modern epidemiology, noted in publications spanning the 1920s and 1930s that life expectancy was generally greatest for moderate drinkers, lower in abstainers, and lowest in heavy drinkers.*

Dufour, M., Introduction: Epidemiological Alcohol Studies, from Alcohol and the Cardiovascular System, NIAAA, DHHS, Washington, D.C., 1996

If extended mortality among drinkers was recognized in the 1920s and 1930s, why is it only being *discovered* at the turn of the following century. Why is this asset virtually rejected by the power elite in medicine? It is time for American medicine to recognize the anomaly of sustaining a vigorous anti-drinking policy that may well cause morbidity and premature mortality to many current moderate drinkers.

A new look at an old problem

A sensible approach to resolving this conflict would be to evaluate the entire range of drinking benefits across all academic disciplines – from mortality and morbidity, from biochemistry through anthropology, from the costs of abuse through the taxes and incomes generated in farming, production and retailing of licensed beverages. With these data, authorities and politicians could establish a legitimate cost/benefit ratio for responsible drinking. Drinking benefits are not just for the weak of heart, nor just for the elderly, nor do they apply exclusively to the paradoxical French. Specific drink benefits have been reported for Japanese-Americans living in Hawaii, construction workers in Germany, individuals who already have suffered heart attacks and a host of other disparate groupings.

At the California Wine Institute, Holmgren prepared the following impressive list of positive cardiovascular mortality studies by region. These studies constitute a profound, international medical consensus on drinking and mortality.

United States
Framingham Heart Study – Kaiser Permanente Studies
Nurses' Health Study – Physicians' Health Study
NHANES Federal Study – Honolulu Heart Study

Europe
Seven Countries Study – British Regional Heart Study
British Doctors Study – Copenhagen Heart Studies
Italian Rural Cohort Study

Asia/Australia
Japanese Physician Study – Busselton Study
Dubbo Study – New Zealand Cohort Study
Shanghai China Cohort Study

What other common food can boast such impressive health validation? In addition to these multi-nation projects, dozens of smaller regional studies come to similar conclusions. In one, Rehm evaluated responses from 5,072 households reported in the 1984-1995 National Alcohol Survey of U.S. Households. He concluded: *A significant influence of alcohol use on mortality was found, with a J-shaped relationship for men and a non-significant relationship of the same shape for women . . . These results emphasize the importance of routinely including measures of drinking patterns in future epidemiological studies . . . Certain drinking patterns, especially episodic heavy drinking or intoxication, (are) more closely related to acute causes of death than average drinking levels* (Rehm 2001.) There is no other way to read this finding than as a ringing support for daily, moderate intake. Health leadership in the U.S. is aware of these data but political correctness and over-reaching fears of mass abuse mitigate against their embrace. Organized medicine seems incapable of confronting the anti-alcohol social and political conventions which have dominated their profession for more than a century.

For reasons outlined in the three concluding chapters of this book, moderate drinking probably will never merit an organized, articulate, ground roots movement working in its behalf. No Mothers for Moderation lobby. No Doctors for Healthy Drinking Research or Citizens for Responsible Consumption. The idea of a responsible drinking society languishes. The great cultural agencies that develop U.S. medical policy are uninterested in social drinking issues. The squeaky wheels of dry advocacy – the Center for Science in the Public Interest, Mothers Against Drunk Driving, the March of Dimes, the many private (government funding dependent?) disease associations and private foundations garner the available op-ed space with their anti-drinking rhetoric.

Noting this apprehension among health institutions, it is important to keep a proper perspective about the significant accomplishments of American medicine. U.S. medical research, surgical advancements and clinical techniques rate among the world's finest. The universal goal to extend life, and quality of life, continues to improve in this blessed land. Data released for 1999 by Health and Human Services in October 2001 place U.S.

life expectancy at 76.9 years and also reports a new record low for infant mortality, a notable problem in this nation. Death rates have dropped for nearly every major disease including cancer, heart disease and stroke. Health care delivery problems remain through an era of systemic change, but every reader should be confident in the essential soundness of American health care.

Despite this deserved praise, responsible drinking remains an orphaned issue in our land. As discussed in the final chapters, no institution seems willing to take leadership in this arena. This book concludes that a critical mass of practicing physicians and informed mothers could enliven this issue, move it off dead center and forge a long-overdue accommodation of responsible drinking.

It helps to be an optimist.

Chapter 23

Osteoporosis

A natural food for stronger bones

Author's abstract: In terms of American public health problems, osteoporosis ranks up there with diabetes, kidney stones and cognition. Over twenty-five million citizens suffer erosion of bone density. Since this disease net is so large, the contribution of drinks to easing the incidence should be better known. Here are some thought provoking findings in the science:

- Higher bone density is found among with consumers of twelve drinks a week
- By seventy-five years of age, one in three men will experience osteoporosis
- Women who drink at least seven ounces of alcohol a week have higher bone densities
- Postmenopausal women drinkers have stronger bones

An article titled "Alcohol and Stronger Bones – The Newly Emerging Evidence" sets the stage for a consideration of drinking and bone disease:

> *Osteoporosis, a leading cause of death and disability in the U.S. affects more than 25 million people.*
>
> *Painful bone fractures caused by a gradual erosion of bone density are responsible for frailty and loss of mobility in the elderly, primarily in women, and can lead to complications culminating in pneumonia.*
>
> *Because a higher rate of fractures is associated with alcohol abuse, researchers assumed for many years that alcohol consumption contributed in a linear fashion to bone loss. But the recent scientific distinction between use and abuse with respect to heart disease and overall mortality prompted researchers to revisit the relationship between alcohol and bone density.*

Alcohol and Stronger Bones – The Newly Emerging Evidence, Wine Issues Monitor, The Wine Institute, San Francisco, 1997

Despite the strong association of osteoporosis with females, men should understand their significant risk. *Harvard Men's Health Watch* notes: *If men think they're immune to osteoporosis, they are badly mistaken. Some 1.5 million American men have osteoporosis, and another 3.5 million are at risk for developing it. Osteoporosis will appear in one of every three men by age 75* (Osteoporosis in men 1999). The Holbrook study found heavier bone density among both men and women who drink moderately. For both men and women, there is evidence of a bias in reporting the research.

Heavy vs moderate drinking

Osteoporosis research demonstrates both positive and negative findings about drinking. Klein represents the negative side: *The habitual consumption of even moderate quantities of alcohol (1 to 2 drinks/day) is clearly linked with reduced bone mass (osteopenia). . . At present, abstinence is the only effective therapy for alcohol-induced bone disease* (Klein 1997). A more liberal interpretation of the data associates bone mass decreases exclusively with chronic alcohol abuse. Kimble notes a difference between use and chronic abuse: *Alcohol has been identified as a risk factor for the development of osteoporosis. Chronic alcohol abuse has been shown to decrease bone mass and increase the incidence of fractures* (Kimble 1997). *Health After 50* suggests moderation of intake: *To maximize bone density, consume 1,200 to 1,500 mg of calcium and 800 mg of vitamin D per day, get daily weight-bearing exercise, don't smoke and limit your alcohol consumption* (Our Strong Recommendation 1997). Odvina: . . . *confirmed a significant decrease in bone mass among chronic alcoholics . . . especially prevalent among those with evidence of liver involvement* (Odvina 1995).

Medicine today employs a highly organized, finely balanced drug culture. Dozens of drug regimens treat what ails us and other drugs and supplements are taken to avoid an onset. Patients are expected routinely to adhere to specified dosages for half a dozen different pills to be taken at various times throughout the day. For the most part, patients measure up to the task.

The *British Medical Journal* published the Holbrook study which was conducted at the University of California, San Diego. It demonstrates benefits for both male and female drinkers.

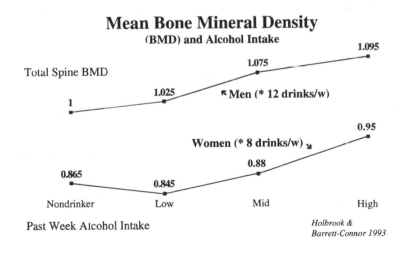

Graph reprinted with permissions of Wine Institute and data used with permission from British Medical Journal, Holbrook et al., A prospective study of alcohol consumption and bone mineral density, 306:1506, 1993

The graph above attests to the following facts: *For the 182 men and 267 women studied, higher bone density was associated with those who consumed an average of 12 drinks per week and eight drinks per week respectively* (Holbrook 1993). The report noted that previous studies linking alcohol intake to osteoporosis had relied on studies among chronic alcoholics, a group which often lacks sufficient dietary nutrients to maintain healthy bones

Felson also found better densities among drinkers: . . . *studied elderly men and women and reported that women who drank at least 7 oz alcohol/week . . . had higher bone densities at most measured sites . . . than women in the lightest consumption category of less than 1 oz/week* (Felson 1995). The difficulty for seniors lies not so much in overdrinking as getting access to these findings. Rapuri discovered: *Moderate alcohol intake was associated with higher BMD in postmenopausal elderly women* (Rapuri 2001). *Wine Issues Monitor* concurs: *Another study on 1,154 participants aged 68 years old from the long ongoing Framingham Heart Study Cohort found that postmenopausal women who consumed alcohol in moderation on a regular basis had stronger bones than women who consumed less.* From the same article: *In an authoritative new book, Osteoporosis, Stanford University School of Medicine Professors David Feldman and Jennifer Kelsy highlight data finding that moderate alcohol consumption is not associated with lower bone density and therefore unlikely to increase osteoporosis risk* (Wine Issues Monitor 1997).

In Copenhagen, Holdrup concluded: . . . *an alcohol intake within the current European drinking limits does not influence the risk of hip fracture, whereas an alcohol intake of more than 27 drinks per week is a major risk factor for men* (Holdrup 1999). Tobe and Laitinen reported that hop compounds in beer delay development of osteoporosis (Tobe 1997 and Laitinen 1999). Franceschi inventoried the status of 1,371 Italian women aged forty to sixty-four looking for causes of low bone density: *The lack of association with alcohol intake (for low bone mineral density) is of special interest since this study was carried out in an area with high intakes of alcoholic beverages among women, thus providing further evidence against any relation between alcohol consumption and osteoporosis* (Franceschi 1996).

In the U.S., Rapuri noted that reports on the effects of drinking on osteoporosis were not consistent. He found significantly higher spine, total body and mid-radius bone density in the drinkers: *Moderate alcohol intake was associated with higher BMD in post menopausal elderly women* (Rapuri 2000). These studies clearly debunk the previous emphasis that any drinking promotes osteoporosis.

More good news

✔ Moderate drinking supports good bone density: " . . . recognized that alcohol abuse is associated with greater risk of fracture in men . . . in men moderate drinking (1 or 2 drinks a day) does not appear to have a detrimental effect on BMD. Even high drinking levels in this older cohort did not appear to decrease BMD" (May 1995).

✔ In Australia, a study of elderly men over 60 determined: ". . . moderate alcohol consumption was one of several factors protective against fracture" (Nguyen 1996).

✔ In Japan, a study supports frequency in drinking: "Drinking less than 3 days per week combined with smoking has a negative effect on radius bone mineral density in older women" (Takada 1997).

✔ A European study also supports frequent consumption: "In older women, regular consumption on more than 5 days per week is associated with a reduced risk" (Naves Diaz 1997).

A recent Hawaiian study utilizes biochemical markers of bone formation to assess the impact of drinks and lifestyle factors and concludes: *These findings suggest that biochemical markers may help to identify life-style factors that affect bone (density) and provide estimates of the relative magnitude of these effects on bone formation and bone resorption, independent of each other. Lifestyle factors like alcohol use may modify bone loss by affecting the remodeling balance during the first year of menopause, when bone turnover is highest* (Hia 2001). Tucker speculated: *This positive association has been hypothesized to be caused by the effects of alcohol on adrenal androgens or estrogen concentrations* (Tucker 2002). Shouldn't menopausal women be aware of these findings?

In Europe, Japan, Australia and the U.S., moderate drinking has been found to strengthen bone density. The *Ninth Special Report to Congress on Alcohol and Health* produced by the National Institute on Alcohol Abuse and Alcoholism and the Department of Health and Human Services briefly acknowledges a linkage of bone health with drinking. However, in over 400 pages of data on health and drinking, the editors could find no space for the extensive positive studies reported here. The government's sole contribution is this less than informative, two-line paragraph:

> *From a broader perspective, clarification of alcohol's effects on estrogen levels will be important in view of studies that show that estrogen and moderate drinking each may have protective effects in preventing post menopausal cardiovascular disease (Gavaler et al. 1991) and studies that show estrogen replacement can deter progression of osteoporosis (Breslau 1994). Thus, potentially beneficial effects of alcohol consumption in preventing cardiovascular disease and osteoporosis must be weighed against the possibility of increased risk for breast cancer and other alcohol-associated endocrine- metabolic disorders.*

Alcohol and the Endocrine System, Ninth Special Report to Congress on Alcohol and Health, DHHS, Washington, D.C., pp 158-163, June 1997

For osteoporosis, the *Ninth Special Report to Congress on Alcohol and Health* follows the politically correct line established by its predecessors (dating from Noble's tenure). Less drinking is better. The federal health agencies must believe that positive health data about drinking would only confuse Congress and America's senior citizens. While noting some undefined "potential beneficial effects," in drinking, the benefits are quickly downgraded by association with breast cancer, endocrine problems and metabolic disorders. Damned with faint praise.

Many medical newsletters and federal health agencies continue to ignore a solid line of favorable bone density research. The twenty million-plus osteoporosis sufferers in America remain oblivious of these data.

Drink therapy. Something to bone-up on.

Chapter 24

Healthy Pleasure

Pleasures enhance
a healthy lifestyle

Author's abstract: A prominent theme through all of Salvatore Lucia's writing is the belief that drinks provide a *plus* value in daily life —mood elevation. Of course, Lucia was an Italian American. Italians are known for their robust, engaging demeanor. For others, especially those reared under conservative Puritanical constraints, the unbridled pursuit of pleasure can be considered an occasion of sin. In its ability to induce euphoria, drinking can be one of those ineffable healthy pleasures.

- Correct alcohol use conveys significant health benefits
- The engine of good health runs on pleasure

America enjoys a unique philosophical and political association with pleasure. The second paragraph of the Declaration of Independence reads:

> . . . that they are endowed by their Creator with certain unalienable rights, that among these are Life,

*Liberty and the Pursuit of Happiness. That to secure
these Rights, Governments are instituted . . .*

The framers of the Constitution believed that governments are
instituted, at least in part, to enhance the pursuit of happiness.
Our constitution ranks happiness up there with life and liberty
– declaring all three to be God-given entitlements. The new
government was empowered to protect and to promote each of
these sacred rights. The document goes on to say that the
government should organize its powers in such form . . . *as to
them shall seem most likely to effect their Safety and Happiness.*
Governments were directed to move beyond providing nourishment, safety and the personal freedoms. Quality of life and the
quest for pleasure were new priorities. This is our heritage.

As this book amply demonstrates, responsible drinking can
yield pleasure while it improves health. A pleasure-endowed,
contented lifestyle promotes good health, as self-indulgence and
squalid living habits engender disease. The similarities, along
with the critical distinction between moderation and excessive
consumption, are nicely articulated in the following quote from
Fermented Food Beverages in Nutrition:

> *Clearly alcohol can serve many purposes through its
> pharmacological and symbolic characteristics. It
> gives pleasure, reduces pain, eliminates fears, raises
> self-esteem, solves conflict and so on. But basically
> the pleasurable experience underlies all alcohol
> problems and perhaps all alcohol use.*

Morse, R., Alcoholism: How Do You Get It?, in Fermented Food Beverages in Nutrition,
Academic Press, N.Y., 1979

This prescient statement supports the premise of this book.
Drinking gives pleasure. The difference between responsible
drinking and abuse lies in the dose. Governments today establish restrictions on the availability and the use of alcohol in the
hope of stemming abuse. But laws and regulations do not alter
human nature. Limitations on the quest for pleasure must ultimately rest with each individual. Americans today avidly seek
novel experiences in food and drink. Similar adaptations of
pleasurable foods and beverages is a common thread through
all human history. In *Tastes of Paradise: A Social History of Spices,*

Stimulants, and Intoxicants, Schivelbusch depicts how various spices and drinks have enjoyed glory days and perpetuity in the pleasuring sun. The author shows how cultures are ever alert for new taste titillations:

> *Spices had a ceremonial as well as a culinary function . . . . Besides being used in food, spices were presented as gifts, like jewels, and collected like precious objects . . . . The symbolic meaning and actual physical taste of medieval spices were closely intertwined. . . . Even though at first the effect is powerfully exciting or intoxicating, it levels off with habitual use. This is true not only for individuals, but also for entire cultures . . . All the exotic spices, stimulants and intoxicants introduced to European civilization in modern times have gone through this process, becoming habitual or domesticated.*

Schivelbusch, W., Tastes of Paradise, A Social History of Spices, Stimulants, and Intoxicants, Pantheon Books, New York, 1992

In the American edition of his book, Schivelbusch expresses astonishment over the fad for bottled water: *. . . for the Yuppie of the eighties, mineral water actually was a gustatory delight. If we assume that every drug stimulates the narcissistic nature of the individual – his self-pleasure – then the fad for mineral waters in the eighties may well have been a unique chapter in the history of drugs.*

Pleasure as guide, proof and triumph

Tiger asserts that the pursuit of pleasure engenders societal stability and continuity both for individuals and for society as a whole. In *The Pursuit of Pleasure,* he concludes: *Pleasure resonates as an imperative . . . . It was and is central to our deepest accountancy, finally as clear-cut as the mysterious certainty of soaring music. Pleasure as guide, pleasure as proof, pleasure as tonic, pleasure as festivity, pleasure as fun and as triumph* (Tiger 1992). Tiger envisions an aesthetic level for pleasure that is uniquely human. All living things great and small seek pleasures beyond mere animal needs. Humans can intellectualize pleasure beyond the reach of plant or animal. Happiness abounds – in the beguiling smile of a child, in the delicate colors of a wildflower along the trail, in vanquishing an opponent in chess, in listening to a rapturous

etude, and, yes, in downing a cold one (or two) with a treasured
friend. Pleasure and good health are as one.

One of the unresolved issues in the new millennium revolves
around how societies should control alcohol and street drugs.
This book separates drinking from the ongoing controversies
surrounding the drug war for one compelling reason. Drinks are
foods which are capable of both therapeutic and life-giving
manifestations. Control programs are more effective in alcohol-
integrated societies because drinks are embedded in the daily
diet. In contrast, nations which lump alcohol and drugs in the
same prevention pot – Norway, Sweden, Great Britain, Ireland,
Australia, Canada and the United States – all have demonstrably more alcohol problems.

To explore these issues, a symposium titled "Permission for
Pleasure: Alcohol and Pleasure from a Health Perspective" was
staged in New York in 1998 by the International Center for
Alcohol Policies (ICAP). ICAP is a Washington, D.C. based
advocacy funded by international drink interests. The event
mingled experts from the social and medical sciences as well as
drinks professionals from thirty nations. Keynoters Peele and
Brodsky suggested the following guidelines to convey to young
people a deserved respect for responsible drinking:

*1. Alcohol is legal and widely available. 2. Alcohol
may be misused with serious consequences. 3. More
people use alcohol in a socially positive way than in
a socially negative way. 4. Alcohol use in this positive
way conveys significant benefits. 5. Individuals need
to develop skills at drinking. 6. Groups with positive
drinking styles should be emulated. 7. Positive
drinking equals something like regular, moderate
consumption in a positive social environment with
people of both genders. 8. Alcohol produces the most
positive benefit within an overall positive structure.*

Peele, S., and Brodsky, A., Permission for Pleasure, Symposium, ICAP, Washington, D.C.,
1998

Ornstein and Sobel recommend a new perspective based upon
the contributions of pleasure to an ordered society:

*Imagine the world without pleasure. Life would
appear colorless and humorless. A baby's smile
would go unappreciated. Foods would be tasteless.
The beauty of a Bach concerto would fall on deaf
ears. Feelings like joy, thrills, delights, ecstasy,
elation and happiness would disappear.*

Ornstein, R., and Sobel, D., Healthy Pleasures, Addison-Wesley Publishing Company,
Reading, Massachusetts, 1989

The authors present research on the benefits of moderate
drinking in the care of the elderly, a manifestation notably
lacking in American medicine (see Chapter 10): *Two months after
the hospital staff began offering an afternoon beer to the geriatric
patients, the number of them who could walk on their own increased
from 21 percent to 74 percent . . . Social interaction tripled, and the
percentage of patients taking Thorazine, a strong tranquilizer, plunged
from 75 percent to zero* (Ornstein 1989). In mysterious ways,
drinking and other innocent pleasures can assuage real or imagi-
nary illnesses. Drinking pleasures are uniquely appropriate for
seniors.

Two seemingly inconsequential studies demonstrate the
power of small gratifications. A study of 7,841 male graduates
of Harvard University reported in the *British Medical Journal*
that: . . . *individuals allowing themselves only one to three candy bars
a month fared the best, having a 36 percent lower risk of death compared
with non-candy eaters.* (British Medical Journal 1998). *HealthNews*
in January 1999 reported on several studies which suggest:
*Women with strong social networks may have less of the artery clogging
that causes heart disease than women who are more socially isolated*
(HealthNews 1999). Candy bars and a social calendar are small
pleasures which combine with other moderate lifestyles for a
grand payoff. Human beings are not automatons. The pleasures
we cultivate can have enormous influence on how we think and
feel, love and laugh, and on how we suffer.

The Associates for Research Into the Science of Enjoyment
(ARISE) sponsored a pleasure-oriented conference in Amster-
dam in 1995 titled "Living is More Than Surviving." Presenters
represented twenty nations. The *London Daily Express* reported:
ARISE holds that health tyrants are turning people into wimps, and

urges people to indulge in more drinking, smoking, sex, sticky puddings and chocolates (A bit of what you fancy 1995). In *Newsweek*, ARISE chairperson Warburton notes: *Guilt creates stress hormones which in turn mobilise fatty acids such as cholesterol* (International scientists advise eat, drink and be merry 1997). A thought provoking book – *Alcohol and Pleasure: A Health Perspective* – was published in 1999 by ICAP (Brunner/Mazel, Philadelphia) containing excerpts from the Permissions for Pleasure symposium. One chapter contributed by alcohol anthropologist Heath takes this position:

> *During much of this century, there has been growing awareness of and concern about the many kinds of harm that can result from drinking —physiological and psychic, as well as social and economic . . . . It is apt that the theme of permission for pleasure be dealt with largely in terms of beverage alcohol as a case study, if only because research and writings on the subject of drinking have for so long been predominantly focused on pathological, negative, or risky aspects, even though the popular consensus on the part of most people is that drinking is positive and pleasurable. It is still, as Bacon (1943) observed over 50 years ago, as if we were trying to understand the role of the automobile by paying attention only to traffic accidents.*

Heath, D., Drinking and Pleasure Across Cultures in Alcohol and Pleasure: A Health Perspective, Peele, S. and Grant, M., editors, Brunner/Mazel, Philadelphia, 1999

In his book *Healthy Pleasures*, Ornstein contends: *. . . the human desire for enjoyment evolved to enhance our survival. Doing what feels right and feeling good are beneficial for health and survival of the species* (Ornstein 1989). These authorities advise embracing many pleasurable avenues – drinking included – which reward in good measure:

> *You possess the ultimate health instrument within yourself, one which runs on pleasure. So, attending to your work, and family, getting an education and helping others not only make you a good citizen, but protects you —perhaps more than diet, more than medicine, more than surgery. It is your relationship to*

> *life itself that brings life . . . . So why not fill your life*
> *with healthy pleasures? (Ornstein 1989)*

Ornstein, R., and Sobel, D., Healthy Pleasures, Addison-Wesley Publishing company,
Reading, Massachusetts, 1989

Many conservatives may question the consideration of a
health potential of "pleasure" in a scientific review. That may
be a key problem in American medicine — too great a dependence upon chemistry and too little adherence to the naturally
endowed healing powers resident in all humans. When the *New
England Journal of Medicine* released Mukamal's recent study
concerning the efficacy of frequent drinking, Tiger responded
in the *Wall Street Journal* with this bon mot: *Why does a society
provide good news with a grim face? No one appears to be the Minister
of Fun around here because no one seems allowed to whoop with pleasure
when a rather cheerful finding is published in the New England Journal
of Medicine to the effect that moderate but relatively frequent drinking
can reduce the risk of heart attack* (Tiger 2003).

"Pleasure cognizant" scientists warmly embrace responsible
drinking, Lucia's "plus" factor.

So do we. In good measure!

Chapter 25

Stress

Drinks and faith can lessen anxiety

■ **Author's abstract**: Common sense and thousands of years of recorded medical history should be sufficient to argue the case that both drinks and religious faith are primary stress relievers. In recent years, medicine has warmed to the idea that religious faith has the potential to help control stress. Here are some positive votes for religious faith and moderate drinking:

■ ➡ Alcohol has been medically prescribed to calm nerves in civilized societies for thousands of years
➡ Faith can help individuals to cope with life's problems
➡ Without the warnings provided by stress hormones, we would be unable to react sufficiently to danger
➡ Alcohol acts to reduce both panic and anxiety

The oldest of all human ailments is anxiety, the offspring of fear. It is still the most universal of all complaints . . . The caveman threatened by the

*sabre-toothed tiger had the same anxiety as the Wall
Street broker in a bear market. The caveman and the
broker have found in naturally fermented products a
certain measure of relief. Every race and tribe that
could get it has used and appreciated this surcease
from worry, depression and stress.*

Wine and Health, in Wine and Medical Practice, Wine Institute, San Francisco, 1979

It is fortuitous that stress falls alphabetically after a discussion
of pleasure. Millions of Americans favor a "wee drop" at quitting
time to shed work-day pressures, to effect a transition from stress
to the pleasurable hours. This generally beneficial ritual, this
same pathway to stress relief — taken one drink too far — can
slip into a pattern of abuse which foments additional stress. No
animal born — from the ponderous elephant to the frustrated
toddler to the majestic lion — is exempt from stress. Stress comes
in many forms. Humans even contrive it where none exists.
Alcohol has provided a unique surcease from life's trifling pressures and, at times, from stress's relentless terrors — for both
man and beast.

The common denominator

It may come as news that the quest for intoxicants encom-
passes the entire animal kingdom. In his authoritative treatise
Intoxication: Life in Pursuit of Artificial Paradise, Siegel writes:
*Intoxicants have been a natural part of the diet of life ever since it began
on this planet. Intoxication, by definition the entry into a state of
toxicity, will never be totally free, but it will always be (Siegel 1989).*
Siegel details how spiders, elephants, birds and tigers, along
with humans, seek out plant sources which produce naturally
fermented alcohol or other psychoactive drugs.

In a 1966 medical text, Leake cites an ancient and honorable
role for alcohol in the relief of stress:

*Although high blood-alcohol concentrations may have
undesirable or dangerous effects on the central
nervous system, it is obvious that lower
concentrations have effects which indicate valuable
clinical applications. Probably the most striking is the
use of alcoholic beverages to reduce emotional*

tension . . . . The use of alcoholic beverages in medicine is suggested at the outset by the fact that these beverages have been prescribed for thousands of years by physicians in nearly every civilized country in the world. Thus, they rank among the oldest drugs known to medicine. Such an endorsement should at least alert modern physicians to the possible applications of alcohol.

Leake, C., and Silverman, M., Alcoholic Beverages in Clinical Medicine, Year Book Medical Publishers, Inc., Chicago, 1966

Religion as stress reducer

A diversion into the role of faith in augmenting good health is warranted. In February 1998, the *Harvard Health Letter* cited religious faith as an ancient therapeutic tool for the relief of human stress:

In another study, Duke University researchers found an association between increased immune function and regular attendance at religious services . . . those who attended services at least once a week were about half as likely as non-attendees to have high blood levels of interleukin-6, a protein that regulates immune and inflammatory responses in the body.

Making a Place for Spirituality, Harvard Health Letter, Vol. 23, No. 4, February, 1998

The article "Can Religion Be Good Medicine" in the November 1998 issue of *The Johns Hopkins Medical Letter* notes: *There are several hypotheses on how religion influences health. One is that religion helps people cope with stress. During any stressful situation, the body's adrenal glands release a flood of chemicals that effectively raise heart rate and blood pressure. Praying or reading religious texts at home seem to help* (Can Religion Be 1998). In "Faith and Longevity: Is There a Link?" *Harvard Men's Health Watch* notes: *The investigators argue for religion, noting that the apparent protection extended beyond cardiovascular disease to include all major causes of death. More study will be needed to determine the relative health impact of religious belief and conventional risk factors* (Faith and Longevity 1997).

In "Ties That Bind: Social Networks and Health," *Harvard Men's Health Watch* discusses stress and religion. In one long-term project, seven thousand subjects of Alameda County, California were observed for nearly three decades: *After 28 years of observation, attendance at religious services was associated with a reduced risk of death. In all, individuals who attended services frequently were 36 percent less likely to die than people who attended infrequently* (Ties That Bind 1999). Drinks promote social intercourse and relaxation, particularly when shared with close friends. Drinking benefits are similar to those realized in the practice of a religious faith. The article above concludes: *The four recent investigations emphasize the link between social supports and good health* (Ties That Bind 1999). These studies emphasize once again that alcohol is not the only arrow in the quiver. But religious faith and moderate consumption join with a bevy of gratifying lifestyle practices which can extend life, and provide robust health along the way.

Another article, "A Health Benefit From the Holidays," appeared in *Harvard Women's Health Watch*. The authors note: *In the California study, those who worshipped regularly tended to have better health practices, more social contacts, and more stable marriages – factors that also bode well for longevity* (A Health Benefit 1999). Is it any wonder that so many religions utilize drinks in worship services, so closely are the goals allied? In "Optimism and Health," *Harvard Men's Health Watch* notes that: . . . *a positive mental outlook can promote good physical health, particularly for the heart and circulation* (Optimism 2001). It is encouraging to find some recognition of unrelated lifestyle research in medical newsletters. This book recommends a great deal more cross-referencing of biomedical studies with the social science disciplines. Epidemiology is proving that the ten thousand year use of alcohol in medical practice was no fluke.

Stress in illness

No one knows the extent of human illness exacted by various dimensions of stress. Neither are there effective tools to measure the benefits of drinks in reducing stress. But stress also has a health-protective dimension. Stress hormones are essential in alerting the body to respond to real or perceived threats. But persistent, unrelieved stress can contribute to many major ill-nesses as found in *Harvard Health Letter: Before Hippocrates (500 B.C.) and until contemporary times, doctors believed that "the pas-sions" played a role in causing disease . . . . Most human research on stress and health has looked at the link between emotions, hypertension and heart disease . . . . There is some, but inconclusive, evidence that stress may somehow be linked to cancer . . . . When experts recommend that people reduce stress in their lives . . . It may simply mean exercising more, expanding your social circle, reaching out to others, joining a support group, or putting traffic jams into perspective* (Can Stress Make You Sick?1998).

Lipton found yet another variation of the U-shaped curve demonstrating benefits in the use of alcohol for stress manage-ment: *Moderate alcohol use may be an indicator of a spectrum of generally moderate behavior which serves to either reduce the effect of stress on depression or suppress the effects of stress* (Lipton   1993).

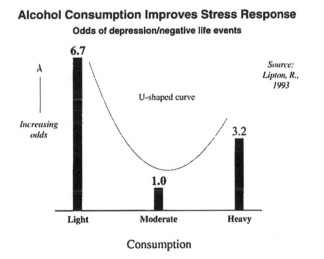

Alcohol Consumption Improves Stress Response
Odds of depression/negative life events

Graph reprinted with permission of Wine Institute from data used with permission of American Journal of Public Health, The effects of moderate alcohol use and the relationship between stress and depression, Lipton, 84:1913–1917, 1994. Copyright by the American Public Health Association, 1994.

Lipton's work is more clinical evidence of Lucia's favorite mood-elevating "plus factor." Note that drinking does not nec-essarily initiate stress. In this study, Lipton followed 928 non-

Hispanic Californians for a year discovering that moderate drinkers also reported lower depression rates.

The *UC Berkeley Wellness Letter* defines the profound role of human stress in balancing the inevitable challenges of human living: *All organisms have to experience stress and adjust to it. Being born is stressful. Being alive is stressful. Without our stress hormones we would be unable to react effectively, or to deal with hunger, crowding, danger, infection, extremes of temperature or the challenges of growing up* (Demystifying stress 1998). In an 1999 article in *Alcohol Research and Health*, Sayette notes: *For centuries, people have used alcohol to relieve stress . . . Alcohol consumption can result in a stress-response dampening (SRD) effect, which can be assessed using various measures* (Sayette 1999). In the same issue, Volpicelli writes: *After a traumatic event, people often report using alcohol to relieve their symptoms of anxiety, irritability, and depression. Alcohol may relieve these symptoms because drinking compensates for deficiencies in endorphin activity following a traumatic experience* (Volpicelli 1999).

Kushner evaluated alcohol consumption and panic disorders and concluded: *Alcohol acts acutely to reduce both panic and anxiety surrounding panic* (Kushner 1996). This may explain why so many instinctively rush to find a drink after experiencing a life-threatening event. Houston Control is famous for providing beer to returning astronauts. Great Britain's ARISE group discovered that social drinkers have a longer life span because they laugh more than their sober-sided associates. Lowe summarizes this argument: *That the mean frequency of laughter score for the group that consumed alcohol was significantly greater than for those who did not consume alcohol* (Lowe 1997).

In a treatise on drinking and longevity published by the American Council on Science and Health, Ellison remarks: *Thus, while the consumption of large amounts of alcohol tends to shorten life, the consumption of small to moderate amounts of alcohol is associated with the prolongation of life* (Ellison 1993).

Alcohol and stress

From these data, it is safe to say that responsible drinking can aid in the relief of harmful stress. It's the reason that humans, birds and elephants seek alcohol fermentations in various plant life. Many studies connect the relief of stress with reduced incidence of major illnesses. *Harvard Men's Health Watch* in "Depression and Other Cardiovascular Diseases" notes: *A study of nearly 3,000 Americans between the ages of 25 and 64 found that depression was associated with an 80 percent increase in the likelihood of developing hypertension* (Depression and Other 1999). Another article, "Mental Stress and Respiratory Infections," reports: *More than a dozen investigations have asked if stress increases susceptibility to the common cold: all have concluded that it does* (Mental Stress 1999). Is this why the drinkers in Cohen's common cold studies were more resistant to cold viruses? Stress relief in drinking ranges from the common cold to hypertension.

HealthNews in "Physical Effects of Stress" reports: *The paper examines more than 100 studies done in the past decade . . . Whether it's the stress of daily life, the pressures of any executive job, frustrations of a lower level position, or even social upheaval in an unstable country . . . Chronic stress also effects the immune system, increasing susceptibility to infections* (Physical Effects 1998). But one must not forget that many other studies link the creation of stress to abusive drinking. One study by Heien notes: *The empirical results based on data from Canada and the United States indicate that ethnic and stress factors strongly influence alcohol abuse* (Heien 1987). These data confirm that moderate drinkers and abusers use identical rationales for drinking, as reported earlier by Morse. Both seek relief from real or imagined stress. In that quest, the abuser vaults the well-defined markers for moderation: *In its nature and quality, however, his drinking has changed from that of a nonalcoholic* (Morse 1979).

"Wine's history as therapy for mankind" lends a scientific rationale for alcohol as stress reliever. Friedman writes:

> A component of wine, ethyl 4-hydroxybutyrate, may explain its ability to reduce emotional tension, relieve anxiety, and produce relaxation. Geriatric studies have shown that the use of wine with meals did reduce the need for sleeping medications and sedatives at nursing homes. Also, it improved appetite and lowered stress and tension.

Friedman, S., Wine's history as therapy for mankind, Wines and Vines, December 2, 1992

The Friedman article discusses a number of chemicals in wine that have distinctive healthful impacts. Spirits and beer have some of the same or similar components. Poikolainen in *Contemporary Drug Problems* finds a positive outcome in responsible use: *To sum up, alcohol may protect healthy persons from stressor-induced anxiety if they also are engaged in activities demanding at least a moderate degree of attention. Alcohol also seems to decrease anxiety among patients with phobias or benign essential tremor* (Poikolainen 1994). (See following chapter on tremors.)

A paper on this issue was delivered to the symposium "Alcohol and Wine in Health and Disease" by Antoshechkin containing the following conclusion:

> *Mild doses of alcohol enhance man's physical performance which is why alcohol is included in the list of banned substances by the International Olympic committee.*
>
> *. . . many people feel psychological tension at the end of their workday, which is a manifestation of light stress. Intake of mild-to-moderate doses of alcohol eliminates these stress manifestations, which provides at least partial motivation for the consumption of alcoholic beverages.*

Physiological Model of the Stimulative Effects of Alcohol in Low-to-Moderate Doses, Anatoly G. Antoshechkin, Annals of the New York Academy of Sciences, 957:288-291, 2002

This research establishes drinks as effective stress reducers. Rodgers, in Canberra, Australia, studied risk factors for depression in abstainers, moderate drinkers and heavy drinkers and reported: *Abstainers have a range of characteristics known to be associated with anxiety, depression and other facets of ill mental health, and these factors may contribute significantly to their elevated levels of depression and anxiety relative to moderate drinkers* (Rodgers 2000).

Despite these cross-disciplinary findings, many physicians are cautious about recommending drinking for the relief of stress because they fear that the patients will overdrink. Sound familiar? Grossarth-Maticek compared 900 subjects who were undergoing stress contrasted with a control group of 806 who were not. The authors dispassionately recounted both the good and the bad news: *People who were not stressed and drank for pleasure had the lowest mortality rate, while those who were stressed and drank to drown their sorrows had the highest mortality rate* (Grossarth-Maticek 1991). This is balanced reporting, but Gordis, in another NIAAA Alcohol Alert, "Alcohol and Stress", has nothing positive to contribute: *Drinking alcohol produces physiological stress, that is, some of the body's responses to alcohol are similar to its responses to other stressors . . . Why people should engage in an activity that produces effects similar to those they are trying to relieve is a paradox that we do not yet understand* (Gordis 1996). The government's constant refrain – less is better.

There is no question that drinking can produce physiological stress. Heien notes: *The empirical results based on data from Canada and the United States indicate that ethnic and stress factors strongly influence alcohol abuse. The stress variables include the rates of unemployment and divorce* (Stress, Ethnic and Distribution Factors 1987). But it is not the mere presence of drinks in society that predicates physiological stress. Other factors – unemployment, marital discord, mental illness – foment the stress that generates alcohol abuse.

The clinical physician has a formidable task in determining whether a patient will exercise discretion or binge-out to drown sorrows if any drinking is recommended. This is perhaps why physicians have leaned on the century-old "Anstie's Limit." Anstie resolved the drinking riddle by informing his patients – male and female – to consume no more than 1 1/2 ounces of absolute alcohol in any twenty-four-hour period, the equivalent of three standard drinks.

The Anstie tradition has been replaced in the U.S. by the recommendation of no more than one drink daily for women and two for men (see Chapter 31). Government policies which discourage all drinking, without distinction as to amount or merit, likely add in some degree to human stress. Some clinicians may question the inclusion of faith, personal income and alcohol therapy as stress reducers in a medical text. But, the current interest in complementary and alternative medicine will inevitably bring into consideration anything and everything that has the potential of reducing harmful stress.

I'll drink to that.

Chapter 26

Essential Tremors

A small drink can
work wonders

■ **Author's abstract**: In this extensive aggregation of drinking and health science, no entry pleases me more than this one. Though I include some scientific references, the primary example is provided by a former dentist who developed an essential tremor in one hand which began about twenty years ago.

■ ◦ Many ET sufferers find that a small drink can be a big help

As many as five million Americans, mostly over sixty years of age, suffer from an irritating condition called essential tremor (ET). Essential tremor usually involves the rhythmic shaking of a body part, limb or even the vocal cords. Perhaps the most famous victim of ET is the actress Katherine Hepburn whose tremor dissembles her speech. A 1995 article in *Parade* explains the condition:

It is called essential tremor because that's all there is — a tremor. It has no known cause or cure and is often confused with other ailments, particularly Parkinson's disease, a seriously debilitating condition.

Stern, C., If Your Hand Trembles, Parade Magazine, July 23, 1995

Another informative article in the *Mayo Clinic Health Letter* advises:

Not everyone with essential tremor needs to see a doctor. If your shaking is only a mild irritation, you probably don't need medical attention. However, if the tremors are affecting your lifestyle, or you have other concerns, your physician can help you decide whether you need treatment. Diagnosing essential tremor involves ruling out other causes that can result in hand, head or voice tremors.

Essential Tremor, Mayo Clinic Health Letter, Vol. 15, No. 3, March, 1997

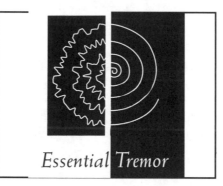

Reprinted with permission of the International Tremor Foundation, Overland Park, Kansas .

The logo here appears on *ET: A Patient Information Handbook* published by the International Tremor Foundation. It portrays a common clinical test for hand tremors. The patient draws a continuous concentric circle with the tremor-afflicted hand. In the logo, the jagged lines of the hand with a tremor fade into the neater lines drawn by an unaffected hand. The Mayo Clinic article explains how a very small number of people with disabling tremors may choose corrective surgery.

Another common therapy omitted in the Mayo article might be called drink therapy. An acquaintance of mine was afflicted by tremors in one hand several decades ago. The tremor became so pronounced that he had to give up a flourishing dental practice. I asked him to prepare a short commentary on his experiences. In the 1970s, he was referred to the Mayo Clinic to make certain that the tremor was not Parkinson's related or some other life-threatening condition.

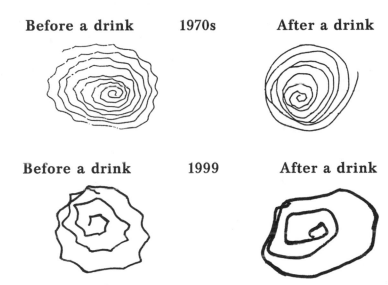

Before a drink 1970s **After a drink**

Before a drink 1999 **After a drink**

Drawings from a confidential source

Following the revelation of ET, the attending physician at Mayo Clinic advised my source to take the above test:

At the Mayo Clinic, one of the attending physicians, Dr. F. M. Howard, suggested I go down to the hotel bar and see what effect alcohol (in moderation) would have on my tremor. So my wife and I did go to the Elizabethan Room of the Kahler Hotel in Rochester, MN and, at 6:00 PM (I kept detailed notes of that entire week), I drank a double screwdriver. At 6:20 PM, twenty minutes later, I determined that I was able to draw with my right hand concentric circles with almost no oscillating type of irregular lines —circles that one hour earlier were

*characterized by the squiggley, jagged lines typical
of my tremor.*

Confidential source

My friend retained the first test and produced the second set of circles shown above for this book nearly thirty years later. Obviously, over a span of several decades, the mild drink therapy continues to work for him. My friend's report is what scientists would call anecdotal data. It was not part of a scientifically controlled study. But it is certainly encouraging information that could be passed on to patients newly afflicted with ET.

Some readers may question why *Mayo Clinic Health Letter* article does not mention this common therapy. Their article continues: *Most people with essential tremor don't need treatment . . . . Medication and surgery aren't cures for essential tremor, but they can help bring it under control* (Essential Tremor 1997). Surely for a clientele mostly over sixty years of age, the risk of consumptive drinking when taken for the relief of tremors must be very, very slim. The omission of this therapy in informative advisories has to be deliberate and short-sighted. Ironically, it was a Mayo physician who passed on the original advice to my friend nearly thirty years ago.

When I submitted a draft of this book to a nephew physician for review and comment, I was provided another anecdotal evidence of the efficacy of drink therapy for ET. My nephew wrote: *He is a 63 year old patient with a history of what was diagnosed as benign essential tremor . . . He responded partially to a trial of a commonly used prescription drug but did not like the dry mouth and fatigue side effects. So, after starting a regularly scheduled use of 1 - 2 glasses of red wine daily, he noted at least 50 percent, usually 75 percent subjective improvement. On days when he would have one glass with lunch and one with dinner he was better. Now he is more functional in terms of fine motor coordination and writing* (Ford 2003).

These two anecdotal reports testify to the long history in clinical practice of alcohol therapy for ET. A 1999 article in *HealthNews*, published by *The New England Journal of Medicine*, "Grasping Essential Tremor," does mention alcohol but, for totally obtuse reasons, it recommends against its use for tremors:

Some people have accidentally found improvement with alcohol consumption (though this route is not recommended) (Grasping Essential Tremor 1999). Why would major medical newsletters discourage a non-invasive and demonstrably safe remedy which has served my friend (and undoubtedly thousands of others) for nearly thirty years? The recommendation to avoid alcohol shows an unreasonable depth of medical ambivalence.

I found some validation for alcohol therapy in the professional literature, but not much. Boecker studied the effect of ethanol on essential tremor patients and concluded: *Alcohol-associated increases of regional cerebral blood flow were observed in the inferior olivary nuclei in the patients but not in the control subjects. We conclude that alcohol-induced suppression of essential tremor is mediated via a reduction of cerebellar synaptic over activity resulting in increased afferent input to the inferior olivary nuclei* (Boecker 1996). In less complex verbiage, the therapy works!

In earlier chapters, I have noted several instances in which medical newsletters are relaxing their apparent opposition to drinking. An article "Setting a Steady Course for Benign Essential Tremor" in the December 1999 issue of the *Johns Hopkins Medical Letter* represents this trend: *Although alcohol worsens some forms of tremor, and tremor is a symptom of alcohol withdrawal, a small amount of alcohol improves essential tremor in about three quarters of patients. Therefore, many sufferers have a drink shortly before meals or social events. But alcohol should be used judiciously and should not be taken with anti-tremor medications* (Setting a Steady 1999). This is the kind of balanced reporting we should expect from all medical authority. Alcohol doesn't work for all tremors and the dose is very much the thing.

A Q&A series in the August 1998 issue of *Harvard Men's Health Watch* provides an interesting response to this question, "My wife is worried that I am becoming an alcoholic. I'm not drinking any more than usual, but I do really seem to need a drink to steady my nerves in the evenings. Without the drink, my hands shake so much that it's hard to eat or drink without spilling things." The *Health Letter* responded:

Your response to alcohol is quite typical; many people with essential tremor find that a small drink is dramatically beneficial, but the effect wears off in an hour or so. Larger amounts of alcohol don't work any better, so you shouldn't increase your intake beyond a safe limit of two drinks a day.

On Call, Harvard Men's Health Watch, August, 1998

This commendable advice suggests a reasonable daily limit without discouraging the therapy. This author assumes that readers can distinguish between a drink or two daily and excess. Would not similar responses have worked in the *Mayo Clinic Health Letter* and *HealthNews* articles? If alcohol can ease an ET sufferer's embarrassment and lessen social stress, its use rivals the relief obtained from diazepam, clozapine or alprazolam, each of which has its own risky or pesky side effects.

A small drink may resolve a very shaky problem.

Chapter 27

Ulcers

Protection against ulcer bacteria

■ **Author's abstract**: This chapter reports on one of the strange twists that often turn medicine on its ear. What was thought for decades to be an irritant for — or even the cause of — stomach ulcers turns out to provide protection against them. The risks for some ulcers are lower among moderate drinkers. The breakthrough was the identification of a common bacteria responsible for the bulk of ulcers.

■ ↦ Nine out of ten ulcers are caused by a bacteria
  ↦ Emotional stress can raise ulcer risk
  ↦ An inverse relationship exists between alcohol and duodenal ulcers
  ↦ Alcohol may exert a protective effect against H. pylori

For decades, stress was considered a causal agent for gastric and duodenal ulcers. Alcohol was implicated in the etiology of both stress and ulcers. The previous chapter on stress established that drinking can both create damaging stress and moderate its deleterious effects, depending upon usage patterns. Here a *Johns Hopkins Medical Letter Health After 50* article discusses the bacterium H. pylori. It is depicted as the primary causal agent for many ulcers:

> *A recent survey on ulcers by the Centers for Disease Control and Prevention found that 60% of people still blame stress for ulcers, while only 25% are aware that the true culprit is a bacterium . . . . Research now shows that 9 out of 10 ulcers are caused by infection with H. pylori. In theory, the cure is simple: antibiotics, combined with acid-suppressing medications . . . . And as recently as 1995, only 5% of patients were being appropriately treated.*

Getting the Right Cure for Ulcers, the Johns Hopkins Medical Letter, Health After 50, Vol. 10, Issue 1, March, 1998

"Stress Still Plays A Role in Ulcer Formation" in the September 1999 *Tufts University Health & Nutrition Letter* cautions that stress still can be an causal irritant: *. . . in their haste to label ulcers as an easily treated bacterial infection, many doctors have forgotten that stress can still play a role . . . emotional stress can raise ulcer risk by increasing a person's output of stomach acid* (Stress Still Plays 1999). In addition to stress, over-the-counter pain relievers like the NSAID family (Ibuprofen etc.) represent an ulcer danger. In "Sizing Up the New Arthritis Drugs," *Health After 50* notes: *Every year, more than 75,000 hospitalizations and 7,500 deaths are attributed to stomach ulcers and hemorrhaging induced by NSAIDs. Older people, especially those who take NSAIDs on a daily basis, are at highest risk* (Sizing Up 1999). NSAIDs are commonly used in the treatment of arthritis.

Conventional ulcer treatment today is seen in "Life Sentence Gets Commuted" in the *Harvard Health Letter*: *His doctor treated him for two weeks with a combination of bismuth subsalicylate (the active ingredients in Pepto Bismol) and two antibiotics, tetracycline and metronidazole. This regimen has wiped out H. pylori in about 90% of patients* (Life Sentence 1999).

A bacterium to blame

Ulcers can still be serious business. Over 40,000 individuals each year undergo emergency surgery to stop ulcerous bleeding. The February 1997 issue of *Harvard Men's Health Watch* describes Helicobacter pylori (Hp):

> *H. pylori is a slender, spiral bacterium that appears to spread from person to person, presumably in food or water that has been contaminated by infected human fecal material. As a result, Hp infection is most common in areas with crowded living conditions and poor sanitation.*

Peptic Ulcer Disease: A Curable Infection, Harvard Men's Health Watch, Vol. 1, No. 7, February, 1997

Of even greater interest to this readership is the following speculation by the same authors that:

> *Finally, Hp has been statistically linked to coronary artery disease. Several studies have found that among men with coronary artery disease, 77-84 percent have antibodies that indicate Hp infection, but only 46-59 percent of men without heart disease have these antibodies.*

Here is another cross-disease linkage where drinking can benefit both problems. Drink components reduce the risk of both coronary disease and ulcers. Further cross-referencing suggests that infections like H. pylori, chlamydia, pneumonia, and cytomegalovirus contribute in some way to the development of atherosclerosis. An article and editorial in the December 2001 issue of *HealthNews* titled "H. pylori: What's the Story?" elaborates the positive and negative potential influences of Hp infection. It establishes a very wide base of that infection: *With over half of Americans over age 60 infected with H. pylori – millions of whom will develop stomach ulcers as a result – this lesser-known germ probably affects far more people than anthrax ever will* (H. pylori: What's the Story? 2001).

In the article's editorial, Bickston comments on the clinical trend to eradicate the infection: *But our enthusiasm for eradication has waned as we've learned more about the relation between Hp and conditions other than ulcers. Because Hp infection is so prevalent, it's often present in patients who have common GI problems . . . What has proved surprising is that clearing the germ often doesn't help these conditions — in fact, it may aggravate symptoms!* As is so often the case in research, new findings challenge old assumptions.

Comprehensive, cross-disease evaluation of all of the medical impacts of drinks could help physicians facing ulcers or other problems related to Hp. Many human ailments originate in the complex chemistry of the stomach and vascular system. Proof of a role for red wine in this puzzle was presented by Fugelsang in "The In Vitro Effect of Red Wine on Helicobacter pylori:"

> *Red wine proved superior to aqueous alcohol alone in decreasing the number of viable cells of Helicobacter pylori in vitro. The apparent ability of red wine to decrease viable cell counts of Helicobacter pylori might help explain the salutary effect of red wine on digestion and perhaps explain the lesser incidence of stomach cancer among red wine drinkers . . . . We have demonstrated that red wine is effective against the organism responsible for several aspects of gastric pathology, including cancer.*

Fugelsang, K., and Muller C., The In Vitro Effect of Red Wine on Helicobacter Pylori, Wine Health Symposium, American Society for Enology and Viticulture, Reno, 1996

Other researchers published in recent years agree. Ogihara concludes: *Alcohol may exert a protective antibacterial effect against new infections, it may be bactericidal against existing H. pylori* (Ogihara 2000). Bak Andersen tested clients in northern Europe and found: *Wine seems to be associated with a much lower risk than beer. It could be speculated that wine has a bactericidal or bacteriostatic effect on Helicobacter pylori* (Bak Andersen 2000). Rosenstock did similar studies in Denmark and decided: *Wine drinking is associated with lower rates of H. pylori infection in Danish adults* (Rosenstock 2000). The latter study found a thirty percent reduction of risk among wine drinkers. Brenner's title is interesting, "Alcohol as a gastric disinfectant?" His conclusion answers the question: *These results support the hypothesis that moderate drinking favours the suppression and eventual elimination of H. pylori infection. At higher drinking levels, the antimicrobial effects of alcohol may not outweigh the adverse systemic effects of alcohol, including its adverse effects on immune disease* (Brenner 2001). As have hundreds of researchers in this book, Brenner clearly distinguishes between moderate and abusive drinking. Most patients follow this advice, if given the chance.

There may even be some effects on cancer. Wine, particularly red wine, constitutes one of the most complex beverages in human consumption. In Germany, Brenner revealed: *The odds ratio of infection among subjects who consumed more than 75 g of alcohol per week compared with subjects who did not drink alcohol was 0.31. The inverse relation with H. pylori infection was stronger for alcohol consumed in the form of wine than for alcohol from beer . . . a clear inverse dose-response relationship, which persisted after controlling for potential confounders.*(Brenner 1999). As few as five drinks per week lowered risks. Another study by Russo involved 2,598 blood donors who volunteered to be tested for antibodies against H. pylori. The study found: *Smoking and heavy butter consumption may be risk factors for gastric IM (intestinal metaplasia) in H. pylori-positive individuals while alcohol use is no risk factor* (Russo 2001).

From data gathered in the Physician's Health Study, Aldoori determined a small decrease in the risk of duodenal ulcers for those who drank slightly over two drinks per day: *Adjusting for age, we observed a small inverse relation between alcohol consumption and risk of duodenal ulcer, comparing drinkers of more than 30 gm of alcohol per day with non-drinkers* (Aldoori 1997). H. pylori was discussed in an article by physician-journalist Isadore Rosenfeld in the December 7, 1997 issue of *Parade Magazine*. Rosenfeld provides his usual detailed description of the bacterium and advises those infected to get antibiotic treatment. He warns: *When ulcers are "hot" you should avoid caffeine, tobacco, alcohol and aspirin-like drugs. After that, eat anything you like, even chili peppers. Forget about diets – and psychiatrists* (Rosenfeld 1997). The author could have noted the many findings on how drinks seem to resist infection from the bacteria.

An interesting study released in 2002 reported that individuals who consumed alcohol had the best success rate during a week of conventional drug treatment designed to eradicate H. pylori. Baena and colleagues tested 156 patients in Barcelona, Spain suffering peptic ulcers or gastritis and found: *Eradication success was alcohol dose-dependent, with success rates increasing from 70.1% in teetotalers to 79.3% in patients drinking 4-16g per day and 100% in patients drinking 18-60g daily* (Baena 2002). This study demonstrates Lucia's claim that alcohol can act as an adjuvant to conventional medicines, adding to their total effect. Sixty grams daily is the equivalent of four standard drinks.

This book presents a variety of studies which evidence some positive relationships for many diseases – cardiovascular problems, cancers, stomach distress, tremors, stress, cognition and now even ulcers. Of course, many of these findings for lesser problems have a very shallow base of research. Much more study, definition and elaboration is needed to reach consensus on these early results. However, research dollars for alcohol-favorable studies are very difficult to find.

Alcohol benefits do not rank very high on the national research agenda. Despite this disparity, most of the high priority research projects inventory alcohol consumption so a steady stream of data can be expected in years to come. But the range of favorable findings already reported in this text demonstrate the many complex relationships of drinking to human health.

A story in need of telling.

Chapter 28

Skin Ulcers

An ancient salve rediscovered

■ **Author's abstract**: The likelihood that an attending physician will treat a skin ulcer today with red wine lies somewhere between remote and never. Yet this lone anecdotal report —not an ortho-dox research paper —is too fascinating to pass up. It constitutes a new exposure for a very old practice. For thousands of years, alcohol beverages were employed as antiseptics to cleanse and salve wounds and sores.

As in Chapter 15, this unit cites a single reference about an unheralded and comparatively unimportant alcohol benefit. The data is a reflection of the historic therapeutic uses for wine and other drinks over many long centuries. This report is taken from an issue of the *Bulletin of the Medical Friends of Wine*:

Medical interest in an ancient therapy —irrigation of wounds with wine —has revived internationally since

*Arthritis and Rheumatism published a letter from a
California physician last year.*

*Rheumatologist-internist Richard D. Smith of Walnut
Creek wrote of successfully using a method
prescribed in the Canon of Avicenna (A.D. 980-1037)
to heal patients' skin ulcerations such as bedsores
with wine irrigation and compresses. His letter
mentions the alcohols, acids, phenolic compounds,
and anthocyanins with anti-bacterial activity present
in wine, capable with adequate cleansing of
promoting the healing of wounds. He has used only
white wine, to avoid staining, but thinks reds may
have additional value.*

Wine for Skin Ulcers, Bulletin of the Society of Medical Friends of Wine, Sausalito, 1984

A new finding about wine antioxidants confirms the potential of wine in wound therapy. Khanna notes: *Proanthocyanins and other tannins facilitate wound healing* (Khanna 2002).

Another little related but nonetheless interesting news clipping reported that scientists in southern California have isolated a cannabis-like (marijuana) compound resident naturally in human skin receptors (no science available). The researchers speculated that these chemicals could be reproduced successfully in the laboratory. They plan to explore commercial applications. The proposed product would be applied topically to skin lesions to create therapeutic effects (apparently without the residual side effects of smoking the stuff).

It is doubtful that medical authorities or the public are ready for wine baths or cannabis extracts for an irritated epidermis. Yet it is interesting to know of these therapeutic uses of wine, beer and distilled spirits over the centuries. They were commonly used to treat wounds, to ward off infections and to endure the stress of both. No other remedy enjoyed this range of application. Alcohol-containing beverages have a unique and wide-ranging relationships with human health, even though antibiotics now have preferred status at your skin clinic.

What other drug or food offers as many benefits?

Chapter 29

Vision

Some potential benefits

■ **Author's abstract:** With medicine's myopia concerning drinking, the public has few opportunities to learn of new findings. Reports in the media on drinking and age-related macular degeneration have been few and none. Studies on other vision problems show some promise but most remain speculative. Alcohol is not major in vision care but the AMD studies are interesting.

■ ➡ Protection against macular degeneration may occur with the consumption of wine, beer and spirits
  ➡ Alcohol is associated with reduced prevalence of cortical cataracts
  ➡ Dark beer antioxidants also may lower risks of cataracts

Vision – the next to last of our thirty health conditions – presents an often conflicting panorama of studies and little resolved consensus. These reports suggest both caution and hope concerning drinking's contributions to vision.

Some vision studies have identified excessive drinking with the growth of cataracts, but a 1998 study in *Journal of the American*

Geriatrics Society opened a new vista of speculation for age-related macular degeneration (AMD). At this point, information about drinking and AMD is at the hypothesis stage. But anything that offers promise with this very troubling condition among the aging is worthy of pursuing.

A recent study reported in *Harvard Health Letter* casts doubt upon Obisesan's earlier findings discussed below: . . . *the Harvard based study that has tracked the health and habits of 120,000 nurses for over two decades, found that low to moderate alcohol consumption was not protective against age-related macular degeneration* (What You Can Do to Protect Your Eyes 2000). Nonetheless, the Obisesan study represented a new frontier for the analysis of macular degeneration. Once again, conflicting studies demonstrate the danger in depending upon the results of any single study.

As background, a November 1999 *Harvard Health Letter* article advised taking precautions against exposure to ultraviolet rays. It alluded also to the ingestion of antioxidants, such as lutein, in an article titled "Living With Low Vision:"

> *Age-related macular degeneration (AMD) — deterioration of the macula, an area in the back of the eye that is responsible for sharp, central vision — is the leading cause of low vision. . . . Protect your eyes from cataracts and age-related macular degeneration by wearing sunglasses with ultraviolet protection and not smoking. And while the verdict is still out on the protective effects of beta carotene and antioxidants like vitamins C and E, it never hurts to eat more fruit and vegetables.*

Living With Low Vision, Harvard Health Letter, Vol. 25, No. 1, November, 1999

The association of antioxidants with macular degeneration opens another avenue for flavonoids in wine and other alcohol beverages. Obisesan and colleagues evaluated reports of 3,072 adults aged forty-five to seventy-four years who participated in the first National Health Nutrition and Examination Survey (NHANES-1). From these data, they determined an association between alcohol intake and the risk of developing AMD. Their report in the *Journal of the American Geriatric Society* notes:

*Moderate wine consumption is associated with
decreased odds of developing AMD. Health promotion
and disease prevention activities directed at
cardiovascular disease may help reduce the rate of
AMD-associated blindness among older people. The
nature and pathophysiology of this association
warrant further investigation.*

Obisesan, T., Hirsch, R., Kosoko, O., Carlson, L., and Parrott, M., Moderate Wine
Consumption is Associated with Decreased Odds of Developing Age-related Macular
Degeneration in NHANES-1, Journal of the American Geriatric Society, 46:1-7, 1998

The Obisesan graph below clearly favors drinkers similar to
a number of disease comparisons through this book. In this
graphic, all drinkers fared better than nondrinkers with wine
showing the best results. The column on the left shows the
percent of individuals suffering AMD. Seniors who now consume alcohol with the view of lowering the risk of cardiovascular
diseases would enjoy knowing about this unrelated vision potential — another argument for cross-disease referencing.

Type of Alcohol

The raging controversy over hormone replacement treatment
(HRT) in the media today demonstrates how such cross-referencing can help patients to evaluate treatment decisions. Obisesan doesn't claim his findings are definitive. He recommends
additional studies to test these AMD observations. An editorial
by Miles speculates on the importance of all AMD findings: . .

. there are no known strategies for the prevention of visual impairment caused by AMD, and no curative therapies are available once the condition is diagnosed . . . This observation suggests that the protection may stem not from exposure to alcohol per se but to another element present in red wine. One recent report suggests that the phytoalexin resveratrol may be the candidate molecule (Miles 1998). Once again a wine antioxidants are credited.

Though some scientists remain dubious of any effects of beverage-borne antioxidants, Miles presses the unanswered questions. At this point, it doesn't matter which specific constituents in drinks may be responsible. The question is whether there is a discernible protection against AMD in drinking. Antioxidant research is presented in numerous chapters. The search goes on.

Other papers report mixed messages about alcohol impact on AMD. Smith studied 3,654 subjects and noted: *Neither alcohol or beer significantly related to age-related maculopathy although specific positive association was found between consumption of spirits and early-age relative maculopathy* (Smith 1996). In the Beaver Dam Eye Study, Ritter raises questions about the effects of beer: *Because there are few epidemiologic data examining the relationship between alcohol use and age-related maculopathy, we investigated this relationship . . . . Current consumption of neither wine nor liquor was related to early or late age-related maculopathy. . . The data suggest a relationship between beer consumption and greater odds of having exudative macular degeneration. Whether this is from a toxic effect specific to beer or from other unknown confounders cannot be determined. (Ritter 1995).* Analysis of more Beaver Dam data by Moss revealed: *Except for an association of beer drinking with retinal drusen in men, consumption of alcoholic beverages is not likely to be an important risk factor for incidence of ARM (age-related maculopathy)* (Moss 1998). Drinking's potential benefits obviously need more study. But they remain of interest, nonetheless.

Possible cataract protection

"Diet Might Help Prevent Cataracts" in the December 1999 *Tufts University Health & Nutrition Letter* demonstrates the importance of foods to organ health:

Harvard researchers made the finding in two large studies involving more than 110,000 men and women.

> *Those who ate the most foods rich in lutein and*
> *zeaxanthin were significantly less likely to develop*
> *age-related cataracts. . . . Earlier research has*
> *suggested that these same two substances may also*
> *play a role in warding off macular degeneration — the*
> *leading cause of irreversible blindness among older*
> *Americans.*

Diet Might Help Prevent Cataracts, Tufts University Health & Nutrition Letter, Vol. 17, No. 10, December, 1999

Yet another authority speculating reductions in risk for both AMD and cataracts from dietary contributions. The article repeats previous commentary that food sources are much preferable to antioxidant supplements:

> *The research may lead you to believe that taking*
> *so-called eye care supplements is a good idea,*
> *especially since pills containing lutein and other*
> *substances are now being heavily promoted. Don't*
> *bother. What we have at this point are associations*
> *between foods rich in certain nutrients and a reduced*
> *risk for eye problems, not cause-and-effect proof*
> *about particular compounds (Diet Might Help 1999).*

In fact, the article recommends at least three servings a week of foods such as broccoli, kale and winter squash, which are rich in lutein. What harm would result if the editors also mentioned antioxidant contributions in wine, beer and other drinks, such as quercetin, resveratrol and other antioxidants? This omission is particularly troubling in view of Obisesan's findings and the evidence for relief of cardiovascular diseases, Alzheimer's, osteoporosis and other aging diseases. When it comes to drinks, the mantra prevails – don't ask, don't tell.

At the 2000 convention of the International Chemical Congress of Pacific Basin Societies, researchers from Canada and the U.S. reported that darker ales and stouts may reduce the incidence of atherosclerosis and cataracts by as much as fifty per cent. In an article titled "Beer cuts risk of cataracts and heart disease," Trevithick noted: *Antioxidants protect the mitochondria against this damage. We think that may be one of the factors that's contributing to the lower risk of cataracts in people who have one drink a day* (Trevithick 2000). As these data accumulate, one wonders how long the medical system can resist their recognition.

Other projects support the possibility of benefits for cataracts. Cuming investigated the associations between alcohol consumption, smoking and cataracts of 3,654 individuals aged forty-nine to ninety-seven years and reported: *Alcohol was associated with a reduced prevalence of cortical cataract . . . . Consistent with other studies, smoking was associated with a higher prevalence of nuclear and posterior subcapsular cataracts. The only adverse effect of alcohol was among smokers: people who smoked and drank heavily had an increased prevalence* (Cuming 1997). Munoz commented on a study by Johns Hopkins scientists: *. . . those who drank less than seven drinks a week were not at increased risk while those who drank more than seven drinks were 4.6 times more likely to have posterior subcapsular cataracts* (Munoz 1996). Obviously, with cataracts, much more work needs to be done before either benefits or risks can be ascribed.

With glaucoma, another common vision malady among seniors, Klein, in the Beaver Dam Study, concluded that neither heavy drinking nor cigarette smoking behavior was related to the prevalence of open-angle glaucoma. *This finding reflected a real absence of pathologic effect* (Klein 1993). In sum, what can be said now is that the positive data developed from the NHANES survey and by Obisesan deserves more serious study. And certainly more recognition. Other relationships between drinking and vision remain more clouded.

The medical newsletters seem more open to positive research in the vision field. As example, the July 2001 *Harvard Men's Health Watch* has a comprehensive report titled "Macular Degeneration: Looking Age in the Eye." Included is the following comment: *Alcohol is controversial: one study suggests that drinking beer increases risk, another that wine may help* (Macular Degeneration 2001). Another article titled "Macular Degeneration" in *The Johns Hopkins Medical Letter* makes no reference to dietary factors but a *Tufts University Health & Nutrition Letter* indicates that "Diet Might Help Prevent Cataracts." It specifically mentions antioxidant research and promotes the use of: *. . . dark green leafy vegetables namely spinach, broccoli, collard greens, kale, mustard greens and winter squash as well as corn and peppers* (Diet Might

Help 1999). The *UC Berkeley Wellness Letter* of April 1998 in a tongue-in-cheek "Weakly news" reports: *Drinking wine may halve the risk of macular degeneration, the leading cause of blindness in older people. But the study was flawed and inconclusive . . . Warrants further investigation was the bottom line – an understatement* (Weakly news 1998).

Miles in the *Journal of the American Geriatrics Society* titled "Should My Mother Take a Drink? raises an important question:" *Reports have appeared suggesting that one or two glasses of red wine on a daily basis decreases the risk of heart disease . . . As Obisesan and colleagues point out, alcohol type (wine, beer, liquor) varies in the degree of association . . . This observation suggests that the protection may stem not from exposure to alcohol per se but to other elements present in red wine. One recent report suggests that the phytoalexin resveratrol may be the candidate molecule . . . Should my mother take a drink? The evidence for that recommendation is still evolving* (Miles 1998). The article presents a balanced report that cross-references heart disease, suggests antioxidative action, and advises caution awaiting further studies. Not a negative or inflammatory thought about drinks in the entire piece. Refreshing, that.

A pleasant aside

My personal ophthalmologist recently provided a research paper which repeats the ancient myth about the discovery of champagne. That stellar event is often attributed to Dom Perignon (1681-1715), a famed monk and wine cellarmaster at a monastery in Hautvillers, France. Bullock's article compares the current state of ocular pathology with Dom Perignon's era:

> *Today, causes of mid-to-late-onset blindness include cataracts, glaucoma, macular degeneration, diabetic retinopathy, adult retinitis pigmentosa, multiple sclerosis, and retinal detachment among others. In 17th century Europe, the most common causes of reduced vision were probably infection, cataracts, and glaucoma.*

Bullock, J., Wang, J., and Bullock, G., Was Dom Perignon Really Blind?, Survey of Ophthalmology, Vol. 42, No. 42, March-April, 1998

Bullock reports that champagne is reputed (and disputed) to have been discovered when Dom Perignon pulled a cloth stopper from a bottle which had undergone a secondary fermentation releasing a profusion of new carbonation in the bottle. Regaling in the profusion of luscious bubbles, the venerable wine maker (who was by then nearly blind) is reputed to have shouted to associates, "Come quickly. I am seeing stars."

While drinking to excess can "blind" one from seeing stars, or anything else, there is genuine hope in vision research that moderate drinking might someday enable older folks to keep on seeing those radiant stars.

Let's toast to that possibility.

Chapter 30

Weight

Drinks can enhance weight maintenance

■ **Author's abstract**: America's flagellation of choice is weight control. Anything that promises to maintain healthy weight is worth a try. Here are some findings concerning drinks and weight.

■ ➤ Moderate consumption does not cause weight gain
 ➤ Alcohol can cause gains when consumed in excess
 ➤ Alcohol consumers were leaner than abstainers
 ➤ Excess alcohol calories are often compensated for by an increase in energy expenditures

Americans have a deadly serious weight problem. The June 2000 issue of *Health After 50* has these alarming statistics:

Weight loss is big business in the United States. More than $30 billion is spent annually on services and products aimed at people eager to be thinner. Perhaps more significant, the complications of excessive weight —including type 2 diabetes, high blood pressure, heart disease, gall bladder disease, *and sleep apnea (intermittent cessation of breathing during sleep) —are a leading cause of preventable deaths, second only to tobacco-related complications. . . At any given moment, almost 38% of men and more than 43% of women are trying to lose weight.*

A Weight Loss Prescription for Longer Life, Health After 50, June, 2000

A recent University of Alabama study led by Fontaine reported in the *Journal of the American Medical Association* states that being obese at age 20 could cut up to 20 years from a life span. Body mass constitutes a combination height-weight ratio. As example, a 5-foot, 4 inch person would have a BMI of 45 but would appear as large as a sumo wrestler. A body mass of 45 was found to exact 13 years from a white person and 20 years from a black person. The study concluded: *Obesity appears to lessen life expectancy markedly, especially among younger adults* (Fontaine 2003). A companion study by Manson, "Obesity in the United States: A Fresh Look at its High Toll," warns: *Obesity has become pandemic in the United States . . . Obesity accounts for more than 280,000 deaths annually in the United States and will soon overtake smoking as the primary preventable cause of death* (Manson 2003).

More statistics from the American Heart Association's *1997 Heart and Stroke Statistical Update* embellish the problem:

Based on NHANES-III (1988-91) data, nearly 62 million American adults (28.1 million men and 33.9 million women) are 20 percent or more above their desirable weight, an increase of 36 percent over 1960-62 examination data.

Heart and Stroke Statistical Update, American Heart Association, Dallas, 1997

Indolence is a contributor. Expendable income is another. Snack food is a prodigious third. The American Heart Association estimates that thirty-three percent of overweight men and forty-one percent of overweight women are not physically active during leisure time. A *Harvard Health Letter* article "Weight and Longevity" explains body mass and obesity:

> *. . . researchers from the University of North Carolina, Chapel Hill, evaluated mortality rates of more than 324,000 white adults, age 30-74 . . . Desirable weight was defined as a body-mass index (BMI) of 21, which translates to 147 pounds for a man of 5 feet 10 inches and 123 pounds for a woman 5 feet 4 inches. . . . People are considered obese when their BMI is above 27. The more people exceeded their desirable weights, the higher their rate of death from cardiovascular disease and all causes.*

Weight and Longevity, Harvard Health Letter, 1998

The March 2000 issue of the *UC Berkeley Wellness Letter* provides a simple formula for calculating a BMI: *The body mass index (BMI) evaluates weight in relation to height. . . . Multiply your weight (in pounds) by 705; divide the result by your height (in inches); then divide again by your height. That will give you your BMI. A "healthy" BMI range is between 19 and 25. Between 25 and 30 is considered moderately overweight; 30 and above, obese. For a man or woman 5'6", that works out to a healthy range of 118 to 155 pounds, with obesity starting at 185* (Figuring your BMI 2000).

A positive role for drinking

Individuals who are obese should be made aware of the positive research data concerning drinking. In a cross-sectional study of 486 obese women and men, Dixon recorded: *Light-to-moderate drinking is associated with a more favourable CVD risk profile in severely obese people . . . Therefore, moderate drinking should not be discouraged in severely obese people* (Dixon 2002).

In 1987, following the second NHANES survey, Williamson questioned the common belief that drinking should be avoided in weight control programs: *Current recommendations indicate alcohol consumption should be reduced in order to lower body weight. Our findings, and those of other studies, do not support these recommendations. However, it is important that further research be directed* (Williamson 1987). The authors continued: *. . . alcohol has a substantial, independent association with lower body weight in women . . . alcohol has only a slight independent association with body weight* *in men.* Other findings on weight control over the past decade support Williamson's conclusions. Stevens had the following comments in the *New England Journal of Medicine* on January 1, 1998:

> *Whether recommended body weight should remain constant throughout adulthood or should be higher for older adults is controversial. The Department of Agriculture's 1990 Dietary Guidelines for Americans recommended age-specific ranges of weight for height, with heavier weights indicated for people 35 years of age or older, but age-specific weight recommendations were omitted from the 1995 Dietary Guidelines for Americans, presumably because the information to support the need for different recommended weights was inadequate.*

Stevens, J., Cai, J., Pamuk, E., Williamson, D., Thun, M., and Wood, J., The Effect of Age on the Association Between Body-Mass Index and Mortality, The New England Journal of Medicine, Vol. 338, No., 1, January 1, 1998

Weight more tolerable as we age

The study came to this conclusion: *Taken together, these studies support the hypothesis that the relative risk of death associated with excess adiposity is lower for older than for younger adults* (Stevens 1998). Another article in *Harvard Health Letter* finds data in the Nurses' Health Study warning against even slight gains in BMI:

> *This study indicates that even moderate weight gain after age 18 significantly increases a woman's risk of heart attack. The researchers — including Harvard Heart Letter editorial-board members Walter Willett and Charles Hennekens — also found that regardless of a woman's weight at age 18, the weight attained at mid-life (30-55 years of age) appears to have the greatest impact on risk of artery disease.*

Weight Gain and Heart Risk, Harvard Heart Letter, 1998

Controversy about whether high school body weight should be maintained through life continues in the literature. Blair evaluated a survey of 12,025 Harvard University graduates with an average age of sixty-seven. Participants were asked how often they dieted: *Those who said "always" had a heart disease rate of 23.1*

*percent, more than double the 10.6 rate of those who answered never.
The men who always dieted had a 38.3 percent rate of hypertension
and 14.6 (per cent) rate of diabetes compared to a 23.4 percent rate of
hypertension and 3 percent rate for diabetes for those who said they
never dieted* (Staying stout 1994).

Moderate drinking is not directly linked to weight gain. In
1997, Cordain studied weight regulation and metabolism with
fourteen male subjects, average age thirty-two. The regimen
called for two glasses of red wine with evening meals: *No significant changes in body weight, body fat by hydrostatic weighing or body
fat by multiple skin fold thickness measurements were noted after the
wine-added periods* (Cordain 1997). In 1996, an analysis by Mannisto which was part of the American Cancer Society study of
79,236 adults: . . . *found that on average there was very little difference
in weight between drinkers and nondrinkers, and moderate daily drinkers were the leanest, even when compared to abstainers* (Mannisto
1996).

Finkel in "Nutrition, Weight, and Wine" points to critical
physiological factors which come into play in weight control
planning: *What you drink and whether you are a woman or a man
may determine the destiny of the calories you consume. Most of us have
observed that men preferentially deposit extra calories (as fat) on their
bellies. Women tend to cushion their posteriors* (Finkel 1999). Finkel
continues: *How the body handles the calories of alcohol remains
something of a mystery and source of argument. It appears that men and
women may be different in their metabolism of alcohol, and that the
metabolism of alcohol may change when consumption increases from
moderate to heavy, resulting in energy wastage, and, thus, less weight
gain than would be predicted for the number of calories consumed.*

A Mannisto report released in 1997 incorporated data from a
1992 Finnish cardiovascular survey: *Alcohol consumers were leaner
than abstainers, and wine drinkers in particular had more antioxidants
in their diet* (Mannisto 1997). Sonko reported on the biological
aspects of drinking: *It is concluded that alcohol has a fat-sparing
effect similar to that of carbohydrate and will only cause fat gain when
consumed in excess of normal energy needs* (Sonko 1994). Kahn, from
the American Cancer Society, studied weight gain with alcohol
consumption and reported: *This study confirms the results of the
recent Colorado State University study (Cordain 1997), which found*

the addition of two glasses of red wine with dinner for men does not influence any measured variable which may adversely affect body weight (Kahn 1997).

A novel conclusion was presented by Orozco: *This study suggests that excess alcohol calories are compensated by an increase in energy expenditure, as evidenced indirectly by increased heart rates occurring between the hours of 2300 and 0700, increased self-reported nightly restlessness, increased wake-time, and exercise* (Orozco 1994). Murgatroyd agreed: *Alcohol ingested in addition to other foods appears not to lead to adiposity; in women drinking alcohol, even a decrease in adiposity has been found* (Murgatroyd 1996). Chyou identifies the very real dangers of over-consumption of all foods: *The most important finding of this study was that . . . extreme (high or low) BMI values and high alcohol consumption are each potentially harmful to health* (Chyou 1997). But Istvan reports: *There were no significant differences in BMI between alcohol drinks in either men or women* (Istvan 1995).

Liu commented on the many arguments swirling around drinking and body weight. Her cohort study was developed from 7,230 participants in the first NHANES study (1971-1975) who were re-weighed ten years later:

> **Because drinkers tend to have a higher energy intake than nondrinkers, drinking has been assumed to be a risk factor for developing obesity . . . In summary, for the US adult population, alcohol was found to be inversely related to body weight among women, and both male and female drinkers over the 10-year follow-up period. These data suggest that alcohol intake does not increase the risk of obesity.**

Liu, S., Serdula, M., Williamson, D., Mokdad, A., and Byers, T., A prospective study of alcohol intake and change in body weight among U.S. adults, American Journal of Epidemiology, 140:912-920, 1994

In sum, moderate drinkers appear advantaged. The April 1998 issue of *UC Berkeley Wellness Letter* provides the best advice: *Don't gain too much weight in the first place. Stay physically active and eat more fruits, vegetables, and grains in order to maintain a healthy weight, or to lose weight if you need to* (Best Advice 1998).

Solid advice.

Chapter 31

Myths, Misperceptions and Inertia

Inertia — a fixed resistance to change

■ **Author's abstract**: The dictionary describes inertia as, "Resistance to motion, action or change." Nothing in the world so resists change as ingrained cultural myths and misperceptions. The dictionary also notes that inertia can be broken only by an "external force." This chapter considers research from the social sciences which challenges the prevailing Temperance myths. Readers who see the need to challenge these myths will find support in the analyses of six prevailing Temperance myths.

The previous thirty chapters provide compelling evidence that moderate drinkers are among the world's healthiest people. Yet, nowhere has this book recommended drinking. It recommends informed choice. The final three chapters address the socio-political aspects of alcohol ambivalence.

America's Temperance movement grew from a genuine need. Many Americans turned to destructive drinking as the new nation's economy virtually collapsed following the Revolutionary War. Wives, preachers and physicians joined hands, quite literally, to save the American family. When the economy rebounded by the middle of the Eighteenth Century, mindless drinking abated. Despite this progress, the Temperance movement continued its efforts to expunge all drinking through legislative fiat. Though it required another half century, Temperance advocacies achieved national Prohibition through the Eighteenth Amendment to the Constitution. Prohibition was a wild, socially corruptive, but thankfully short-lived experiment in governmental control. Seventy years after Repeal, vestiges of this radical political aspiration still hold a vise-like grip on the American political psyche. A majority of Americans are torn between a desire to drink and a fearful sway of some or all the following myths rising from Temperance thinking:

1. *All drinking is risk taking.*
2. *The U.S. is a heavy drinking nation.*
3. *The suggested daily drinking limits make sense.*
4. *Alcohol abuse can be lowered by reducing all (per capita) drinking.*
5. *Alcohol abuse costs the nation $148 billions annually.*
6. *Alcohol is correctly grouped with street drugs.*

In myriad ways from early childhood, these assumptions are drilled into us with all the fervor of the three Rs. There is no impetus for the engines of popular culture – education, medicine, politics, think tanks, the media, foundations, government or religion – to challenge these thoroughly ingrained beliefs. Alcohol inertia will reign forever in our land, short of a vigorous public discussion about the health properties in drinks. Human health is the key to initiate a new era of responsible drinking.

Conditions are ripe for public support of this concept. Polls in the U.S. and Canada show that most people believe that drinking (at least red wine) can benefit heart health. Kitson in New Zealand reviewed the world's literature and claimed: *There is thus little doubt now, based on statistical evidence, that the consumption of alcohol in moderate amounts can produce health benefits. The*

*acceptance of this fact has produced an upsurge of interest in research
with the aim of finding an explanation as to how alcohol consumption
may produce health benefits* (Kitson 2001). Prominent physicians,
researchers and social scientists support moderate consumption
(see Epilogue). We live in an era of heightened health conscious-
ness. The wine boom, the microbrew craze and the coffee, tea
and bottled water fads represent fascination with exotic drinks
and diets. Conditions are ideal for a reassessment of alcohol
ambivalence based in a public discussion of the burgeoning
epidemiology of healthy drinking.

Many authorities in this chapter represent academic disciplines far afield from the biomedicines. Their competencies lie
in sociology, economics, anthropology and political science.
Their findings offer new dimensions and unique insights into
why and how people drink. Social scientists are epidemiologists
of everyday life. They look for behavioral answers in the patterns which structure the way we live, work and play.

1. Moderate drinking is "risk taking"

A great debate has ensued in the abuse and treatment fields
in recent decades over the "disease theory" of alcoholism. Weiner in *The Politics of Alcoholism* quotes a proponent of this
concept: *Alcohol is a drug. We don't talk about responsible drugs. If
there is addiction . . . a little alcohol is also dangerous* (Weiner 1981).
One might extrapolate from this concept that modern medicine
also is a "risk-taking" enterprise since it involves the use of
dangerous, even lethal drugs. The "disease" theorists perceive
alcohol as a pathogen. A pathogen is an agent (bacterium,
fungus) that causes a disease to develop. That idea makes any
use of alcohol more than a little dangerous. It becomes always
a "risk-taking" practice. It rejects the idea of responsible use.

The traditional perception of responsible drinking was enun-
ciated by Morris Chafetz, M.D. founding director of the National Institute on Alcohol Abuse and Alcoholism in the *Second
Special Report to Congress on Alcohol and Health* which states: . . .
*should the choice be to drink, the individual assumes a responsibility
not to destroy himself or others. That in the broadest sense is responsible
drinking* (Weiner 1981). Chafetz assumes that risks to health lie

The Drinker's Inevitable Fate   Circa 1919

in the manner of use, not in the substance itself. Further, drinks can and do manifest health-giving properties for the vast majority of drinkers. Around this conflict the debate should ensue since risk anxiety is the foundation of all alcohol ambivalence and our cultural inertia to change.

Responsible drinking proponents believe that an individual can − and that most people do and will − choose safe drinking limits. Moderates understand that a percentage of drinkers will inevitably abuse no matter what society does to control the availability of the product. Risk-mongering was the primary tool of the Prohibition era as seen in the popular Currier & Ives poster. Peele sees this as a prevailing myth: *For what is at best a shallow half-truth, the notion of an inexorable progression from tasting forbidden fruit to self destruction has had a remarkably enduring appeal for Americans* (Peele 1997).

Up to ninety percent of American drinkers consume regularly over a lifetime without serious problems. Alcoholism specialists in many nations report that from three to five of every 100 drinkers are addicted to alcohol. Another three to five percent are periodic abusers. These estimate are confirmed in a series of surveys on alcohol control policies conducted by the Brewers Association of Canada. The *Alcohol Beverage Taxation and Control Policies, Ninth Edition,* summary notes: *The proportion of the population considered to be at risk from misuse of alcoholic beverages in Australia, Germany, the Netherlands, Switzerland, Canada and Japan has been estimated at or below two per cent. In Austria, Portugal, England, Scotland and Wales, between three to five percent of the population are considered to be at risk or alcoholic, and in Italy, Mexico and the United States, ten per cent or greater* (Alcoholic Beverage Taxation 1997).

If all drinkers were truly risk-prone, high per capita consuming nations such as France, Germany, Italy and Spain would be overwhelmed by alcoholism and abuse problems. With some variation, societies that integrate drinking into family and social life experience less overall abuse. The reality is that the majority of drinkers globally are at very low risk of addiction.

That is not to say drinking is risk-free for anyone. Nor are dozens of other work and recreational activities we engage in − freeway driving, flying, bicycling, heavy construction work, hang-gliding, off-road vehicle jaunts, automobile racing, and skiing – to name but a few. Even rushing down the stairs to breakfast involves the risk of a serious fall. Human life is a tenuous, risky enterprise at best. We accept many relative risks without stigmatizing the involved activities, as government and medicine do with drinking. We don't require ski resorts to erect billboards near ski lifts warning of the risk of broken limbs or mandate airlines to include plane crash statistics in their advertisements. Public health programs today seek reductions in per capita drinking but condone increases in skiing, jogging and bicycling as healthy exercising though each carries significant physical risks.

Of course, under sufficient stress any drinker can lose control and overindulge. But the same is true of nondrinkers who succumb to road rage or a violent marital dispute. Temptation is a given. Safe drinking cautions are praiseworthy. But maintaining a policy that all drinkers are at equal risk is *reductio ad absurdum*. No medical literature validates such an assumption. Barr presents a broader, more rational perspective:

> *For ten thousand years, ever since human beings settled down to the cultivation of cereals and vines, alcohol has played a fundamental role in society. It has served as an object of religious ritual, a focus of secular ceremonies and a lubricant of social intercourse; it has been employed as an aid to the digestion of food, a means of slaking thirst without risk of contracting disease and as a source of nutrition in its own right; it has been used in the treatment of wounds and disease and as both a stimulant and a sedative —as well as being valued for its taste.*

Barr, A., Drink, Bantam Press, New York, 1995

Even addiction science supports responsible use. In a formidable book, *The Natural History of Alcoholism*, Vaillant summarizes a forty-year project in which he and colleagues at Harvard University Medical School followed a cohort of alcoholics in New York City. This highly acclaimed study states: *Introducing children to the ceremonial and sanctioned use of low-proof alcoholic beverages taken with meals in the presence of others, coupled with social sanctions against drunkenness and against drinking at unspecified times would appear to provide the best protection against future alcohol abuse* (Vaillant 1983). Vaillant's study supports responsible youth drinking as a *preventive* measure, to *avoid* drinking problems later in life. Why isn't this study widely communicated?

In 1991, the Center on Alcohol Studies at Rutgers University published an 800-page monograph including comments from over forty international prevention scholars. This monograph backs Vaillant's assumption: *Societies with low alcohol abuse problems a) portray any alcohol abuse or overindulgence as unacceptable, and b) make drinking of alcohol beverages an adjunct to sociability and not the focus of an occasion* (Rutgers Monograph Stresses 1991). We should emulate those societies which have fewer abuse problems. Hanson suggests consideration of the European integrative approach: *Rather than simply focusing upon the negative consequences of alcohol consumption, we need to be encouraging moderate consumption for those who choose to drink. Encouraging the moderate use of alcohol simultaneously discourages immoderate use* (Hanson 1996).

To sum up, few American drinkers are at real risk of addiction and many alcoholics suffer from unrelated mental or social problems which foster their abusive patterns. By disavowing the risk myth, government programs could focus on those at genuine risk.

2. The U. S. is a heavy drinking nation

Again, not so. By the advent of the Civil War, American consumption had retrenched to acceptable drinking levels. Through wars, epidemics, good times and bad – even through the Prohibition era – Americans have maintained comparatively moderate levels of per capita consumption. Surprised?

Post-Revolutionary War drinking patterns were fueled by an abysmal economy in the struggling new nation. Cut adrift from a preferential trade with Great Britain, the nascent American economy literally fell apart. Employment took a nose-dive. The most important unit of wealth was land and what it could produce. Rye and corn whiskey became a highly valued, relatively cheap harvest, as well as a common medium in a largely barter economy. At times, a gallon of whiskey could be procured for twenty-five cents — less than a gallon of milk. Many sought solace at the bottom of a jug. Alcohol historian Rorabaugh reconstructed drinking statistics from those forlorn days through modern times. His research reveals the terrible burdens that economic and social disruption can have on any society:

> *Alcohol was pervasive in American society; it crossed regional, sexual, racial and class lines. Americans drank at home and abroad, alone and together, at work and at play, in fun and in earnest. . . . They drank in their youth, and, if they lived long enough, in their old age.*

Rorabaugh, W., The Alcoholic Republic, Oxford University Press, New York, 1979

Rorabaugh's data shows that the consumption spike which followed the war did not abate fully until the 1840s. Over those decades, new industries and commercial opportunities developed under the impetus of the Industrial Revolution. The annual U.S. per capita consumption in gallons is seen below for selected years from 1710 to 1975 as excerpted from *The Alcoholic Republic*.

1710	2.7	1830	3.9	1900	1.4
1790	3.1	1835	2.8	1915	1.6
1800	3.5	1840	1.8	1935	1.1
1810	3.7	1850	1.0	1975	2.0

By 1840, annual alcohol consumption was slightly less than two gallons per person, a moderate pattern that persisted through both the nineteenth and twentieth centuries. Polls taken since Repeal by the Gallup organization record a pattern of about sixty-five percent of U.S. adults as drinkers. This is a smaller percentage of drinkers to population than in most developed western nations. Ironically, Prohibition was a failed, costly social intrusion designed to solve a problem that no longer existed. Over the twentieth century, the U.S. ranked in the mid-level in per capita consumption.

One common measure of alcoholism lies in the number of cirrhosis deaths per 100,000 population. In *Alcohol, Policy and the Public Good*, Edwards compares cirrhosis fatalities in Europe and America. At 11.6 per 100,000, the U.S. ranked lower than most European nations. The range was from a high of 54.8 deaths in Hungary and 48.6 in Mexico, to a mid range of 9.3 in Canada, and a low of 2.9 deaths in Ireland. This is more evidence that the U.S. is statistically a temperate society.

However, the raw data does not reveal the manner of consumption. France, at nearly thirteen liters annually, consumes almost twice as much alcohol as the U.S. Over ninety percent of French adults drink compared to our sixty-five percent. By integrating drinking with meals and other communal activities, the French experience less disruptive drinking. France has a high cirrhosis rate overall, particularly in the Norman regions in the north while the wine drinking regions have very low cirrhosis rates. So drinking volumes alone are meaningless — as are the federal efforts to reduce per capita drinking. Americans drink far too much when alone and without the tempering of food but the myth that Americans are heavy drinkers is nonsense.

3. Daily drinking limits should be two drinks for men and one for women

This will likely become the most controversial section in this tome. The medical fraternity and government health agencies have pretty much settled on a one-fits-all mandate recommending no more than one daily drink for women and two for men. If that limitation works for you, more power. This book conscientiously avoids recommending anything. This intake would likely reap the health benefits attributed to drinking.

The following remarks are meant more to amplify than to dispute, to inform rather than to disparage. Much of the data on drinking levels is fractious because study participants tend to understate their real drinking proclivities. Studies scattered through this book find benefits in a much wider range, particularly those conducted in the heavier drinking nations like

France, Spain and Italy. Many nations have initiated drinking
limits over the past two decades influenced by neoprohitionary
fervor. Overall, this has been a commendable effort.

But, in their simplicity and rigidity, arbitrary mandates fail to
recognize a variety of social, cultural and physiological factors
which attend drinking. Arbitrary limits fail to consider the
following: 1) the range of healthy drinking levels found in the
research, 2) differences in body size, 3) variability in blood
alcohol levels and alcohol elimination rates, 4) how alcohol
tolerance moderates toxicity levels, 5) gender differences, 6)
how food moderates absorption rates and, finally, 7) how environment, time and place – what sociologists call the set and
setting – shape the outcome of any drinking episode. Here are
comments on each.

Consider the levels found in the research. In the preceding thirty chapters, health benefits were found in as little as
several drinks a week to as much as three to five drinks per day.
Quite a range:

> *American Heart Association — daily 2 for men, 1 for women*
> *Amer. Coll. of Cardiology — daily 1-3 for lowest heart risk*
> *Australian survey — daily 1-4 for men, 1-2 for women*
> *Anstie's Limit — daily 1 1/2 ounces alcohol (3 drinks)*
> *British Physicians — weekly 21 units for men, 14 for women*
> *Chou in NIAAA study — 2-5 for men, 1-3 for women*
> *Federal health agencies — daily 2 for men, 1 for women*
> *Gose for European males — 6 daily lowest heart risk*
> *Klatsky/Kaiser Permanente — up to 3 daily for heart risk*
> *Mayo Clinic Health Letter — 2 for men, 1 for women*
> *Heart Assoc. — lowest mortality consumers 1-2 daily*
> *Rehm in U.S. — 6 daily had 50 percent less coronary risk*
> *Renaud in France — 2 to 5 daily glasses the healthiest*
> *Turner survey in U.S. — daily wine 25 oz, beer, 75 oz, spir-*
> *its 7 oz*

The American Heart Association supports the government's
recommendations. At the opposite end, Turner's review of the
literature found that as much as a bottle of wine, a six pack or
seven cocktails a day permissible for men. In December 1995,
U.K. physicians adjusted their recommended levels upward,
partially because of Doll's studies which found the longest-lived
British physicians drank eight to twenty-four units per week.

The U.K.'s unit (drink) contains eight grams of ethanol compared to our 14 gram drink.

An International Council on Alcohol Policies study on drink limits shows a befuddling range in standard drinks: *Australia, 10 grams of alcohol; Canada, 13.5 grams; Japan, 19.75 grams* (Safe Alcohol Consumption 1996). The U.S. daily limit of 28 grams for men and 14 for women contrasts with Australia's 40 gram top. Basque authorities recommend no more than 70 grams. Italy and Japan top off at 39.5 grams. Several Italian studies report that the healthiest citizens consume close to the 70 grams daily. All nations have access to the same science. Obviously, government limits reflect as much political science and prevailing culture as the medical science of drinking.

One has to factor in the food that is consumed while drinking. When drinks are taken with food, less alcohol reaches the bloodstream. Italian Spanish, and French cuisines encourage drinking as compared to the U.S. and Great Britain. Klatsky wisely cautions against inaccuracy of drinking surveys: *It also should be kept in mind that many persons underestimate the amount (i.e. minimize) their alcohol drinking when responding to survey queries. Thus, by making some heavier drinkers appear to be lighter drinkers, underestimation blurs the accuracy of true thresholds for harmful alcohol effects, which are likely to be higher than the levels found in epidemiologic studies* (Klatsky 1996). The point is that drinking is often underestimated in scientific studies. The apocryphal example concerns the lady who assured her physician that she takes but a single glass of vodka daily, failing to mention her glass was a mason jar!

Consider body size. Inelastic drink limits fail to accommodate for body size as do drunk driving laws. For driving, intoxication relates to specific, arbitrary levels of BAC (blood alcohol concentration).

A person's BAC is a precise measurement of the amount of alcohol circulating in the bloodstream. The BAC chart below was published and distributed by the Washington State Liquor Control Board. It demonstrates an increasing capacity to consume alcohol and remain under legal intoxication levels as the person's body size increases. As weight increases, the vascular system enlarges supplying more blood to ameliorate the intoxication.

Consequently, on the Washington chart, a 250 pound man can consume twice the alcohol over a similar period as a 125 pound man. Since all drinking is done for physical effect (whether to get high or make the food taste better), drinking limits which fail to accommodate for a range of body sizes likely will be ignored, at least by large-bodied drinkers. Drunk driving levels make both legal and physical sense.

BLOOD ALCOHOL CONCENTRATION (B.A.C.) CHART
(PERCENT OF ALCOHOL IN BLOODSTREAM)

YOUR WEIGHT ▼	NUMBER OF DRINKS CONSUMED *								
	1	2	3	4	5	6	7	8	9
100	.029	.058	.088	.117	.146	.175	.204	.233	.262
120	.024	.048	.073	.097	.121	.145	.170	.194	.219
140	.021	.042	.063	.083	.104	.125	.146	.166	.187
160	.019	.037	.055	.073	.091	.109	.128	.146	.164
180	.017	.033	.049	.065	.081	.097	.113	.130	.146
200	.015	.029	.044	.058	.073	.087	.102	.117	.131
220	.014	.027	.040	.053	.067	.080	.093	.106	.119
240	.012	.024	.037	.048	.061	.073	.085	.097	.109

USE CAUTION
Response time affected

DRIVING IMPAIRED
Crash risk quadrupled at .080%

LEGALLY DRUNK

DO NOT DRIVE

-756-

* ONE DRINK EQUALS:
  1 oz. of 80 proof alcohol; 12 oz. bottle of beer
  2 oz. of 20% wine; 3 oz. of 12% wine

The above BAC Chart was released before the Washington legislature lowered legal intoxication from .10 percent BAC to .08 percent BAC, an arbitrary political decision that varies from nation to nation. The chart measures the toxicity of drinks consumed in a *single hour* related to an individual's body weight. A 100 pound person reaches an "impaired driving zone" after two drinks in an hour but will not be legally intoxicated until consuming the 4th drink in that single hour. In many states, a person who is observed driving erratically can be charged with drunk driving, even at lower than legal intoxication levels.

Moderate drinkers do not consume four drinks in a single hour. A 220 pound body does not reach reach legal intoxication until the eighth drink in an hour! The Washington BAC card notes that one hour is needed to eliminate every single drink. Therefore, body size and period consuming are crucial determinants for safe drinking and drinking limits. A good BAC chart is the moderate driver/drinker's best friend. If everyone learned how to maintain their BACs at or below .05 BAC, the risk for many kinds of accidents would be reduced.

A systematized approach to the maintenance of a safe level of BAC was offered by alcohol abuse professionals Vogler and Bartz in the early 1980s in *The Better Way to Drink: The basic rule of successful and enjoyable drinking can be stated clearly: savor the good effects as your blood alcohol is rising up to a maximum of 55 [BAC] and then quit drinking* (Vogler 1982). Their compact paperback provides easy-to-use charts on number of drinks permissible according to body weight. Unfortunately, this system was never embraced by the abuse prevention officials or the public safety bureaucracy.

The Limits of Binge Drinking published by the International Center for Alcohol Policies (ICAP), sums up the weakness of arbitrary drink limits: . . . *defining a drinking pattern solely by the number of drinks consumed also falls short of being adequate. This approach fails to take into account the context of drinking, the individual engaging in the behavior (a 250-lb male is likely to experience very different consequences from five drinks than is a 100-lb female), and the salience of alcohol within the drinking occasion* (The Limits of 1997).

Consider alcohol familiarity. Familiarity is another way of saying physiological tolerance. Tolerance is defined as the body's capacity to endure or resist the intoxicative influence of any drug. Tolerance is extremely difficult to measure and it is widely misunderstood. In *Alcohol Tolerance and Social Drinking*, Vogel-Sprott suggests: *Tolerance to the behavioral effects of alcohol can occur during early stages in its social use* (Vogel-Sprott 1992). A novice drinker, no matter the body size, gets high quicker and from less exposure. Moderate alcohol tolerance develops naturally over time in the same manner as bodily adjustment to other toxic foods or drugs — say jalapena peppers.

Arbitrary volume limits fail to distinguish between novice and experienced drinkers. After a single drink, a teenage driver will feel twice as "high" as an alcohol-tolerant adult who has consumed moderately over many years. Some research papers suggest that introducing young people to alcohol *before* granting driving privileges. Novice drivers would have gained some tolerance to alcohol before taking command of an automobile. The many issues involved in drunken and/or sober, impaired driving are extremely difficult to resolve. Ross in *Deterring the Drinking Driver* notes the inevitable injustice of focusing on the drunken driver as compared to the errant driver: *The killer drunk gets his due, but in the vast majority of cases of alcohol-impaired driving, the prohibited behavior is not seen as warranting highly punitive sanctions . . . Since the practicality of deterrence in the long run is questionable and its justice arguable, other approaches to the reduction of death and injury related to drinking and driving ought to be considered by policy makers* (Ross 1982).

A realistic adaptation might be to allow drinking at nineteen but to ban driving with *any* alcohol in the bloodstream before the age of twenty-one. In a 1986 study, Asch made these comments: *What we suggest as an appropriate view of the drinking-and-driving problem may in fact appear startling. The problem arises not because we permit people to drink when they are "too young," but rather because we permit them to experience the novelty of "new drinking" at a time when they are legally able to drive. The suggestions is very likely impractical in political and social terms. But if the objective is saving lives . . . this type of policy change deserves more study* (Asch 1986). There is little likelihood that state legislatures will give serious consideration to this advice, but a better understanding of the role of alcohol familiarity could help parents to set firm policies of no alcohol (or drugs) before handing over the keys to the car.

Consider gender. As reported in Chapter 18, in addition to smaller vascular systems, women are believed to generate lower levels of the dehydrogenase enzyme which breaks down alcohol. An appropriate warning is posed by Gilson: *It is known that, pound for pound of body weight, women reach higher peaks than men from the same quantity of alcohol* (Gilson 1989). In her textbook *Pharmacology of Alcohol,* Goldstein notes: *Small people, women and teen-agers may be expected to eliminate ethanol more slowly* (Goldstein 1983).

In *Alcohol and Women: Creating a Safer Lifestyle,* Gilson and Bennett have assembled vital female-oriented research from many sources on the impacts and conditions which shape responsible female drinking. The book offers different absorption charts for women and men. Their Table 2.3 below provides "Proposed Daily Upper Limits of Moderate Drinking for Women." Both body weight and beverage types determine recommended upper limits of daily consumption in ounces. The figures are based in the original 1981 research (The Beneficial Side of Moderate Alcohol Use, Turner T., Bennett, V., and Hernandez, H., The Johns Hopkins Medical Journal, 148 (2):53-63, 1981). Note that a 170 pound woman's limit (4.1 ounces of 80 proof spirits) is almost twice that suggested for a ninety pound female (2.2 ounces of spirit). The weight factor comes to the same conclusion as the Washington State BAC chart.

The findings in *Alcohol and Women* deserve serious consideration. Gilson and Bennett repeatedly stress that epidemiological statistics are no more than averages for a certain group of individuals. Important, sometimes unique, personal factors need to be considered in determining whether to drink and how much. In a opening note, they stress the importance of personal and family experiences:

The book Alcohol and Women: Creating a Safer Lifestyle is designed for women as a summary of conclusions to be drawn from a large amount of published data on the effects of alcohol. It is not meant to offer or replace medical advice. Physical condition and other influences, such as medication and estrogen levels, can cause reactions to alcohol to vary on different occasions. Also some women are more or less tolerant of alcohol than others. These guidelines should thus be regarded as the "norm" for answering personal quantity-risk questions . . .

Gilson, C., and Bennett, V., Alcohol and Women:Creating a Safer Lifestyle, Fusion Press, A Publishing Service of Authorlink (www.authorlink.com), Irving, Texas, 2000

Table 2.3

Proposed Daily Upper Limits of Moderate Drinking for Women - Not to be Exceeded -			
Body Weight in Pounds	Oz. 80-proof Spirits	Oz. 12% Wine	Oz. 4.5% Beer
90	2.2	7.3	19.5
100	2.4	8.1	21.7
110	2.7	8.9	23.8
120	2.9	9.7	25.9
130	3.2	10.5	28.1
140	3.4	11.3	30.3
150	3.7	12.2	32.5
160	3.9	13.0	34.6
170	4.1	13.8	36.8

*The table is based on 0.5 grams of alcohol per kilogram (2.2 pounds) body weight for women, as opposed to 0.7 for men as used in the 1981 analysis. ibid

Reprinted with permission from Alcohol and Women: Creating a Safer Lifestyle, Gilson, C and Bennett, V., (Authorlink on the Internet) Fusion Press, Irving, Texas, 2001

The authors suggest that the gentler sex should demonstrate their gentility by drinking less and tarrying longer between drinks. The authors worked for years with Thomas Turner, M.D. former dean of the Johns Hopkins Medical School and founding president of the Alcoholic Beverage Medical Research Foundation. There is no similarly comprehensive text for women available in the English language. This is a unique and valuable addition to gender specific drinking literature and should be placed in every medical research library (and on the desks of thoughtful physicians) for its insights and referencing.

Consider food as a protector. It is wise to consume some solid food when drinking. Foods slow down alcohol absorption from the stomach into the bloodstream and thereby reduce the prevailing BAC levels. The illustration below demonstrates various absorption rates for various drinks. It is taken from Leake's 1966 text *Alcoholic Beverages in Clinical Medicine.* The chart also reflects lower BACs and quicker elimination when wine and beer are taken with a meal.

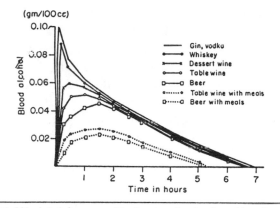

Typical blood-alcohol curves resulting from ingestion of various spirits, wines and beer, each at amounts equivalent to 0.6 gm of alcohol per kilogram of body weight. (From *Alcoholic Beverages in Clinical Medicine,* by Chauncey D. Leake and Milton Silverman, Year Book Medical Publ., Inc., Chicago, 1966).

Reprinted with permission of Year Book Publishing/W. B. Saunders Company. Shows typical blood-alcohol curves for various drinks at 0.6 grams per kilogram of body weight.

Commenting on the absorption chart, Scholten, a San Francisco physician-journalist with long-experience in drinking issues, notes:

Few physicians of my acquaintance are aware of what the graph shows. It depicts the marked differences in the alcoholic effects of various beverages, which it is government policy and the policy of alcohol-research laboratories to ignore.

Scholten, P., Wine and Health, Wines and Vines, Vol. 10, No. 8, August, 1989

Robinson comments on absorption: *If . . . there is food in the digestive system, the alcohol has to take its turn with the masticated food to reach the wall of the stomach, and more particularly the first two feet of small intestine leading from it, where most alcohol is absorbed* (Robinson 1988). Undoubtedly this is why European traditions strongly associate eating with drinking. Food tempers the drink. Obviously this is not new science. BACs are lower when food accompanies consumption.

Consider the setting. Sociologists stress the impact environments have on drinking. This factor is seldom considered in biomedical research. Social scientists study the places, the time involved, and companionship which combine to constitute a "set and setting." A solitary drinker in a skid road tavern is more of a public threat than an amiable, ambulatory group sharing champagne and canapes at a symphony orchestra fund raiser. It matters very much where and how drinking occurs, how much time transpires between drinks, whether and what kind of food is involved, and the amiability (or hostility) among the individuals sharing the drinks.

Caregivers should become familiar with these data when counseling patients. They should stress tolerance, explain the male/female absorption tendencies, the need to eat something when drinking, analyze the patients history and pattern of drinking, and stress the impact of the atmosphere in which the person drinks.

Limits must be imposed on drinking. Arriving at a personal levels can be frustrating unless all the foregoing contributing factors are considered. The government takes the easy way out by announcing arbitrary, one-fits-all limits. Undoubtedly this sort of practicality influenced Anstie, the nineteenth century British physician, as well as the government health officials in our day. Anstie recommend that his patients not to exceed 1 1/2 ounces of absolute alcohol on any single day – the equivalent of three standard drinks. Klatsky says of Anstie's rule: *Modern scientific advances have added little: the threshold for net harm in most population studies is exactly where Anstie, using common sense observations, placed his limit* (Klatsky 2002).

The best advice is to practice moderation in all things.

4. Abuse is tied to per capita consumption

This is the least defensible of all Temperance myths. And probably the most widely held. At first blush, it seems logical. But the logic falters on investigation.

The concept was devised by a French alcoholism researcher Sully Ledermann. Today it is warmly embraced by those public health agencies committed to lowering per capita consumption. They argue a simplistic premise. If everyone consumed less, abusive drinking would decline proportionately. Brunn discusses the rudiments of the theory: *If a government aims at reducing the number of heavy consumers, this goal is likely to be attained if the government succeeds in lowering the total consumption of alcohol* (Brunn 1975). This "control of availability" doctrine holds that all ships rise and fall on the same tide. If drinking goes up, abuse will increase. If drinking falls, the society experiences less abuse. Dozens of studies in the U.S. in and in many other nations have totally refuted the premise in real life.

This nation's sad experience in Prohibition and Premier Gorbachev's attempt to reduce Russian indulgence by shutting down vodka production and curtailing hours of sale show how theory often differs from experience. Both of these nationally enforced programs ultimately increased abusive levels of drinking. The ingenuity of private entrepreneurs doomed both efforts. In Russia's case, a national shortage of sugar resulted from the increase of moonshining.

Federal health officials ignore these experiences in pushing their control of availability agenda. Gmeil suggests that since control of availability has so abjectly failed that another approach should be adopted: *If more evidence is accumulated which fails to support his (Ledermann's) assumptions, different types of alcohol policy and prevention strategy should be sought* (Gmeil 2000). The evidence is incontrovertible. Efforts to reduce per capita drinking do not prevent abuse; they add to its incidence.

A Midanik drinking survey conducted at the University of Michigan reports that 73.4% of twenty-three to twenty-six year-olds and 67.9% of twenty-seven to thirty-year-olds say they disapprove of people over eighteen having one to two drinks nearly every day (Midanik 1999). This is a remarkable sentiment in a small population segment responsible for twenty-seven percent of all beer consumed in our nation. It is easy to recommend less drinking while bending one's own elbows at a furious rate.

In four previous surveys taken between 1979 and 1994, Midanik found: *Despite significant increases in abstention rates, declines in heavy drinking rates and a nearly 20% drop in per capita absolute alcohol consumption since 1980, reports of negative social consequences and/or symptoms of alcohol dependence did not change much* (Midanik 1999). Federal policies have reduced overall consumption in the past thirty years but abuse rates have remained relatively static. The government's program is counterproductive. Selden Bacon, a noted pioneer of the alcoholism treatment systems in the U.S. was for many years director of the Center of Alcohol Studies at Rutgers University. In 1967, Bacon wrote these prophetic words:

> *However, the impact of the Classic Temperance Movement was and is today so great that we can only speak of the current situation vis-a-vis alcohol problems in the U.S.A. as being in flux . . . there still remains a cycling or repetition of old maneuvers, sometimes under new names: Prohibition is finally gone from all the States, but often enough it is replaced by little prohibitions . . . just teaching 16- and 18-year olds that "they mustn't drink" is increasingly recognized as silly, but what should be taught instead remains uncertain and frightening.*

Bacon, S., The Classic Temperance Movement of the U.S.A.: Impact Today on Attitudes, Action and Research, British Journal of Addiction, Vol. 62, pp5-18, 1967

Bacon came to this bleak conclusion forty years after Repeal. In the intervening thirty-four years since his plaintive statement, public policy has drifted steadily back to prohibitionary programs. The dry myths prevail. Inertia rules.

Government programs fail because they ignore the reasons why individuals over-drink. Alcohol abuse is a complex behavioral pattern. In "Comorbidity of Mental Disorders With Alcohol and Other Drug Abuse," Regnier found a high correlation of mental illness among those suffering alcoholism: . . . *among those with alcohol disorders, 36.6% had at least one other mental disorder and 21.5% had another drug abuse-dependence disorder in their lifetime* (Regnier 1996). Reducing the availability of drinks does nothing to help disturbed people who drink to escape serious personal burdens. Alcohol abuse correlates with and is caused by problems and pressures which have little or nothing to do with accessibility of alcoholic beverages.

In a 1986 study, "Drinking Norms and Alcohol-Related Problems in the United States," Linsky established six criteria from data commonly gathered by cities and states which demonstrate socially disruptive drinking: 1) death rate from cirrhosis of the liver, 2) alcohol consumption: average gallons per person, 3) alcohol consumption corrected for tourism: gallons per person, 4) driving while intoxicated (DWI) arrest rates, 5) other alcohol-related arrests such as vagrancy, drunkenness and disorderly conduct, and 6) the percentage of all alcohol arrests divided by total arrests.

Linsky's criteria were formulated into a "score" relating to each state's degree of these six alcohol-related behavioral problems. Here are selected listings of the seven worst and the seven least problem-prone states. The Bible-belt states — Mississippi, Utah, Kentucky and Georgia — had the highest levels of disruptive problems. Remarkably, heavier drinking states — Nevada, Wisconsin, Vermont and Alaska — had the fewest alcohol disruptions. All states (and nations) experience drinking problems but jurisdictions where authorities most fear drinking experience the most problems. The highest disruption scores emerged in states which employ the most restrictive laws — laws which conform to the control of availability mandates promoted by federal health agencies.

RANK	STATE	SCORE	RANK	STATE	SCORE
1	Mississippi	99	44	New Jersey	32
2	Utah	95	45	Montana	30
3	Kentucky	90	46	Penn.	28
4	Georgia	88	47	Alaska	28
5	Tennessee	87	48	Vermont	24
6	Alabama	81	49	Wisconsin	24
7	S. Carolina	81	50	Nevada	17

This is irrefutable evidence that atmosphere – the set and setting – counts. Vindictive and repressive laws *cause* more problems than those they seek to solve. While myriad social and political factors contribute both to the enactment of such laws and to the severity of their enforcement, Linsky's critique shows how pejorative policies and procedures can be counter-productive. Prohibition fostered many proscriptive regulations. Prohibition ultimately became a social disaster. Neoprohibition and the linkage of drinking with the drug war has instituted dozens of new problems in recent decades including binge drinking on the nation's campuses.

Hanson concludes: . . . *that all attempts to stigmatize alcohol as a dirty drug, or as a substance to be abhorred or shunned should be ended; that governmental agencies formulate and implement policies that incorporate the concept of moderate or responsible drinking with the choice of abstinence* (Hanson 1995).

Responsible drinking? It's worth a try.

5. Alcohol abuse costs $148 billion plus

The Department of Health and Human Services alcohol abuse cost estimates come perilously close to tightly edited fiction. Granting the tendency of any government agency to heighten the problems it is instituted to resolve, the gyrating cost estimates published by the National Institute on Alcohol Abuse and Alcoholism over the past two decades betray a total disregard of accounting standards. The latest estimate $148 plus billions is simply indefensible.

Since 1975, when the agency first initiated alcohol abuse cost estimates, the totals have bounced from $42.5 billion (1975) to $148 billion (1998). That's an escalation of more than threefold during a period of gradually eroding per capita consumption. Economist Heien and sociologist Pittman utilized standard accounting methods to determine annual societal costs of drinking abuse to be around $9.5 billion annually. That's about seven percent of the NIAAA figure. Obviously the economic pot needs a bit more stirring.

By choosing to ignore any drinking benefits – a true cost/benefit analysis – the NIAAA makes a mockery of the process. If they didn't perceive some benefits, people would not drink. The most egregious example of creative elaboration is the NIAAA's concept of "lost productivity." No doubt the work absences of heavy drinkers could drag down a company's productivity. But *who* loses *what* during such absences? The abuser and his or her family may lose wages and opportunities for career advancement. The employer may, or may not, lose actual productivity depending on the ability of others to pick up the slack. In real life, the heaviest burdens fall upon the abuser, not society. Nearly half of the $148 billion NIAAA estimates is chalked-up to lost productivity, a fictitious, specious concept.

Barsby explains the ruse of lost productivity: *Take, for example, a Manhattan advertising executive who leaves a hefty annual salary of $225,000 for a high school teaching position in rustic Vermont that pays $25,000 per year. Is there a public loss of $200,000 annually through the executive's remaining working career? Of course not. Yet that is the nonsense which NIAAA wants us to believe* (Barsby 1990).

Weinberg provides a whimsical but telling comparison. He poses a counter-assumption that moderate drinkers *earn* more than either abstaining or abusing workers. Chapter 20 demonstrates that real wages of moderate drinking workers exceed those of abstainers by about seven per cent. Weinberg calls this factor "increased productivity." He discusses an earlier NIAAA projection of abuse costs of $116.8 billion and compares it to the "increased productivity" of America's moderate drinkers:

> I will take their $117 billion and say, all right, there is also a plus side to drinking. I will make the logical assumption that there is a modest increase in workers' productivity because of moderate alcohol use. I might use the Gross National Product as my relative scale . . . Now that cost figure of $116.8 billion is actually 1.2 percent of the total $9.7 trillion receipts of all business. Therefore I am making the simple assumption that the over one hundred million moderate drinkers enjoy an increase in productivity equal to the 1.2 percent of all business receipts — a total of $116.9 billion.

Weinberg, S., Benefits of Alcohol Use Wash Out the Costs of Use Says Noted Economist, Moderate Drinking Journal, Vol. 1, No. 5, September/October, 1987

Voila, NIAAA's "lost productivity" and Weinberg's "increased productivity" constitute an economic wash. No gain; no loss. In a more serious vein, Heien rejects lost productivity using the accounting concepts of internal and external costs: *The methodology employed by the NIAAA in making their estimates of the costs of alcohol abuse basically ignores the distinction between external and internal costs. In the NIAAA approach, no attempt is made to distinguish these costs separately* (Heien 1993).

External costs apply to non-involved individuals or institutions. Lost productivity has no bearing because it is an external cost with no loss to the institution. Cook even challenges the assumption that all alcoholics are less productive in the work place: *There is little credible evidence . . . that heavy drinkers are less productive than other members of the labor force* (Cook 1990).

A study conducted by Lewin-VHI in 1994 found that current levels of wine consumption in the United States account for nearly $1 billion in *reduced* health care expenditures. This conclusion was based upon a comparison of medical expenditures among moderate wine drinkers compared to non-drinkers. These are not phantom figures. Projecting these data to potential new drinkers, the study concluded that a shift of low risk, non-drinkers to one glass of wine per day would save another $2.2 billion in current health care costs (The Benefits for Health-Care Expenditures from Moderate Wine Consumption 1994).

The NIAAA refuses to incorporate these real savings in health care expenditures by moderate drinkers. Further, there is no recognition of the very significant tax contributions to state and national treasuries as well as those generated by the vast agriculture and retail economies in licensed beverages. All these figures are all relevant to a cost/benefit analysis. No serious assessment can be made of alcohol abuse costs without references to counter-balancing benefits.

It is irresponsible for the NIAAA to ignore benefits and to fabricate lost productivity costs. They do so with impunity because our public interest watchdogs and media don't care about drinking issues. Inertia reigns.

6. Alcohol is just another drug

"Alcohol and other drugs" has become as familiar as "mom and apple pie." This intentionally demeaning phrase was introduced by the Department of Health and Human Services in the late 1980s as a key component of the control of availability agenda. Two examples of this type of guilt-by-association advertising by DHHS funding are seen on the following page.

The "alcohol and other drugs" misnomer was the brainchild of Otis Bowen, M.D., Secretary of the Department of Health and Human Services. Bowen established the linkage in a speech in the nation's capitol on November 17, 1987. For thirty years, DHHS and other federal agencies, notably the Surgeon General's office, had been linking drinking with smoking as part of the World Health Organization campaign to reduce use of both. Bowen's clever syntactical strategy tied all three reduction targets together — alcohol, tobacco and illicit drugs.

Alcohol is placed first in this litany of "drugs" for a reason. No matter what drug problem is addressed, Bowen mandated that "alcohol" would be seen first. DHHS eliminated all language modifiers which previously distinguished acceptable use from abuse such as "excessive drinking" or "abusive drinking." Drinking was wedded with the nation's most feared, addictive scourges. Words do matter. The resulting imagery is perniciously negative. The strategy opened federal drug funds to many dry lobby agencies fighting "alcohol and other drugs."

Bowen asserted in his speech: *Nearly 5 million adolescents, or 3 of every 10, have problems with alcohol today . . . it's the "gateway" theory at work . . . one out of 15 kids will eventually become alcoholic* (Bowen 1987). Bowen's "facts" are, to be kind, gross hyperbole.

A decade or more of serious, heavy drinking is required to develop the classic symptoms of alcoholism as defined by the American Medical Association. Teen-agers do abuse alcohol daily at addictive levels, but they are not, strictly speaking, addicted alcoholics. In fact, through the 1990s, underage alcohol abuse was in a gentle decline.

In the *American Journal of Drug and Alcohol Abuse,* Kaufman disputes the existence of an alcohol and drug gateway: *The*

Here are two advertisements generated by federal and state drug war funds. The first implies children are corrupted by the simple act of fetching a beer bottle. The second, transforms a beer bottle into a drug hypodermic needle. Both are egregious overstatements typical of the federal control of availability agenda.

When some parents crave their favorite drug, they'll even use their own kids to get it.

IT'S ONLY BEER.

Beer contains alcohol. Alcohol is a drug. Alcohol is the number one drug problem in this country. Not marijuana. Not cocaine. Alcohol. Get the point?

Make the choice to make a change.

*steppingstone hypothesis was presented as a primary danger of mari-
juana in that it led to the use of "hard" drugs . . . We propose that
neither alcohol nor marijuana are truly steppingstones in that they
seduce a non-predisposed individual down the path to hard drugs.
Rather, they are both very commonly used in our society and are used
and abused more frequently by those who eventually go on to "harder"
drugs* (Kaufman 1982). Golub notes that: *The gateway phenomenon
reflects norms prevailing among youth at a specific place and time and
that the linkages between stages are far from causal* (Golub 2000).
Government rhetoric has conditioned society to fear youth
drinking, to raise alcohol taxes to exorbitant rates, and to restrict
both the availability and hours of service. If it's booze that's
being bashed, no one dares, or cares, to object. Inertia reigns.

A 1987 debate on the meaning of "alcoholism" in the prestig-
ious *British Journal of Addiction* reflected the developing acri-
mony, even in the professional literature. Room complained
that the term "problem drinker" inferred that all drinking is
"risk-taking:" *As the term "problem drinker" came into more general
use in the U.S., it tended to be co-opted by champions of a disease
concept of alcoholism . . . Instead of two classes of drinkers, "alcoholics"
and "social drinkers," there were now three, with "problem drinkers"
as an in-between "pre-alcoholismic" category* (Room 1987). Clever,
that.

The tenacity of cultural myths

Physician and *London Times* columnist Stuttaford provides a
perspective on this ongoing battle for the public mind:

*Approximately 90 percent of men and 80 percent of
women in this country enjoy drinking alcohol from
time to time. Only a tiny fraction drink to excess . . .
Opponents of drinking are selective in their reporting:
they seize upon the disasters which overtake the
minority who drink too much and draw conclusions
from their behaviour and health which are then
applied to the population as a whole. This way of
generating statistics is unsound, and their misleading
of the public is unjustifiable. The medical advantages
of alcohol have been hidden from the general public
for thirty years, and the reason usually advanced for
this obfuscation is the patronizing one that alcohol,*

delightful as it is to take and good as it is for the heart, cannot be entrusted to the masses lest they drink themselves to death.

Stuttaford, T., To Your Good Health! The Wise Drinker's Guide, Faber & Faber, London, 1997

Stuttaford's conclusions echo those of his British colleague Sir Richard Doll, M.D. found in the opening chapter of this book: *People should be treated as adults and told the facts* (Doll 1999). Instead of facts, Americans are treated like children and fed generous doses of anti-drinking spin.

The pot is boiling. This book seeks new energy and involvement from the two segments of society most responsible for the day to day delivery of health care in our nation– doctors and mothers.

The final two chapters are "how to" for physicians and parents.

Chapter 32

The Clinician's Conundrum

A medical problem

■ **Author's abstract**: The Journal of the American Medical Association framed the critical issue in an editorial titled "The Clinician's Conundrum." It concluded that lives would be saved if the public was better informed about drinking and cardiovascular disease. This chapter challenges practicing physicians and alternative caregivers in this nation to demand improved communication of positive alcohol research in medical and public health communications.

■ ◦→ Caregivers are inadequately informed today about the health effects of moderate consumption.

The *American Heritage Dictionary* describes a conundrum as a problem admitting of no satisfactory solution. Healthy drinking research presents a significant conundrum for the medical communication systems. Traditional antipathies to drinking smother objective science and discourage its dissemination to caregivers and the health-interested public.

Addressing the conundrum in a seminar for practicing physicians in Texas, Juergens reviewed the findings of a survey undertaken by the American Wine Alliance for Research and Education (AWARE): . . . *physicians today are not adequately informed about the current medical and scientific data on the health effects of moderate alcohol consumption. A review of the professional literature showed that of the more than 2,000 scientific articles published annually about alcohol, less than 15% address the positive effects of moderate consumption* (Juergens 1998). AWARE is a research advocacy of physicians and scientists which promotes wider communication of healthy drinking research within the medical professions. Juergens addressed the imbalance in total research. This book suggests that fair and complete communication of that fifteen percent favorable to responsible drinking would turn the tide.

The clinician's conundrum

On September 28, 1994, three years following the CBS telecast on the French paradox, the *Journal of the American Medical Association* published a remarkable editorial admitting that healthy drinking science presents a "clinician's conundrum." Pearson wrote:

> The stance that the medical community should take on alcohol consumption is seemingly a conundrum of the highest order. On the one hand, extensive observational data document the finding that total mortality is reduced in those who consume one or two drinks per day, as compared with teetotalers. Numerous attempts have failed to show these data to be artifactual.

Pearson, T., and Terry, P., What to Advise Patients About Drinking Alcohol: The Clinician's Conundrum, Journal of the American Medical Association, Vol. 272, No. 12, September 28, 1994

Few in medicine today doubt this editorial's premise that responsible drinking can lessen heart disease. But the bombshell in the editorial was a computation made by the authors speculating about drinking's impact on real mortality.

> *We applied estimates from 13 cohort studies of
> alcohol consumption and coronary heart disease
> mortality in moderate consumers, who make up the
> largest proportion of all drinkers. . . to develop
> ranges of estimates of coronary heart disease deaths
> that would result from nationwide abstinence from
> alcohol. Estimates ranged from 11,556 to 135,884
> additional coronary heart disease deaths that would
> occur because of abstinence (Pearson 1994).*

As many as 135,884 additional annual coronary deaths could occur if the government succeeded in reducing alcohol consumption to zero. The obvious conclusion is that drinking now protects 135,884 individuals from premature heart failure. This estimate refers solely to coronary *mortality.* No calculation was made on how much additional cardiovascular *illness* would occur. Nor was there an estimate (or recognition) of illness and death that total abstention might provoke in osteoporosis, cancer, diabetes, gallstones, stress, early loss of cognition, increased kidney and gall stones along with new demands for acute and clinical hospital services. By choosing indifference and cooperation with government programs medicine is, in effect, reducing the public's health! By their own accounting!

Pearson closed his editorial with the commendable recommendation that practicing physicians: . . . *tailor the message to each individual in the same way that counseling is given on diet, physical activity, sexual practices and so on.* Excellent advice but how can a "generally uninformed" physician corps tailor pertinent advice about drinking?

A serious conundrum indeed.

Where it all started

Alcohol ambivalence in American medicine traces its roots to a regrettable but understandable policy decision rendered by an American Medical Association meeting on June 6, 1917 at the apex of the Prohibition campaign. In keeping with the temper of the times, the AMA passed the following:

> *WHEREAS, We believe that the use of alcohol as a
> beverage is detrimental to the human economy and,
> WHEREAS, its use in therapeutics, as a tonic or a
> stimulant, or as a food has no scientific basis,*

therefore be it
RESOLVED, that the American Medical Association
opposes the use of alcohol as a beverage; and be it
further
RESOLVED, That the use of alcohol as a therapeutic
agent should be discouraged.

The previous year, federal health authorities had removed alcohol from the *U.S. Pharmacopoeia*. These actions mirrored a turbulent time in American society. Repeal of Prohibition in 1933 was virtually meaningless for the myriad alcohol prohibitions ensconsed within American medicine. Indifference to favorable drinking science today is rooted in the 1917 resolution.

The communication gap redux

Wodak sums up the communication dilemma: *There can be little doubt that our knowledge of health effects of immoderate alcohol consumption far exceeds our understanding of the impact of moderate alcohol consumption* (Wodak 1994). Recall that Lucia championed more healthy drinking research and better communication of the findings. Hundreds of epidemiological studies have justified Lucia's early confidence. Doctors know they are being short-changed on drinking issues. They see the fragmented reports in *U.S.A. Today* and *Time* magazine along with the rest of us. Harrison notes physician dissatisfaction with alcohol research censorship among Canadian physicians: *A large majority of delegates voted in favour of publishing information on the health benefits of moderate drinking* (Harrison 1998). Physicians are aware also of the more liberal medical attitudes in European nations which still employ levels of alcohol therapy. Commenting on the AMA's 1917 rejection resolution, Sinclair writes:

If the American Medical Association had really
believed that alcohol was detrimental to the human
economy, its condemnation would have been just. But
alcohol was still being widely prescribed as a
medicine in 1917. It was recommended by many
doctors in cases of fainting, shock, heart failure,
exposure, and exhaustion. It was believed to be an
antidote to snake bite, pneumonia, influenza,
diphtheria, and anemia. It was used as a method of
feeding carbohydrates to sufferers from diabetes. It

> *was given to cheer and build up the aged . . . Nothing
> was said in the resolution about the fact that small
> quantities of alcohol taken with meals might aid the
> digestion and relax the mind.*

Sinclair, A., Era of Excess, Harper Colophon Books, New York, 1964

Sinclair continues: *The prohibitionists exploited the medical and sexual terrors of the people of America in order to further their cause.* Today the federal government pressures the medical system to support inflated risks. Since government money permeates medical education, research and care delivery, breaking away is indeed a challenge. But it is a challenge that science and good public health demands.

Pessimism and mixed messages

In "Physician's Perspective," Hennekens argues: *Assumptions that the average person should begin to have a drink a day are premature, or even misguided. None of us is the mythical average person . . . The health benefits of an alcoholic drink a day are substantially smaller than those offered by exercise and eating right* (Hennekens 1998). The millions of Americans who drink moderately are not "mythical" either. They are made up of flesh and bone which now enjoys a range of benefits from conservative drinking practices. Shouldn't everyone have that choice?

No one espouses universal consumption. There are many health, religious or simple prejudicial reasons for abstention. But better communication of the science would permit individuals to make informed choices, in concert with their caregivers. The national surveys conducted by the American Cancer Society, the government's NHANES surveys, the work of Ellison, Renaud, Klatsky, Kaplan and many others conclude that individuals who exercise regularly, eat correctly *and drink moderately* are the healthiest. The public should be aware of these studies. Hennekens is right in that none of us is a "mythical average person," but neither are we "wanna-be drunks." Pessimism about the public's genuine temperance is unwarranted.

Medical mixed messages abound. A *Health After 50* article "The Facts About Drinking to Your Health" establishes certain benefits for heart disease and "non-cardiac benefits as well" and then virtually destroys the good news with:

> *While USDA guidelines and health organizations like the American Heart Association say that it is safe and perhaps even healthy for men to have up to two alcohol drinks per day and women to have one, they do not recommend that anyone who doesn't already drink start in order to achieve a possible health benefit. And neither do we. The potential drawbacks of excessive alcohol consumption and the possibility of dependence are too great.*

The Facts About Drinking to Your Health, Health After 50, Vol. 12, Issue 5, July, 2000

If medical writers and researchers were better schooled in the anthropology and sociology of drinking, perhaps they would be less fearful of the relative risks of mass alcohol dependence. From three to five percent of all drinkers are dependent in a clinical sense and most of them have underlying problems. An article in the *UC Berkeley Wellness Letter* titled "Healthy hearts without hormone therapy" has this troubling advice: *Consider alcohol. Moderate drinking – for a woman, no more than one drink a day – may reduce the risk of developing CHD. . . Nondrinkers should probably not start drinking just for potential heart benefits* (Healthy hearts 2000).

Why not? Shouldn't women evaluate all options for better health? Several hundred research papers published in the past fifteen years have deduced that moderates have healthier hearts and live longer than abstainers and even survive better following a heart attack. Aren't avoidance of infarctions and extended life worthy aspirations? Clinical medicine needs to grapple with the alcohol conundrums passed on by the clogged medical arteries. As Britain's Doll advises, adults in a free society deserve the truth.

In "Alcohol, health and the heart," Chick advises: *The balance of risk to benefit appears to favour giving medical advice to some patients in middle life with uncontrollable risk factors for coronary heart disease . . . There is also the theoretical risk of a ripple in the population such that more people may move into harmful drinking* (Chick 1998). Atherosclerosis problems begin in the teens and develop over a lifetime. If drinks help to maintain healthy arteries why wait until the middle-years when plaque has become an "uncontrollable risk factor?" Drinking will not eliminate the hundred and one other lifestyle choices that contribute to corroded arteries but it is one factor known to lower that risk.

An article in the *Canadian Family Physician* by Ashley recommends: *While moderate drinking might protect some older people . . . those who currently abstain from alcohol should not begin drinking in order to reduce their risk of health problems* (Ashley 1997). Has Ashley missed the copious literature which shows health benefits across the span of life for up to thirty different conditions? If broccoli, exercise and leisure activities are recommended routinely because they "reduce the risk of health problems," why exclude drinks which are already taken regularly by the healthiest segments of the society? Ashley should be informed of Smart's Ontario study which concluded: *Most respondents believed that wine drinking protects against heart disease. Most of them (78%) had heard that drinking wine or other alcoholic beverages reduces the risk of CHD . . . A vast majority (87.6%) said that having one or two drinks a day would reduce their risk of heart disease. Belief in the health benefits was most common among men, more frequent drinkers and wine drinkers* (Smart 2002). The Canadian citizen is far ahead of the medical system on this issue.

The most egregious of mixed messages discourages drinking by ennobling abstention. This is prime Temperance-think. An article in the Johns Hopkins Medical School's *Health After 50* exemplifies this technique: *One glass of wine or spirits daily is acceptable and may even provide some cardiovascular benefit. But if you don't drink, don't start* (Prescription for Longevity 1998). The clear implication is that it is healthier to abstain than to drink moderately. That's nonsense. Many findings in this book challenge this assumption. One must wonder why so many of these articles address exclusively cardiovascular benefits when the science favors drinking for cognition, diabetes, osteoporosis, stress and so on. Why should any adult be discouraged from the moderate intake of foods with such benefits?

Clinical physicians need to shake up the system. It's failing them and the public.

Dueling European epidemiologies

Any journalist starts out to assemble facts and figures that are beyond the view of cursory reading or electronic viewing. This book presents a meager sampling of evidence that U.S. medical publications and newsletters routinely neglect telling the whole story of healthy drinking science. Every physician knows that any book represents but a smattering of data, an anthill of information compared to the mountainous body of facts and figures in biomedicine.

In all this interesting data, one line of study stands out as uniquely promising — that of drink antioxidants. A review of U.S. studies on phenolic compounds is presented in Chapter 2. Quotes from Waterhouse, Gorinstein, Agewall, Bagchi, Frankel, Demrow, Bertelli, Duthie, and a panel of chemists reporting in *Wine: Nutrition and Therapeutic Benefits* including Watkins and Maxwell outline the extraordinary work being done by American scientists in this developing field. European antioxidant research has bifurcated into two parallel but similar paths, one studying wine impacts and the other evaluating beer's role.

Physicians should applaud — as does this writer — a healthy diversity in research funding. But the European undertakings are of special importance. First, European nations enjoy highly profitable agricultures, local commerce and international trade in licensed beverages. Wine and brandy exports from Italy, Spain and France, liqueurs and brews from Germany, Holland, and Scotch and beer from UK are high-priority items to their respective governments. Second, the medical establishments in these countries generally support responsible drinking. Drink therapy is common in clinical practice. Despite continuing efforts to reduce per capita drinking by the World Health Organization and its public health cadres, Europeans still treasure their drinks. Because of these critical differences, advances in antioxidant research in Europe are likely to be government funded and easily incorporated into medical practice.

In the December 14, 2001 issue of *Wine Spectator*, senior editor Per-Henrik Mansson updates the impressive work of a cooperative team of wine-oriented European scientists. The titular head of this multi-talented ensemble is Serge Renaud whose pioneering epidemiology is quoted in this book. Mansson reports that

Renaud was challenged by U.S. government health officials to verify his assertions on the CBS *60 Minutes* French Paradox telecast that wine consumption could reduce coronary disease. The scientist's response came in the form of an article in *The Lancet* (Renaud 1992). That report employs data from the MONICA study which compared annual coronary heart disease deaths per 100,000 population in nine cities or regions including the cities of Toulouse and Lille in France and Stanford in the U.S.

Lille had 89 deaths per 100,000 citizens (78 male and 11 female) compared to 232 in Stanford (182 male and 48 female). Renaud comments: *It must be emphasized that alcohol is a drug that, studies suggest, should be used regularly but only at moderate doses of about 20-30 g[rams] per day. At this level of consumption, the risk of CHD can be decreased by as much as 40% . . . The average consumption of alcohol in Toulouse is about 38 g[rams] per day, 34 g[rams] in the form of wine whereas Stanford [consumption level] is not known but can be expected to be much lower* (Renaud 1992). Residents in Lille apparently average about 2 1/2 standard American drinks daily.

Why should citizens in the U.S. endure nearly three times the annual CHD deaths as the residents of Lille, France? That's the puzzle of the French paradox, an anomaly evaluated in hundreds of studies. Renaud's pioneering assumptions have been validated many times over. Yet the prevailing sentiment in American medicine, as evidenced over and over in this book, remains generally negative and dissuasive. "If you don't drink now, don't start for *health's* sake." For *heaven's* sake, why not? Without other medical contraindications, why shouldn't Americans consider wine in the same manner as they choose other fruits and vegetables known to reduce coronary risk? This does not imply that everyone in America should begin drinking wine daily. That's absurd. It does imply that everyone *not at risk* should be given the option of informed choice in view of the overwhelming evidence now on the table. Only physicians have sufficient clout to challenge this negative framework common to their profession. As the editors for JAMA pointed out, alcohol ambivalence raises mortality risk.

According to Mansson, members of the European wine consortium have presented a major funding proposal for this research to the European Union. He notes: *In recent years, research teams, many based in Europe, have provided fresh insights into the health benefits and unique characteristics of wine. As their results become better known, these scientists are influencing European culture by inspiring chefs and wine lovers to apply their discoveries to a lifestyle that integrates healthier drinking, eating and living patterns* (Mansson 2001). Their findings are impacting American culture as well.

The beer-oriented findings were revealed in a symposium staged by The Brewers of Europe – an association known as the CBMC (*www.cbmc.org*). Their symposium "Beer and health: the latest benefits" was held in Brussels in October, 2001. Medical experts discussed new findings on a several scientific fronts to an audience which included policy makers of the European Parliament and the European Commission. Oliver James, chair of the event and professor at the School of Clinical Medical Studies in the U.K., noted: *Beer plays a part, along with other alcoholic drinks, in reducing the risk of heart disease. There is also preliminary evidence of benefits of beer consumption, which may be different from those of other drinks, which warrants more detailed investigation* (Beer and health benefits 2001).

The "dueling" beer and wine epidemiologies in Europe will inevitably generate new interest in responsible drinking among medical decision makers across the globe. Their findings will enrich us all. Mansson reveals a contagious enthusiasm among the wine fraternity. He quotes Joseph Vercauteren, head of the pharmacology department at the University Victor Segalen in Bordeaux. Vercauteren sets an inspiring tone: *We have a sense that we are dealing with the essentials of being . . . Oxidation, breathing, cell life: We are dealing with the preservation of life* (Mansson 2001). The CBMC web site reports similar enthusiasm by Shahidi, Pagagni and Bourne who suggest that beer has equally profound but somewhat different oxidative consequences: *Beer is also a source of antioxidants which play a role in the fight against cancer . . . Per drink (of equivalent alcohol content), beer contains more than twice as many antioxidants as white wine, although only half the amount in red wine. However, many of the antioxidants in red wine are large molecules and may be less readily absorbed by the body than the smaller molecules found in beer . . . research has shown that the*

*antioxidant material in beer is more readily available to the body than
from solid foods* (Potential Benefits of Beer 2001). The research
pot boils over.

What excites these scientists, as well as the producers of wine,
beer and spirits in Europe, is the beneficial relationship of
drinks when employed as common foods for heart health, cancer and other illnesses. Not as "street drugs" but as foods. In the
"Questions Still To Be Answered" page of the the CBMC web
site, there is this challenging statement: *There is a dilemma for the
medical profession: Is it ethical to advocate drinking alcoholic drinks?
Is it ethical not to when the benefits are well established?* (Questions
still to be answered 2001). Chapter 2 of this book concludes
with: . . . *drinks are pleasant foods which provide nourishment,
tranquillity and an abundance of antioxidants. As with green leafy
vegetables, moderate consumption couldn't hurt.*

Antioxidant research is demonstrating that American clinicians today do have a genuine conundrum that challenges traditional medical antipathies. It's time for clinical action.

Breaking with bad traditions

The first step in resolving the dilemma lies in opening up the
information channels within all sectors of the health system and
with media that target a general audience. There is no need to
silence those who oppose drinking. They are important to the
debate. But contemplate the impact if one-hundred subscribing
physicians communicated with the editors of the medical newsletters. Genuine and informed concern expressed about a lack
of coverage or bias on healthy drinking issues would alert
editors of a potential readership problem. What if a thousand
doctors wrote, called or e-mailed? How about ten-thousand? Are
there ten thousand clinical physicians out of 600,000 physicians
out there who are concerned about these issues?

Remember that physicians are not the only readers of *UC
Berkeley Wellness Letter, Harvard Health Watch* or *Health After 50*
and others. Medical journalists (including this writer) and thousands of private citizens subscribe to these publications. The
ramifications of more open presentation of responsible drinking
issues in the popular newsletters are incalculable. Peele outlines
the fundamental problem in the *American Journal of Public Health*:

Today there is a public health debate in America over how to deal with beverage alcohol. The dominant approach, the disease model of alcoholism, emphasizes the biological —probably inherited —nature of problem drinking. This model is challenged by the public health model which strives to limit alcohol consumption for everyone in order to reduce individual and social problems. The first approach is medical and treatment-oriented and the second is epidemiological and policy-oriented; however, both present alcohol in fundamentally negative terms.

Peele, S., The Conflict Between Public Health Goals and the Temperance Mentality, American Journal of Public Health, Vol. 83, No. 6, June, 1993

The medical voice is negatively framed. Only a few scattered medical authorities speak of drinking in objective, positive terms. Juergens stresses the crying need for better understanding of drinking issues among physicians: *Americans are confident when they turn to their physicians for advice. They expect that it will be both accurate and current. . . . (research) has demonstrated that physicians today are not adequately informed about the current medical and scientific data on the health effects of moderate alcohol consumption* (Juergens 1998). Peele and Juergens are right. The transition to open communication must begin within medicine itself and it must proceed on many fronts. Here are some suggestions from an journalistic outsider looking in:

1. A long-range priority should be the restructuring of the 1917 resolution of the AMA House of Delegates that ejected alcohol from medical education and clinical practice. Every member of the AMA has a piece of the organization's power.

2. Physicians, dentists, nurses, chiropractors, therapists, nutritionists, acupuncturists, hypnotists, naturopathic practitioners, psychologists and other health professionals belong to professional societies and subscribe to publications that periodically discuss alcohol use and abuse. It only takes a few moments to drop a letter or e-mail to the editor of your chosen publications when something is omitted

*or a gratuitous, overblown negative is attached to
such articles.*

*3. Professionals are urged to become more informed,
more widely read and articulate on drinking issues.*

*4. Those with the resources, experience and
inclination are urged to participate in or mount
research projects in their own disciplines as did the
German lumbar surgeon reported in Chapter 15.*

Regier sums up the current standoff in drinking communication: *The current situation in alcohol education and research is analogous to conditions following the collapse of the Tower of Babel. We speak in a plethora of different tongues, and our progress is impeded by the absence of a common language* (Regier 1990). Caregivers can cast out the babbling tongues by asking for new, uncluttered, straightforward language that distinguishes decisively between the benefits of alcohol use and the dangers of alcohol abuse. Weill points to the oddity of American medicine being held hostage by a specious political theory that lacks any scientific credibility: *Ledermann's theory has no valid theoretical basis, has not been experimentally validated and does not take abstainers into account. It should remain a matter of scientific debate but not an instrument of health policy* (Weill 2001).

Vaillant's monumental, 40 year study of alcoholism suggests a more open, family-oriented approach: *A second conclusion is that if culture does play such an important role in the genesis of alcoholism, we must try to uncover ways of socializing healthy drinking practices, so that such practices will remain for a lifetime under an individual's conscious choice. Introducing children to the ceremonial and sanctioned use of low-proof alcoholic beverages taken with meals in the presence of others, coupled with social sanctions against drunkenness and against drinking at unspecified times, would appear to provide the best protection against future alcohol abuse* (Vaillant 1983). This is the European system of responsible drinking.

It's probably "illegal, fattening or causes cancer"

Opening the communication gates will require time, patience and good will. In the 1997 Christmas issue of the *British Medical Journal,* in "Just what the doctor ordered – more alcohol and sex: Anything I want to do is illegal, fattening, or causes cancer in mice," Clare advocated one of our nation's treasured Constitutional privileges. The pursuit of human pleasure:

> *But what of the presence of pleasure . . . So, what do we tell our patients now? We are left with a paradox . . . what we thought was bad for you may actually be good for you, but it may not be good to tell you, in case you do it too much, and it is certainly not good to tell you it is good for you if you do too much of it already—assuming we could agree what was too much in the first place.*

Clare, A., and Wessely, S., Just what the doctor ordered – more alcohol and sex: Anything I want to do is illegal, fattening, or causes cancer in mice, British Medical Journal, Vol. 315, Vol. 7123, December, 1998

Clinical physicians can ask, at a minimum, for a change in the pejorative syntax, the very language with which drinking is discussed. Lawrence, a pioneer cardiologist and immunochemist at the University of California, expresses a lost faith in America's moderate consuming majority:

> *I remember once asking a dermatologist how often I should wash my hair. "As often as you wish," he replied. "Isn't that how often you wash your hands?" My concept of moderate consumption of alcohol is the same. I drink as much as I wish, and I have been doing so for decades . . . . I believe that a normal person should drink as much as he or she wishes, whether the drink be a cocktail before dinner, wine with dinner, brandy or a dessert wine after dinner, or all of the above. If you are not a problem drinker, you will not often exceed the basic limits and the few times you do will teach you to be more restrained in the future, for you will not like the way overindulgence makes you feel.*

Lawrence, S., What is Moderate Drinking, Healthy Drinking, 1994

In concluding his survey of the literature, de Lorimier concurs with Lawrence: *However, it is inappropriate to advocate consumption of beverage alcohol for those who are prone to addiction, who have religious reasons for abstaining, in individuals who are taking medication that adversely interact with alcohol, for people who have repugnant reactions, for those who have had pancreatitis, and perhaps during pregnancy. It should be a priority in our educational system to define consumption in moderation and to deplore abuse of alcohol* (de Lorimier 2000).

Antoschechkin's *Alcohol: Poison or Medicine?* makes the important distinction between responsible use and the craving for a "pharmacological effect" when drinking. He concludes: *A moderate drinker feels a requirement to take an alcohol dose that eliminates tension and mental fatigue and that is sufficient for him. An alcoholic has a need to reach a pharmacological effect to reduce a depressive state, which results from genetically determined abnormalities . . . A popular belief that regular alcohol consumption, even in moderate amounts, leads to alcoholism does not have substantial grounds of support . . . alcohol in low-to-moderate doses can be used an unlimitedly long time as a remedy (for) . . . stress, anxiety, depression, risk of coronary artery disease, thrombosis, type II diabetes and some other stress-related diseases* (Antoschechkin 2002).

This book argues for nothing more than the distribution and discussion of a developing science. Hardly revolutionary. It has no quarrel whatsoever with the need for strong public and private prevention and treatment programs for abuse and alcoholism. Physicians who agree that this is a fight worth waging are urged to use this book as a handy tool to stem misperceptions in the media and to promote a wider understanding of the truly impressive breadth of healthy drinking science. Physicians are urged to photocopy freely from its pages. The short chapters are designed to facilitate distribution to editors and commentators. Other informative background books are listed in the Recommended Reading section. For those with handy desktop computers, here are several excellent Internet sources which provide a variety of up-to-date resources and commentaries on healthy drinking. Articles and references can be downloaded from these web sites and sent on to publication editors in moments.

A great example of enlightened drinking in North American can be found in the Province of Quebec. Educ'alcool (Alcohol Education) conducts a major study of drinking in the province every five years: *Eight out of ten Quebecers aged 15 and older (82%) drink alcohol . . . Alcohol is assuming an increasingly normal place in Quebec Society, as it becomes more accepted and acceptable part of day-to-day affairs* (Quebecers and Alcohol 2002). Eighty-two percent drink compared to sicty-five percent in the U.S. For answers, contact Educ'alcool at www.educalool.qc.ca.

One never knows what might happend as a consequence of a publication such as this one which speaks to a very large body of professionals. One can hope, however, that a better comprehension of this body of favorable research might stimulate all sorts of unanticipated actions. There is one thing that any concerned physicians can do. That is to monitor the following web sites for the latest in healthy drinking research and pass data along to medical newsletters or other sources of medical updating which omit or downplay its significance.

David Hanson's Alcohol Problems and Solutions
www.alcoholinformation.org

Alcohol in Moderation
AIM-Digest.com

American Wine Alliance for Research and Education
www.alcohol-aware.com

Gene Ford's Science of Healthy Drinking
www.scienceofhealthydrinking.com

International Center for Alcohol Policies
www.icap.org

The Society of Medical Friends of Wine
www.medicalfriendsofwine.org

The Wine Institute
www.wineinstitute.com

Have at it. You've nothing to lose but a conundrum!

Chapter 33

The Family Challenge

A return to
genuine temperance

■ **Author's abstract**: Temperance culture has remained a vital political force in our land for two centuries. Through this long period, governments and alcohol control agencies sought in various ways to reduce drinking. This chapter challenges the parents of America —our de facto nutritionists and caregivers — to rise to a new challenge. This time the goal is to return to the primal motivations of Temperance —to promote responsible consumption among those who choose to drink.

■ ➡ To develop a consensus distinguishing use from abuse
➡ To reconstruct a genuine temperance ethic

Admittedly, the challenge in this book is a whopper. Fixed cultural attributes are resistant to change. But it is an achievable goal. The majority of Americans drink so there is no fundamental problem with alcohol consumption. What is lacking is comprehension of drinks as wholesome foods.

The last chapter posed a specific challenge to physicians and other caregivers to work for unbiased communication of drinking research within the medical and alternative care systems. This chapter moves the same challenge to American mothers and fathers — the individuals who determine the family diet and render in-home health care. Consider how the range of science presented in this book could alter these two domestic tasks:

1. Health benefits in responsible drinking extend across the entire cardiovascular cluster of diseases and apply in varying degrees to youth, to the middle-aged and to seniors.

2. Surveys conducted by the American Cancer Society, government agencies and epidemiologists in many nations show moderate drinkers having lower rates of heart disease and cancer than abstainers or heavy drinkers.

3. The uncertain links between drinking and breast cancer are less than those for female heart disease. Both risk factors need to be evaluated.

4. Studies favor moderate drinking for many other conditions. While many of these do not reach a scientific consensus, they combine to present a multi-faceted array of health advantages enjoyed by moderate drinkers.

5. Physicians, alternative caregivers and food nutritionists are poorly informed of these findings. This research communication gap reduces effective clinical care and alcohol abuse counseling.

6. Most government and private health agencies promote a control of availability which seeks a national reduction in per capita drinking, a policy which fails to distinguish use from abuse.

One can argue with any one, or with many, of the over 600 scientific quotations in this text, or with the additional hundreds of citations in the reference section. But any objective perusal of this mass confirms the book's premise. Our nation is needlessly hung up on drinking. Other nations and cultures enjoy more health benefits from responsible consumption. This impasse constitutes America's "clinical conundrum."

Nothing in this book diminishes addiction science which addresses the human misery occasioned by alcohol abuse. Nothing denies the vulnerability of significant segments of the population to any alcohol use. ICAP published a review of such "at risk" populations titled *Alcohol and Special "Populations:" Biological Vulnerability.* The November 2001 study reports: . . . *a biological predisposition makes them especially susceptible . . . genetic vulnerability means low tolerance to alcohol and the inability to process it . . . Such information is included in the drinking and dietary guidelines published by a number of countries (Alcohol and "Special Populations"* 2001). It is important to respect the evidence that some individuals should refrain from drinking.

Alcohol abuse or alcohol vulnerability are not addressed in this book. The objective posed here is to open up the channels of health communication relating to the interests of responsible drinkers. If that single goal is met, substantial change will evolve in how we perceive drinking. The pre-Prohibition distinctions between use and abuse will again be honored in our land. Whether you are a physician, an alternative caregiver, a nurse, a mom, a dad or other responsible family person, your participation is warmly solicited, much needed. This task can be accomplished in your home, at your leisure. No experience or special training required. The sole requirement is a willingness to learn a bit more about a specific body of science. With that grounding, anyone can challenge the encrusted, indifferent public health system. An informed and convinced advocate is one of nature's irresistible forces.

A Temperance primer

A few comments on the meaning and history of Temperance in America will be useful. If pioneer Temperance workers had stuck to their guns and promoted *moderation* for those who chose to drink, American drinking history would have been dramatically different. Temperance by definition is "the exercise of moderation and self-restraint." Every scientist quoted in this book has stressed moderation. Adoption of genuine temperance practices is an entirely scientific plan today.

In colonial times, nearly everyone – young, old and most in-between – consumed some form of alcohol every day. Beer and wine were known as the beverages of health. Misgivings developed about distilled spirits because hard liquor was associated with the most pressing drinking problems. An addicted drinker will always seek the most potent source available. When no high proof can be had, the addict settles for the next best or any other source of alcohol, even for after-shave lotion.

Since almost everyone consumed some alcohol, the original thrust of temperance pioneers was not abstinence. Pioneer temperance workers encouraged the use of "moderate" beverages – wine, beer, cider and other fermented drinks. This manner of drinking was endorsed by both religion and medicine. Early temperance programs sought to switch drinkers from hard liquor. Lender makes this point in *Drinking in America*:

> The sticking point was hard liquor and, more specifically, the realization that its use was becoming so prevalent that (at least in the eyes of some observers) society was losing the ability to control drinking excesses. As the eighteenth century advanced, it became increasingly clear that the social norms that previously had controlled individual behavior with remarkable success were loosening.

Lender, M., and Martin, J., Drinking in America, The Free Press, New York, 1982

Following the American Revolution, Congress began to establish national laws and regulations to be carried out in all states. Lender notes that this shift of power and influence from state assemblies and local social institutions to the Congress created jurisdictional tensions, some of which endure to this day: *It had ushered in new leaders, hastened the decline of the established churches, stimulated Western migration and allowed egalitarian ideals to challenge hierarchical social relations as never before* (Lender 1982). Federal excise taxes on liquor were imposed soon after the hostilities to pay the debts incurred in the war.

The original Temperance campaign was nurtured by Calvinist ministers around 1810 when drinking problems had reached truly epidemic levels. Lender reports . . . *the chief credit for popularizing the temperance message before the mid-1820s must go to the Protestant churches, whose social influence and sheer numbers began to have a national impact* (Lender 1982). The clergy's goal was uncomplicated – to shore up the endangered family structure. Their proposals were enthusiastically embraced by wives and mothers who often waited and watched as family resources were dissipated in local taverns. Thus women became prime movers in the Temperance movement. The first formal Temperance organization was assembled in 1826 as the American Society for the Promotion of Temperance. Note that temperate drinking was to be *promoted*. Lender continues: *The early temperance movement, then, was not a prohibitionary crusade. But the split between moderation and abstinence was present even among the earliest leaders* (Lender 1982). This bit of history provides a strong argument for returning to the original roots – genuine temperance.

Soon an ultimate solution emerged for the hard-nosed drys. Moderation gave way to a ruling passion to outlaw drinking altogether. Kobler reports that as early as 1812, a band of sixty-nine Portland, Maine Quaker women mounted a campaign to outlaw any drinking in that state: *Abstinence groups gained strength in town after Maine town* (Kobler 1973). By the 1840s, per capita drinking had fallen steadily but support remained high for legislation which would protect against future drinking excesses. Ironically, Maine finally enacted prohibition in 1851, when the ban no longer made much sense.

When discussing this issue, assure others that medical leadership originally supported true temperance. Benjamin Rush, M.D. of Philadelphia, the most honored physician of the period, was also a prominent Temperance leader. He supported responsible drinking but opposed spirit-based drinks in his famous thermometer (see below) published in 1784 in *An Inquiry in the Effects of Spirituous Liquors*. Rush encouraged consumption of lighter beverages for good health and sociability. Rush and others in medicine argued that health reasons favored the lower potency beverages.

Rush pronounced wine and small beer: . . . *pleasant and wholesome liquors ideal for human consumption . . .Unlike ardent spirits which render the temper terrible* (Rush 1784). He classified small beer, apple cider, pear wine, porter and strong beer as promoters of: *Cheerfulness, strength and nourishment*. He depicted hard liquors as contributing to: . . . *vice, disease, civic problems ranging from jailing to blackened eyes, a life in prison.*

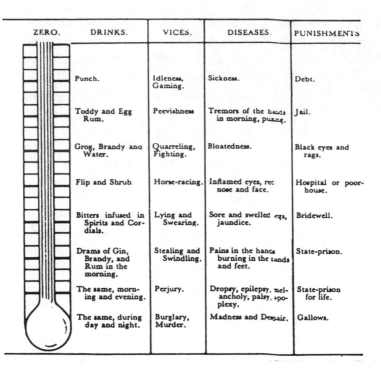

ZERO.	DRINKS.	VICES.	DISEASES.	PUNISHMENTS
	Punch.	Idleness, Gaming.	Sickness.	Debt.
	Toddy and Egg Rum.	Peevishness	Tremors of the hands in morning, puking.	Jail.
	Grog, Brandy and Water.	Quarreling, Fighting.	Bloatedness.	Black eyes and rags.
	Flip and Shrub.	Horse-racing.	Inflamed eyes, red nose and face.	Hospital or poor-house.
	Bitters infused in Spirits and Cor-dials.	Lying and Swearing.	Sore and swelled legs, jaundice.	Bridewell.
	Drams of Gin, Brandy, and Rum in the morning.	Stealing and Swindling.	Pains in the hands burning in the hands and feet.	State-prison.
	The same, morn-ing and evening.	Perjury.	Dropsy, epilepsy, mel-ancholy, palsy, apo-plexy.	State-prison for life.
	The same, during day and night.	Burglary, Murder.	Madness and Despair.	Gallows.

As the nineteenth century waned, the more radical leadership in Temperance joined hands with the populist, rural political forces, a band of conservative clerics and others who feared the influx of heavy drinking immigrant populations flooding Eastern seaboard cities. This largely rural political tide joined the prohibitionary tide in fostering national prohibition. Business interests joined in visualizing Temperance as an method to maintain a sober labor force. Ultimately, Temperance became more of a political manifestation than a health crusade. Populism always looks to government to resolve social problems. This faith still runs very deep in the American political psyche.

The dry coalition promulgated the myth that any drinking leads eventually to addiction – a credo which resonates today in the "risk-taking" theme promoted by public health. Lender recounts this commitment in an 1832 Methodist publication which asserted: . . . *there is no safe line of distinction between the moderate and the immoderate use of alcohol* (Lender 1982). In 1825, during this evolving strategy, famed preacher Lyman Beecher published *Six Sermons on Intemperance* which were delivered from his Litchfield, Connecticut pulpit. Total abstinence was Beecher's target: *You might as well cast loose in a frail boat before a hurricane, and expect safety. You are gone, gone irretrievably, if you do not stop* (Beecher 1826).

Abstinence as a political tactic was formalized in an 1826 Temperance gathering in Hector, New York. A compromise was struck between those present who supported responsible drinking – the moderate wets – and the total abstainers. All who pledged abstinence had the letter T placed after their names on the society's roster. Thus the concept of "a pledged teetotaler" was hatched. As the teetotaling segment of the movement gained prestige and political power, governmental prohibitions became the central focus of Temperance.

American prohibitionary movements

There have been three great prohibitionary periods in our history. The original movement achieved many state and local legal prohibitions and restrictions on availability through the mid- and late-1800s. National prohibition was enacted in 1919 and lasted a brief, tumultuous thirteen years. The third crusade – dubbed neoprohibition – began in the early 1970s and continues today. Neoprohibition was fostered by and is supported financially by the federal health agencies. In place of debate, compromise and resolution of drinking issues, neoprohibition sustains irrational fears of drinking and blurs the distinctions between use and abuse.

No rational person objects to prudent government controls over the commerce in licensed beverages. In the interest of good order and public health, governments should discourage abuse, assist those suffering addiction and abuse problems, protect life and property from indiscretions of abusers, and, in the process, reap reliable tax revenues to accomplish these goals. But the Public Health Model advocates today espouse really radical controls. Mosher defines the philosophical underpinnings of neoprohibition in "New Directions in Alcohol Policy." He argues that governmental controls should extend over the product, the drinker and the environments in which drinking takes place. This global vision imposes bureaucratic decision-making over marketing, advertising, packaging and even pricing strategies, a virtual abrogation of the commercial rights guaranteed by the Constitution for both merchant and drinker:

> *In recent years, alcohol and public health researchers have placed these alcohol control strategies solidly in the public health tradition . . . In addition . . . to the host — i.e. the individual drinkers . . . this "public health model" of alcohol-related problems calls attention to the role of environmental factors (the social and physical structures within which alcohol problems occur) and agent factors (the presentation of alcohol, including alcohol packaging, labeling and price) in the spread of alcohol problems.*

Mosher, J., and Jernigan, D., New Directions in Alcohol Policy, Annual Review of Public Health, 10:245-279, 1989

In contrast, the European Integration Model offers no panacea for the banishment of alcohol abuse. It accepts the inevitability of some level of abuse. We learned in the Prohibition cycle that there is no escape from the availability of wines, beers and spirits since drinks are so easily produced, in the home or in clandestine factories. But, over time, the cultural integration of drinks into society has proved more effective for alleviating abuse problems. The strongest attribute of integration is a tradition of self-restraint — genuine temperance. No self-respecting Spaniard or Frenchman would appear before his parents or peers while intoxicated. This doesn't imply that Spanish and French societies are free of alcohol or drug abuse. They're not. It merely observes that peer pressures dictate levels of conduct and restraint among the majority. Safe drinking deportment is the expected norm. Across the age spectrum, peers discourage aberrant behavior. Social disdain for drunken behavior becomes a powerful constraint. Smith elaborates this concept:

> *According to this model, alcohol-related problems are more likely where drinking is not fully integrated into the local norms for social and cultural life. It is argued that where alcohol is considered to be a*

"forbidden fruit," it will have more serious consequences for those who persist in drinking. It follows that if drinking can somehow be more fully integrated into the prevailing culture, the prevalence of problems can be reduced.

Smith, C., The wrath of grapes: the health-related implications of changing American drinking practices, Area, Vol. 17, No. 2, pp.97-108, 1985

A significant cadre of medical professionals in America now openly support responsible drinking (see Epilogue). The three *60 Minutes* telecasts, medical school symposia on healthy drinking issues and the spate of books by physicians supporting moderate consumption exemplify this new trend. But these exposures have yet to warrant serious consideration in political, medical and public health councils. Recall that forty years ago a little known researcher named Rachel Carson wrote a book titled *Silent Spring* which eventually spawned the vast environmental movement. What this issue needs is similar exposure of the facts, of the research. While few medical authorities today openly dispute the science, responsible drinking is discouraged as demonstrated throughout these chapters.

A primer on genuine temperance

In *Alcohol and Pleasure*, Heath discusses how social harmony is engendered when drinking is a valued, comfortable part of family life and social intercourse:

Drinking together, even more than eating together, serves to bind members of a group in ways that other joint activities do not. In medieval guilds, drinking together was an important symbol of acceptance among those who moved from apprenticeship to membership, and much the same process occurs among groups ranging from college fraternities to dueling clubs, to neighborhood ethnic groups, to professional organizations, and among fishermen, lumberjacks, or cowboys, in the between-job camaraderie.

Heath, D., Drinking and Pleasure Across Cultures, in Alcohol and Pleasure, Brenner/Mazel, Philadelphia, 1999

Apart from health considerations, genuine temperance provides a powerful avenue for social bonding. The distinction
between use and abstention – and support of both – was a
guiding principle of the first NIAAA administration. Founding
director Morris Chafetz espoused virtually identical objectives
to those set forth by Benjamin Rush in the 1780s. In 1972, in the
Second Special Report to Congress on Alcohol and Health, Chafetz
published the following guidelines for the NIAAA programs:

> *Provide support for those people who choose to take
> alcohol in moderation or to abstain. Reduce the guilt
> feelings surrounding alcohol when taken in
> moderation.*

Second Special Report to Congress on Alcohol and Health, DHHS, Washington, D.C., 1974

The over-riding goal at hand is to get the good news out. To
generate new interest among physicians, the media and the
political system for the "rest of the story." Americans are skilled
at sifting the wheat from the chaff. That's why, despite a wide
diversity of opinions on many public issues, this society has
survived and prospered so well. We are capable of handling
controversy and change. We revel in public debate. Physician,
educator and author Whitten made this appeal to his conferes
in a 1987 meeting of the Society of Medical Friends of Wine:

> *It is up to us, the enlightened and knowledgeable, to
> educate our patients, but more importantly, our
> colleagues and political representatives, of the
> important health and social benefits of wine. I would
> like to see everyone here share their knowledge of
> reality with friends, family, colleagues and patients.
> We must not be afraid to join battle with and
> challenge those who would stack the deck politically
> and distort the truth.*

Whitten, D., Wine & Healthy Lifestyles, A Symposium on Wine, Culture & Healthy
Lifestyles, The Wine Institute, New York, May 1, 1987

An encouraging article in the *Journal of Studies on Alcohol*, by
alcohol historian Engs suggests that the current anti-drinking
campaign has peaked. If so, a campaign to spread knowledge
about the developing research is just what the doctor ordered.

Engs echoes Selden Bacon's appeal to reason made thirty-some years ago that the time had arrived for thinking the "unthinkable:"

> *Because of the cresting of the anti-alcohol wave, now is the time to re-evaluate the restrictive policies and educational programs implemented during the past 15 years. There should be changes in education programs and public policy, measures that allow for different values concerning alcohol and its consumption . . . In terms of public policy, there needs to be a lowering of the legal purchase age to 19, the age at which many young adults are involved with post-secondary education away from home. Parents need to be allowed to serve alcohol to their children in public places such as restaurants. As a society, we need to begin working toward the development of a consensus as to what constitutes positive and negative alcohol use.*

Engs, R., Cycles of Social Reform: Is the Current Anti-Alcohol Movement Cresting?, Journal of Studies on Alcohol. Vol. 58, pp223-224, 1997

Is age nineteen for drinking unthinkable? Or all-age family drinking in public restaurants? Shouldn't parents be heard on this issue? Americans who have traveled to Europe have observed such routine, disciplined family drinking in public restaurants. On the CBS French Paradox telecast Morley Safer interviewed a French mother and her teenage daughter in a Bordeaux restaurant. Both were sipping from their own glasses of red wine. Americans initially may be apprehensive about Eng's "unthinkable" suggestions, but they deserve serious consideration. Parents who believe in teaching proper habits and responsible behavior to their offspring should be able to provide small amounts of wine or beer when eating out – as they do at home. We might be able to shed some of the "hidden fruit" challenge of clandestine boozing among our teenagers.

Why do we allow government to enforce mistrust of drinking among teens? The Judeo/Christian tradition fosters a symbiotic marriage of food and drinks. Corinthians I, Chapter 10 suggests: *Whatever you eat, whatever you drink, whatever you do at all, do it for the glory of God.* Can we regain this noble dietary tradition or are we doomed to endure another century of niggling myths? Hanson votes for a positive expectation:

> *Rather than simply focusing upon the negative consequences of excessive alcohol consumption, we need to be encouraging moderate consumption for those who choose to drink. Encouraging the moderate use of alcohol simultaneously discourages its immoderate use. For example, Jewish and Italian-American children typically learn to drink in moderation at home with the encouragement and good example of their parents as appropriate role models. While most Jews and Italians drink, very few experience any difficulties arising from alcohol.*

Hanson, D., and Engs, R., It's Better to Drink Moderately Than to Abstain: www.potsdam2.edu/alcohol-info

Epidemiology will continue to generate new evidence of healthy drinking. About this there is no doubt or debate. The epidemiological spigot cannot be closed because, as Doll maintains, the evidence already is massive and nearly every new study inventories alcohol consumption. As early as 1993, Peele states the obvious. There is little to fear in this prospect:

> *Americans would not drink more even if we told them to. Health professionals seem to live in fear that on hearing that it is good to drink, people will rush out and become alcoholics. They may be reassured to know that according to the Gallup poll, "Fifty eight percent of Americans are aware of recent research linking moderate drinking to lower rates of heart disease, but only 5 percent of all respondents say the studies are more likely to make them drink moderately."*

Peele, S., The Conflict Between Public Health Goals and the Temperance Mentality, American Journal of Public Health, Vol. 83, No. 6, June, 1993

Consider again the inventive approach of Engs:

> *The failure of the reduction of consumption theory suggests the need for an alternative approach based on the experience of peoples around the world . . .By analyzing those who use it successfully, we can*

> *apply their techniques in our own use of alcohol.*
> *Italians, Greeks, Jews and many others tend to share*
> *three common keys to success . . . First, there is an*
> *absence of emotionality associated with alcohol*
> *which is seen as neither poison on the one hand nor*
> *as a magic elixir on the other. Second, there is little*
> *or no social pressure to drink. Abstaining and*
> *drinking in moderation are seen as equally desirable*
> *or acceptable choices. . . . Third, young people learn*
> *at home from their parents and their parents' good*
> *example how to handle alcohol responsibly.*

Engs, R., and Hanson, D., Reduction of Consumption Theory: A Test Using the Drinking Patterns and Problems of Collegians in the United States, 1983-1994, College Student Journal, Vol. 33, No. 3, September, 1999

A coalition of practicing physicians and informed parents could shatter the long-standing wall of medical ambivalence. In the above quote, historian Engs assures us that the current public health advocacy of control of availability has run its course — a failure waiting to be challenged by informed physicians armed with healthy drinking science as the new rationale.

But physicians and parents need to be convinced that a responsible drinking ethic will reap benefits for their families and for society as a whole. The first step in this process lies with committed parents who can pass on the messages in this book to their own physicians. Clinical physicians form the front line of medicine, where care delivery meets patient needs, where medical politics take a back seat to acute issues. When a critical mass of practicing physicians insist on more and better communication of healthy drinking research from institutional leadership, the medical die will be cast. The responsible drinking debate will commence.

This book (and others in the recommended reading section) can be an enormously helpful in formulating and arguing the right questions. Parents are urged to send pertinent photocopies of book sections to their doctors or to take the book along to their next appointment. Chapters have been kept small for ease of reading and duplication. Parents should raise questions about specific research findings that speak to their own family health issues. That's where the doctor/family coalition will emerge. Focusing on specific research findings.

The warmest phrase in the publishing world is "*You oughta read this book!*" Respecting, of course, that this text is not for anyone who has clinical depression, has had drinking or addiction problems, or has religious scruples concerning alcohol. Each reader has family members, friends, or business associates who could profit from exposure to these arguments.

Family care givers can also spark media interest in these issues by sending photocopies of chapters to columnists, editors and publishers when articles fail to accord proper coverage or over-state drinking abuse risks. Media sources should be encouraged to visit the web sites presented at the end of the previous chapter for reliable data on healthy drinking research.

Moderate drinkers can then take comfort in Heath's wise counsel in *Drinking Occasions: But those who want to drink moderately, for whatever among the many benefits of ethanol may suit them at a given time, should be confident that their behavior is neither deviant nor drug-addicted, but fits well in the vivid panorama of human history* (Health 2000).

Healthy drinking science is a rapidly developing, highly credible health care instrumentality – perhaps the only factor of sufficient depth to overcome America's endemic alcohol ambivalence. This book presents no alcohol nirvana. It raises no false promises that all drinkers will enjoy diminished heart disease, arrested cancers or better bone mass. It offers no magical resolutions for the ravages of alcohol abuse. But it does present scientific verity in responsible drinking.

A new social compact favoring genuine temperance will surely advantage our nation's "vivid panorama of history."

Remember the clarion call: *You oughta read this book!*

Epilogue

This book has argued two hypotheses – that there exists a little recognized but impressive scientific literature of health benefits in drinking, and that the systems responsible for communicating vital data remain indifferent to its dissemination.

The January 2002 issue of *Time* magazine proves this case! In a thirty-eight page feature – "How to Keep the Doctor Away" – the nation's most widely read news weekly demonstrates great competence across a wide spectrum of health issues but woefully little grasp of healthy drinking science.

In "10 Foods that Pack a Wallop," the authors include red wine saying that its polyphenols can elevate good cholesterol helping to reduce hardening of the arteries. The article fails to mention evidence of similar traits for other types of drinks. To no surprise, there is the obligatory, overstated warning: *Wine may be great for the heart, but it's been blamed for everything from cirrhosis of the liver to hemorrhagic stroke, fetal alcohol syndrome and possibly breast cancer, so consumption should be limited to no more than several glasses a week* (How to Keep the Doctor Away 2002).

Compare this negative coloration with the confident findings of Ruitenberg in *The Lancet* published one week later than the above *Time*. In a six year study of senior citizens in the Netherlands, the authors found that: *Light-to-moderate alcohol consumption is associated with lower risks of coronary heart disease, ischemic stroke, and total mortality in elderly men and women . . . These findings suggest that light-to-moderate alcohol consumption is associated with a reduced risk of dementia in individuals aged 55 or older. The effect seems to be unchanged by the source of alcohol* (Ruitenberg 2002). Ruitenberg joins many other reports seen in Chapter 10. Obviously *Time* writers have not been exposed to the bevy of positive findings cited in this book, many of which attribute benefits to all types of drinks. That's the communication problem. If *Time* reporters don't know about it, medicine isn't reporting it. Note, however, that *Time* classifies red wine as a *food* – better than all the nutrition sources found in Chapter 14 are willing to do.

However, in failing to discuss findings of *lowered* risks for cirrhosis, hemorrhagic stroke, the common cold, kidney stones, diabetes, acute hospitalization, mortality and osteoporosis for *moderate* drinkers, the magazine demonstrates how poorly this science is communicated — and, consequently, how unbalanced the *Time* coverage is. The conventional places where health journalists look for information — medical association publications and medical school and clinic newsletters — routinely fail to communicate the depth and breadth of drink research.

The above issue of *Time* also contains nine full page ads for drugs (Paxil for anxiety, Zocor for cholesterol, Zoloft for depression, etc.), each followed by another page of small print warning of the drug's many side effects! Swartzberg in the February, 2002 issue of the *U.C. Berkeley Wellness Letter* says about contemporary pharmaceutical advertising: *The number of prescriptions for the 50 drugs most heavily advertised to patients grew at a rate of six times that for other drugs . . . Remember, someone's trying to sell you something . . . talk to your doctor. Don't be disappointed if he/she recommends a different, more appropriate brand or generic. Or no drug at all* (Swartzberg 2002). Shades of the barnstorming medicine men of yesteryear.

Physicians who are willing to speak out against the flood of high-priced pharmaceuticals should be first in line to speak up for more honest reporting of healthy drinking science. Americans are being cheated of study findings generated largely by tax dollars.

The ambivalent mindset

A final example of corruptive ambivalence is seen in the *New England Journal of Medicine's HealthNews.* A January, 2001 editorial references two heart attack studies among senior citizens which appeared in the *Journal of the American Medical Association.* The first by Mukamal found better survival statistics among 1,913 heart attack victims who continued a pattern of moderate drinking following their heart seizures: *. . . were about 30 percent more likely to be alive after four years than those who abstained* (Mukamal 2001). The second by Abramson involved over 2,000 individuals, sixty-five years of age and over, who: *. . . drank 21 to 70 ounces of alcohol during the month preceding the study (about one* *and a one-half drinks each day) had about half the risk of developing heart failure during the 14-year study* (Abramson 2001). These studies confirm that – at least for seniors – drinking before and after a heart attack, drinks can provide some risk reduction.

Virtually ignoring any benefits, the *HealthNews* editorial chose to discourage consumption: . . . *doctors agree that nondrinkers should not take up drinking to preserve their health . . . Plus alcohol has been linked to the development of breast cancer, gastrointestinal ailments, and birth defects, so there are trade-offs with alcohol that everyone should consider* (Alcohol Update 2001). On what basis do "doctors agree" that seniors should not drink to advantage heart health? Do the editors suggest that senior citizens are unaware of breast cancer or GI problems common to their age group, or that alcohol abuse risks are unknown to them in their sixth and seventh decades? Or that birth defects have much relevance to their ages? Recall the run-around that Jonathan Rauch experienced from doctors in the opening essay on epidemiology. Seeking advice for his aging father about drinking to lessen hypertension, he got "muttering:" *I think the message most people would get from (these) sources is: Drinking isn't all bad, but eschew it anyway . . . To continue today's policy of muttering and changing the subject verges perilously on saying not just that too much alcohol is bad for you but that ignorance is good for you* (Rauch 1998).

Indecision and muttering from health care industry seeds alcohol ambivalence in the media. A headline in the June 20, 2001 issue of *Beverage Alcohol Market Report* tells of a major corporate gift to reduce drunken driving. The headline reads "General Motors Grants $2.5 Million To MADD." Despite its signal accomplishment of focusing national attention on drunk driving, MADD has evolved (as did early Temperance) into one of the most strident voices for neoprohibition in private advocacy.

In recent years, MADD has adopted a hardline agenda capable of attracting big bucks from government and private industry. The above article notes: *On the surface, and in the press, the GM grant appears to be the right thing at the right time . . . GM says that it does not endorse MADD's position on higher taxes (for alcohol beverages), linking beverage alcohol to illegal drugs, cutting down hours of store operation and licensing, and government censorship of adver-*

tising . . . But, on the other hand, once MADD has the money, there's nothing GM can do to stop its being used for those purposes (General Motors Grants 2001). Over $2 million dollars may not constitute an endorsement but its a good bit more than petty cash. Ambivalence — and inertia — reigns in the media and the public mind. The dry lobby profits.

Corporate interests, the media, law enforcement, the justice systems and the public are sucked into the dizzying vortex of anti-drinking advocacy. For those who believe in genuine temperance and in the rights of individuals to make informed health choices, here is a roster of medical, academic and religious leadership which has long argued for a more enlightened and encompassing approach to drinking.

Voices for accommodation

As epilogue to the untenable status quo outlined in this book, here are brief quotes — some extending back a half-century — from medical professionals and others who support responsible drinking. Most ideas have their specific time and place in history. In these, calm, thoughtful medical professionals, I rest my own case. They, and I, argue that the time has come for the U.S. to repeal alcohol ambivalence.

1931. U.S. pathologist, researcher and physician, Timothy Leary, M.D.: *It seems paradoxical that a pathologist should be called upon to address a clinical meeting on the therapeutic value of alcohol . . . Alcohol has been used in medicine as a food and as a drug. . . Clinical observation, however, from long ages, has brought in a verdict favorable on the whole to the use of alcohol in disease* (Leary 1931).

1967. U.S pioneer alcoholism professional, director of the Center of Alcohol Studies at Rutgers University, Selden Bacon: *The impact of the Classic Temperance Movement was and is today so great that we can only speak of the current situation vis-a-vis alcohol problems in the U.S.A. as being in flux . . . Prohibition is finally gone from all the States, but often enough it is replaced by little, local and partial prohibitions . . . just teaching 16- and 18-year olds that "they mustn't drink" is increasingly recognized as silly, but what should be taught instead remains uncertain and frightening* (Bacon 1967).

1968. U.S. physician, researcher, educator and author, Robert C. Stepto, M.D., Ph.D.: *Young physicians should be encouraged to* *explore the scientific mysteries of alcohol and wine. These explorations will open new vistas to them and make them better physicians and better citizens* (Stepto 1968).

1971. U.S. professor of preventive medicine and author, Salvatore P. Lucia, M.D.: *Hippocrates was one of the earliest believers in wine as a medicine. He used it as a nourishing dietary beverage, as a cooling agent for fevers, as a purgative and a diuretic . . . the teachings of Hippocrates are worthy of his famous oath* (Lucia 1971).

1974. U.S. psychiatrist, author and first director of the NIAAA, Morris E. Chafetz, M.D.: *All-in-all, the data on general mortality suggest that for the amount of drinking . . . there may be some kind of threshold below which mortality is little affected. In the absence of further evidence, in fact, the classical "Anstie's limit" (up to 3 drinks per day) seems still to reflect the safe amount of drinking which does not substantially increase the risk of early death* (Chafetz 1974).

1977. U.S. pioneer alcoholism specialist and philosopher, E.M. Jellinek: *Wines, spirituous liquors and beers have long been considered "blood builders." . . . Blood and alcoholic beverages mean two things to men: the restoration of health, i.e., medicine, and the maintenance of good health, i.e., food. Blood is par excellence the stream of life. Accordingly, the alcoholic beverage, too, becomes the stream of life, and the stream-of-life symbolism means power. All these important properties of the alcoholic beverage — medicine, food, stream of life, power, and death (the corollary of the blood-alcohol equation) — result in a tremendous prestige being attached to it* (Jellinek 1977).

1980. U.S. physician, researcher and educator, Ronald E. La Porte, M.D.: *Each individual study could be criticized for possible biases. What is important is that a pattern emerged across the diverse studies employing numerous methodologies, various populations, and different definitions of alcohol consumption. The pattern is that moderate alcohol consumption appears to be associated with a lower risk of heart disease than either non drinking or heavy drinking* (La Porte 1980).

1981. U.S. educator, researcher and founding director of the Alcoholic Beverage Medical Research Foundation, Thomas B. Turner, M.D.: *Evidence is accumulating that the moderate use of alcohol as defined in this paper is associated with certain beneficial effects on health . . . heart disease, especially myocardial infarction, is lower in persons who use alcohol moderately . . . intake seems to have* *a favorable physiological impact on the elderly . . . alcoholic beverages contribute significantly to the American diet* (Turner 1981).

1981. Editor, British Journal on Alcohol and Alcoholism, H.D. Chalke, M.D.: *It is important to acknowledge that drinking by most members of society is not accompanied by problems and may ease the loneliness of old age, the burden of intolerable pain, foster healthy psycho-sexual attitudes, or encourage social intercourse* (Chalke 1981).

1981. U.S. nutritionist and public health professional, Janet T. McDonald, Ph.D., R.D.: *. . . more than just a beverage containing alcohol, and when consumed principally with and as food, can be safely and beneficially included in the diets of most people. A reasonable estimate of a safe limit consumption, that would not displace essential nutrients in a regular diet, is ten percent of the total energy intake necessary to maintain ideal body weight* (McDonald 1981).

1984. U.S. sociologist, researcher and author, Harry Gene Levine: *Further, both 19th and 20th century formulations have a tendency to blame drinking and individual behaviour for many problems which have much broader political and economic causes. The alcohol problem, or alcohol abuse, as it is commonly understood today, is not a thing, or a number of things — it is a relationship. Or, more precisely, it is the relationship one sees when one views alcohol as the cause of many personal and social problems and many diseases and illnesses. This medical, scientific and popular way of viewing of alcohol is nearly 200 years old — but no older* (Levine 1984).

1985. U.S. historian and prohibition expert, David E. Kyvig, Ph.D.: *Only the Thirteenth and Eighteenth Amendments represented fundamental departures from previous American governmental principles. They destroyed large-scale private property holdings and economic arrangements — slave holdings in one case, an entire industry for the other — for the object of social restructuring. . . . Adoption of the Eighteenth Amendment set a new standard for governmental intervention into personal lives, a step long discussed but not taken until 1919 . . . Prohibition as a constitutional experiment was a gaudy failure* (Kyvig 1985).

1985. Pioneer alcohol abuse expert and editor of the *Journal of Studies on Alcohol*, Mark Keller: *Recent biomedical literature too is again filled with articles that blame alcohol, articles proclaiming that alcohol directly damages the brain, the heart, the stomach, the liver,* *the pancreas, the muscles, the testicles, the metabolism, and, of course, the fetus . . . After fifty years in the alcohol field – I began in 1933– I still believe that solutions are more likely to come from science than from legislation, from evolution of mores rather than the enactment of laws* (Keller 1985).

1986. Pastor, lecturer and Biblical scholar, Kenneth L. Gentry, Jr., Th.D.: *It is often argued that Christians should totally abstain from alcohol . . . the character of the Christian witness must be molded by biblical truth. The truth of the matter is that the Bible does not condemn moderate consumption . . . The biblical witness to the world relative to alcohol should be that of moderation* (Gentry 1986).

1986. U.S. economist, researcher and consultant, Dale Heien, Ph.D.: *. . . from an economist's point of view, individuals voluntarily parting with their income to buy a product derive utility from this product. They find it useful, and certainly this can be said about alcoholic beverages. We use them to celebrate some of our most sacrosanct occasions such as weddings, anniversaries, so forth. We use them in business settings; we use it to relieve tensions at the end of the day and so forth. Alcoholic beverages can be seen as a valued economic good which people buy on the market* (Heien 1986).

1987. U.S. educator, author and physician, David N. Whitten, Ph.D., M.D.: *. . . it is primarily the physicians of this country who need especially to to know the things I have talked of tonight. It is up to us, the enlightened and knowledgeable, to educate our patients, but more importantly, our colleagues and political representatives, of the important health and social benefits of wine* (Whitten 1987).

1987. U.S. physical anthropology specialist: Solomon N. Katz, Ph.D.: *In a broad historic sense, the domestication of the grape along with other fruits marked an important . . . dividing line in human antiquity– as clear as the Neolithic revolution which led to the original domestication of cereal grains and animals . . . the early introduction of wine as a fermented food and beverage resulted in substantial changes of the food combinations being consumed* (Katz 1987).

1991. Leading French researcher in cardiology, panelist on the CBS-TV 60 Minutes telecast, Serge Renaud, Ph.D.: *It's well-documented that an intake of alcohol prevents coronary heart disease by as much as 50 per cent. I mean there is no other drug that is being so efficient as the moderate intake of alcohol* (Renaud 1991).

1991. U.S. cardiologist, author and educator, Norman M. Kaplan, M.D.: *As for moderate consumption, usually defined as less than three drinks or 1.5 ounces of ethanol per day, the dangers appear to be exaggerated and often misrepresented . . . most Americans drink in moderation and are thereby in no danger* (Kaplan 1991)

1992. U.S. cardiologist and physician, Arthur L. Klatsky, M.D.: *To conclude, current evidence about lighter drinking and health suggests that . . . we cannot yet define precisely the optimal amount of alcohol but that it is below 3 drinks a day; and it doesn't seem to matter what type of alcoholic beverage is taken* (Klatsky 1992).

1992. U.S. alcohol anthropologist and author, Dwight B. Heath, Ph.D.: *But, as is so often the case, there is another side to the coin. How many people profit from occasional use of small doses of alcohol as an effective, short-term tranquilizer that does no bodily harm. How many fights are avoided because alcohol helps some people to avoid depression. And how do we weigh the obvious medical costs of alcohol-related illness against the equally obvious medical benefits of alcohol-related wellness?* (Heath 1992).

1994. U.S. physician and author, Martin R. Lipp, M.D.: *Risk! . . . 4% to 7% of myocardial infarctions are exercise associated . . . . somewhere between 25 and 50 thousand sudden cardiac deaths . . . over 100,000 are injured seriously by automobiles in a given year. Risk! Everything in life involves risk! There may be some risk associated with light, regular wine consumption, but when you compare it with other strategies for lowering risk of our single greatest killer, the moderate consumption of wine compares very, very favorably* (Lipp 1994).

1995. U.S. author, researcher, and educator, Ruth C. Engs, R.N., Ph.D.: *Much of the literature concerning drinking in the United States during the 1980s focused upon serious or sensational problems caused by alcohol. Few authors discussed normal drinking patterns or how alcohol has been an intrinsic part of Western culture. This is despite the fact that only a small proportion of people who drink have alcohol-related problems, while the vast majority of drinkers (90%) consume alcohol in moderation without problems* (Engs 1995).

1995. British writer and physician, M. J. Griffith, M.D.: *The message is reaching the public through the mass media, but not the medical profession. Part of the reason that this information is suppressed lies in North America, where the temperance mentality holds sway . . . We have a duty to tell our patients and the wider public what* *lifestyle changes may be beneficial to them. The benefits of a change to a regular, moderate intake of alcohol are equivalent to giving up smoking and are far greater than regular exercise or diet* (Griffith 1995).

1995. U.S. sociologist, author and educator, David J. Hanson, Ph.D.: *In stigmatizing alcohol, control proponents may inadvertently trivialize the use of illegal drugs and thereby encourage their use. Or, especially among younger students, they may create the false impression that parents who use alcohol in moderation are drug abusers* (Hanson 1995).

1996. U.S. alcohol and addiction specialists Stanton Peele, Ph.D., and Archie Brodsky, Ph.D.: *It is long past time to tell the American people the truth about alcohol, instead of a destructive fantasy that too often becomes a self-fulfilling prophecy . . . transforming a culture of abstinence warring with excess into a culture of moderate, responsible, healthy drinking* (Peele 1996).

1996. U.S. health journalist, Jacob Sullum: *Today's public health measures are attempts to control illness and injury by controlling behavior thought to be associated with them. Treating behavior as if it were a communicable disease is problematic. First of all, behavior cannot be transmitted to other people against their will. Second, people do not choose to be sick, but they do choose to engage in risky behavior. The choice implies that the behavior, unlike a viral or bacterial infection, has value and that attempts to control the behavior will be resisted* (Sullum 1996).

1997. British physician and journalist, Thomas Stuttaford, M.D.: *The medical advantages of alcohol have been hidden from the general public for thirty years, and the reason usually advanced for this obfuscation is the patronizing one that alcohol, delightful as it is to take and good as it is for the heart, cannot be entrusted to the masses lest they drink themselves to death . . . most people are healthy and a drink is more likely to do good than harm* (Stuttaford 1997).

1997. British cardiologist, researcher and physician, Sir Richard Doll, M.D.: *The evidence for a beneficial effect is now massive. It includes not only a reduction of about a third in risk for vascular disease, but also . . . a reduction in total mortality. People should be treated like adults and told the facts* (Doll 1997).

1998. U.S. preventative medicine educator, researcher and panelist on *60 Minutes* telecast on the CBS-TV French Paradox,

R. Curtis Ellison, M.D.: *From the data now available, we know that a population that drinks moderately generally lives longer than a population that does not drink but otherwise has essentially the same lifestyle . . . We should try to make sure that the medical community, the public and our policy makers are up to date on the scientific findings* (Ellison 1998).

1998. U.S. oncologist, researcher and educator, Harvey E. Finkel, M.D.: *In general, we may conclude that consistent moderation is harmless, often beneficial . . . Evidence of benefit is strongest for the prevention of cardiovascular disease . . . Wine is not a medicine, but an enricher of life* (Finkel 1998).

2000. U.S. surgeon and wine maker, Alfred A. de Lorimier, M.D.: *It is important that a distinction is made between use in moderation of alcohol and abuse of alcohol. . . it is inappropriate to advocate consumption of beverage alcohol for persons who are prone to addiction, who have religious reasons for abstaining, who are taking medication that adversely interacts with alcohol . . . It should be a priority in our educational system to define consumption in moderation and to deplore abuse of alcohol* (de Lorimier 2000).

For the curious physician, a good place to begin research is the de Lorimier paper quoted above (Alcohol, Wine and Health, American Journal of Surgery, 180:357-361, 2000). de Lorimier and the other voices here present a rich mix of competencies – medicine, sociology, religion, history and political science, alcoholism and abuse treatment, anthropology, nutrition, psychiatry, addiction, and medical journalism. Their arguments should resound at the highest levels of public policy.

I began this book with a quote from anthropologist Dwight Heath. I close with comments of another academician, Joseph Gusfield who, like Heath, has devoted a long career in research and teaching to the sociology of drinking in America. In "Why I Am Often Introduced As An Expert In Alcoholism But Am Not," Gusfield writes:

My academic absorption with issues of alcohol and drinking in the United States dates from the late nineteen-forties . . . Most people who drink are not pathological drinkers. Such drinking is part of how many leisure pursuits involve "escapes" or retreats from sober areas of life. . . I have still not answered the question of why the United States is an exception to most Western societies in its most severe public condemnatory attitudes towards drinking, as well as other moral issues . . . Part of solving this intellectual puzzle, I believe, lies in understanding the cultural aspects of leisure use in differing groups.

The focus on the alcoholic as a troubled person remained, and remains a major part of alcohol studies and, as such, has had a modest place on the public agenda. In the eighties it gave way to a concern for drinking driving. With that phenomenon drinking became, for a few years, higher on the public agenda. It shifted away from medicalization to criminalization and doctors left as police came in. Now the object of attention was not a troubled but a troubling person.

In the present (January, 2001) alcohol is very low on the list of issues and problems with which governments are concerned. It has been lumped together in many states into offices of Substance Abuse along with smoking and illicit drug use. In many ways it now rides on the back of the illicit drug issue in American politics.

Gusfield, J., Why I Am Often Introduced As An Expert On Alcoholism But Am Not, The Social History of Alcohol Review, 15:3-4, Spring/Summer, 2001

This is why doctors must become involved. Healthy drinking science is a missing component in American culture.

No one in the above group argues — nor does this book — that the neglect of healthy drinking research is the most compelling problem in American medicine or American public policy. As Gusfield notes, it ranks low on the agenda. Dozens of other health care issues and public concerns dwarf its importance. Nor does this book of "medical journalism" claim to be other than one reporter's assembling of random findings in the scientific journals. But drinking is of genuine significance to more than 130 million Americans who opt to consume, as well as to many fearful abstainers. Drinking can advantage or damage health and well-being. This majority deserves more from government and medicine than specious warnings and "muttering."

America needs to adopt the common sense found in the U.K.'s review of the literature compiled in *Health Issues Related to Alcohol Consumption*. It's prologue concludes: *The idea of an optimal level of alcohol intake is based in epidemiological evidence that overall mortality in a population, or mortality and morbidity due to specific causes, is lower among those who drink lightly than among abstainers or heavier drinkers* (Macdonald 1999). That's a message America's moderate drinkers need to hear.

For my own bimonthly Internet magazine *Healthy Drinking* and reprints from other publications on drinking issues on a continuing basis, look to www.healthydrinkingscience.com

Gene Ford 2003

Good Reading

This selection bring to bear many voices and diverse opinions about drinking in history and the benefits of responsible consumption.

Barr, A., *Drink: A Social History of America*, Carroll & Graf Publishers, Inc. New York, 1999 – A copious, highly annotated review of political and social attitudes toward drinking in the U.S.

Edell, D., *Eat, Drink & Be Merry*, Harper Collins, New York, 1999 – A common sense, witty approach to responsible drinking presented by a popular radio/TV physician/journalist

Engs, R. *Clean Living Movements: American Cycles of Health Reform,* Praeger Publishers, Westport, 2000 – How the contemporary anti-drinking saga in the U.S. is related to and differs from previous Temperance crusades and opportunities for change

Ford, G., *The Benefits of Moderate Drinking: Alcohol Health and Society,* and *The French Paradox & Drinking for Health,* Wine Appreciation Guild, South San Francisco, 1988 – Two discussions of medical, social and political factors in U.S. alcohol control policies

Gentry, K., *God Gave Wine: What the Bible Says About Alcohol,* Oakleafs Books, 2000 – A penetrating and scholarly discussion of drinking in the Bible and its application to modern cultures

Gilson, C., and Bennett, V., *Alcohol and Women: Creating a Safer Lifestyle,* Fusion Press, Irving, 2001 – A unique compilation of drinking research from a female viewpoint

Hanson, D., *Preventing Alcohol Abuse: Alcohol, Culture and Control,* Praeger, Westport, 1995 – An extensive sociological treatise on American drinking with reasoned recommendations for future policy

Heath, D., *Drinking Occasions: Comparative Perspectives on Alcohol and Culture,* Brunner/Mazel, Philadelphia, 2000 – Drinking practices in many cultures from an informed anthropological viewpoint

Lucia, P., *Wine and Your Well-Being,* Popular Library, New York, 1971 – This fifth in his remarkable series on the medical aspects of drinking is a primer which presents alcohol therapy for a range of illnesses

MacDonald, I., Ed., *Health Issues Related to Alcohol Consumption,* International Life Sciences Institute, Blackwell Science, – A ranging discussion of the social, cultural and medical issues on drinking with contributions of over thirty noted researchers

Peele, S., and Grant, M., *Alcohol and Pleasure: A Health Perspective,* Brunner/Mazel, Philadelphia, 1999 – Thirty presenters representing twenty countries commenting on the role of human pleasure in responsible drinking

Lewis Perdue, Keith Marton and Wells Shoemaker, *The French Paradox and Beyond,* Renaissance Publishing, Sonoma, 1992 – The unvarnished facts about drinking, food and health in a fact-packed book

Pittman, J., and White H., Eds., *Society, Culture and Drinking Patterns Re-examined,* Rutgers Center on Alcohol Studies, New Brunswick, 1991 – An invaluable compilation including commentaries from over thirty noted authors on every aspect of drinking

Robinson, J., *On The Demon Drink,* Mitchell Beazley Publishers, London, 1988 – An informative outline of British drinking practices

Roman, P., (Ed.), *Alcohol: The Development of Sociological Perspectives on Use and Abuse,* Rutgers Center of Alcohol Studies, New Brunswick, 1991 – A scholarly compilation of articles written in memory of the pioneering alcoholism work of Seldon Bacon

William Rorabaugh, *The Alcoholic Republic,* Oxford University Press, New York, 1979 – A dlightful but deeply erudite romp through America's love and hate affair with drinking

Sinclair, A., *Era of Excess: A Social History of the Prohibition Movement,* Harper Colophon Books, New York, 1962 – The only book on Prohibition you'll ever need to read

Skovenborg, Erik, Vin og Helbred: Myter og facts (Wine and Health: Myths and Facts) Denmark, 2000 – A cleverly illustrated, comprehensive survey of the health benefits of responsible drinking

Stuttaford, T., *To Your Good Health! The Wise Drinkers Guide,* Faber & Faber, London, 1997 – A humorous, science-based essay on drinking and health from a leading British physician/journalist

Vogler, R. and Bartz, W., *The Better Way to Drink,* Simon & Schuster, New York, 1982 – A common sense guide to moderation based on blood alcohol content replete with graphs tables, and guides

Whitten, D., and Lipp, M., *To Your Health! Two Physicians Explore the Health Benefits of Wine,* HarperCollinsWest, New York, 1994 – A uniquely inviting American perspective on drinking and health issues written for a general audience by two California physician/educators

References

The following 1,400 plus references concerning drinking and health were assembled from personal files, from contemporary professional journals, medical newsletters and other media for the first draft of the book. About half that number remain in the final draft. The entire list is printed here for physicians, alcohol researchers and journalists interested in the field.

A bit of what you fancy, London Daily Express, 1995

A Bite Out of Cancer, HealthNews, Vol 6., No. 8, August, 2000

A Health Benefit From the Holidays, Vol. VII, No. 4, December, 1999

A Healthful Diet Goes Beyond This or That Food, Tufts University Health & Nutrition Letter, June, 2000

A meta-analysis underlines an increase of the risk, Vin, Nutrition & Sante, November 31, 1998

A New Sight-Saving Option, Health After 50, Johns Hopkins, Vol. 11, Issue 12, February, 2000

A Scientific Perspective on the Latest Wine and Breast Cancer Research, Wine Institute News Release, July 26, 1993

A Spirited Discussion with Journalists and Scientists, DISCUS, National Press Club, Washington, D.C., December 15, 1999

A Weight Loss Prescription for Longer Life, Health After 50, June, 2000

Abel, E., Fetal Alcohol Syndrome, Medical Economics Books, Oradell, New Jersey, 1990

Abel, E., Fetal Alcohol Syndrome: The American Paradox, Alcohol and Alcoholism, 33: 195-201, May, 1998

Abel, E., Moderate drinking during pregnancy: cause for concern? Clinica Chimica Acta, 246:149-154, 1996

Abel E., and Hannigan, J., J-shaped relationship between drinking during pregnancy and birth weight: re-analysis of prospective epidemiological data, Alcohol and Alcoholism, 30:345-355, 1995

Abel, E., Kruger, M., and Friedl, J., How do physicians define "light" and "heavy" drinking?, Alcohol Clinical and Experimental Research, 22:979-984, 1998

Abel, E., and Sokol, R., Is Occasional Light Drinking During Pregnancy Harmful?, Internet www2.potsdam.edu/alcohol-info

Abou-Agag, L., Aikens, M., Tabengwa, E., et al., Polyphenolics increase t-PA and u-PA gene transcription in cultured human endothelial cells, Alcohol Clinical and Experimental Research, 25:155-162, 2001

Abramson, J., Williams, A., Krumholz, H., and Vaccarino, V., Moderate alcohol Consumption and Risk of Heart Failure Among Older Persons, JAMA, Vol. 285, No. 15, April 18, 2001

Abu-Amsha, R., Phenolic content of various beverages determines the extent of inhibition of human serum and low-density lipoprotein oxidation in vitro: Identification and mechanisms of action of some cinnamic acid derivatives from red wine, Clinicial Science, 91: 449-58, 1996

Actual vs. Perceived Health Risks in Women, HealthNews, Vol. 6, No. 8, August, 2000

Adams, W., Alcohol-Related Hospitalizations Common Among Elderly, News Release, American Medical Association, September 7, 1993

Addiction journals: Amazing happenings, landmark meeting, historic consensus, evolving process, Addiction, 92(12):1613-1616, 1997

Adult Changes in Thought, statistics gathered from Monthly Vital Statistics Report, Vol. 46, No. 1, 1998

Advances in Diagnosing and Treating Alzheimer's Disease, Health After 50, September, 1998

Advisory, Journal of the National Cancer Institute, Vol. 89, No. 21, pp1570-1571, 1997

Aging, Memory and the Brain, Harvard Women's Health Watch, July, 2000

Ajani, U., Gaziano, J., Lotufo, P., et al., Alcohol consumption and risk of coronary heart disease, Circulation, 102:500-505,2000

Akhter, M., Medicine and Public Health Working Together to Meet Health Care Challenges, Media Advisory, American Medical Association, Chicago, December 2, 1997

Alar scare-mongering revisited 10 years later, Editorial, The Seattle Times, February 26, 1999

Alarming news on cardiac arrest, Seattle Post Intelligencer, March 2, 2001

Albertsen, K., Gronbaek, M., Does amount or type of alcohol influence the risk of prostate cancer?, Prostate, 52:297-304, 2002

Alcohol and Cognition, Alcohol Alert, NIAAA, No. 4, PH 258, May, 1989

Alcohol and Coronary Heart Disease, Alcohol Alert, No. 34, NIAAA, October, 1999

Alcohol and Diabetes, New England Journal of Medicine HealthNews, Vol. 5, No. 10, August 15, 1999

Alcohol and Health, Mayo Clinic Health Letter, Vol. 17, No. 4, April, 1999

Alcohol and Health, The New England Journal of Medicine, Vol. 4, No. 4, March 31, 1998

Alcohol and Nutrition, ADAMHA NEWS, May 1987

Alcohol and "Special Populations:" Biological Vulnerability, ICAP Reports 10, Washington, D.C., November, 2001

Alcohol and

Stress, Alcohol Alert, NIAAA, Washington, D.C., No. 32, PH 363, April, 1996

Alcohol and Stroke: Too Much of a Good Thing?, The Cleveland Clinic Heart Advisor, Vol. 1, No. 7, July, 1998

Alcohol and Stronger Bones– The Newly Emerging Evidence, Wine Issues Monitor, The Wine Institute, San Francisco, January/February, 1997

Alcohol and the Endocrine System, Ninth Special Report to Congress on Alcohol and Health, DHHS, pp158-163, Washington, D.C., June, 1997

Alcohol and the Heart: Consensus Emerges, Harvard Heart Letter, Vol. 6, No. 5, January 1996

Alcohol and the heart in perspective: Sensible limits reaffirmed, Journal of the Royal College of Physicians, London, Vol. 29, No. 4, July/August, 1995

Alcohol and the Liver, Alcohol Alert, NIAAA, No. 19, PH 329, January, 1993

Alcohol and Tobacco, Alcohol Alert, NIAAA, No. 39, Washington, D.C., January, 1988

Alcohol and Tobacco in America, American Council on Science and Health, New York City, June, 2000

Alcohol and Tolerance, Alcohol Alert, NIAAA, No. 28, PH 365, Washington, D.C., April, 1995

Alcohol/Cancer Link is Solid, American Institute for Cancer Research, Spring, 1999

Alcohol Consumption Among Pregnant and Childbearing-Aged Women– US, 1991 and 1995, Morbidity and Mortality Weekly Report, 46:346-350,April 24, 1997

Alcohol factor in 40 percent of US violent crime, Reuters News Service, April 5, 1998

Alcohol Update, HealthNews, Vol. 7, No. 6, June, 2001

Alcohol, Violence, and Aggression, Alcohol Alert, No. 38, National Institute on Alcohol Abuse and Alcoholism, Washington, D.C., October, 1997

Alcohol, Violence and Aggression, Alcohol Alert, NIAAA, No. 38, Washington, D.C., October, 1997

Alcohol/Violence Linkage Emerges as New Anti-Alcohol Strategy, Wine Institute NEWS, May/June, 1994

Alcoholic Beverage Taxation and Control Policies, Brewers Association of Canada, Toronto, August, 1997

Alcoholism in the Elderly: Diagnosis, Treatment, Prevention, American Medical Association, Chicago, 1995

Aldoori, W., Giovannucci, E., Stampfer, M., Rimm, E., Wing, A., and Willett, W., A prospective study of alcohol, smoking, caffeine, and the risk of duodenal ulcer in men, Epidemiology, Vol. 8, No. 4, pp420-424, 1997

Allerdyce, J., Research disputes alcohol link with violence, The Scotsman, May 6, 1995

Alpert, J., HDL on the Rise, HealthNews, Vol. 5, No. 11, September 10, 1999

Alzheimer's Disease, Harvard Women's Health Watch, Vol. VI, No. 1, March, 1999

Amarasuriya, R., Gupta, A., Civen, M., Horng, Y., Maeda, T., and Kashyap, M., Ethanol Stimulates Apolipoprotein A-I Secretion by Human Hepatocytes: Implications for a Mechanism for Atherosclerosis Protection, Metabolism, 41(8), August, 1992

American Academy of Pediatrics, News Release, Alcohol During Pregnancy Associated with Rare Kidney Defects, April 7, 1997

American Heart Association, News Release, Dallas, November 19, 1987

American Heart Association, News Release, Dallas, January 28, 1988

American Heart Association, News Release, Dallas, January 13, 1992

American Medical Association, Moderate Lifestyle Changes Reduce High Blood Pressure in the Elderly, News Release, Chicago, March 17, 1998

American Medical Association: Complete Guide to Men's Health, Perry, A., and Schacht, M., editors, John Wiley & Sons, Inc., New York, 2001

Ames, B., Facts versus phantoms, Moderation Reader, March/April, 1993

Ames, B., Review of Evidence for Alcohol-Related Carcinogenesis, Department of Biochemistry, University of California, Berkeley, 1987

Ames, B., Six Common Errors Relating to Environmental Pollution, Regulatory Toxicology and Pharmacology, 7:379-383, 1987

An eating plan for healthy Americans, American Heart Association Diet Dallas, 1995

Antoshechkin, A., et.al., Physiological Model of the Stimulative Effects of Alcohol in Low-to-Moderate Doses, Annals of the New York Academy of Sciences, 957:288-291, 2002

An Update on Headaches, Wine Issues Monitor, January/February, 1997

Anderson, P., Are there net health benefits from moderate drinking? all-cause mortality, Contemporary Drug Problems, Spring, 1994

Anderson, J., and Garner, S., The effect of phytoestrogens on bone, Nutrition Research, 17:1617-1632, 1997

Andrianopoulos, G., and Nelson, R., Alcohol and Breast Cancer, The New England Journal of Medicine, Vol. 317, No. 20, November 12, 1987

Another disease affected by habits, editorial in the Seattle Post Intelligencer, August 11, 2001

Another Reduction: Study Calculated 4.6 Million With Alcohol Disorders in 1980, Alcohol Issues Insights, Vol. 7, No. 12, December, 1990

Anstie, F., On the Uses of Wine in Health and Disease, Macmillan and Company, 1877G35

Antioxidant Overhaul, HealthNews, Vol. 6, No. 5, May, 2000

Antioxidant Supplements and the Heart: What Went Wrong, Harvard Men's Health Watch, Vol. 5, No. 9, April, 2001

Antioxidants May Curb Macular Degeneration, HealthNews, Vol. 7, No., 12, December, 2001

Antioxidants: troublemakers, too, UC Berkeley Wellness Letter, Vol. 14, Issue 10, July, 1998

Antoschechkin, A., Alcohol: Poison or Medicine?, 1st Books Library, Bloomington, IN, 2002

Antoschechkin, A., Physiological Model of the Stimulative Effects of Alcohol in Low-to-Moderate Doses, Annals of the New York Academy of Sciences, Vol. 957:288-291, May, 2002

Appel, L., et al., A Clinical Trial of the Effects of Dietary Patterns on Blood Pressure, New England Journal of Medicine, 336:1117-1123, April 17, 1997

Applegate, L., in The Truth About Losing Body Fat, Better Homes and Gardens, March, 1999

Arbuckle, T., Chaikelson, J., and Pushkar, D., Social drinking and cognitive functioning revisited: the role of intellectual endowment and psychological distress, Journal of Studies on Alcohol, 55:352-361, 1994

Are Mental Stress Tests Next?, Harvard Men's Health Watch, March, 1997

Arimoto-Kobayashi, S., Sugiyama, C., Hrad, N., Takeuchi, M., Takemura, M., and Hayatsu, H., Inhibitory effects of beer and other alcoholic beverages on mutagenesis and DNA adduct formation induced by several carcinogens, Journal of Agricultural and Food Chemistry, Vol., 47, No. 1, pp221,230, 1999

ARISE, Dietary Disarray: Contradictions and Confusion in International Food and Drink Guidelines, www.arise.org/dietary.html

Armstrong, M., and Klatsky, A., Alcohol Use and Later Hospitalization Experience, Medical Care, Vol. 27, No. 12, December, 1989

Arnot, B., The Breast Cancer Prevention Diet, Little Brown and Company, Boston, 1998

Artalejo, F., Guallar-Castillon, P., Banegas, J., De Andres Monzano, B., and del Ray Calero, J., Consumption of fruit and wine and the decline in cerebrovascular disease mortality in Spain (1975-1993), Stroke, 29:1556-1561, 1998

Asch, T., and Levy D., The Minimum Legal Drinking Age and Traffic Fatalities, NIAAA Report, Rutgers University, 1986

Ascherio, A., Foods rich in potassium may help cut stroke risk, Seattle PI, September 22, 1998

Ashley, M., Alcohol Consumption, Ischemic Heart Disease and Cerebrovascular Disease, Journal of Studies on Alcohol, Vol. 43, No. 9, 1982

Ashley, M., Ferrence, R., Room, R., Bondy, S., Rehm, J., and Single, E., Moderate drinking and health, Canadian Family Physician, Vol. 43, April, 1997

Ask Tufts Experts, Tufts University Health & Nutrition Letter, Vol. 17, No. 6, August, 1999

Aspirin to Prevent Strokes: Fact or Fiction?, HealthNews, Vol. 6, No. 5, May, 2000

Atherosclerosis definition, Harvard Men's Health Watch, Vol. 2, No. 7, February, 1998

Atkinson, H., Follow Up, HealthNews, January, 2002

Atkinson, H., How Medical Research Becomes News, New England Journal of Medicine, Vol. 4, No. 10, August 15, 1998

Attention Glucophage Users, Seattle Post Intelligencer, April 5, 2001

Attili, A., Scafato, E., Marchioli, R., Marfisi, R., and Festi, D., Diet and gallstones in Italy: the cross-sectional MICOL results, Hepatology, Vol. 27, No. 6, pp1492-1498, 1998

Avorn, J., Forty Percent of Cholesterol-Lowering Drug Prescriptions Are Not Filled Annually, JAMA, 279:1458-1462, 1998

AWARE, Alcohol & the GI System, Fall, 1997

B Vitamins and Heart Disease, Harvard Health Letter, Vol. 23, No. 12, October, 1998

B Vitamins, Harvard Health Letter, Vol. 27, No. 2, December, 2001

B Vitamins and the Heart: What Men Can Learn from Women, Harvard Men's Health Watch, Vol. 12, No. 11, June, 1998

Bacon, S., The Classic Temperance Movement of the U.S.A.: Impact Today on Attitudes, Action and Research, British Journal of Addiction, Vol. 62, pp5-18, 1967

Baena, J., Lopez, C., Hidalgo, A., et al., Relation between alcohol consumption and the success of Helicobacter pylori eradication therapy using omeprazole, clarithromycin and amoxicillin for 1 week, European Journal of Gastroenterology Hepatol 14:291-296, 2002

Bagchi, D., Have No Fear-Activin is Here, The Wine Investor, April 12, 1997

Bak Andersen, I., Jorgensen, T., Bonnevie, T., Gronbaek, M., and Serrensen, T., Smoking and alcohol intake as risk factors for bleeding and perforated peptic ulcers: a population-based cohort study, Epidemiology, 11:434-439, 2000

Bakalinksy, A., Sulfites, Wine and Health, Symposium on Wine and Health, American Society for Enology and Viticulture, Reno, June 24, 1996

Balkau, B., Eschwege, F., Eschwege, E., Ischemic heart disease and alcohol-related causes of death: a view of the French Paradox, Annals of Epidemiology, 7: 490-497, 1997

Balzer, H., NPD (survey) finds alcohol on more American dinner tables than coffee for the first time ever, Business Wire, September 21, 1998

Bandera, E., Freudenheim, J., Marshall, J., et al., Diet and alcohol consumption and lung cancer risk in the New York State Cohort, Cancer Causes Control, 8:828-840, 1997

Barboriak, J., Anderson, A., Rimm, A., Tristani, F., Alcohol and coronary arteries, Clinical and Experimental Research, 3:29-32, 1979

Barnard, N., Doctors group says food pyramid racially biased, The Seattle Times, September 17, 1998

Barnes, G., Farrell, M., and Cairns, A., Parental Socialization Factors and Adolescent Drinking Behaviors, Journal of Marriage and the Family, 48:27-36, February, 1986

Baron, J., Farahmand, B., Weiderpasse, E., et al., Cigarette Smoking, alcohol consumption and risk of hip fracture in women, Archives of Internal Medicine, 161:983-988, 2001

Baron, J., Sandler, R., Haile, R., Mandel, J., Mott, L., Greenberg, E., Folate intake, alcohol consumption, cigarette smoking, and risk of colorectal adenomas, Journal of the National Cancer Institute, Vol. 90, No. 1, pp.57-62, 1998

Barr, A., Drink: A Social History of America, Carroll & Graf Publishers, New York, 1999

Barr, A., Drink: A Social History of America, Carroll & Graf Publishers, Inc., New York, 1999

Barrett-Connor, E., Caffeinated Coffee Linked to Lower Bone Mass in Women, Media Advisory, American Medical Association, Chicago, January 25, 1994

Barsby, S., A review of the Heien and Pittman study on the costs of alcohol abuse, Moderation Reader, January/February, 1990

Baum-Baicker, C., The Psychological Benefits of Moderate Alcohol Consumption: A Review of the Literature, Drug and Alcohol Dependence, Vol. 15, 1985

Becker, J., Taxed to the Limit, All About Beer, Vol. 20, No. 5, November, 1999

Becker, P., and Cesar, J., Happy-Hour Therapy, Human Behavior, June, 1974

Beer and health benefits, cbmc/org

Beer's Benefits, HealthNews, July, 2000

Beer cuts risk of cataracts and heart disease, www.webmaster@bigfy.com, December 23, 2000

Beer is Good for Your Heart, All About Beer, Vol. 22, No. 6, January, 2002

Beilin, L., Puddey, I., Burke, V., Alcohol and hypertension– kill or cure?, Journal of Hypertension, 10: 1-5, 1996

Bekelman, J., Li, Y, and Gross, C., Financial Relationships among Industry, Scientific Investigators, and Academic Institutions Widespread, with Potential Influence on Research Process, JAMA, 289:454-465, 2003

Bell, D., Alcohol and the NIDDM patient, diabetes care, Vol. 19, No. 5, pp509-513, 1996

Bellantani, S., Saccoccio, G., Tiribelli, C., Costa, G., Manenti, F., Sodde, M., Saveria, C., Croce, L., Sasso, F., Pozzato, G., Cristianini, G., and Brandi, G., Drinking habits as cofactors of risk for alcohol induced liver damage, But, Vol. 41, No. 6, pp845-850, 1997

Bellia, J., Birchall, J., and Roberts, N., Beer-A Useful Source of Silicon, The Lancet, January 22, 1994

Bellido-Blasco, J., Arnedo-Pena, A., Cordero-Cutillas, E., Canos-Cabedo, M., Herro-Carot, C., and Safont-Adsuara, L., The effect of alcoholic beverages on the occurrence of a Salmonella food-borne outbreak, Epidemiology 13:228-230, 2002

Ben-Eliyahu, S., Page, G., Yirmiya, R., and Taylor, A., Acute alcohol intoxication suppresses natural killer cell activity and promotes tumour metastatsis, Nature Medicine, Vol. 2, pp457-460, 1996

Bengtsson, A., Rylander, L., Hagmar, L., Nived, O., and Sturfelt, G., Risk factors for developing systemic lupus erythematosus: a case - control study in southern Sweden, Rheumatology, 41:563-571, 2002

Bennett, W., et al., Body Count: Moral Poverty . . . And How to Win America's War Against Crime and Drugs, Simon & Schuster, New York, 1996

Ben-Shlomo, Y., et al., Stroke risk from alcohol consumption using different control groups, Stroke, 23(8): 1093-1098, 1992

Bereczki, D., Alcohol Consumption and the Risk of Silent Brain Infarct and Stroke, Stroke, Vol. 32, 2001

Berge, K., Editorial, Mayo Health Clinic, Oasis, Internet www.mayoclinic.org

Berger, K., Ajani, U., Kase, C., et al., Light-to-moderate alcohol consumption and risk of stroke among U.S. male physicians, New England Journal of Medicine, 341:1557-1564, 1999

Bertelli, A., et al.., Plasma and tissue resveratrol concentrations and pharmacological activity, Drugs, Experimental and Clinical Research, Vol. 24, No. 3, pp133-138, 1998

Best Advice, UC Berkeley Wellness Letter, April, 1998

Beta Carotene, Harvard Health Letter, Vol. 25, No. 1, November, 1999

Beverage Alcohol and Women, Beverage Alcohol Market Report, Vol. 18, No. 6, March 22, 1999

Bijur, P., One-Third of Injuries to Children, Adolescents are Sports-Related, News Release, American Medical Association, Chicago, 1998

Blackburn, G., Building a Better Food Pyramid, HealthNews, Vol. 8, No. 2, February, 2002

Blackburn, H., Wagenaar, A., and Jacobs, D., Alcohol: Good for Your Health?, Epidemiology, Vol. 2, No. 3, May, 1991

Blackwelder, W., Yano, K., Rhoads, G., Kagen, A., Gordon, T., and Palesh, Y., Alcohol Mortality: The Honolulu Heart Study, American Journal of Medicine, 68: 164-169, 1980

Blair, S., Staying stout may be healthier than dieting, The Seattle Times, March 20, 1994

Bleich, S., Bleich, K., Dropp, S., et al., Moderate alcohol consumption in social drinkers raises plasma homocysteine levels: a contradiction to the French Paradox? Alcohol alcohol, 36:189-192, 2001

Blood Pressure and Alzheimer's, HealthNews, Vol. 4, No. 15, December 15, 1998

Blow, F., Walton, M., Barry, K., Coyne, J., Mudd, S., and Copeland, L., The relationship between alcohol problems and health functioning of older adults in primary care settings, Journal of American Geriatric Society, 48:769-774, 2000

Blume, S., Levy, R., Kannel, W., and Takamine, J., JAMA, Vol. 256, No. 23, December 19, 1986

Bobak, Martin, et al., Effect of Beer Drinking on Risk of Myocardial Infarction: Population-based Case-control Study, British Medical Journal, Vol. 320, May, 2000

Bode, C., and Bode, J., Alcohol's role in gastrointestinal tract disorders, Alcohol Health Research World, 21:65-75, 1997

Bode, C., Bode, J., Erhardt, J., French, B., and French, S., Effect of the type of beverage and meat consumed by alcoholics with alcoholic liver disease, Alcoholism: Clinical and Experimental Research, Vol. 22, No. 8, pp1803-1845, 1998

Boecker, H., et al., The effect of ethanol on alcoholic-responsive essential tremor: a positron emission tomography study, Annals of Neurology, 39:650-658, 1996

Boffetta, P., and Garfinkel, L., Alcohol Drinking and Mortality Among Men Enrolled in an American Cancer Society Prospective Study, Epidemiology, Vol. 1, No. 5, 1990

Bolumar, F., et al., The effect of moderate intake of alcohol during pregnancy on the weight of the newborn, Med Clin, 102:765-768, 1994

Bond, G. et al., Alcohol, Aging and Cognitive Performance in a Cohort of Japanese-Americans Aged 65 and Older, The Kame Project, International Psychogeriatrics, Vol. 13, No. 2, pp207-223, June, 2001

Bondy, S., and Rehm, J., The interplay of drinking patterns and other determinants of health, Drug and Alcohol Review, Vol. 17, No. 4, pp399-411, 1998

Bourne, L., Paganga, G., Backter, D., Hughes, P., and Rice-Evans, C., Bioavailability of ferulic acid from beer, Free Radical Research, 2000

Bowden, S., Brain impairment in social drinkers? No cause for concern, Alcoholism, Clinical and Experimental Research, Vol. 15, 1985

Bowden, S., Cerebral Deficients in Social Drinkers and the Onus of Proof, Australian Drug and Alcohol Review, 6:87-92, 1987

Bowen, O., Speech to National Conference on Alcohol Abuse and Alcoholism, from Department of Health and Human Services, Washington, D.C., November 12, 1987

Braddock, C., Patients decisions lack data, study says, Seattle Times, December 21, 1999

Breast Cancer, AIM-Digest, Vol. 11, No. 4, February/March, 2003, Excerpts of Reeves, G., from British Medical Journal and Doll. R., from Annals of Internal Medicine

Breast Cancer, Medical Essay, Mayo Clinic Health Letter, October, 1994

Breast cancer prevention: exercise and diet?, UC Berkeley Wellness Letter, Vol. 17, Issue 10, July, 2001

Breast cancer: what 1-in-8 means, UC Berkeley Wellness Letter, Vol. 15, Issue 11, August, 1999

Breast Cancer Prevention: What's Realistic?, Harvard Women's Health Watch, Vol. 6, No. 4, December, 1998

Brenner, H., et al., Coronary Heart Disease Risk Reduction in a Predominantly Beer-Drinking Population, Epidemiology, Vol. 12, pp390-395, 2001

Brenner, H., Berg, G., Lappus, N., Kliebech, U., Bode, G., and Boeing, H., Alcohol consumption and Helicobacter pylori infection: results from the German national health and nutrition survey, Epidemiology, Vol. 10, No. 3, pp214-218, 1999

Brenner, H., Bode, G., Adler, G., Hoffmeister, A., Koenig, W., and Rothenbacher, D., Alcohol as a gastric disinfectant? The complex relationship between alcohol consumption and current Helicobacter pylori infection, Epidemiology, 12:209-214, 2001

Brenner, H., Rothenbacher, D., Bode, G., et al., Inverse graded relation between alcohol consumption and active infection with Helicobacter pylori, American Journal of Epidemiology, 149:571-576, 1999

Brenner, H., Rothenbacher, D., Bode, G., and Adler, G., Relation of smoking and alcohol and coffee consumption to active Helicobacter pylori infection: cross sectional study, British Medical Journal, Vol. 315, No. 7121, pp 1489-1492, 1997

Brenner, H., et al., The Association Between Alcohol Consumption and All-Cause Mortality in a Cohort of Male Employees in the German Construction Industry, International Journal of Epidemiology, 26:85-91, 1997

Brenner, M., Economic Change, Alcohol, Consumption and Heart Disease Mortality in Nine Industrialized Countries, Society, Science and Medicine, Vol. 25, No. 2, pp119-132, 1987

Breslow, R., and Weed, D., Review of epidemiologic studies of alcohol and prostate cancer, Nutrition and Cancer, 30:1-13, 1998

Brismar, B., and Bergman, B., The significance of alcohol for violence and accidents, Alcohol Clinical and Experimental Research, 22(7):Suppl:299S-306S, 1998

Broder, D., Decoding the mysteries of American ambivalence, The Seattle Times, September 26, 1999

Broder, D., Democracy on the ascent, government on the decline, The Seattle Times, January, 2000

Brodsky A., and Peele, S., Psycho-Social Benefits of Moderate Consumption, in Alcohol and Pleasure, Peele and Grant, editors, Bruner/Mazel, Philadelphia, 1999

Brody, J., The Moderate Benefits of Moderate Alcohol Consumption, in The New York Times Book of Health, Random Books, New York, 1997

Brody, J., Wine in a Fit World, A Symposium on Wine, Health and Society, the Wine Institute, Washington, D. C., February 24, 1986

Brody, J., Brown, L., et al., Drinking practices and risk of squamous-cell esophageal cancer among Black and White men in the United States, Cancer Causes & Controls, 8:605-609, 1997

Broe, G., Creasey, H., Jorm, A., Bennett, H., Casey, B., Waite, L., Grayson, D., and Cullen, J., Health habits and risk of cognitive impairment and dementia in old age: a prospective study on the effects of exercise, smoking and alcohol consumption, Australian and New Zealand Journal of Public Health, Vol. 22, No. 5, pp621-623, 1998

Brothers, J., Are You Caught in the Middle?, Parade Magazine, June 28, 1998

Brown, B., Zhao, X., Chait, A., Fisher, L., Cheung, M., Morse, J., Dowdy, A., Marino, E., Bolson, E., Alaupovic, P.,Frolich, J.,

Serafini, L., Huss-Frechette, E., Want, S., DeAngelis, D., Dodek, A., and Albers, J., Simvastatin and Niacin, Antioxidant Vitamins, or the Combination for the Prevention of Coronary disease, The New England Journal of Medicine, Vol. 345:1583-1592, No. 22, November 29, 2001

Bruce, K., Shestowsky, J., Mayerovitch, J., et al., Motivational effects of alcohol on memory consolidation and heart rate in social drinkers, Alcohol: Clinical and Experimental Research, 23: 693-701, 1999

Brummer, P., Coronary Mortality and Living Standard, Acta Medica, 18661-63, 1969

Brunn, K., Edwards, G., et al., Alcohol Control Policies in Public Health Perspective, the Finnish Foundation for Alcohol Studies, Vol. 25, 1975

B_{12}: don't B deficient, UC Berkeley Wellness Letter, March, 1999

Buhler, D., Beer flavour fights cancer, researchers say, Ottawa Citizen, March 16, 1998

Buhner, S., Sacred and Herbal Healing Beers: The Secrets of Ancient Fermentation, Brewers Publications, Boulder, 1999

Building a better pyramid, UC Berkeley Wellness Letter, Vol. 18, Issue 3, December, 2001

Bullock, J., Wang, J., and Bullock, G., Was Dom Perignon Really Blind?, Survey of Ophthalmology, Vol. 42, No. 5, March-April, 1998

Bulpitt, C., Alcohol and blood pressure, British Medical Journal, Vol. 309, 1994

Busy B's: good for your heart?, University of California Berkeley Wellness Letter, Vol. 17, Issue 6, March, 2001

By the Way, Doctor, Harvard Women's Health Watch, February, 1999

Cabernet Each Day Keeps the Doctor Away, Wine Spectator, December 15, 2001

Caces, F., and Harford, T., Time series analysis of alcohol consumption and mortality in the United States, 1934-1987, Journal of Studies on Alcohol, Vol. 59, No. 4, pp455-461, 1998

Calcoya, M., Rodriguez, T., Corrales, C., Cuello, R., Lasheras, C., Alcohol and stroke: a community case-control study in Asturias, Spain, Journal of Clinical Epidemiology, 52:677-684, 1999

Caloric Restriction and Longevity, Harvard Men's Health Watch, Boston, May, 1998

Camargo, C., Medical Advisory Group Conference, Alcoholic Beverage Medical Research foundation, October 23-25, 2000 in "The Health Effects of Moderate Alcohol Consumption" symposium

Camargo, C., et al., Moderate alcohol consumption and the risk for angina pectoris or myocardial infarction in the U.S. male physicians, Annals of Internal Medicine, 126(5), 1997

Camargo, C., Stampfer, M., and Gaziano, J., Prospective Study of Moderate Alcohol Consumption, Smoking and Risk of Peripheral Arterial Disease, American Journal of Epidemiology, 141(11 Suppl):S57, Abstract 227, 1995

Cambon, K., Wine and Otolaryngology, Bulletin of The Society of Medical Friends of Wine, 1968

Campbell, E., Louis, K., and Blumenthal, D., Looking a gift horse in the mouth: corporate gifts supporting life sciences research, Journal of the American Medical Association, Vol. 279, No. 13, pp995-999, 1998

Can antioxidants save your life?, UC Berkeley Wellness Letter, July, 1998

Can Religion Be Good Medicine?, The Johns Hopkins Medical Letter, Vol. 10, Issue 9, November, 1998

Can Stress Make You Sick?, Harvard Health Letter, Vol. 23, No. 6, April, 1998

Can Taking Vitamins Protect Your Brain?, Harvard Health Letter, Vol. 25, No. 10, August, 2000

Cancer: Tamoxifen helps head off recurrences, cuts risk of relapses, Seattle Post Intelligencer, May 19, 2000

Can't Conclude from Current Research, in Alcohol Issues Insights, 1996

Cantril A., and Cantril S., Reading Mixed Signals: Ambivalence in American Public Opinion About government, Woodrow Wilson Center Press, 1999

Carbo, N., et al., Resveratrol, a natural product present in wine, decreases tumour growth in a rat tumour model, Biochemistry and Biophysics, Research Communications, 254:739-743, 1999

Cardiovascular Health, Special Advertising Feature, Time Magazine, June 11, 2001

Carmelli, D., Swan, G., Page, W., et al., WW II veteran male twins who are discordant for alcohol consumption: 24-year mortality, American Journal of Public Health, 85:99-101, 1995

Carmelli, D., Swan, G., Schellenberg, G., and Christian, J., The effect of apolipoprotein, E 4 in the relationship of smoking and drinking to cognitive function, Neuroepidemiology, 18:126-133, 1999

Caroli-Bosc, F., Deveau, C., Peten, E., et al., Cholelithiasis and dietary risk factors: an epidemiological investigation in Vidauban, southeast France, Digest Cis Science, 43:2131-2137, 1998

Carper, J., STOP AGING NOW!, from Wine Issues Monitor, June/July, 1996

Casswell, S., Public discourse on the benefits of moderation: implications for alcohol policy development, Addictions, 88:459-465, 1993

Castellsague, X., Munoz, N., De Stefani, E., et al. Independent and joint effects of tobacco smoking and alcohol drinking on the risk of esophageal cancer in men and women, International Journal of Cancer, 82:657-664, 1999

Cataracts, Mayo Clinic Health Letter, Vol. 16, No. 8, August, 1998

Chafetz, M., The Tyranny of Experts, Madison Books, New York, 1996

Chalke, H., Moderate Drinking– Moderate Damage, British Journal on Alcohol and Alcoholism, Vol. 16, No. 3, Autumn, 1981

Charles Dickens revisited, UC Berkeley Wellness Letter, Vol. 18, Issue 3, December, 2001

Chasokela, C., and Tongue, E., Conclusions in Alcohol and Pleasure, Peele and Grant, editors, Brunner/Mazel, 1999

Cherpitel, C., Regional Differences in Alcohol and Fatal Injury: A Comparison of Data from Two County Coroners, Journal of Studies on Alcohol, 57:244-248, May, 1996

Chick, J., Alcohol, health and the heart: implications for clinicians, Alcohol and Alcoholism, Vol. 33, No. 6, pp576-591, 1998

Chick, J., Can Light or Moderate Drinking Benefit Mental Health?, European Addiction Research, June, 1999

Chiu, B., Cerhan, J., Gapstur, S., et al., Alcohol consumption and non-Hodgkin lymphoma in a cohort of older women, British Journal of Cancer, 80:1476-1482, 1999

Chocolate: The Next Health Food?, Tufts University Health & Nutrition Letter, Vol. 18, No. 3, May, 2000

Cholesterol and Stroke, Harvard Men's Health Watch, November, 1998

Chou, S., Medical consequences of alcohol consumption– United States, 1992, in Alcoholism: Clinical and Experimental Research, Vol. 20, No. 8, 1996

Chou, S., Grant, B., and Dawson, D., Alcoholic Beverage Preference and Risks of Alcohol-Related Medical Consequences: A Preliminary Report from the National Longitudinal Alcohol Epidemiological Survey, Alcohol: Clinical and Experimental Research, Vol. 22, No. 7, pp1450-1455, 1998

Chow, W., Swanson, C., Lissowaka, J., et al.,. Risk of stomach cancer in relation to consumption of cigarettes, alcohol, tea and coffee in Warsaw, International Journal of Cancer, 81:871-876, 1998

Christian, J., Moderate Alcohol Consumption Helps Preserve Reasoning Skills, Journal of Studies on Alcohol, Vol. 56, pp414-416, 1995

Chyou, P., et al., Obesity, alcohol consumption, smoking and mortality, Annals of Epidemiology, 7:311-317, 1997

Cipriani, F., Balzi, D., Sorso, B., and Bulatti, E., Alcohol-related mortality in Italy, Public Health, Vol. 112, No. 3, pp183-188, 1998

Clare, A., and Wessely, S., Just what the doctor ordered— more alcohol and sex, British Medical Journal, Vol. 315, No. 7123, December, 1998

Clarke, R., and Smith, A., Elevated Homocysteine Levels Identified as a Possible Risk Factor for Alzheimer's Disease, Special Report, American Medical Association, October 18, 1998

Clarren, S., Recognition of Fetal Alcohol Syndrome, JAMA, Vol. 248, No. 23, 1981

Cleveland Heart Clinic, October, 1998

Clifford, A., Ebeler S., Ebeler, J., Bills, N., Hinrich, S., Teissedre, P., and Waterhouse, A., Delayed tumor onset in transgenic mice fed an amino acid-based diet supplemented with red wine solids, American Journal of Clinical Nutrition, 64:748-756, 1996

Clinton, P., Alcohol Beverage Industry Needs to be Fundamentally Transformed, Alcohol Issues Insights, Vol. 18, No. 11, November, 2001

Coate, D., Moderate drinking and Coronary Heart Disease Mortality, American Journal of Public Health, 83(6): 888-890, 1993

Cockrell, F., Blunders that Outlawed The Liquor Traffic, The New York Times Current History, November, 1930

Coffee Debate Still Percolating, Harvard Health News, July, 2000

Coffee may help stem Parkinson's disease, Seattle Post Intelligencer, May 24, 2000

Cohen, F., et al., Effects of Alcohol Policy Change, Journal of Alcohol and Drug Education, Winter, 42:69-82, 1997

Cohen, S., Alcohol-Related Injuries: The State of the Art of Interventions, A Background Paper for The Secretary's National Conference on Alcohol-Related Injuries, Newton, Massachusetts, March 23, 1992

Cohen S., Doyle, W., Skoner, D., Rabin, B., and Gwaltney, J., Social Ties and Susceptibility to the Common Cold, JAMA, Vol. 277, No. 24, June, 1997

Cohen, S., Tyrrell, D., Russell, M., Jarvis, M., and Smith, A., Smoking, alcohol consumption, and susceptibility to the common cold, American Journal of Public Health, 83:1277-1283, 1993

Colditz, G and Rosner, B., Cumulative risk of Breast Cancer to Age 70 Years According to Risk Factor Status: Data from the Nurses' Health Study, American Journal of Epidemiology, Vol. 152, No. 10:950-964, 2000

Colditz, G., Branch, L., Lipnick, R., Willett, W., Rosner, B., Posner, B., and Hennekens, C., Moderate alcohol and decreased cardiovascular mortality in an elderly cohort, American Heart Journal, 109(4):886-889, 1985

Cole, P., and Rodu, B., Declining cancer mortality in the United States, Cancer, Vol. 78, No. 10, pp2045-2049, 1996

College chiefs put spotlight on alcohol abuse, The Seattle Times, October 17, 1998

Colon Cancer Prevention, Harvard Health Letter, Vol. 25, No. 1, November, 1999

Comments from Wine Institute to the Food and Drug Administration, The Wine Institute, San Francisco, March, 1996

Conigrave, K., et al., A Prospective Study of Drinking Patterns in Relation to Risk of Type 2 Diabetes Among Men, Diabetes, Vol. 50:2390-2395, 2001

Conn, D., Is it RA or Gout?, Arthritis Today, January/February, 1988

Consumer Reports, On Health, Special Report, 1999

Cook, P., Social costs of drinking, in O.G. Assland (Ed.), Expert meeting on the negative social consequences of alcohol use, Norwegian Ministry of Health and Social Affairs, pp49-94, Oslo, August 27-31, 1990

Cooper, E., Racial differences, Stroke News, Cardiovascular Research Report, No. 29, Winter, 1988/89

Cordain, L., Brian, E., Melby, C., and Smith, M., Influence of Moderate Daily Wine Consumption upon Body Weight Regulation and Metabolism in Healthy Free-Living Males, Journal of the American College of Nutrition, 16:1, 1997

Corder, R., Douthwaite, J., Less, D., et al., Endothelin-1 synthesis reduced by red wine, Nature 414:863-864, 2001

Coronary Artery Disease: A Lifelong Process, Harvard Men's Health Watch, Vol. 4, No. 7, February, 2000

Coronary Heart Disease: New Guidelines for Prevention, Harvard Women's Health Watch, 1999

Corrao, G., Arico, S., Zambon, A., Torchio, P., and De Orio, F., Female sex and the risk of liver cirrhosis, Collaborative Groups for the Study of Liver diseases in Italy, Scandinavian Journal of Gastroenterology, Vol. 32, No. 11, pp1174-1180, 1997

Corrao, G., Ferrari, P., Zambon, A., and Torchio, P., Are the recent trends in liver cirrhosis mortality affected by the changes in alcohol consumption? Analysis of latency period in European countries, Journal of Studies on Alcohol, Vol. 58, No. 5, pp486-494, 1997

Criqui, M., Alcohol and Coronary Heart Disease, at the Symposium Health Effects of Moderate Alcohol Consumption, Good, Bad, or Indifferent?, University of Toronto School of Medicine, December 3, 1994

Criqui, M., Alcohol and the heart: implications of present epidemiologic knowledge, Contemporary Drug Problems, Spring, 1994

Criqui, M., Dowan, L., Tyroler, H., Bangdiwala, S., Heiss, G., Wallace, R., and Cohn, R., Lipoproteins as Mediators for the Effects of Alcohol Consumption and Cigarette Smoking on Cardiovascular Mortality: Results from the Lipid Research Clinic Follow-up Study, American Journal of Epidemiology, 126:629-637, 1987

Croft, K., The chemistry and biological effects of flavonoids and phenolic acids, Annals of the New York Academy of Science, 845:435-442, 1998

Croft, K., Puddey, I., Rakic, V., Abu-Amsha, R., Dimmitt, S., Beilin, L., Alcoholism: Clinical and Experimental Research, Vol. 20, No. 6, 1996

Crumley, F., Substance Abuse and Adolescent Suicidal Behavior, Special Communication, American Medical Association, Chicago, June 13, 1990

Cullen, K., Knuiman, M., and Ward, N., Alcohol and Mortality in Busselton, Western Australia, American Journal of Epidemiology, 137(2): 242-248, 1993

Cuming, R., and Mitchell, P., Alcohol, smoking and cataracts: The Blue Mountain Eye Study, Archives of Ophthalmology, Vol. 115, No. 10, pp1296-1303, 1997

Cupples, L., Weinberg, J., Beiser, A., et al., Effects of smoking, alcohol and APOE genotype on Alzheimer disease: the MIRAGE study, Alzheimer Report, 3:105-114, 2000

Curhan, G., Willett, W., Speizer, F., and Stampfer, M., Beverage use and risk for kidney stones in women, Annals of Internal Medicine, Vol. 128, No. 7, pp534-540, 1998

Curhan, G., et al., Prospective study of beverage use and the risk of kidney stones, American Journal of Epidemiology, 143(3):240-247, 1996

Curtis, K., Savitz, D., and Arbuckle, T., Effects of cigarette smoking, caffeine consumption, and alcohol intake on fecundability, American Journal of Epidemiology, 146:32-41, 1997

Daeschel, M., Headache and Wine, Symposium on Wine and Health, American Society for Enology and Viticulture, Reno, June 24, 1996

Dale, D., Boomers who add weight multiply health risks, Seattle Post Intelligencer, December 18, 1998

Dallongeville, J., Marcecaux, N., Ducimetiere, P., Ferrieres, J., Arveiler, D., Bingham, A., Ruidavets, J., Simon, C., and Amouyel, P., Influence of alcohol consumption and various beverages on waist girth and waste-to-hip ratio in a sample of French men and women, International Journal of Obesity, Vol. 22, No. 112, pp1178-1183, 1998

Damianaki, A., Bakogeorgou, E., Kampa, M., Notals, G., et al., Potent inhibitory action of red wine polyphenols on human breast cancer cells, Journal of Cell Biochemistry, 78:429-441, 2000

Dammerman, M., and Breslow, J., Genetic Determinants of Myocardial Infarction, in Prevention of Myocardial Infarction, Oxford University Press, New York, 1996

Daube, M., Pleasure in Health Promotion, in Alcohol and Pleasure, Peele and Grant, editors, Brunner/Mazel, Philadelphia, 1999

Davies, M., Baer, D., Judd, J., Brown, E., Campbell, W., and Taylor, P., Effects of moderate alcohol intake on fasting insulin and glucose concentrations and insulin sensitivity in postmenopausal women: a randomized controlled trial, JAMA, 287:2559-2562, 2002

Davis, A., et al., The prevalence of alcohol misuse in patients undergoing cataract surgery, Addiction Biology, 3:213-219, 1998

Day, L., and Richardson, G., Comparative Teratogenicity of Alcohol and Other Drugs, Alcohol Health and Research World, Vol. 18, No. 1, 1994

de Lorgeril, M., Renaud, S., Mammelle, N., et al., Mediterranean alpha-linolenic acid-rich diet in secondary prevention of coronary heart disease, The Lancet, 343:1454-1459, 1994

de Lorgeril, M., Salen, P., Boucher, F. de Leiris, J., Paillard, F., Effect of wine ethanol on serum iron and ferritin levels in patients with coronary heart disease, Nutrition Metab Cardiovasc Dis, 11: 176-180, 2001

de Lorgeril, M., Salen, P., Martin, J., Monjaud, I., Boucher, P., and Mamelle, N., Mediterranean Dietary Patter in a Randomized Trial, Archives of Internal Medicine, Vol. 158, June 8, 1998

de Rijke, Y., et al., Red wine consumption does not affect oxidizability of low-density lipoproteins in volunteers, American Journal of Clinical Nutrition, 53:329-334, 1996

de Semir, V., Press Releases Generate Wider Newspaper Coverage of Scientific Articles, JAMA, Vol. 280, No. 305, 1998

Dearwater, S., 1 of 3 Women Experience Emotional or Physical Abuse, JAMA, 280:433-438, 1998

Debakey, S., Stinson, F., Grant, B., and Dufour, M., Liver cirrhosis mortality in the US, 1970-93, NIAAA, Alcohol Epidemiology Data System, Report #41, Washington, D.C., 1996

Decarli, A., Favero, A., La Vecchia, C., Russo, A., Ferrarone, M., Negri, E., and Franchesi, S., Macro-nutrients, energy intake and breast cancer risk: implications from different models, Epidemiology, Vol. 8, No. 4, pp245-428, 1997

Decision-Making Dialogue, HealthNews, Vol. 6, No. 2, February, 1999

Deev, A., Shestov, D., Abernathy, J., Kapustina, A., Muhina, N., and Irving, S., Association of alcohol consumption to mortality in middle-aged U.S. and Russian men and women, Annals of Epidemiology, Vol. 8, No. 3, pp147-153, 1998

Dejinkarlsson, E., Hanson, B., and Ostergren, P., Psychosocial resources and persistent alcohol consumption in early pregnancy— a population study of women in their first pregnancy in Sweden, Scandinavian Journal of Social Medicine, Vol. 25, No. 4, 280-288, 1997

De Labry, L., Glynn, R., Levenson, M., Hermos, J., LoCastro, J., and Vokonas, P., Alcohol Consumption and Mortality in an American Male Population: Recovering the U-Shape curve-Findings from the Normative Aging Study, Journal of Studies on Alcohol, 53: 25-32, 1992

Delmas, D., Jannin, B., Cherkaoui Malki, M., and Latruffe, N., Inhibitory effect of resveratrol on the proliferation of human and rat hepatic derived cell lines, Oncology Reports, Vol., 7:847-852, 2000

de Longeril, M., et al., Wine Drinking and Risk of Cardiovascular Complications After Recent Myocardial Infarction, Circulation, Vol. 106:1465-1469, 2002

De Luca, J., NIAAA's Moderation Research Could Redefine Alcohol's Role in the U.S., Alcohol Issues Insights, Vol. 12, No. 6, June, 1995

De Luca, J., President's Report, Wine Institute, San Francisco, October 16, 1996

Demrow, H., Slane, P., and Folts, J., Administration of wine and grape juice inhibits in vivo platelet activity and thrombosis in canine coronary arteries, Circulation, 91:1182-1188, 1995

Demystifying stress, UC Berkeley Wellness Letter, Vol.. 14, Issue 9, June, 1998

Dennison, E., Eastell, R., Fall, C., Kellingray, S., Wood, P., and Cooper, C., Determinants of bone loss in elderly men and women: a prospective population-based study, Osteoporosis, International, 10:384-391, 1999

Dent, O., Sulway, M., Broe, G., Creasey, H., Kos, S., Jorm, A., Tennant, C., and Fiarley, M., Alcohol consumption and cognitive performance in a random sample of Australian soldiers who served in the second world war, British Medical Journal, Vol. 314, No. 7095, pp1655-1657, 1997

Derr, R., Wine, alcohol, nutrition, and the risk of human mortality: Correlation with rat and baboon studies, Biochemical Archives, Vol. 12, No. 4, pp277-282, 1996

Desenclos, J., et al., The Protective Effect of Alcohol on the Occurrence of Epidemic Oyster-Borne Hepatitis A, Epidemiology, 3(4):371-373, 1994

DeShazo, R., and Kemp, S., Nearly One-Third of Patients May Experience Adverse Drug Reactions, JAMA, 278:1895-1906, 1997

Diabetes, Medical Essay, Supplement to the Mayo Clinic Health Letter, Rochester, February, 1998

Diet and Cholesterol: Foods That Help, Harvard Men's Health Watch, Vol. 3, No. 1, August, 1998

Diet and Exercise: A Partnership That Works, Harvard Men's Health Watch, Vol. 4, No. 1, August, 1999

Diet Might Help Prevent Cataracts, Tufts University Health & Nutrition Letter, Vol. 17, No. 10, December, 1999

Dietary Guidelines for Americans, Health and Human Services and the Department of Agriculture, 1995 Fourth and 2000 Fifth Editions, Washington, D.C.

Different for women, UC Berkeley Wellness Letter, April, 2000

Dingle, G., and Oei, T., Is alcohol a cofactor of HIV and AIDS? Evidence from immunological and behavioural studies, Psychological Bulletin, Vol. 122, No. 1, pp56-71, 1997

Distilled Spirits Council of the U.S., Free Radical Paper, Washington, D.C., 1995

Dixon, J., Dixon, M., and O'Brien, P., Alcohol consumption in the severely obese: relatoinship with the metabolic syndrome, Obesity Research 10:245-252, 2002

Dixon, J., Dixon, M., and O'Brien, P., Reduced plasma homocysteine in obese red wine consumers: a potential contributor to reduce cardiovascular risk status, European Journal of Clinical Nutirtion, 56:608-614, 2002

Djousse, L., Levy, D., Murabito, J., Cupples, L., and Ellison, R., Alcohol consumption and risk of intermittent claudication in the Framingham Heart Study, Circulation, 102:3092-3097, 2000

Djousse, L., Pankow, J., Arnett, D., et al., Alcohol consumption and plasminogen activator inhibitor type 1, the National Heart, Lung, and Blood Institute Family Heart Study, American Heart Journal, 129:704-709, 2000

Do free radicals cause cancer and aging, UC Berkeley Wellness Letter, January, 1988

Do You Have Diabetes?, Harvard Men's Health Watch, Cambridge, December, 1997

Dock, W., Wine and Health, Pacific Coast Publishers, Menlo Park, 1968

Does Nature Know Best?, American Council on Science and Health, New York, December, 1996

Doherty, B., WHO Cares?, Reason, Vol. 33, No. 8, January, 2002

Doll, R., Peto, R., Hall, E., Wheatley, K., and Gray, R., Mortality in relation to consumption of alcohol: 13 years observations on male British doctors, British Medical Journal, 309:911-918, 1994

Doll, R., One For The Heart, British Medical Journal, No. 7123, Vol. 315, December, 1997

Doll, R., The benefit of alcohol in moderation, Drug and Alcohol Review, Vol. 17, No. 4, pp353-363, 1998

Don't Get Shaken by this Manageable Disease, Harvard Health Letter, Vol. 24, No. 5, March, 1999

Don't Ignore Stroke Warning Sign, HealthNews, Vol. 6, No. 4, April, 2000

Dorgan, J., Baer, D., Albert, P., Judd, J., Brown, J., Corle, D., Campbell, W., Hartman, T., Tejpar, A., Clevidence, B., Giffen, C., Chandler, D., Stanczyk, F., and Taylor, P., Serum Hormones and the

Alcohol-Breast Cancer Association in Postmenopausal Women, Journal of the National Cancer Institute, Vol. 93, No. 9, pp710-715, May 2, 2001

Doty, L., Women's health overlooked as medicine focuses mainly on men, The Seattle Times, Wednesday March 4, 1998

Drinkers Less Likely than Abstainers to be Hospitalized, Use Outpatient Services, Alcohol Issues, Insights, Vol. 17, No. 9, September, 2000

Drinking a couple of beers daily found to be a health benefit, Business Wine, April 9, 1999

Drinking Age Limits, ICAP Reports 4, International Center for Alcohol Policies, Washington, D.C., March, 1998

Drinking Alcohol and Glucose Control, The Diabetes Cafe at Virginia Mason, www.About.com, 1999

Drinking and diabetes, Johns Hopkins Medical School, intelihealth.com, 1999

Drinking to get drunk seen on rise at U.S. colleges, The Seattle Times, September 10, 1998

Drugstore Aisle, Johns Hopkins Medical Letter, April, 1988

Du V Florey, et al., A European Concerted Action: Maternal Alcohol Consumption and its Relation to the Outcome of Pregnancy and Child Development at 18 Months, International Journal of Epidemiology, Vol. 21, No. 4 (Suppl. 1), 1992

Duffy, J., Alcohol consumption and all-cause mortality, International Journal of Epidemiology, Vol. 24, No. 1, pp100-105, 1995

Dufouil, C., et al., Sex differences in the association between alcohol consumption and cognitive performance, American Journal of Epidemiology, 146(5):405-412, 1997

Dufour, M., Are there net health benefits from moderate alcohol consumption? morbidity and other parameters of health, Contemporary Drug Problems, Spring, 1994

Dufour, M., Introduction: Epidemiological Alcohol Studies, from Alcohol and the Cardiovascular System, NIAAA, Washington, D.C., 1996

Dufour, M., Archer, L., and Gordis, E., Clinics in Geriatric Medicine, NIAAA, Division of Biometry and Epidemiology, Epidemiologic Report, Washington, D.C., June/July 1992

Dull, R., and Giocopassi, D., An Assessment of the Effects of Alcohol Ordinances on Selected Behaviors and Conditions, The Journal of Drug Issues, 16(4): 511-521, 1986

Duthie, G., Pedersen, M., Gardner, P., Morrice, P., Jenkinson, A., McPhail, D., and Steele, G., The effect of whisky and wine consumption on total phenol content and antioxidant capacity of plasma from healthy volunteers, European Journal of Clinical Nutrition, 52:733-736, 1998

Dykstra, D., Drinking warning, Pacific Northeast, November 15, 1998

Eat Your Heart Out, Time, July 19, 1999

Eating Mediterranean, Mayo Clinic Health Letter, Vol. 17, No. 6, June, 1999

Ebeler, C., et al., Delayed tumor onset in transgenic mice fed an amino acid-based diet supplement with red wine solids, American Journal of Clinical Nutrition, Vol. 64:748-756, 1966

Ebeler, S., and Weber, M., Wine and Cancer, Wine in Context Symposium, American Society for Enology and Viticulture, Reno, June, 1996

Ebeler, S., Clifford, A., Ebeler, J., Bills, N., and Hinrichs, S., An In Vivo Experimental Protocol for Identifying and Evaluating Dietary Factors That Delay Tumor Onset, in Wine: Nutritional and Therapeutic Benefits, American Chemical Society, Washington, D.C., 1997

Eckardt, M., File, S., Gessa, G., Grant, K., Guerri, C., Hoffman, P., Kalant, H., Koob, G., Li, T., and Tabakoff, B., Effects of Moderate Alcohol Consumption on the Central Nervous System, Alcoholism: Clinical and Experimental Research, Vol. 22, No. 5, pp998-1040, 1998

Eckardt, M., Harford, T., Kaelber, T., Parker, E., Rosenthal, L., Ryback, R., Salmiraghi, G., Vanderveen, E., and Warren, K., Health Hazards Associated with Alcohol Consumption, Journal of the American Medical Association, Vol. 246, No. 6, August 7, 1981

Eckhardt, F., Alcohol Liberated, All About Beer, Vol. 20, No. 1, March 1, 1999

Economic Costs of Alcohol and Drug Abuse Estimated at $246 Billion in the United States, NIDA Media Advisory, NIDA/NIAAA, Washington, D.C., Wednesday, May 13, 1998

Edell, D., Eat, Drink & Be Merry, HarperCollins, New York, 1999

Edelstein, S., Kritz Silverstein, D., and Barrett Connor, E., Prospective association of smoking and alcohol use with cognitive function in an elderly cohort, Journal of Women's Health, Vol. 7, No. 10, pp1271-1281, 1998

Edwards, G., Alcohol Policy and the Public Good, Oxford Medical Publications, New York, 1994

Edwards, G., If the drinks industry does not clean up its act, pariah status is inevitable, British Medical Journal, Vol. 317, No. 7154, p336, 1998

Effects of Alcohol on Behavior and Safety, Ninth Special Report to Congress on Alcohol and Health, DHHS, Washington, D.C. June, 1997

Egeland, G., Perham-Hester, K., Gessner, B., Ingle, D., Berner, J., and Middaugh, J., Foetal alcohol syndrome in Alaska, 1977 through 1992; an administrative prevalence derived from multiple data sources, American Journal of Public Health, Vol. 88, No. 5, pp781-786, 1998

Eight good bets for preventing colon cancer, UC Berkeley Wellness Letter, December, 1998

Eisenberg, D., 4 of 10 People Use Alternative Medicine in the United States, JAMA, 280:1569-1575, 1998

Ekpo, E., et al., Demographic, life style and anthropometric correlates of blood pressure of Nigerian urban civil servants, factory and plantation workers, Journal of Human Hypertension, 6(4): 275-80, 1992

Elias, P., Elias, M., D'Agostino, R., Silbershatz, H., and Wolf, P., Alcohol Consumption and Cognitive Performance in the Framingham Heart Study, American Journal of Epidemiology, Vol. 150, No. 6, pp580-589, 1999

Ellison, R., Alcohol Consumption: Beneficial to your health?, Wine in Context Symposium, American Society of Enologist and Viticulturists, Reno, June, 1996.

Ellison, R., Alcohol in the Mediterranean diet, American Journal of Clinical Nutrition, (6S):1378S-1282S, 1995

Ellison, R., Cheers!, Epidemiology, Vol. 1, No. 5, September, 1990

Ellison, R, Does Moderate Alcohol Consumption Prolong Life?, American Council on Science and Health, New York, 1993

Ellison, R., Exploring the French Paradox, Speech to the National Press Club, Washington, D.C., May 5, 1992

Ellison, R, Presentation to the National Press Club, Washington, D.C., September 26, 1994

Ellison, R., Speech to The Society of Medical Friends of Wine, Pacific Union Club, San Francisco, January 6, 1993

Ellison, R., Zhang, Y., McLennan, C., and Rothman, K., Exploring the Relation of Alcohol Consumption to Risk of Breast Cancer, American Journal of Epidemiology, Vol. 154, No. 8:740-747, 2001

Elwood, P., Gallagher, J., Hopkinson, C., Pickering, J., Rabbitt, P., Stollery, B., Brayne, C., Huppert, F., and Bayer, A., Smoking, drinking, and other lifestyle factors and cognitive function in men in the Caerphilly cohort, Journal of Epidemiology and Community Health, Vol. 53, No. 1, pp9-14, 1999

Emboden, W., Narcotic Plants, Collier Books, New York, 1979

Emeson, E., Manaves, V., Emeson, B., et al., Alcohol inhibits the progression as well as the initiation of atherosclerotic lesions in /6 hyperlipidemic mice, Alcohol Clinical and Experimental Research, 24:1456-1466, 2000

Engs, R., Cycles of Social-Reform: Is the Current Anti-Alcohol Movement Cresting?, Expert Opinions, www2.potsdam.edu/alcohol-info, reprinted from Journal of Studies on Alcohol, Vol. 58, 1997

Engs, R., Do Traditional Western European Drinking Practices Have Origins in Antiquity, Addiction Research, Vol. 2, No. 3, pp227-239, 1995

Engs, R., Women, alcohol and health: a drink a day keeps the heart attack away?, Current Opinion in Psychiatry, 9:217-220, 1996

Engs, R., and Aldo-Benson, M., The Association of Alcohol Consumption with Self-Reported Illness in University Students, Psychological Reports, 76:727-736, 1995

Engs, R., and Hanson, D., Reduction of Consumption Theory: A Test Using the Drinking Patterns and Problems of Collegians in the United States 1983-1994, College Student Journal, Vol. 33, No. 3, September, 1999

Eriksson, C., et al., Estrogen-related acetaldehyde elevation in women during alcohol intoxication, Alc Clin Exp Research, 20:1192-1195, 1996

Essential tremor, Mayo Clinic Health Letter, Vol. 15, No. 3, March, 1997

Estifeeva, T, MacFarlane, G., and Robertson, C., Trends in cancer mortality in central European countries— The effect of age, birth cohort and time-period, European Journal of Public Health, Vol. 7, No. 2, 1997

Estrin, R., Parkinson's study raises serious ethical issues, Seattle Post Intelligencer, March 27, 1998

Estrogen, Affluence and Alcohol: Breast Cancer Risk Factors?, The Wine Institute, Research News Bulletin, Vol. 2, No. 5, September, 1993

ET: A Patient Information Handbook,International Tremor Foundation, Overland Park, Kansas 66212-1803

Even "Normal" Blood Pressure May Be Too High, Tufts University Health & Nutrition Letter, Vol. 18, No. 1, March, 2000

Exercise and the Prostate: Can You Run Away from Trouble, Harvard Men's Health Watch, Vol. 5, No. 10, May, 2001

Facchini, F., Chen, Y., and Reaven, G., Light-to-Moderate Alcohol Intake is Associated with Enhanced Insulin Sensitivity, Diabetes Care, Vol. 17, No. 2, February, 1994

Fagan, J., Influences of Alcohol on the Social Context of Violent Events, in Alcohol and Violence, Monograph No. 2, Alcoholic Beverage Medical Research Foundation, December 7, 1994

Fagan, J., Interactions among drugs, alcohol and violence, Health Affairs, Vol. 12, No. 4, 1993

Faith and Longevity: Is There a Link?, Harvard Men's Health Watch, September, 1997

Farb, P., and Armelagos, G., Consuming Passions: The Anthropology of Eating, Houghton Mifflin Company, Boston, 1980

Farchi, T., Fidanza, F., Bimapaoli, S., Mariotti, S., and Menotti, A., Alcohol and survival in the Italian rural cohorts of the Seven Countries Study, International Journal of Epidemiology, 29:667-671, 2000

Farchi, G., Fidanza, F., Mariotti, S., and Menotti, A., Alcohol and Mortality in the Italian Rural Cohorts of the Seven Countries Study, International Journal of Epidemiology, 21:74-81, 1993

Farrer, L., from Boston University Medical School presentation at World Alzheimer's Congress, Washington, D.C., 2000

FDA Drug Bulletin, Surgeon General's Advisory on Alcohol and Pregnancy, Vol. 11, No. 2, July, 1981

Feinstein, A., Scientific standards in epidemiological studies, Science, Vol. 212, December 2, 1988

Felson, D., Zhang, Y., Hannan, M., Kannel, W., and Kiel, D., Alcohol intake and bone mineral density in elderly men and women, The Framingham Study, American Journal of Epidemiology, 142(5):485-492, 1995

Ferrarone, M., et al., Alcohol Consumption and Risk of Breast Cancer: a Multicentre Italian Case-Control Study, European Journal of Cancer, 34:1403-1409, August, 1998

Ferrence, R., Truscott, S., and Whitehead, P., Drinking and the Prevention of Coronary Heart Disease: Findings, Issues and Public

Ferrero, M., Bertelli, A., Fulgenzi, A., Pelligatta, F., Corsi, M., Bongrate, M., Ferrara, F, Caterina, R., Giovannini, L., and Bertelli, A., Activity in vitro of resveratrol on granulocyte and monocyte adhesion to endothelium, American Journal of Clinical Nutrition, 68:1208-1214, 1998

Ferrieres, J., Comments and reflections, Wine, Nutrition & Health, No. 44, 1999

Feskanich, D., Korrick, S., Greenspan, S., Rosen, H., and Colditz, G., Moderate alcohol consumption and bone density among postmenopausal women, Journal of Women's Health, Vol. 8, No. 1, pp65-73, 1999

Feskanich, D., Singh, V., Willett, W., and Colditz, G., Vitamin A Intake and Hip Fractures Among Postmenopausal Women, JAMA, Vol. 287, No. 1, January 2, 2002

Fetal Alcohol Syndrome Fact Sheet, National Organization on Fetal Alcohol Syndrome, 1815 H Street NW, Washington, D.C., 2000

Fewer than one-third of American women of child-bearing age take daily supplements of the B vitamin folic acid, UC Berkeley Wellness Letter, Vol. 16, Issue 12, September, 2000

Figuring your BMI, UC Berkeley Wellness Letter, Vol. 6, Issue 6, March, 2000

Fillmore, M., Carscadden, J., and Vogel-Sprott, M., Alcohol, cognitive impairment and expectancies, Journal of Studies on Alcohol, 59:174-179, 1998

Final Report, 2, A Summary, Task Force on Responsible Decisions About Alcohol, Education Commissions of the States, Denver, 1973

Fingarette, H., Heavy Drinking: The Myth of Alcoholism as a Disease, University of California Press, 1988

Finkel, H., Alcohol and the Aging Brain, The Chronicle, Society of Wine Educators, 1998

Finkel, H., Cancer: Does Alcohol Cause It? Does Wine Protect Against It? Society of Wine Educators Bulletin, 1997

Finkel, H., In Vino Sanitas?, Society of Wine Educators, Savage, Maryland, 1998

Finkel, H., Is the French Paradox true? Some don't want to believe, Healthy Drinking, July/August 1995

Finkel, H., Nutrition, Weight, and Wine, Health Update, Bulletin of the Society of Wine Educators, Vol. 20, No. 2, July, 1999

Finkel, H., What's Your Doctor's View of the French Paradox?, The Chronicle, Society of Wine Educators, Vol. 19, No. 1, March, 1998

Firms told to add folic acid to food,Seattle Times, March 1988

First world recommendation for a programme of education "Wine and Society," Wine, Nutrition & Health, OIV, No. 46, 1999

Fisher, M., Translation of Brilliatt-Savarin's The Physiology of Taste, Harcourt Brace Jovanovich, New York, 1978

Fitzgerald, E., and Hume, D., the Single Chemical Test for Intoxication: A Challenge to Admissibility, Massachusetts Law Review, Vol. 66, No. 1, Winter 1981

Five Keys to Diabetes Control, the Johns Hopkins Medical Letter Health After 50, Vol. 9, Issue 12, February, 1998

Five Nutrition Topics Worth Considering for Your Health and Well-Being, Supplement, Tufts University Health & Nutrition Letter, Vol. 7, No. 5, 1999

Flanagan, D., Moore, V., Godsland, I., Cockington, R., Robinson, J., and Phillips, D., Alcohol consumption and insulin resistance in young adults, European Journal of Clinical Investigation, 30:297-301, 2000

Flavonoids, the Next New Thing?, Harvard Health Letter, Vol. 26, No. 2, December, 2000

Fletcher, D., More women are turning to drink and cigarettes, Daily Telegraph, p4, March 26, 1998

Flood, A., Caprario, L., Chaterjee, N., Lacey, Jr., J., Schairere, C., and Schatzkin, A., Folate, methionine, alcohol, and colorectal cancer in a prospective study of women in the United States, Cancer Causes and Control, 13:551-561, 2002

Follow Up: Natural Prostatitis Treatment, Health News, Vol. 6, No. 3, March, 2000

Folts, J., American College of Cardiology 47th Convention, Atlanta, 1998

Fontaine, K., Redden, D., Wang, C., Westfall, A., and Allison, D., Years of Life Lost Due to Obesity, JAMA. Vol. 289:187-193, 2003

Foppa, M., Fuchs, F., Preissier, L., Andrighetto, A., Rosito, G., and Duncan, B., Red wine with the noon meal lowers post-meal blood pressure: a randomized trial in centrally obese, hypertensive patients, Journal of Studies on Alcohol, 63:247-251, 2002

Ford, G., Midcourse Revision of Healthy People 2000, Letter to M. McGinnis of DHHS, November 25, 1994

Ford, G., Moderation Defined, Healthy Drinking, March/April, 1995

Ford, G., The Benefits of Moderate Drinking: Alcohol, Health and Society, Wine Appreciation Guild, San Francisco, 1988

Ford, G., The French Paradox & Drinking for Health, Wine Appreciation Guild, San Francisco, 1993

Foreman, J., Health care on the Internet: a wealth of info— and risks, The Seattle, Times, January 24, 1999

Formica, J., Review of the biology of quercetin and related bioflavonoids, Food and Chemical Toxicology, Vol. 33, No. 12, pp1061-1080, 1995

Forrest, F., Du V Florey, C., and Taylor, D., Maternal Alcohol Consumption and Child Development, International Journal of Epidemiology, Vol. 21, No. 4(Suppl 1), 1992

Forrest, F., du V Florey, C., Taylor, D., McPherson, F., and Young J., Reported social alcohol consumption during pregnancy and infants' development at 18 months, British Medical Journal, Vol. 303, July 6, 1991

Forsander, O., Dietary Influences on Alcohol Intake: A Review, Journal of Studies on Alcohol, 59:26-31, 1998

Forsham, P., The Impact of Wine On Diabetes Mellitus, Bulletin of the Society of Medical Friends of Wine, Vol., 29, No. 1., San Francisco, November 5, 1986

Forsham, P., Wine and Diabetes, presentation in Wine, Health & Society Symposium, Wine Appreciation Guild, San Francisco, November 13, 1981

Fox, B., To Your Health: The Healing Power of Alcohol, Diane Publishing, 2000

Franceschi, S., et al., The influence of body size, smoking, and diet on bone density in pre and post menopausal women, Epidemiology, 239:229-304, 1996

Frank, J., The Determinants of Health and the Prevention Paradox in Alcohol Research, Alcoholic Beverage Medical Research Foundation Journal, Vol. 7, N0. 3, 1997

Frankel, E., Waterhouse, A., Kinsella, J., Inhibition of Human LDL Oxidation by Resveratrol, The Lancet, 341, April 24, 1993

Frankel, E., Waterhouse, A, and Teissedre, L., Principal Phenolic Phytochemicals in selected California Wines and their Antioxidant Activity in Inhibiting Oxidation of Human Low-Density Lipoproteins, Journal of Agricultural Food Chemistry, 43:890-894, 1995

Fraser, G., Anderson, J., Foster, N., Goldberg, R., Jacobs, D., and Blackburn, H., The Effect of Alcohol on Serum High Density Lipoprotein, (HDL): A Controlled Experiment, Atherosclerosis, 46:275-286, 1983

Fremont, L., Biological Effects of Resveratrol, Life Sciences, 66:663-673, 2000

French, M., and Zarkin, G., Is moderate alcohol use related to wages?, Evidence from four work sites, Journal of Health Economics, 14:319-344, 1995

Freudenheim, J., et al., Lifetime Alcohol Consumption and Risk of Breast Cancer, Nutrition and Cancer, 23:1-11, 1995

Frezza, M., de Padova, C., Pozzato, G., Terpin, M., Baraona, E., and Lieger, C., High Blood Alcohol Levels in Women, The Role of Decreased Gastric Alcohol Dehydrogenase Activity and First-Pass Metabolism, New England Journal of Medicine, Vol. 322, No. 2, 1990

Fried, L., Sex, Income, Disability Important Predictors of Mortality, JAMA, 279:585-592, 1998

Friedman, G., Selby, J., Quesenberry C., Armstorng, M. and Klatsky, A., Precursors of essential hypertension: body weight, alcohol and salt use, and parental history of hypertension, Preventive Medicine, (4): 387-402, July, 1988

Friedman, G., and Klatsky, A., Is Alcohol Good for Your Health, The New England Journal of Medicine, Vol. 329, No. 25, December 16, 1993

Friedman, L., and Kimball, A., Coronary Heart Disease Mortality and Alcohol Consumption in Framingham, American Journal of Epidemiology 124(3): 481-489, 1986

Friedman, S., Wine's history as therapy for mankind, Wines and Vines, December, 1992

Friends May be Good for Your Heart, HealthNews, Vol. 5, No. 1, January, 1999

Fuchs, F., Chambless, L., Whelton, P., Nieto, F., and Heiss, G., Alcohol consumption and the incidence of hypertension: the Atherosclerosis risk in Communities Study, Hypertension, 37:1242-1250, 2001

Fuchs, C., Stampfer, M., Colditz, G., Giovannucci, E., Manson, J., Kawachi, I., Hunter, D., Hankinson, S., Hennekens, C., Rosner, B., Speizer, F., and Willett, W., Alcohol consumption and mortality among women, New England Journal of Medicine, Vol. 3332, No. 19, pp1245-1250, 1995

Fugelsang, K., Recent research on SO_2, Wines and Vines, Vol. 70, No. 8, August, 1989

Fugelsang, K., and Muller C., The In Vitro Effect of Red Wine on Helicobacter pylori, Wine Health Symposium, American Society for Enology and Viticulture, Reno, 1996

Fuhrman, B., et al., Consumption of red wine with meals reduces the susceptibility of human plasma and low density lipoprotein to lipid peroxidation, American Journal of Clinical Nutrition, 61:549-554, 1995

Fuller, R., Littell, A., Witschi, J., et al., Calorie and nutrient contribution of alcoholic beverages to the usual diets of 155 adults, American Journal of Clinical Nutrition, 24(9):1042-1052,

Galanis, D., Joseph, D., Masaki, K., et al., A Longitudinal Study of Drinking and Cognitive Performance in Elderly Japanese American Men: The Honolulu-Asia Aging Study, American Journal of Public Health, Vol. 90, No. 8, August, 2000

Gallup Alcohol Update, Gallup Polls, Vol. 62, No. 20, September, 1997

Gapstur, S., Patten J., Sellers, T., et al., Increased risk of breast cancer in postmenopausal women, American Journal of Epidemiology 136(10):1221-1231, 1992

Garcia, C., Rodriguez, A., Vilar, A., Ganegas, J., del Rey, C., Wine consumption and ischaemic heart disease mortality in Spain, Medica Clinica, Vol. 111, No. 4, pp142-144, 1998

Gardner, G., and McKinney, R., The Great American War on Drugs: Another Failure of Tough-Guy Management, The Journal of Drug Issues 21(3), 605-616, 1991

Garg, R., et al., Alcohol consumption and risk of ischemic heart disease in women, Archives of Internal Medicine, 153:1121-1216, 1993

Garland, M., Hunter, D., Colditz, G., et al., Alcohol consumption in relation to breast cancer risk in a cohort of United States women 25-42 years of age, Cancer Epidemiological Biomarkers Prevention, 8:1017-1021, 1999

Gavalier, J., and Van Thiel, D., The Association Between Moderate Alcoholic Beverage Consumption and Seru Estradiol and Testosterone Levels in Normal Postmenopausal Women: Relationship to the Literature, Alcohol: Clinical and Experimental Research, 16(1): 87-92, 1992

Gaziano, J., Gaziano, T., Glynn, R., et al., Light-to-moderate alcohol consumption and mortality in the Physicians' Health Study enrollment cohort, Journal of the American College of Cardiology, 35:96-105, 2000

Gaziano, M., et al., Moderate alcohol intake, increased levels of high-density lipoprotein and its subfractions, and decreased risk of myocardial infarction, The New England Journal of Medicine, 3239(25) 1829-1834, 1993

Gaziano, M., et al., Potential Mortality Benefits for Drinkers with Previous Heart Attacks, The Lancet, Vol. 352, 1993

Gaziano, M., Hennekens, C., Godfried, S., Sesso, H., Glynn, R., Breslow, J., and Buring, J., Type of alcoholic beverage and risk of myocardial infarction, American Journal of Cardiology, Vol. 83, No. 1, pp52-57, 1999

Gaziano, M., American Heart Association Conference Presentation Reinforces Potential Health Benefits of All Beverage Alcohol, News Release, DISCUS, November 21, 1995

Gazmanian, et al., More than One-Third of Elderly HMO Enrollees Have Inadequate Health Literacy, JAMA, 281:543-549, 1999

Gehm, B., Resveratrol, a polyphenolic compound found in grapes and wine, is an agonist for the estrogen receptor, Proceedings of the National Academy of Science, 94:141-143, 1997

Gender Differences in Diseased, Harvard Women's Health Watch, Vol. VI, No. 5, January, 1999

General Motors Grants $2.5 Million to MADD, Beverage Alcohol Market Report, Vol. 20, No. 10, June 29, 2001

Gentry, K., God Gave Wine: What the Bible Says About Alcohol, Oakleafs Books, 2000

Gentry, K., The Christian and Alcoholic Beverages, Baker Bookhouse, Grand Rapids, 1986

Geoffroy-Perez, B., and Corier, S., Fluid consumption and the risk of bladder cancer: results of a multicenter case-control study, International Journal of Cancer, 93:880-887, 2001

Gerety, T., Wine Insight, in Alcohol Issues Insights, 1993

Getting the Right Cure for Ulcers, the Johns Hopkins Medical Leter Health After 50, Vol. 10, Issue 1, March, 1998

Ghiselli, A., Natelia, F., Guidi, A., Montanari, L., Fantozzi, P., and Scaccini, C., Beer increases plasma antioxidant capacity in humans, Journal of Nutritional Biochemistry, 11:78-80, 2000

Giancola, P., and Zelchner, A., The biphasic effects of alcohol on human physical aggression, Journal of Abnormal Psychology, 106:598-607, 1997

Gifford, K., Battling Radicals, Oldways Exchange Newsletter, Vol. 2, Issue 4, August, 1999

Gilder, P., Challenging the Collegiate Rite of Passage: A Campus-Wide Social Marketing Campaign to Reduce Binge Drinking, Journal of Drug Education, Vol. 31, No. 2:207-220, 2001

Gill, J., Zezulka, A., Shipley, M., Gill, S., and Beevers, D., Stroke and Alcohol, The New England Journal of Medicine, Vol. 315, No. 17, October, 1986

Gillman, W., et al., Relationship of alcohol intake with blood pressure in young adults, Hypertension, 25:1106-1110, 1995

Gillman, W., Cupples, L., Millen B., Ellison, R., and Wolf, P., Inverse Association of Dietary Fat with Development of Ischemic Stroke in Men, JAMA, 278:2145-2150, 1997

Gilson, C., and Bennett, Virginia, Alcohol and Women, Creating a Safer Lifestyle, Fusion Press, Irving, Texas, 2000

Gilson, C., With Women Alcohol is Different, ACA Journal, 1989

Gmel, G., Rehm, J., and Ghazinouri, A., Alcohol and suicide in Switzerland– an aggregate-level analysis, Drug and Alcohol Review, Vol. 17, No. 1, pp27-37, 1998

Attention Glucophage Users, advertisement, Seattle Post-Intelligencer, Thursday, April 5, 2001

Goldberg, B., Bias: A CBS Insider Exposes How the Media Distort the News, Regnery Publishing, Inc., Washington, D.C., 2002

Goldberg, D., Does wine work?, Clinical Chemistry, 41(1): 14-16, 1995

Goldberg, D., Garovic-Kocic, V., Diamandis, E., and Pace-Asciak, C., Wine: Does the colour count?, Clin Chim Acta, 246(1-2):183-193, March 15, 1996

Goldbert, I., To Drink or Not to Drink?, New England Journal of Medicine, Vol. 348, January 9, 2003

Goldberg, J., Older Americans Should Enjoy Their Meals, Media Advisory, American Medical Association, Chicago, September 18, 1997

Goldberg, R., Burchfield, C., Reed, D., et al., A prospective study of the health effects of alcohol consumption in middle-aged and elderly men, Honolulu Heart Study, Circulation, 89(2):651-659, February, 1989

Goldbohm, R., van den Brandt, P., van't Veer, P., Dorant, E., Slumans, R., and Hemus, R., Cancer Case Control, 5:95-104, 1994

Goldman, L., Cholesterol Reduction, in Prevention of Myocardial Infarction, Oxford University Press, New York, 1996

Goldstein, D., Pharmacology of Alcohol, Oxford University Press, New York, 1983

Golub, A., and Johnson, B., Alcohol is not the gateway to hard drug use, Journal of Drug Issues, 28:971-984, 2000

Golub, A., and Johnson, B., Variation in Youthful Risks of Progression from Alcohol and Tobacco to Marijuana and to Hard Drugs Across Generations, American Journal of Public Health, Vol. 91, No. 2, 2000

Good News, Time, p117, November 19, 1999

Gordis, E., Alcohol and Nutrition, Alcohol Alert No. 22, PH346, Washington, D.C., October, 1993

Gordis, E., Alcohol and Stress, Alcohol Alert No. 32, NIAAA, PH 363, Washington, D.C., April, 1996

Gordis, E., Alcohol Research and Public Health Policy, Alcohol Alert, No. 20, NIAAA, PH 330, April, 1993

Gordis, E., Fetal Alcohol Syndrome, Alcohol Alert, NIAAA, No. 13, Washington D.C., July, 1991

Gordis, E., Moderate Drinking, Alcohol Alert, NIAAA, No. 16, Washington, D.C., April, 1992

Gordis, E., The Genetics of Alcoholism, Alcohol Alert No. 18, PH328, October, 1992

Gordon, T., and Doyle, J., Drinking and Mortality, the Albany Study, American Journal of Epidemiology, Vol. 125, No. 2, 1987

Gordon, T., and Kannel, W., Drinking habits and cardiovascular disease: The Framingham Study, American Heart Journal, April, 1983

Gorinstein, S., Zemser, M., Berliner, M., et al., Moderate beer consumption and positive biochemical changes in patients with coronary atherosclerosis, Journal of Internal Medicine, 242: 219-224, 1997

Gorman, C., Where's the Proof?, Time, January 27, 2003

Gough, M., Beneficial Effects of Consumption of Low Levels of Alcohol, Competitive Enterprise Institute, Washington, D.C., 1999

Goverde, H., Dekker, H., Janssen, H., Bastiaans, B., Rolland, R., and Zielhuis, G., International Journal on Fertility, 40:135-138, 1995

Gout, w.w.w.dietitian.com

Gout: New Views of an Old Ailment, Harvard Men's Health Watch, November, 1997

Goverde, H., et al., Semen quality and frequency of smoking and alcohol consumption— an explorative study, International Journal of Fertility Menopause Studies 40: 135-138, 1995

Government Policies on Alcohol and Pregnancy, International Center for Alcohol Policies, Report 6, January, 1999

Graham, K., Wilsnak, R., Dawson, D., and Vogeltanz, N., Should alcohol consumption measures be adjusted for gender differences?, Addiction, Vol. 93, No.8, pp1137-3347, 1998

Grant, B., The Ale Master, Sasquatch Books, 1998

Grant, B., Harford, T., Chou, P., Pickering R., Dawson, D., Stonson, F., and Noble, J., Epidemiologic Bulletin No. 27, Prevalence of DSM-III-R alcohol abuse and dependence, Alcohol Health & Research World 15(1):91-96, 1991

Grant, M., Gwinner, P., Alcoholism in Perspective, Croom Helm, London, 1979

Grasping Essential Tremor, HealthNews, Vol. 5, No. 12, October 1, 1999

Graves, K., and Hines, A., Ethnic differences in the association between alcohol and risky sexual behavior with a new partner: an event-based analysis, AIDS Education Prevention, 9:219-237, 1997

Great news about avoiding diabetes, UC Berkeley Wellness Letter, Vol. 18, Issue 2, November, 2001

Green, black, and red: the tea-total evidence, UC Berkeley Wellness Letter, Vol. 16, Issue 6, March, 2000

Greenfield, T., Midanik, L., and Rogers, J., A 10-year national trend study of alcohol consumption, 1984-1995: Is the period of declining drinking over?, American Journal of Public Health, 90:47-52, 2000

Greenwald, J., Herbal Healing, Time Magazine, November 23, 1998

Grodstein, F., Goldman, M., and Cramer, D., Infertility in Women and Moderate Alcohol Use, American Journal of Public Health, Vol. 84, No. 9, 1994

Grodstein, F., Manson, J., and Stamfer, M., Postmenopausal Hormone Therapy, in Prevention of Myocardial Infarction, Oxford University Press, 1996

Groffoti, V., Alcoholism may be inherited, Financial Times, p15, November 26, 1998

Gronbaek, M., et al., Type of alcohol consumed and mortality from all causes, coronary heart disease, and cancer, Annals of Internal Medicine, 133(6):411-419, 2000

Gronbaek, M., Deis, A., Becker, U., Schnorr, H., Jensen, G., Borch Johansen, K., and Sorensen, T., Alcohol and mortality: is there a U-shaped relation in elderly people, Age and Aging, vol. 27, No. 6, pp739-744, 1998

Gronbaek, M., Deis, A., Sorensen, T., Becker, U., Borch-Johansen, K., Muller, C., Schnorr, H., and Jensen, G., Influence of sex, age, body mass, index, and smoking on alcohol intake and mortality, British Medical Journal, 308:302-306, 1994

Gronbaek, M., Deis, A., Sorensen, T., Becker, U., Schnorr, P., Jensen, G., Mortality associated with moderate intakes of wine, beer, or spirits, British Medical Journal, 310: 1165-1169, 1995

Gronbaek, M., Iversen, L., Olsen, J., Becker, P., and Sorensen, T., Sensible drinking limits, Ugeskrift for Laeger, Vol. 159, No. 40, pp5939-5945, 1997

Gronbaek, M., Becker, U., Johansen, D., Tonnesen, H., Hensen, G., and Sorensen, E., Population based cohort study of the association between alcohol intake and cancer of the upper digestive tract, British Medical Journal, 317:844-848, 1998

Gross, L., How Much is Too Much: The Effects of Social Drinking, Random House, New York, 1983

Grossarth-Maticek, R., et al., Personality, stress and motivational factors in drinking as determinants of risk for cancer and coronary heart disease, Psychological Reports, 69(3 pt 1):1027-1043, December, 1991

Grunewald, P., et al., Drinking and Driving: Explaining Beverage Specific Risks, Journal of Studies on Alcohol, Vol. 61, No. 4, pp515-523, July, 2000

Guallar-Castillon, P. et al., Consumption of Alcoholic Beverages and Subjective Health in Spain, Journal of Epidemiology and Community Health, Vol 55, pp648-652, September, 2001

Guidelines for sensible wine drinking, Oldways Preservation & Exchange Trust, Cambridge, Massachusetts, 1996

Gupta, S., Are Old Drugs Better than New?, Time, May 13, 2002

Gupta, S., Rx: Not for the Elderly, Time, December 24, 2001

Gusfield, J., Drinking, University of California Press, Berkeley, 1991

Gusfield, J., Symbolic Crusade, University of Illinois Press, Urbana, 1963

Gusfield, J., Why I Am Often Introduced As An Expert On Alcoholism But Am Not, The Social History of Alcohol Review, 15:3-4, Spring/Summer, 2001

Guthrie, H., Nutrition: Past, Present and Future, Priorities, Vol. 10, No. 2-3, 1998

H. pylori: What's the Story?, HealthNews, Vol. 7, No. 12, December, 2001

Haapanen-Niemi, N., Millunpalo, S., Vuori, I., et al., The impact of smoking, alcohol consumption and physical activity on use of hospital services, American Journal of Public Health, 89:691-698, 1999

Hadley, J., A unified call to end war on drugs, Seattle Post Intelligencer, December 13, 2001

Hakim, I., Mediterranean Diets and Cancer Prevention, Archives of Internal Medicine, Vol. 158, June 8, 1998

Hall, W., Changes in the public perceptions of the health benefits of alcohol use, 1989 to 1994, Australian and New Zealand Journal of Public Health, Vol. 20, No. 1, pp93-95, 1996

Hamilton, V., et al., Alcohol and earnings: does drinking yield a wage premium?, Canadian Journal of Economics, 1:135-151, February, 1997

Hammar, N., Romelsjo, A., and Alfredsson, L., Alcohol consumption, drinking pattern and acute myocardial infarction. A case referent study based on the Swedish Twin Register, Journal of Internal Medicine, Vol. 241, No. 2, 1997

Handa, K., Sasaki, J., Saku, K., Kono, S., Arakawa, K., Alcohol Consumption, Serum Lipids and Severity of Angiographically Determined Coronary Artery Disease, American Journal of Cardiology, 62: 287-289, 1990

Haney, D., Scientists smell success with cold medicine, Seattle, Post Intelligencer, December 18, 2001

Haney, D., Too much vitamin C may harden arteries, Seattle Post Intelligencer, March 3, 2000

Haney, D., Why life saving drugs can kill victims of heart attacks, Seattle Post Intelligencer, March 9, 2000

Hanson, D., Preventing Alcohol Abuse: Alcohol, Culture and Control, Praeger, Westport, 1995

Hanson, D., Prohibitionist Approach Toward Alcohol, Brewers' Advocate, January, 1999

Hanson, D., Science vs. Ideology: The Drinking Age Paradox, Brewers Advocate, 1997

Hanson, D., and Engs, R., It's Better to Drink Moderately Than to Abstain, Expert Opinions, www.potsdam2.edu/alcohol-info

Harburg, E., Davis, D., and Caplan, R., Parent and Offspring Alcohol Use, Journal of Studies on Alcohol, Vol. 43, No. 5, 1982

Harding, A., et al., Cross-sectional association between total level and type of alcohol consumption and glycosylated haemoglobin level, European Journal of Clinical Nutrition, Vol. 56:882-890, 2002

Harding, R., An Approach to a Sensible Drinking Message, Wine and Health Symposium, American Society for Enology and Viticulture, Reno, June 24, 1996

Harnack, L., Anderson, K., Zheng, W., Folsom, A., Sellers, T., Kushi, L., Smoking, alcohol, coffee and tea intake and incidence of cancer of the exocrine pancreas: the Iowa Women's Health Study, Cancer: Epidemiology, Biomarkers and Prevention, Vol. 6, No. 12, pp1081-1086, 1997

Harris, R., and Wynder, E., Breast Cancer and Alcohol Consumption, JAMA, Vol. 259, No., 19, May 20, 1988

Harrison, P., Royal college debates whether M.D.s should promote moderate consumption of alcohol, Canadian Medical Association Journal, Vol. 159, No. 10, pp1289-1290, 1998

Hart, C., et al., Alcohol consumption and mortality from all causes, coronary heart disease and stroke: results for a prospective study of Scottish men with 21 years of follow up, British Medical Journal, 318:1725-1729, June 26, 1999

Harty, L., Caporaso, N., Hayes, R., Winn, D., Bravo-Otero, E., Blot W., Kleinman, D., Brown, L. Armenian, H., Fraumeni, J., and Shields, P., Alcohol dehydrogenase 3 genotype and risk of oral cavity and pharyngeal cancers, Journal of the National Cancer Institute, Vol. 89, No. 22, pp1698-1705, 1997

Hawkes, N., Doctors link lifestyle to onset of Alzheimer's, London Times, January 10, 1996

Hawkes, N., Drinkers' longevity relies on the genes, Times, p5, January 9, 1996

Hayes, R., et al., Alcohol use and prostate cancer risk in US blacks and whites, American Journal of epidemiology, Vol. 143, No. 7, pp692-697, 1996

Hayward, L., Zubrick, S., and Silburn, S., Blood alcohol levels in suicide cases, Journal of Epidemiology and Community Health, 46(3):256-260, June, 1992

HDL Cholesterol: 7 Ways to Get More of a Good Thing, Harvard Men's Health Watch, Vol. 1, No. 6, January, 1997

He, J., et al., Aspirin Therapy Increases Risk of Brain Hemorrhage, JAMA, 280:1950-1951, 1998

Health After 100: Secrets of the Centenarians, Health After 50, Vol. 13, Issue 9, November, 2001

Health for Life, Newsweek Cover Story, December 2, 2002

HealthNews, Women's social networks, 1999

Health Policy, Journal of Studies on Alcohol, Vol. 47, No. 5, 1986

Health Report, One More Drink, Time, p36, April 13, 1998

Healthy Eating After 70, Health News, Vol. 5, No. 5, April 15, 1999

Healthy hearts without hormone therapy, UC Berkeley Wellness Letter, Vol. 16, Issue, 10, July, 2000

Healthy People 2000, U. S. Department of Health and Human Services, Washington, D.C., Publication No. (PHS) 91-50212, 1990

Healthy People 2010, Draft Initiative, Office of Disease Prevention and Health Promotion, U.S. Department of Health and Human Services, Washington, D.C., Updated November 1, 1998

Healthy Public Policy, Report on the Adelaide Conference, 2nd International Conference on Health Promotion, Adelaide, South Africa, World Health Organization, Copenhagen, April, 1988

Heart and Stroke Facts, American Heart Association, Dallas, 1999

Heart and Stroke Statistical Update, American Heart Association, Dallas, 2001

Heath, D., Alcohol link with violence is unproved, The Addiction Letter, Vol. 10, No. 2, February, 1994

Heath, D., Alcohol, risk taking, and the quest for commonalities, Moderation Reader, May/June, 1992

Heath, D., Alcohol use, 1970-1980, in Constructive Drinking, Cambridge University Press, 1987

Heath, D., An Anthropological View of Alcohol and Culture in International Perspective, in International Handbook on Alcohol and Culture, Greenwood Press, Westport, 1995

Heath, D., in the book Self-Regulatory Behavior and Risk Taking: Causes and Consequences, Ablex Publishing Corporation, Norwood, 1991

Heath, D., An Anthropological View of Alcohol and Culture in International Perspective, in International Handbook on Alcohol and Culture, Greenwood Press, Westport, 1995

Heath, D., Drinking and Pleasure Across Cultures, in Alcohol and Pleasure: A Health Perspective, Peele, S., and Grant, M., editors, Brunner/Mazel, Philadelphia, 1999

Heath, D., Drinking Occasions: Comparative Perspectives on Alcohol and Culture, Brunner/Mazel, Philadelphia, 2000

Heath, D., Moderate Alcohol Intake, Priorities, Vol. 10, No. 2-3, 1998

Heath, D., The New Temperance Movement: Through the Looking Glass, Moderation Reader, May/June 1990

Hegele, R., Pathogenesis of Atherosclerosis, Health Effects of Moderate Consumption,: Good, Bad, or Indifferent? Canadian Atherosclerosis Society, University of Toronto, December 3, 1994

Heien, D., Health Consequences and Tax Initiatives, A Symposium on Wine, Health and Society, The Wine Institute, Washington, D.C., February 14, 1986

Heien, D., The External Costs of Alcohol Abuse, Journal of Studies on Alcohol, 54:302-307, 1993

Heien, D., The Relationship Between Alcohol Consumption and Earnings, Journal of Studies on Alcohol, 57:336-342, 1996

Heien, D., and Pompelli, G., Stress, Ethnic and Distribution Factors in a Dichotomous Response Model of Alcohol Abuse, Journal of Studies on Alcohol, 48:450-455, 1987

Hein, H., Sorensen, H., Suadicani, P., and Gyntelberg, F., Alcohol Consumption, Lewis Phenotypes and Risk of Ischaemic Heart Disease, The Lancet, 341:392-396, 1993

Hein, H., Suadicani, P., and Gyntelberg, F., Alcohol consumption, serum low density lipoprotein cholesterol concentration, and risk of ischaemic heart disease: six year follow up in the Copenhagen male study, British Medical Journal, Vol. 312, No. 7033, 1996

Hellenbrand, W., Boeing, H., Robra, B., Seidler, A., Vieregge, P., Nishcan, P., Joerg, J., Oertel, W., Schneider, E., and Ulm, G., Diet and Parkinson's disease II: A possible role for the past intake of specific nutrients, Neurology, 47:644-650, 1996

Hellman, K., Alcohol: a carcinogenic risk?, in Drinking to Your Health, Social Affairs Unit, London, 1989

Helping the Patient by Helping the Caregiver, Johns Hopkins Medical Letter, Vol. 12, Issue 5, July, 2000

Hendrie, H., Gao, S., Hall, K., Hui, S., and Unverzagt, F., The relationship between alcohol consumption, cognitive performance, and daily functioning in an urban sample of older black Americans, Journal of the American Geriatrics society, Vol. 44, No. 10, pp1158-1165, 1996

Hendriks, H., Report of the 30thj International Medical Advisory Board Conference, Belgium, 13-16 October, 2002, Alcohol Research, Vol. 7:239, December 2002

Hendriks, H., van Haaren, M., Leenen, R., et al., Moderate alcohol consumption and postprandial plasma lipids in men with different risks for coronary heart disease, Alcohol clinical and Experimental Research, 25:563-570, 2001

Hendriks, H., Veenstra, J., van Tol, A., Groener, J., Schaafsma, G., Moderate doses of alcoholic beverages with dinner and postprandial high density lipoprotein composition, Alcohol and Alcoholism, Vol. 33, No. 4, pp403-410, 1998

Henley, J., Scientists discover smokers holy grail, Guardian, January 9, 1998

Hennekens, C., Alcohol and Health: The Harvard Experience with Cohort Studies, Conference on The Medicinal Virtues of Alcohol in Moderation, Sydney, Australia, October 30, 1991

Hennekens, C., Alcohol in Prevention of Coronary Heart Disease, W. B. Saunders Company, Philadelphia, 1983

Hennekens, C., Drink a Little and Help Your Heart, News Release, American Heart Association, Dallas, November 19, 1987

Hennekens, C., Study Points to Value of Aspirin Therapy for Careful Use, The A.H.A. Says, News Release, American Heart Association, Dallas, January 28, 1988

Hennekens, C., The Physician's Perspective, The New England Journal of Medicine HealthNews, Vol. 4, No. 4, March 31, 1998

Hennekens, C., Buring J., O'Connor, G., et al., Moderate Alcohol Consumption and Risk of Myocardial Infarction, Circulation, 76(Supple. IV), IV-501, 1987

Hennekens, C., Gaziano, M., Manson, J., and Buring, J., Antioxidant vitamin cardiovascular disease hypotheses is still promising, but still unproved: the need for randomized trials, American Journal of Clinical Nutrition, 62(Suppl) 1995

Hennekens, C., Willett, W., Rosner, B., Cole, D., and Mayrent S., Effects of Beer, Wine and Liquor, Journal of the American Medical Association, 242:1973-1974, 1979

Hertog, M., Kromhout, D., Fidanza, F., Menotti, A., et al., Flavonoid Intake and Long-Term Risk of Coronary Heart Disease and Cancer in the Seven Countries Study, Archives of Internal Medicine, 155(4):381-386, 1995

Hewlett, G., Education model vs control model, Moderation Reader, May/June, 1993

Hewlett, G., Interview, Moderate Drinking Journal, August, 1987

Hia, M., Davis J., Ross, P., Yates, A., and Wasnich, R., The relation between lifestyle factors and biochemical markers of bone turnover among early post-menopausal women, Calcif tissue Int 68:291-296, 2001

Hillbom, M., Numminen, H., and Juvela, S., Recent heavy drinking of alcohol and embolic stroke, Stroke 30:2307-2312, 199

Hirvonen, T., Pietinen, P., Virtanen, M., Albanes, D., and Virtamo, J., Nutrient intake and use of beverages and the risk of kidney stones among male smokers, American Journal of Epidemiology, 150:187-194, 1999

Hoaken, P., Assaad, J., and Pihl, R., Cognitive functioning and the inhibition of alcohol-induced aggression, Journal of Studies on Alcohol, 59:599-607, 1998

Hochman, J., Tamis, J., Thompson, T.,Weaver, W., White, H., Van de Werf, F., Aylward, P., Topol, E., and Califf, R., New England Journal of Medicine, Vol. 341, No. 4, July, 1999

Hoffmesiter, H., Schelp, F., Mensink, G., Dietz, E., and Bohning, D., The relationship between alcohol consumption, health indicators and morality in the German population, International Journal of Epidemiology, 28(6):1066-1072, 1999

Holbrook, T., Barrett-Connor, E., A prospective study of alcohol consumption and bone mineral density, British Medical Journal, 306:1506-1509, 1993

Holdrup, S., Gronbaek, M., Gottschau, A., et al., Alcohol intake, beverage preference, and risk of hip fracture in men and women, American Journal of Epidemiology, 149:993-1001, 1999

Holman, C., English, D., Milne, E., and Winter, M., Meta-analysis of alcohol and all-cause mortality: a validation of NHMRC recommendations, Journal of Medicine, 164:141-145, 1996

Holman, C., and English, D., Ought low alcohol intake to be promoted for health reasons?, Journal of Research in Social Medicine, 89:123-9, 1996

Holmgren, E., A Scientific Perspective on the Latest Wine and Breast Cancer Research, Wine Institute, San Francisco, July 26, 1993

Holmgren, E., Health Issues, in Wines & Vines, August, 1993

Holmgren, E., Health Issues, in Wines & Vines, October, 1993

Homocysteine, Mayo Clinic Health Letter, December, 1997

Homocysteine & Heart Disease, HealthNews, Vol. 6, No. 10, October, 2000

Homocysteine: The New Cholesterol, Cleveland Clinic Heart Advisor, Vol. 2, No. 2, February, 1999

Honigmann, J., Alcohol in its Cultural Context, Beliefs, Behaviors & Alcoholic Beverages, University of Michigan Press, Ann Arbor, 1979

How Age Affects Breast Cancer, HealthNews, February 25, 1999

How many calories do you burn?, UC Berkeley Wellness Letter, March, 1999

How to calculate your BMI, Mayo Clinic Health Letter, September 1998

How to Keep the Doctor Away, Time, January 21, 2002

How to Stop Living on the Edge, Harvard Health Letter, Vol. 23, No. 9, July, 1998

hPylori and Dyspepsia, HealthNews, Vol. 5, No. 14, November 20, 1999

Hsing, A., McLaughlin, J., Crocco, P., Co Chien, H., and Fraumeni, J., Risk factors for male breast cancer, Cancer Causes Control, 9:269-275, 1998

Hu, F., et al., Diet, Lifestyle and the Risk of Type 2 Diabetes Mellitus in Women, The New England Journal of Medicine, Vol. 345, No. 11, pp790-797, 2001

Hu, F., et al., How to reduce heart disease by 82%, Seattle Post Intelligencer, November 9, 1999

Huang, Z., et al., Avoiding Weight Gain May Prevent Some Breast Cancer, JAMA, 278:1407-1411, 1997

Huber, P., Galileo's Revenge, Basic Books, New York, 1991

Hulley, S., Estrogen Quandary, News Release, American Medical Association, Chicago, August 18, 1998

Humidity Increases The Danger, Lifetime Health Letter, Vol. 5, No. 8, August, 1993

Hurst, W., Gregory, E., and Gussman, T., Alcoholic Beverage Taxation and Control Policies, Ninth Edition, Brewers Association of Canada, Ottawa, 1997

Hypertension, The Johns Hopkins White Papers, Johns Hopkins Medical Institutions, Baltimore, 1997

ICAP, Minimum age drinking, www.icap,org

IHD Data, Centers for Disease Control, Trends in Ischemic Heart Disease Deaths– United States 1990-1994, Morbidity and Mortality Weekly Report, February 21, 1996

Imagine if you could plan your day around your life instead of your arthritis plan, VIOXX advertisement, Seattle Post Intelligencer, September 13, 2000

Inflammation, Infection and Coronary Artery Disease, Harvard Men's Health Watch, February, 1988

Interim Report Number 4 (A Summary), Task Force on Responsible Decisions About Drinking, Education Commission of the States, Denver, 1973

International scientists advise eat, drink and be merry, Newsweek, December 22, 1997

International Wine and Health Conference, Medically, is wine just another alcoholic beverage?, Sydney, Australia, June 12, 1996

in't Veld, B., Ruitenberg, A., Hofman, A., Launer, L., van Duijn, C., Stijenen, T., Breteler, M., and Stricker, B., Nonsteroidal Anti inflammatory Drugs and the Risk of Alzheimer's Disease, The New England Journal of Medicine, Vol. 345:1515-1521, No. 21, November 22, 2001

Is Alcohol Good For You?, Mayo Clinic Heart Book, William Morrow and Company, Inc., New York, 1993

Is Moderate Alcohol Use Related to U.S. Wage Levels? Wine Issues Monitor, the Wine Institute, San Francisco, May/June, 1994

Ishimitsu, T., Yoshida, K., Nakamura, M., et al., Effects of alcohol intake on organ injuries in normotensive and hypertensive human subjects, Clinical Science, 93:541-547, 1997

Isner, J., Genes inserted into heart muscle raise blood flow, Seattle Post Intelligencer, 1998

Istvan, J., Murray, R., and Voelker, H., The relationship between patterns of alcohol consumption and body weight, International Journal of Epidemiology, Vol. 24, No. 3, 1995

Jackson, R., Stewart, A., Beaglehole, R., and Scragg, R., Alcohol Consumption and Blood Pressure, American Journal of epidemiology, Vol. 122, No. 6, pp1037-1044, 1985

Jackson, R., Scragg, R., and Beaglehole, R., Alcohol Consumption and Risk of Coronary Heart Disease, British Medical Journal, Vol. 303, July, 1991

Jacobs, D., Popular suicide myth debunked by expert, Infoseek-Reuters, October 19, 1997

Jacobson, J., Jacobson, S., and Sokol, R., Increased vulnerability to alcohol-related birth defects in the offspring of mothers over 30, Alcoholism: Clinical and Experimental Research, Vol. 20, No. 2, 1996

Jain, M., Ferrec, R., Rehm, J., et al., Alcohol and breast cancer mortality in a cohort study, Breast Cancer Research Treatment, 64:201-209, 2001

Jain, M., Hislop, G., Howe, G., Burch, J., and Ghadrian, P., Alcohol and other beverage use and prostate cancer risk among Canadian men, International Journal of Cancer, Vol. 78, No. 6, pp707-711, 1998

Jang, M., et al., Cancer chemopreventive activity of resveratrol, a natural product derived from grapes, Science, 275:218-220, 1997

Jaret, P., New Reasons to Love Olive Oil, People advertising supplement, February 8, 1999

Jenkens, D., Psychosocial and Behavioral Factors, Prevention of Coronary Heart Disease, W.B. Saunders Company, 1983

Jensen, C., Stories That changed America, Seven Stories Press, New York, 2000

Jensen, M., Andersen, A., Serensen, T., Becker, U., Thorsen, T., and Gronbaek, M., Alcoholic beverage preference and risk of becoming a heavy drinker, epidemiology 13:127-132, 2002

Jensen, T., Hjollund, H., Henriksen, T., Scheike, T., Kolstad, H., Giwercman, A., Ernet, E., Bonde, J., Skakkebaek, N., and Olsen, J., Does moderate alcohol consumption affect fertility? Follow up study among couples planning first pregnancy, British Medical Journal, Vol. 317, No. 7175, pp505-510, 1998

Jepson, R., Fowkes, R., and Housley, E., Alcohol Intake as a Risk Factor for Peripheral Arterial Disease in the General Population in the Edinburgh Artery Study, European Journal of Epidemiology, 11:9-14, 1995

Johansen, K., Skorpe, S., Olsen, J., and Osterud, B., The effect of red wine on the fibrinolytic system and the cellular activation reactions before and after exercise, Symposium Nordisk Koagulasjonsmote, 1998

Johnson, E., What change? letter to Gene Ford, in Moderation Reader, September/October, 1993

Johnston, L., Monitoring the Future Study, Institute for Social Research, 1975-1998, University of Michigan, Ann Arbor, 1998

Johnston, L., et al., National Survey Results on Drug Use from the Monitoring the Future Study, 1975-1995, USDHHS, Publication #96-4140, Washington, D.C., 1997

Jones, F., The Save Your Heart Wine Guide, St. Martin's Press, New York, 1996

Jones-Webb, R., Jacobs, D., Flack, J., and Liu, K., Relationships between depressive symptoms, anxiety, alcohol consumption, and blood pressure: results from the CARDIA Study, Alcoholism: Clinical and Experimental Research, Vol. 20, No. 3, 1996

Josephson, E., Trends in Problem Drinking, Columbia University School of Public Health, in An Assessment of Statistics on Alcohol-Related Problems, May 5, 1980

Joshipura, K., and Brustman, B., Eating More Fruits and Vegetables Associated with Reduced Ischemic Stroke Risk, JAMA, 282:1233-1239, 1999

Journal of the American Medical Association, Editorial, The Clinician's Conundrum, September 28, 1994

Juergens, J., Facts and Fiction: Health Professional's Knowledge About Alcohol and Health, speech to Alcohol and Health Seminar, AWARE, Dallas, November 7, 1998

Just one drink a week can lower stroke risk in men, Seattle Post-Intelligencer, November 18, 1999

Just what exactly is the Mediterranean diet?, UC Berkeley Wellness Letter, April, 1999

Kahn, H., et al., Stable behaviors associated with adults' 10-year change in body mass index and likelihood of gain at the waist, American Journal of Public Health, 87(5):747-754, 1997

Kalish, G., Wine can cause and reduce headache pain, Wine Spectator, May 1, 1982

Kalish, G., Wine in moderation key to gout sufferers, Wine Spectator, June, 1981

Kannel, W., Ellison, R., Alcohol and coronary heart disease: The evidence for a protective effect, Clinica Chimica Acta, 246:59-76, 1996

Kaplan, N., Bashing booze: The danger of losing the benefits of moderate alcohol consumption, Moderation Reader, July/August, 1991

Kaplan, N., Foreword in The French Paradox & Drinking for Health, Wine Appreciation Guild, San Francisco, 1993

Kaplan, N., Bashing booze: The danger of losing the benefits of moderate alcohol consumption, American Heart Journal, June, 1991

Kaplan, N., and Stamler, J., Hypertension, in Preventing Coronary Heart Disease, W. B. Saunders Company, 1983

Kastenbaum, R., In Moderation, Alcohol & Drugs Generations, Summer, 1988

Kastenbaum, R., Wine and Health, Wine Advisory Board, San Francisco, 1969

Kastenbaum, R., Wine and the Elderly Person, Wine, Health & Society, The Wine Institute, San Francisco, November 13, 1981

Katella, K., Good Health in a Tea Cup?, Arthritis today, 1:13, 1998

Katsouyanni, K., et al., Ethanol and Breast Cancer: An Association That May Be Both Confounded and Causal, International Journal of Cancer, 58:356-361, 1994

Katsuyuki, M., Daviglus, M., Dyer, A., Kiang, L., Garside, D., Stamler, J., and Greenland, P., Relationship of Blood Pressure to 25-year Mortality Due to Coronary Heart disease, Cardiovascular Diseases, and All Causes in Young Adult Men, Archives, Journals of the AMA, Vol. 161, No. 12, June 25, 2001

Katz, F., ATF Approves Wine Institute's Health Label Statement, The Wine Investor, Vol. III, No. 2, February, 1999

Katz, S., Wine and the Origins of Cuisine, A Symposium on Wine, Culture & Healthy Lifestyles, The Wine Institute, New York, May 1, 1987

Katz, S, and Voight, M., Bread and Beer, Expeditions, Vol. 28, No. 2, 1986

Kaufman, E., The Relationship of Alcoholism and Alcohol Abuse to the Abuse of Other drugs, American Journal of Alcohol Abuse, 9(1), pp1-17, 1982

Keen on beans: a new soy label, UC Berkeley Wellness Letter, Vol. 16, Issue 5, February, 2000

Kesse, E., Clafel-Chapelon, F., Slimani, N., van Liere, M., and the E3N Group, Do eating habits differ according to alcohol consumption. Results of a study of the French cohort of the European Prospective Investigation into Cancer and Nutrition, American Journal of Clinical Nutrition, 74:322-327, 2001

Keevil, J., Osman, H., Reed, J., and Folts, J., Grape juice, but not orange juice or grapefruit juice, inhibits human platelet aggregation, Journal of Nutrition, 130:53-556, 2000

Keil, U., Chambless, L., Doring, A., Filipiak, B., and Stieber, J., Biertrinker erleiden seltener Herzinfarkte. Massige bierkonsum senkt Infarktinzidenz und Gesamtmortalitat, Fortschritte der Medizin, Vol. 116, No. 4, pp19-20, 1998

Keil, U., Chambless, L., Doring, A., Filipiak, B., and Steiber, J., The relation of alcohol intake to coronary heart disease and all-cause mortality in a beer drinking population, Epidemiology, 8(2):150-156, 1997

Keller, M., in Law, Alcohol and Order, Kyvig, D., ed., Greenwood Press, Westport, 1983

Kelsey, J., and Baron, J., Understanding the relationship between weight and breast cancer important, JAMA, 278:1448-1449, 1997

Kenneth, S., A Population-Based Twin Study of Alcoholism in Women, JAMA, Vol. 268, No. 14, pp1877-1882, 1992

Khanna, S., Gordillo, G., et al., Oxygen, Oxidants and Antioxidants in Wound Healing, Annals of the New York Academy of Sciences, Vol. 957, 2002

Kidney Stones, Harvard Men's Health Watch, Vol. 4, No. 9, April, 2000

Kidney stones: myths & facts, University of California, Berkeley Wellness Letter, p5, March, 1998

Kiechl, S., Willett, J., Rungger, G., Egger, G., Oberhollenzer, F., and Bonora, E., Alcohol Consumption and Atherosclerosis: What is the Relation?, Stroke, May, 1998

Kimble, R., Alcohol, cytokines, and estrogen in the control of bone remodeling, Alcohol Clinical and Experimental Research, 21:385-391, 1997

King, W., Health Page, Seattle Times, June 24, 2001

Kinney, A., Millikan, R., Lin, V., Moorman, P., and Newman, B., Alcohol consumption and breast cancer among black and white women in North Carolina, Cancer Causes and Control, 11:345-357, 2000

Kitamura, A., et al., Potential heart benefit linked to ethanol in beverage alcohol– type of drink not significant, from American Journal of Epidemiology January 1998 as reported in a News Release, DISCUS, January 27, 1998

Kitson, K., and Stanley, C., Report to Winegrowers of New Zealand on Evidence for Health Benefits of Moderate Wine Consumption, Institute of Food, Nutrition and Human Health, College of Sciences, Masseyh University, New Zealand, 2001

Klatsky, A., Alcohol and Cardiovascular diseases, Annals of the New York Academy of Sciences, Vol., 95, 2002

Klatsky, A., Alcohol and Cardiovascular Disorders: Abstinence May be Hazardous to Some Persons, Speech to the National Press Club, Washington, D.C., June 10, 1991

Klatsky, A., Alcohol and hypertension, Clinical Chim Acta, 246:91-105, 1996

Klatsky, A., Alcohol and Mortality: A Ten Year Kaiser Permanente Experience, Annals of Internal Medicine, 95:139-145, 1981

Klatsky, A., Alcohol, coronary disease, and hypertension, Annual Review of Medicine, 47:149-60, 1996

Klatsky, A., Alcoholic Beverage Choice and Coronary Artery Disease: Do Red Wine Drinkers Fare Best?, Presentation to American Heart Association, New Orleans, November 17, 1992

Klatsky, A., Alcoholic Beverage Choice and Risk of Coronary Artery Disease Mortality: Do Red Wine Drinkers Fare Best?, the American Journal of Cardiology, 71: 467-69, 1993

Klatsky, A., Epidemiology of Coronary Heart Disease: Influence of Alcohol, Alcoholism: Clinical and Experimental Research, 18(1): 88-97, 1994

Klatsky, A., Health Effects of Moderate Alcohol Intake: Alcohol, Hypertension, and Stroke, Abstract of presentation: RSA?ISBRA Meeting, June 25, 1996

Klatsky, A., Is Drinking Healthy, in Alcohol and Pleasure, Peele and Grant, editors, Brunner/Mazel, 1999

Klatsky, A., Wine is Part of New Healthy Eating Pyramid, News Release, Wine Institute, San Francisco, June 22, 1994

Klatsky, A., Should Patients With Heart Disease Drink Alcohol, JAMA, Vol. 285, No. 15, April 18, 2001

Klatsky, A., and Armstrong, M., Alcohol use, other traits, and risk of unnatural death: a prospective study, Alcohol, Clinical and Experimental Research, 17:1156-1162, 1993

Klatsky A., Armstrong, M., and Friedman, G., Red Wine, White Wine, Liquor, Beer, and Risk for Coronary Artery Disease Hospitalization, American Journal of Cardiology, 80:416-420, 1997

Klatsky A., Armstrong, M., and Friedman, G., Relations of Alcoholic Beverage Use to Subsequent Coronary Heart Disease Hospitalizations, American Journal of Cardiology, 98:710-714, 1986

Klatsky, A., Armstrong, M., Friedman, G., and Sidney, S., Alcohol drinking and risk of hemorrhagic stroke, Neuropepidemiology 21: 115-122, 2002

Klatsky, A., Armstrong, M., and Kipp, H., Correlates of Alcohol Beverage Preference: Traits of Persons Who Choose Wine, Liquor, British Journal of Addiction, Vol. 85, 1990

Klatsky, A., and Freidman, A., Alcohol use and cardiovascular disease: The Kaiser-Permanente experience. Circulation, 64:(Supple III):32-41, 1981

Klatsky, A., et al., Red wine, white wine, liquor, beer and risk for coronary artery disease hospitalization, American Journal of Cardiology, 80:416-420, 1997

Klatsky, A., et al., Risk of Cardiovascular Mortality in Alcohol Drinkers, Ex-Drinkers, and Non-Drinkers, The American Journal of Cardiology, Vol. 66, Nov. 15, 1999

Klein, B., Klein, R., and Ritter, L., Relationship of drinking alcohol and smoking to prevalence of open-angle glaucoma, Ophthalmology, 100(11):1609-1613, 1993

Klein, H., Changes in college students' use and abuse of alcohol, and in their attitudes toward drinking over the course of their college years, Journal of Youth and Adolescence 23:251-259, 1994

Klein, R., Alcohol induced bone disease: impact of ethanol on osteoblast proliferation, Alcohol Clinical and Experimental Research, 21:392-399, 1997

Knapik-Smith, M., and Bennett, G., Moderate Drinking in Women: A Concept Analysis, Issues in Mental Health Nursing, 18:285-301, 1997

Knupfer, G., Abstaining for foetal health: The fiction that even light drinking is dangerous, British Journal of Addiction, 86:1063-1073, 1991

Kobler, J., Ardent Spirits, Michael Joseph, Ltd., London, 1973

Koehler, K., Baumgartner, R., Garry, P., et al., Association of folate intake and serum homocysteine in elderly persons according to vitamin supplementation and alcohol use, American Journal of Clinical Nutrition, 73:628-637, 2001

Kolb, F., Wine and Gout– Myth or Reality, Speech to Society of Medical Friends of Wine, San Francisco, January 4, 1984

Kono, S., Eguchi, H, Honjo, S., et al., Cigarette smoking, alcohol use, and gallstone risk in Japanese men, Digestion, 65:177-183, 2002

Kono, S., Ikeda, M., Tokudome, S., Nishizumi, M., and Kuratsune, M., Alcohol and Mortality: A Cohort Study of Male Japanese Physicians, International Journal of Epidemiology, 14(4):527-532, 1986

Konrat, C., Mennen, L., Cades, E., et al., Alcohol intake and fasting insulin in French men and women, The DESIR study, Diabetes Metabolism, (Paris), 28:116-123, 2002

Kreiger, L., Ads for pharmaceutical products arm patients with useful information, New York Times Copyright, Seattle Post Intelligencer, December 9, 1998

Kropp, S., Becher, H., Nieters, A. and Chang-Claude, J., Low-to-Moderate Alcohol consumption and Breast cancer Risk by Age 50 Years among Women in Germany, American Journal of Epidemiology, Vol. 154, No. 7:624-634, 2001

Kubota, M., Nakazaki, S., Hirai, S., Saeki, N., Yamaura, A., and Kusaki, T., Alcohol consumption and frontal lobe shrinkage: study of 1432 non-alcohol subjects. Journal of Neurology, Neurosurgery, and Psychiatry, 71:104-106, 2001

Kunz, J., Alcohol Use and Reported Visits to Health Professionals, An Exploratory Study, Journal of Studies on Alcohol, 58:474-479, September, 1997

Kushi, L., et al., Health implications of Mediterranean diets in light of contemporary knowledge: meat, wine, fats and oils, American Journal of Clinical Nutrition, 61:(6S):1416S-1427S, 1995

Kushner, M., Mackenzie, T., Fiszdon, J., et al., The effects of alcohol consumption on laboratory-induced panic and state anxiety, Archives of General Psychiatry, 53:264-270, 1996

Kusserow, R., Youth and Alcohol: Laws and Enforcement, Office of Inspector General, DHHS, Washington, D.C., September, 1991

Kyvig, D., Law, Alcohol and Order, Greenwood Press, Westport, 1985

La Porte, R., et al., Coronary Heart Disease and Total Mortality, in Recent Developments in Alcoholism, 1985

La Porte, R., Cresanta, L., and Kuller, L., The Relationship of Alcohol Consumption to Atherosclerotic Heart Disease, Preventive Medicine, 9:22-40, 1980

La Vecchia, C., Alcohol in the Mediterranean Diet, International Journal for Vitamin and Nutrition Research, 65(1):71-72, 1995

La Vecchia, C., Decarli, A., Franceshci, S., Ferraroni, M., and Pagano, R., Prevalence of chronic diseases in alcohol abstainers, Epidemiology, Vol. 6, No. 4, pp436-438, 1995

Laitinen, C., and Kardinaal, A., Alcohol and Bone in Health Issues Related to Alcohol Consump[tion, 2nd Ed., Macdonald, I., ed., Blackwell Science Ltd. London

La Vecchia, C., Franchesi, S., Cuzick, J., Alcohol and Breast Cancer, The Lancet, March 13, 1982

La Vecchia, C., Decarli, A., Franceschi, S., Pampaliona, S., and Tognone, G., Alcohol Consumption and the Risk of Breast Cancer in Women, JNCI, Vol. 75, No. 1, July, 1985

Labouvie, E., Bates, M., and Pandina, R., Age of First Use: Its Reliability and Predictive Utility, Journal of Studies on Alcohol, 58:638-643, 1997

Lacoste, L., Hung, J., and Lam, J., Acute and delayed antithrombotic effects of alcohol in humans, American Journal of Cardiology, 87:82-85, 2001

Lammers, S., Emancipation of drinking behaviour?, Alcohol Digest, Vol. 12, No. 47, May, 1995

Langer, R., Criqui, M., Reed, D., Lipoprotein and Blood Pressure as Biological Pathways for Effect of Moderate Alcohol Consumption on Coronary Heart Disease, Circulation, 85(3):910-915, 1992

Lantz, P., House, J., Lepkowski, J., Williams D., Mero, R., and Chen, J., Socioeconomic factors, health behaviours, and mortality: Results from a nationally representative prospective study of US adults, Journal of the American Medical Association, Vol. 279, No. 21, pp1709-1708, 1998

Lardinois, C., Proper Nutrition Helpful in Treating Hypertension, News Release, American Medical Association, Chicago, August 14, 1995

Lasser, K., Allen, P., Woodhandler, S., Himmelstein, D., Wolfe, S., and Bor, D., Timing of New Black Box Warnings and Withdrawals for Prescription Medications, JAMA, Vol. 287, No. 17, May 1, 2002

Latest Government Report on Alcohol & Health Recognizes Moderation's Benefits, But Still Leans Toward Control, Alcohol Issues Insights, Vol. 14, No. 9, September, 1997

Launer, L., et al., Smoking, drinking and thinking: The Zutphen Elderly Study, American Journal of Epidemiology, 143(3):219-227, 1996

Laurance, J., Pregnant women may drink– in moderation, London Times, March 3, p2, 1997

Law, M., and Wald, N., Why heart disease mortality is low in France: the time lag explanation, British Medical Journal, 318:1470-1480, May, 1999

Lawrence, S., What is Moderate Drinking, Healthy Drinking, 1994

Lazarus, N., Kaplan, G., Cohen, R., and Leu, D., Change in Alcohol Consumption and Risk of Death From All Causes and Ischemic Heart Disease, British Medical Journal, 303:553-556, 1991

Lazarus, R., et al., Alcohol intake and insulin levels, The Normative Aging Study, American Journal of Epidemiology, 145:909-916, 1997

Leighton, T., Research News Bulletin, Wine Institute, Vol. 1, No. 2, May, 1992

Leake, C., and Silverman, M., Alcoholic Beverages in Clinical Medicine, Year Book Medical Publishers, Chicago, 1966

Leary, T., The Therapeutic Value of Alcohol, New England Journal of Medicine, 205:231-242, 1931

Lee, I-Min, British Medical Journal, December, 1998

Lieber, C., alcoholism: Clinical and Experimental Research, 24:417-418, 2000

Leibovici, C., Ritchie, K., Ledesaert, B., and Tuchon, J., The effects of wine and tobacco consumption on cognitive performance in the elderly: a longitudinal study of relative risk, International Journal of Epidemiology, 28:77-81, 1999

Letenneru, L, Wine Consumption in the Elderly, excerpted from, Annals of Internal Medicine, Vol. 118, No. 4, February, 1993

Leibel, R., Dufour, M., Hubbard, V., et al., Alcohol and calories: a matter of balance, Alcohol, 10:427-434, 1993

Leitzmann, M., Giovannucci, E., Stampfer, M., et al., Prospective study of alcohol consumption patterns in relation to symptomatic gallstone disease in men, Alcohol Clinical and Experimental Research, 23:835-841, 1999

Lender, M., and Martin, J., Drinking in America, The Free Press, New York, 1982

Leppala, J., Paunio, M., Viramo, J., et al., Alcohol consumption and stroke incidence in male smokers, Circulation, 100:1209-1214, 1999

Letenneur, L., and Orgogozo, J., Wine Consumption in the Elderly, AIM, 1997

Levine, H., The Alcohol Problem in America, From Temperance to Alcoholism, British Journal of Addiction, 1983

Levine, H., The Committee of Fifty and the Origins of Alcohol Control, Journal of Drug Issues, Winter, 1983

Lewin-VHI, Health Benefits of Moderate Wine Consumption, 9302 Lee Highway, Suite 500, Fairfax, VA 22031, 1994

Lewis, J., Interview with Noble, E., Journal of Studies on Alcohol, Vol. 37, No. 9, 1976

Lex, B., Greenwald, N., Lukas, S., Slater, J., and Mendelson, J., Blood Ethanol Levels, Self-Rated Ethanol Effects and Cognitive-Perceptual Tasks, Pharmacology, Biochemistry and Behavior, Vol. 29, pp.509-515, 1988

Li, W., Zheng, T., and Altura, B., Antioxidants prevent ethanol-induced contractions of canine cerebral vascular smooth muscle: relation to alcohol-induced grain injury, Neuroscience Lett, 301:91-94, 2001

Life Sentence Gets Commuted, Harvard Health Letter, Vol. 25, No. 1, November, 1999

Lifestyle and aging, Mayo Clinic Health Letter, Vol. 17, No. 7, July, 1999

Light, D., Costs and Benefits of Alcohol Consumption, Society, September/October, 1975

Light, Moderate and Heavy Drinkers Have Lower Death Rates than Abstainers: American Cancer Society Study, Alcohol Issues Insights, Vol. 14, No. 12, December, 1997

Lindegard, B., Correspondence, The New England Journal of Medicine, Vol. 317, No. 20, 1987

Linsky, A., Colby, J., and Straus, M., Drinking Norms and Alcohol-Related Problems in the United states, Journal of Studies on Alcohol, No. 5, 1986

Lipp, M., To Your Health! Two Physicians Explore the Health Benefits of Wine, Speech to Society of Medical Friends of Wine, San Francisco, April 6, 1994

Lipsey, M., Wilson, D., Cohen, M., and Dryer, J., Is there a causal relationship between alcohol use and violence, in Recent Developments in Alcoholism, Plenum Press, New York, 1977

Lipton, R., The effect of moderate alcohol use on the relationship between stress and depression, American Journal of Public Health, 84:1913-1917, 1994

Lipton, R., The Stress Buffering Role of Moderate Alcohol Use on the Relationship Between Stress and Depression, paper presented at Society for Behavioral Medicine, March 11, 1993, San Francisco

Little, R., Anderson K., Ervin, C., Worthington-Roberts, B., and Clarren, S., Maternal Alcohol Use During Breast-Feeding and Infant Mental and Motor Development at One Year, New England Journal of Medicine, 321:425-430, 1989

Littlewood, J., Glover, V., Davies P., Gibb, C., Sandler M., and Rose, F., The Lancet, March 12, pp558-559, 1988

Liu, S., Serdula, M., Williamson, D., Mokdad, A., and Byers, T., A prospective study of alcohol intake and change in body weight among US adults, American Journal of Epidemiology, 140:912-920, 1994

Living by the numbers: how to gauge your risks, UC Berkeley Wellness Letter, Vol. 6, Issue 9, June, 2000

Living to 100: What's the Secret?, Harvard Health Letter, Vol. 27, no. 3, January, 2002

Living With Low Vision, Harvard Health Letter, Vol. 25, No. 1, November, 1999

Lloyd-Jones, D., and Levy, D., Lifetime risk of heart disease charter for men and women, from the Framingham Study, January, 1999

Locher, R., Suter, P., and Vetter, W., Ethanol suppresses smooth muscle cell proliferation in the postprandial state: a new antiatherosclerotic mechanism of ethanol?, American Journal on Clinical Nutrition, 67:338-341, 1998

Lolli, G., Serianni, E., Golder, G., and Luzzatto-Fegiz, P., Alcohol in Italian Culture, The Free Press, Glencoe, Illinois, 1958

Longevity Facts, Johns Hopkins Medical Letter, Health After 50, Vol. 12, Issue 2, April, 2000

Longnecker, M., Alcohol Consumption and Risk of Cancer in Humans: An Overview, Alcohol, Vol. 12, No. 2, pp87-96, 1995

Longnecker, M., Associations Between Alcoholic Beverage Consumption and Hospitalization, 1983 National Health Survey, American Journal of Public Health, Vol. 78, No. 2, 1988

Longnecker, M., and Enger, S., Epidemiologic data on alcoholic beverage consumption and risk of cancer, Clin Chimica Acta, 246:121-141, 1996

Low-Dose Aspirin for Everyone? Health After 50, Vol. 14, Issue 8, October 2002

Lowe, G., and Taylor S., Effects of alcohol on responsive laughter and amusement, Psychological Reports, 80:1149-1150, 1997

Lower risk of gallstones, Healthy Drinking, January/February, 1994

Lower Your LDL with Nuts?, HealthNews, Vol. 6, No. 5, May, 2000

Lucia, S., A History of Wine as Therapy, J.B. Lipincott Company, Philadelphia, 1963

Lucia, S., Wine and Your Well Being, Popular Library, New York, 1971

Lucia, S., Wine as Food and Medicine, The Blakiston Company, Inc., New York, 1954

Lui, S., A prospective study of alcohol intake and change in body weight among US adults, Liu, S., Serdula, M., Williamson, D., Mokdad, A., and Byers, T., American Journal of Epidemiology, 140:912-920, 1994

Lui, T., Waterbor, J., and Soong, S., Relationships between beer, wine and spirits consumption and suicide rates in United States from 1977 to 1988, Omega– Journal of Death and Dying, Vol. 32, No. 3, pp227-240, 1996

Lui, Y., Tanaka, H., Sasazuki, S., et al., Alcohol consumption and severity of angiographically determined coronary artery disease in Japanese men and women, Atherosclerosis, 156:177-183, 2001

Luik, J., Wardens, Abbots, and Modest Hedonists: The Problem of Permission for Pleasure in a Democratic Society, in Alcohol and Pleasure, Peele and Grant, editors, Brunner/Mazel, Philadelphia, 1999

Lumey, L., et al., Alcohol Use and Prostate Cancer in US Whites, Prostate, 36:250-255, September 1, 1998

Lundberg, G., JAMA Readers and Medical Experts Differ on What Topics to Emphasize, JAMA, 280:296-298, 1998

Lundsberg, L., Bracken M., and Saftlas, A., Low-to-moderate gestational alcohol use and intrauterine growth retardation, low birth weight, and preterm delivery, Annals of Epidemiology, 7:498-508, 1997

Lynch, M., Killer Tomatoes, Reason, Vol. 32, No. 3, July, 2000

Maalej, N. Demrow, H., Slane, P., and Folts, J., Antithrombotic Effect of Flavonoids in Red Wine: Nutritional and Therapeutic Effects, American Chemical Society, Washington, D.C., 1997

Macdonald, I., Editor, Health issues related to alcohol consumption, 2nd ed., Blackwell Science, Oxford, 1999

MacFarlane, G., MacFarlane, T., and Lowenfels, A., The influence of alcohol consumption on worldwide trends in mortality from upper aerodigestive tract cancers in men, Journal of Epidemiology and Community Health, Vol. 50, No. 6, 1996

Maclure, K., et al., Weight, Diet and the Risk of Symptomatic Gallstones, New England Journal of Medicine, August, 1989

Macular Degeneration, The Johns Hopkins Medical Newsletter, July, 2001

Macular Degeneration: Looking age in the Eye, Harvard Men's Health Watch, Vol. 5, No. 12, July, 2001

Major Congestion in Seattle, advertisement for Allegra-D in The Post-Intelligencer, April 10, 2001

Making a Place for Spirituality, Harvard Health Letter, Vol. 23, No. 4, February, 1998

Malarcher, A., et al., Alcohol Intake, type of Beverage, and the Risk of Cerebral Infarction in Young Women, Stroke, Vol. 32, No. 1, pp77-83, January, 2001

Males, M., Adolescents: daughters or alien sociopaths?, Adolescence, Vol. 349, March, 1997

Mangioni, T., JSI Research and Training Institute, Boston University School of Public Health, 1997

Mannisto, S., et al., Reported alcohol intake, diet and body mass index in male smokers, European Journal of Clinical Nutrition, 50:239-245, 1996

Mannisto, S., Usitalo, K., Roos, E., Fogelholm, M., and Pietinen, P., Alcohol beverage drinking, diet and body mass index in a a cross-sectional survey, European Journal of Clinical Nutrition, Vol. 51, No. 5, pp326-332, 1997

Manson, J., and Bassuk, S., Obesity in the United States: A Fresh Look at its High Toll, JAMA, Vol: 289, No. 2, 2003

Manson, J., Gaziano, M., Ridker, P., and Hennekens, C., Summary and Conclusions, in Prevention of Myocardial Infarction, Oxford University Press, New York, 1996

Manson, J., et al., Medical Progress: The Primary Prevention of Myocardial Infarction, New England Journal of Medicine, 326(21),
May, 1992

Mansson, N., Rastam, L., Eriksson, K., and Israelsson, B., Alcohol
consumption and disability pension among middle-aged men, Annals of Epidemiology, 9:341-348, 1999

Manual on Alcoholism, American Medical Association, Chicago,
1967

Margen, S., The Wellness Encyclopedia of Food and Nutrition, Rebus, New York, 1998

Margolis, S., and Saudek, C., Diabetes Mellitus, The Johns Hopkins
White Papers, Johns Hopkins Medical Institutions, Baltimore, 1998

Margolis, S., Diabetes Mellitus, The Johns Hopkins White Papers,
Johns Hopkins Medical Institutions, Baltimore, 2002

Margolis, S., and Wilder, L., Nutrition and Longevity, The Johns
Hopkins White Papers, Baltimore, 1998

Margolis, S., and Wityk, R., Stroke, The Johns Hopkins White Papers, Baltimore, 1998

Marinkovich, V., Allergy to Wine, Symposium on Wine and Health,
American Society for Enology and Viticulture, Reno, June 24,
1996

Marmot, M., Rose, G., Shipley, M., and Thomas, B., Alcohol and
Mortality: A U-Shaped Curve, The Lancet, (8220), 580-583, 1981

Marmot, M., and Brunner E., Alcohol and Cardiovascular Disease:
The Status of the U-Shaped Curve, British Medical Journal,
303:565-568, 1991

Marques-Vidal, P., Ducimetiere, P., Evans, A., Cambou, J., and
Arveiler, D., Alcohol consumption and myocardial infarction: a
case-control study in France and Northern Ireland, Vol. 143, No.
11, 1089-1093, 1996

Marrugat, J., et al., Women at greater risk of death after first heart attack than men, JAMA, 280:1405-1409, 1998

Mars, S., Klein, C., and Klein, B., The association of alcohol consumption with the incidence and progression of diabetes retinopathy, Ophthalmology, 101(12):1962-1968, 1994

Marshall, Mac, Conclusions, Beliefs, Behaviors, & Alcoholic Beverages, University of Michigan Press, Ann Arbor, 1979

Martin, G., Alcohol and the Heart, Heart Corps, November/Decem-
ber 1989

Marton, K., Alcohol and Breast Cancer: the Jury is Still Out, To
Your Health!, August/September, 1996

Marton, K., The Future of Wine and Health, Society of Medical
Friends of Wine, Vol. 40, No. 1., May, 1998

Marton, K., The Impact of Moderate Use, Wines & Vines, May, 1990

Marton, K., Wine and Health, A Doctor Speaks Out, Grand Cru,
Newsletter, Spring, 1989

Marty, A., La Hierarchie de la Fourchette et al Maladie Cornarienne, Indiana Medicine, Vol. 80, No. 8, August, 1987

Masarei, J., Puddly, I., Rouse, I., Lynch, W., Vandongen, R., and Beilin, L., Effects of Alcohol Consumption on Serum Lipoprotein-Lipid and Apolipoprotein Concentrations, Atherosclerosis, 60:78-79, 1986

Maskarinec, G., Meng, L., and Kolonel, L., Alcohol intake, body weight, and mortality in a multiethnic prospective cohort, Epidemiology, Vol. 9, No. 6, pp654-661, 1998

Matser, E, et al., Head Injuries in Soccer, JAMA, 282:971-973, 1999

Mattes, R., Dietary compensation by humans for supplemental energy provided as ethanol or carbohydrates in fluids, Physiological Behavior 59:179-189, 1996

Mattson, S., Riley, E., Gramling, L., Delis, D., and Jones, K., Heavy prenatal alcohol exposure with or without physical features of foetal alcohol syndrome leads to IQ deficits, Journal of Pediatrics, Vol. 131, No. 5, pp718-721, 1997

Maugh, II., T., Study finds genetic link to addiction, Los Angeles Times, March 4, 1998

Maury, E., Wine is The Best Medicine, Sheed Andrews and McMeel, Kansas City, 1974

Maxwell, S., Wine Antioxidants and Their Impact on Antioxidant Activity In Vivo, In Wine: Nutritional and Therapeutic Benefits, American Chemical Society, Washington, D.C., 1997

May, H., et al., Alcohol consumption and bone mineral density in older men, Gerontology, 41:152-158, 1995

May I recommend the pill de Roussillon, sir, The Times, www.thetimes,.co.uk/article/0,,3-2001192723,00.html

McConnell, C., and McConnell, M., The Mediterranean Diet, Wine, Pasta, Olive Oil and a Long, Healthy Life, W. W. Norton & Company, 1987

McConnell, M., et al., Effects of a single daily alcoholic beverage on lipid and hemostatic markers of cardiovascular risk, American Journal of Cardiology, 80:1226-1228, 1997

McDonald, J., Nutrition, A Symposium on Wine, Health and Society, Wine Institute, Washington, D.C., February 24, 1986

McDonald, J., Wine and Human Nutrition, a Symposium on Wine, Health & Society, The Wine Institute, San Francisco, November 13, 1981

McDonald, J., McElduff, P., and Dobson, A., How much alcohol and how often?, Population based case control study of alcohol consumption and risk of major coronary event, British Journal of Addiction, 314:1159-1164, 1997

McDonald, J., and Margen, S., Wine versus ethanol in human nutrition, The American Journal of Clinical Nutrition, 29:1093-1103, 1976

McDonald, P., Williams, R., Dawkins, F., and Adams-Campbell, L., Breast cancer survival in African American Women: is alcohol consumption a prognostic indicator?, Cancer Cases and Control, 13:543-549, 2002

McGovern, P., Earliest Evidence Dates Wine Back at Least 7000 Years, Wine, Culture and Society Series, The Wine Institute, Vol. 1, No., 1, June, 1996

McPherson, K., Cavalo, F., and Rubin, E., Alcohol and Breast Cancer, in Health Issues Related to Alcohol Consumption, Second Edition, MacDonald, I., editor, Blackwell Science, Oxford, 1999

Mediterranean Diet for Cancer Prevention, New England Journal of Medicine Health News, Vol. 4, No. 9, July 25, 1998

Mediterranean Diet Reduces Risk of Second Heart Attack, The Cleveland Clinic Heart Advisor, Vol. 2, No. 7, July, 1999

Meijers, R., Lamzin, V., and Cedergren-Zeppezauer, E., The role of a hydroxide ion in alcohol oxidation, Alcohol Research, Vol. 7, No. 3, June 2002

Meis, P., Goldenberg, R., Mercer, B., et al., The preterm prediction study: risk factors for indicated preterm births, American Journal of Obstetrics and Gynecology, 178:562-567, 1998

Memory, Mayo Clinic Health Letter, Vol. 7, No. 9, September, 1999

Mendelson, J., and Mello, N., Alcohol: Use and Abuse in America, Little Brown and Company, Boston, 1985

Mennen, L., Balkau, B., Vol, S., Cases, E., and Eschwege, E., Fibrinogen may explain in part the protective effect of moderate drinking on the risk of cardiovascular disease, Arteriosclerosis Thrombosis Vascular Biology, 19:887-892, 1999

Mental Stress and Respiratory Infections, Harvard Men's Health Watch, January, 1999

Messner, T., and Petersson, B., Alcohol consumption and ischaemic heart disease mortality in Sweden, Scandinavian Journal of Social Medicine, Vol. 24, No. 2, 1996

Mezzano, D., Leighton, F., Martinez, C., et al. Complementary effects of Mediterranean diet and moderate red wine intake on haemostatic cardiovascular risk factors, European Journal of Clinical Nutrition, 55:444-451, 2001

Michaud, D., Giovannucci, E., Willett, W., et al., Coffee and alcohol consumption and risk of pancreatic cancer in two prospective United States cohorts, Cancer Epidemiological Biomarkers Prev, 10:429-437, 2001

Midanik, L., Drunkenness, Feeling the Effects and 5+ Measures, Addiction, Vol. 94, No. 6, pp887-897, 1999

Midanik, L., Perspectives on the Validity of Self-Reported Alcohol Use, British Journal of Addiction, 84:1419-1423, 1989

Miles, T., Should My Mother Take a Drink?, Journal of the American Geriatric Society, 46:114, 1998

Miller, D., Rosenberg, A., Clarke, A., and Shapiro, S., American Journal of Epidemiology, Vol. 126, No. 4, P.436, 1987

Miller, H., When Worlds Collide: Science, Politics and Biotechnology, Priorities, Vol. 9, No. 4, 1997

Miller, W., and Cervantes, E., Gender and patterns of alcohol problems, Journal of Clinical Psychology, 53:263-277, 1997

Mingardi, R., Avogaro, A., Noventa, F., Stazzabosco, M., Stocchiero, C., Tiengo, A., and Erle, G., Alcohol intake is associated with a lower prevalence of peripheral vascular disease in non-insulin dependent diabetic women, Nutrition, Metabolism and Cardiovascular Diseases, Vol. 7, No. 4, 1997

Miranda, C., Stevens, J., Helmrikch, A., et al., Antiproliferative and cytotoxic effects of prenylated flavonoids from hops in human cancer, Food and Chemical Toxicology, 37(4):271-285, 1999

Mishara, B., and Kastenbaum, R., Alcohol and Old Age, Grune & Stratton, New York, 1980

Mishara,B., Miyame, M., Figueredo, V., et al., Regular alcohol consumption mimics cardiac preconditioning by protecting against ischemia-reperfusion injury, Proceedings of the National Academy of Sciences, 94:3235-3239, 1997

Mitchell, Jr., M., Commentary: Moderate Alcohol Intake, Alcoholic Beverage Medical Research Foundation, Vol. 4, No. 3, 1994

Miyake, Y., and the Fukuoka Heart Study Group, Risk factors for non-fatal acute myocardial infarction in middle-aged and older Japanese, Japanese Circulation, 64:103-109, 2000

Miyami, M., Figueredo, V., et al., Regular alcohol consumption mimics cardiac preconditioning by protecting against ischemia-reperfursion injury, Proceedings of the National Academy of Sciences, 94:3235-3239, 1997

Moderate Drinking, Alcohol Alert, NIAAA, No. 16, PH 315, April, 1992

Moderate Drinking and Health, Joint Policy Statement, Addiction Research Foundation of Ontario, Canadian Centre on Substance Abuse, Toronto, April 30, 1993

Monique, G., Hill, C., Kramar, A., and Flamant, R., Alcoholic Beverage Consumption and Breast Cancer in a French Case-Control Study, American Journal of Epidemiology, Vol. 120, No. 3, 1984

Montgomery, K., Alcohol and Tobacco Sites on the Internet Appeal to Youth, News Release, American Medical Association, March 19, 1999

Moore, D., Alcohol and Nutrition: Many Gastric Disorders Traced to Overuse of Alcohol, ADAMHA NEWS, May, 1987

Moore, N., Facts About Nutrition, New York State Journal of Medicine, 51:1283-1284, 1951

Moore, R., and Pearson, T., Moderate Alcohol Consumption and Coronary Artery Disease, Medicine, No. 65, No. 4, 1986

Moore, T., Lifespan, Simon & Schuster, New York, 1993

Moore, T., The Cholesterol Myth, Atlantic Monthly, September, 1988

More Adults Are Drinkers, Alcohol Issues Insights, Vol. 17, No. 1, January, 2000

More good fiber news: from JAMA, in Seattle Times, June 20, 1999

More News About Potential Benefits Linked to Alcohol in Spirits, Beer or Wine, Press Release, Distilled Spirits Council of U.S., Washington, D.C., May 6, 1996

More than a contraceptive, UC Berkeley Wellness Letter, Vol. 15, Issue 12, September, 1999

More than 300 new medicines being tested for cancer, other ills, Seattle Post Intelligencer, April 11, 1998

Morrow, L., After All the Smoke Cleared, Time, September 27, 1999

Morse, R., Alcoholism: How Do You Get It? in Fermented Food Beverages in Nutrition, Academic Press, New York, 1979

Mortensen, E., Jensen, HJ., Sanders, S.., and Reinisch, J., Better psychological functioning and higher social status may largely explain the apparent health benefits of wine, Archives of Internal Medicine, 161:1844-1848, 2001

Mosher, J., and Jernigan, D., New Directions in Alcohol Policy, Annual Revue of Public Health, 10:245-279, 1989

Moss, S., Klein, R., Klein, B., Jensen, S., and Meuer, S., Alcohol consumption and the 5-year incidence of age-related maculopathy: the Beaver Dam eye study, Ophthalmology, Vol. 105, No. 5, pp798-794, 1998

Motoaki, S., Maulik, G., and Ray, P., et al., Cardioprotective effects of grape seed proanthocyanidin against ischemic reperfusion injury, Journal of Molecular Cell Cardiology, 31:1289-1297, 199

Moulton, K., Economic Benefits of Moderate Wine Consumption, AIM, Vol. 4, No. 3, October/November, 1995

Mukamal, K., Muller, J., Maclure, M., Sherwood, J., and Mittleman, M., Lack of effect of recent alcohol consumption on the course of acute myocardial infarction, American Heart Journal 138:926-933, 1999

Mukamal, K., Conigrave, K., Mittleman, M., Camargo, C., Meir, J., Willett, W., and Rimm, E., Roles of Drinking Pattern and Type of Alcohol Consumed in Coronary Heart Disease in Men, The New England Journal of Medicine, Vol. 348:109-118, 2003

Mulford, H., and Fitzgerald, M., Per Capita Alcohol Sales: Heavy Drinker Prevalence and Alcohol Problems in Iowa for 1958-1985, British Journal of Addiction, 1988

Muller, C., and Fugelsang, K., Take Two Glasses of Wine and See Me in the Morning, The Lancet, 343:1428-1429, 1994

Muller, C., and Fugelsang, K., Take two glasses of wine and see me in the morning, in a letter to The Lancet, Vol. 3443, No. 8910, pp1428-142-, 1994

Munoz, B., et al., Posterior subcapsular cataracts, Archives of Ophthalmology, January, 1996

Munoz, S., Navarro, A., Lantieri, M., et al., Alcohol methylxanthine-containing beverages, and colorectal cancer in Cordoba, Argentina, European Journal of Cancer, Prev. 7:207-213, 1998

Muntwyler, J., Hennekens, C., Buring, J., and Gaziano, J., Mortality and light to moderate alcohol consumption after myocardial infarction, The Lancet, Vol. 352, No. 9144, pp1882-1885, 1998

Murgatroyd, P., van den Ven, M., Goldberg, G., and Prentice A., Alcohol and the regulation of energy balance: overnight effects on diet-induced thermogenesis and fuel storage, British Journal of Nutrition, 75:33-45, 1996

Murray, R., et al., Alcohol and Morbidity in the Lung Health Study, Journal of Studies on Alcohol, 59:250-257, May 1998

Muthen, B., and Muthen, L., The development of heavy drinking and alcohol-related problems from ages 18 to 37 in a U.S. national sample, Graduate School of Education, University of California, Los Angeles, Studies of Alcohol, 2000:290-300, 2000

Nagata, C., Shimizue, H., Kametani, M., Takeyama, N., Chnuma, T., and Matsushita, S., Cigarette smoking, alcohol use, and colorectal adenoma in Japanese men and women, Dis Colon Rectum, 42:337-342, 1999

Nagaya, T., Yoshida, H., Takahashi, H., Matsuda, Y., and Kawai, M., Dose-response relationships between drinking and serum tests in Japanese men aged 40-59 years, Alcohol, 17:133-138, 1999

Nakahashi, N., Nakamura, K., Ichikawa, S., Suzuki, K., and Tatara, K., Relationship between lifestyle and serum lipoprotein levels in middle-aged Japanese men, European Journal of Epidemiology, 15:341-348, 1999

Namekata, T., Moore, D., Suzuki, K., et al., Biological and lifestyle factors, and lipid and lipoprotein levels among Japanese Americans in Seattle and Japanese men in Japan, International Journal of Epidemiology, 26:1203-1213, 1997

Nanchahal, K., Ashton, W., and Wood, D., Alcohol consumption, metabolic cardiovascular risk factors and hypertension in women, International Journal on Epidemiology, 29:57-64, 2000

Nanji, A., Alcohol and Ischemic Heart Disease: Wine, Beer, or Both?, International Journal of Cardiology, Vol. 8, 1985

Nascetti, S., Elosua, R., Pena, A., et al., Variables associated with fibrinogen in a population-based study: interaction beween smoking and age on fibrinogen concentration, European Journal of Epidemiology, 17:953-958, 2002

Natural Prostatitis Treatment, Health News, Vol. 6, o. 3, March 2000

Naves Diaz, M., O'Neill, T., and Silman, A., The influence of alcohol consumption on the risk of vertebral deformity, Osteoporosis Int., 7:65-71, 1997

Neergaard, L., Fight urged against germs, Seattle Post Intelligencer, December 15, 1998

Nelson, H., et al., Smoking, alcohol and neuromuscular and physical function of older women, JAMA, 272(23):1825-1831, 1994

Nelson, R., Levine, A., Marks, G., and Bernstein, L., Alcohol, tobacco and recreational drug use and the risk of non-Hodgkin's lymphoma, British Journal of Cancer, 76:1532-1537, 1997

Nestle, M., Alcohol Guidelines for Chronic Disease Prevention: From Prohibition to Moderation, Social History of Alcohol Review, 32-33, 1996

Nevill, A., et al., Modeling the associations of BMI, physical activity and diet with arterial blood pressure, some results from the Allied Dunbar National Fitness Survey, Annals of Human Biology, 24:229-47, 1997

New Blood Test a Strong Predictor of Heart Disease, Tufts University Health & Nutrition Letter, Vol. 18, No. 3, May, 2000

New Diabetes Drugs: Which One is Right for You?, Health After 50, Vol. 10, Issue 11, January, 1999

New Guidelines for Prevention, Harvard Women's Health Watch, Vol. VI, No. 12, August, 1999

New Tools for Taking Control of Alzheimer Disease, Health After 50, Vol. 13, Issue 10, December, 2001

New Treatment for Heart Attack, HealthNews, July, 2000

Newcomb, P., Trentham-Dietz, A., and Storer, B., Alcohol consumption in relation to endometrial cancer risk, Cancer: Epidemiology, Biomarkers and Prevention, Vol. 6, No. 10:775-778, 1997

Newnham, H., and Silberger, J., Women's hearts are hard to break, The Lancet, Vol. 349, March, 1997

Newport, Frank, More than a Third of Americans Report Drinking Has Caused Family Problems, The Gallup Organization, November 3, 1999

Nguyen, T., et al., Risk factors for osteoporotic fracture in elderly men, American Journal of epidemiology, 144(3):255-263, 1996

Nigdikar, S., Williams, N., Griffin, B., Howard, A., Consumption of red wine polyphenols reduces the susceptibility of low-density lipoproteins to oxidation in vivo, American Journal of Clinical Nutrition, Vol. 68, pp258-265, 1998

Nine Strategies for Cutting Your Heart attack, Risk, Health After 50, Vol. 4, Issue 12, February, 1993

Ninth Special Report to the U.S. Congress on Alcohol and Health, DHHS, Washington, D.C., June, 1997

Noble, E., Prevention by and for All to Make a Safer Future, The Bottom Line, 1986

Norman, P., Bennett, P., and Lewis, H., Understanding binge drinking among young people: an application of the theory of planned behaviour, Health Education and Research, 13:163-169, 1998

Norstrom, T., Effects on criminal violence of different beverage types and private and public drinking, Addiction, Vol. 93, No. 5, pp689-699, 1998

Norton, R., Batey, R., Dwyer, T., and MacMahon, S., Alcohol Consumption and the Risk of Alcohol-Related Cirrhosis in Women, British Medical Journal, 295:80-82, 1987

Obisesan, T., Hirsch, R., Kosoko, O., Carlson, L., and Parrott, M., Moderate Wine Consumption is Associated with Decreased Odds of Developing Age-Related Macular Degeneration in NHANES-I, Journal of the American Geriatric Society, 46:1-7, 1998

Odvina, C., Safi, I., Wojtowicz, C., Barengolts, E., Lathon, P., Skapars, A., Desai, P., and Kukreja, S., Effect of heavy alcohol intake in the absence of liver disease on bone mass in black and white men, Journal of Clinical Endocrinology Metabolism, 80(8):499-503, 1995

Ogihara, A., Kikuchi, S., Hasegawa, A., et al., Relationship between Helicobacter pylori infection and smoking and drinking habits, Journal of Gastroenterology and Hepatology 15:271-276, 2000

Okamoto, M., Yamagata, Z., Takeda, Y., Yoda, Y., Kobayashi, K., and Fujino, M., The relationship between gallbladder disease and smoking and drinking habits in middle-aged Japanese, Journal of Gastroenterology 37:455-462, 2002

Olds, R., et al., The Relationship of Adolescent Perceptions of Peer Norms and Parent Involvement to Cigarette and Alcohol Use, Journal of School Health, Vol. 71, No. 6, pp223-228, August, 2001.

Oldways Preservation & Exchange Trust, What is Oldways, Cambridge, 1995

Olive Oil Lowers Blood Pressure, HealthNews, Vol. 6, No. 5, May, 2000

Olsen, J., Bolumar, F., Boldsen, J., and Bisanti, L., Does moderate alcohol intake reduce fecundability? A European multicentre study on infertility and subfecundability, Alcoholism: Clinical and Experimental Research, Vol. 21, No. 2,

Olsen, J., and Tuntiseranee, Is moderate alcohol intake in pregnancy associated with the craniofacial features related to foetal alcohol syndrome?, Vol. 23, No. 3, pp56-161, 1995

On Call, Harvard Men's Health Watch, August, 1998

Open and Say "Ah." , Smart Money, September, 1999

Orgogozo, M., et al., Wine consumption and dementia in the elderly: A prospective community study in the Bordeaux area, Revue Neurologique, Vol. 153, No. 2, 1997

Orgogozo, M., Wine & Health Research in Bordeaux, Bordeaux International, 1997

Ornstein, R., and Sobel, D., Healthy Pleasures, Addison-Wesley Publishing Company, Reading, Massachusetts, 1989

Orozco, S., and de Castro, J., Effect of spontaneous alcohol intake on heart rate and dietary intake of free-living women, Pharmacology Biochemistry and Behavior, Vol. 49, No. 3, pp629-638, 1994

Osler, M., Jergensen, T., Davidsen, M., et al., Socioeconomic status and trends in alcohol drinking in the Danish MONICA population, 1982-92, Scandinavian Journal of Public Health, 29:40-43, 2001

Osmon, H., Maalej, N., Shanmuganayagam, D., and Folts, J., Grape juice but not orange juice or grapefruit juice inhibits platelet activity in dogs and monkeys, Journal of Nutrition, 128:2307-2312, 1998

Osteoporosis in Men, Harvard Men's Health Watch, Vol. 3, No. 7, February, 1999

Osteoporosis: Know Your Risk and How to Lessen It, Tufts University Health & Nutrition Letter, Supplement, May, 2000

Ostermann, J., et al., Effects of Alcohol consumption on Disability among the Near Elderly,: A Longitudinal Analysis, The Milbank Quarterly, Vol. 79, No. 4, 2001

Our Strong Recommendation for Bone Density Testing, Health After 50, Johns Hopkins Medical Publications, October, 1997

Paasilta, M., Kervinene, K., Rantala, A., Savolainen, M., Reunanen, A., and Kesaniemi, Y., Social alcohol consumption and low Lpa lipoprotein concentrations in middle-aged Finnish men: population based study, British Medical Journal, Vol. 316, No. 7131, 1998

Paganga, G., Miller, N., and Rice-Evans, C., The polyphenolic content of fruit and vegetables and their antioxidant activities. What does a serving constitute, Free Radical research, 30:153-162, 1999

Paganini-Hill, A., Risk factors for Parkinson's disease: the Leisure World Cohort Study, Neuroepidemiology, 20:118-124, 2001

Pahor, M., Guralnik, J., Havlik, R., Carbonin, P., Salive, M., Ferrucci, L., Coriti, M., and Hennekens, C., Alcohol consumption and risk of deep venous thrombosis and pulmonary embolism in older persons, Journal of the American Geriatrics Society, Vol. 44, No. 9, 1996

Pajarinen, J., Karhunen, P., and Savolainene, V., Moderate alcohol consumption and disorders of human spermatogenesis, Alcoholism: Clinical and Experimental Research, Vol. 20, No. 2, pp333-337, 1996

Pancioli, M., Public Education Needed to Increase Awareness of Stroke Warning Signs, JAMA, 279:1307-1308, 1998

Park, R., Universities well-schooled in politics of pork, the Seattle Post Intelligencer, August 24, 1999

Parsons, O., and Nixon, S., Cognitive Functioning in Sober Social Drinkers: A Review of the Research Since 1986, Journal of Studies on Alcohol, 59:180-190, 1998

Partner or Foe? The Alcohol Industry, Youth Alcohol Problems, and Alcohol Policy Strategies, Alcohol Issues, The American Medical Association, 2001

Passaro, K., Little, R., Savitz, D., and Noss, J., The effect of maternal drinking before conception and in early pregnancy on infant birthweight, Epidemiology, Vol. 7, No. 4, pp77-383, 1996

Pasternak et al., Task Force 3, Spectrum of risk factors for coronary heart disease, Journal of American College of Cardiology, 27(5): 961-962

Patients' decisions lack data study says, Seattle Times, December 21, 1999

Paulson, T., Possible Rx for stroke: Irish coffee, Seattle Post Intelligencer, October 13, 1999

Paying for the Golden Age of Medicine, Harvard Health Letter, Vol. 25, No. 3, January, 2000

Pear, R., Medical research still shorts women, new studies say, New York Times, in The Seattle Times, April 30, 2000

Pearson T., AHA Science Advisory, American Journal of Clinical Nutrition, Vol. 65, No. 5, pp1567-1569, 1997

Pearson, T., and Terry, P., What to Advise Patients About Drinking Alcohol: The Clinician's Conundrum, JAMA, Vol. 272, No. 12, September, 1994

Peatfield, R., Headache, Vol. 35, No. 6, pp355-357, 1995

Peele, S., Culture, alcohol and health: the consequences of alcohol consumption among Western nations, December 1, Morristown, New Jersey, 1995

Peele, S., Should Physicians Recommend Alcohol to their Patients, Priorities, Vol. 8, No. 1, 1996

Peele, S., The Conflict Between Public Health Goals and the Temperance Mentality, American Journal of Public Health, 83:805-810, June, 1993

Peele, S., The Pleasure Principle in Addiction, Journal of Drug Issues, Vol. 15, No. 2, pp193-201, Spring, 1985

Peele, S., and Brodsky, A., Exploring psychological benefits associated with moderate alcohol use: a necessary corrective to assessments of drinking outcomes?, Drug and Alcohol Dependence, 60:221-247, 2000

Peele, S., and Brodsky, A., Gateway to Nowhere, Addiction Research, Vol. 5, No. 5, pp419-426, 1997

Peele, S., and Brodsky, A., presentation at Permission for Pleasure Symposium, ICAP, Washington, D.C., 1998

Peele, S., and Grant, M., Alcohol and Pleasure: A Health Perspective, Brunner/Mazel, Philadelphia, 1999

Pekkanen, J., et al., Ten-Year Mortality From Cardiovascular Disease in Relation to Cholesterol Level Among Men with and without

Pre-existing Cardiovascular Disease, The New England Journal of Medicine, Vol. 322, No. 24, June 14, 1990

Pengelley, B., Stale Beer Part III: The Role of Polyphenols in Beer Oxidation, The New Brewer, September/October, 2002

Peptic Ulcer Disease: A Curable Infection, Harvard Men's Health Watch, Vol. 1, No. 7, February, 1997

Peptic ulcers, Mayo Clinic Health Letter, Vol. 17, No. 9, September, 1999

Percent of Individuals Having Alcohol With Dinner at Home at Least Once Within a two-Week Period, Market Watch, March/April, 1999

Perdue, L., Wine May Have Protected Passengers from Infection, Wine Business Monthly, Sonoma, October, 1994

Perry, H., Horowitz, M., Fleming S., et al., The effects of season and alcohol intake on mineral metabolism in men, Alcoholism: Clinical and Experimental Research, 23:214-219, 1999

Peyret, E., One French person in four dies before the age of 65, Liberation, p23, February 16, 1996

Pezzuto, J., An Anti-cancer activity in grapes and wines, Wine Nutrition and Health, OIV, Bordeaux, 1997

Physical Effects of Stress, The New England Journal of Medicine Health News, Vol. 4, No. 2, February, 17, 1998

Piendl, A., Beer and Health, Brauwelt International, September 10, 1998

Piendl, A., and Wagner, I., Beer and health– Part I. Effect of diet on high blood pressure, Brauindustrie, 71(5)205-209, 1986

Pikaar, N., Wedel, M., van der Beek, E., van Dokkum, W., Kluft C., Ockhuizen, T., and Hermuss, R., Effects of Moderate Alcohol Consumption on Platelet Aggregation, Fribrinolysis, and Blood Lipids, Metabolism, 36(6): 538-543, 1987

Pittman, D., American Attitudes About Wine, A Symposium on Wine, Culture & Healthy Lifestyles, The Wine Institute, New York, May 1, 1987

Pittman, D., Chapter 40, Society, Culture and Drinking Practices, Rutgers Center of Alcohol Studies, New Brunswick, 1991

Pittman, D., Chapter VI: An Analysis of the Control of Consumption Model, Primary Prevention of Alcohol Abuse and Alcoholism, Social Science Institute, Washington University, St. Louis, 1980

Pittman, D., Cross Cultural Aspects of Drinking, Alcohol Abuse, and Alcoholism, Wine in Context: Nutrition, Physiology, Policy, American Society for Enology and Viticulture, Reno, 1996

Pittman, D., The New Temperance Movement, Society, Culture and Drinking Patterns Re-examined, Rutgers Center of Alcohol Studies, New Brunswick 1991

Pittman, D., U.S. Consumption Guidelines Deemed Restrictive, in Wine Issues Monitor, 1995

Plant, M., Drinking and Pregnancy, Tavistock Publications, London, 1987

Plotkin, G., The Physician's Perspective in Grasping Essential Tremor, Vol. 5, No. 12, October, 1999

Poikolainen, K. et al., Phenolic content of various beverages determines the extent of inhibition of human serum and low-density lipoprotein oxidation in vitro: Identification and mechanisms of action of some cinnamic acid derivatives from red wine, Clinicial Science, 91:449-58, 1996

Poikolainen, K., Alcohol and mortality: a review, Journal of Clinical Epidemiology, 48(4): 455-465, 1995

Poikolainen, K., Vartiainen, E., and Korhonen, H., Alcohol intake and subjective health, American Journal of Epidemiology, Vol. 144, No. 4, pp346-350, 1996

Poikolainen, K., The other health benefits of moderate alcohol intake, Contemporary Drug Problems, Spring, 1994

Poldrugo, F., Alcohol and criminal behaviour, Alcohol, 33:12-15, 1998

Polomaki, H., and Kaste, M., Regular light-to-moderate intake of alcohol and the risk of ischemic stroke, Is there a beneficial effect?, Stroke, 24(2): 1828 1832, December, 1993

Polygenis, D., Wharton, S., Maimberg, C., et al., Moderate alcohol consumption during pregnancy and the incidence of fetal malformations: a meta-analysis, Neurotosociology & Teratology, 20:61-67, 1998

Popelka, M., et al., Moderate Alcohol Consumption and Hearing Loss: A protective Effect, Journal of the American Geriatric Society, Vol. 48, No. 10pp1273-1278, 2000

Potential Benefits of Beer, cbmc.org

Potter, J, Hazards and Benefits of Alcohol, The New England Journal of Medicine, Vol. 337, No. 24, December 11, 1997

Power, C., U-shaped relation for alcohol consumption and health in early adulthood and implications for mortality, The Lancet, Vol. 352, September 12, 1998

Pre-emptive Strikes, Harvard Health Letter, Vol. 25, No. 6, April, 2000

Prescott, E., Gronbaek, M., Becker, U., Serensen, T., Alcohol intake and the risk of lung cancer: Influence of type of alcoholic beverage, American Journal of Epidemiology, 149:463-470, 1999

Prescription Drugs: Playing It Safe, HealthNews, Vol. 4, No. 9, July 25, 1998

Prescription for Heart Attack Survivors, John Hopkins Health After 50, Vol. 13, Issue 4, June, 2001

Prescriptions increase as drug makers spend more on ads, USA today, February 21, 2001

Preserving Memory Through the Years, Harvard Health Letter, Vol. 23, No. 10, August, 1998

Preventing Brain Attack, Harvard Health Letter, Vol. 26, No. 8, June, 2001

Preventing Cancer, Harvard Men's Health Watch, Vol. 3, No. 4, November, 1998

Pritchard, K., Breast cancer: the real challenge, The Lancet, Vol. 349, March, 1997

Probert, C., Emmett, P., and Heaton, K., Quarterly Journal of Medicine, 88:311-315, 1995

Profile of the Wine Drinker, Issue In Focus, The Wine Institute, San Francisco, November, 1991

Progress against heart disease: an advance you can live with, UC Berkeley Wellness Letter, November, 1999

Psychologists say too many people feel guilty about pleasure, Seattle Times, November, 1996

Puddy, I., et al., Alcohol, hypertension and the cardiovascular system: a critical appraisal, Addition Biology, 2:159-170, 1997

Putnam, S., Carhan, J., and Parker, A., et al., Alcohol consumption and prostate cancer in a cohort of Iowa males, American Journal of Epidemiology, 147:Suppl:165, 1998

Quercetin: An apple a day, UC Berkeley Wellness Letter, Vol. 19, Issue 4, 2003

Questions still to be answered, cbmc.org/ukpages/beer-health/page6.htm

Radford, T., Daily glass of wine could help stave off Alzheimer's, Guardian, p7, January 7, 1999

Rakic, V., et al., Influence of pattern of alcohol intake on blood pressure in regular drinkers: a controlled trial. Journal of Hypertension, 16:165-174, 1998

Ramsey, L., et al., Alcohol and Myocardial Infarction in Hypertensive Men, American Heart Journal, 1979

Rapuri, P., Gallagher, J., Balhorn, K., and Ryschon, K., Alcohol intake and bone metabolism in elderly women, American Journal of Clinical Nutrition, 72:

Rasmussen, C., Lumbar disc herniation: favourable outcome associated with intake of wine, European Spine Journal, Vol. 7, No. 1, pp24-28, 1998

Rauch, J., Temperance Kills, www.slate.com 08/18/98

Razay, G., Heaton, K., Bolton, C., and Hunges, A., Alcohol consumption and its Relation to Cardiovascular Risk Factors in British Women, British Medical Journal, 304(6819): 80-3, 1992

Reaney, P., Diet plan brings fat back from exile, Seattle Times, 1999

Recht, J., Wine and Women, Wine East, 1997

Regarding Women, Virginia Mason Medical Center, Seattle, Spring, 1990

Regier, D., Farmer, M., Rae D., Locke, B., Keith, S., Judd, L., and Goodwin, F., Comorbidity of Mental Disorders With Alcohol and Other Drug Abuse, JAMA, Vol. 264, No. 19, November 1990

Rehm, J., Ashley, M., and DuBois, G., Alcohol and health: individual and population perspectives, Addiction, 92:(Supplement I), ppS109-S115, 1997

Rehm, J., Bondy, S., Sempos, C., and Vuong, C., Alcohol consumption and coronary heart disease morbidity and mortality, American Journal of Epidemiology, Vol. 146, No. 6, 1997

Rehm, J., and Sempos, C., Alcohol consumption and all-cause mortality, Addiction, 90:471-480, 1995

Rehm, J., Greenfield, T., and Robers, J., Average volume of alcohol consumption, patters of drinking, and all-cause mortality: results from the U.S. National Alcohol Survey, American Journal of Epidemiology, 153:64-71, 2001

Reich, T., Edenberg, H., Goate, A., Williams, J., Rice, J., Van Erdewegh, P., Foroud, T., Hesselbrock, V., Schuckit, M., Bucholz, K., Porjesz, B., et al., Genome-wide search for genes affecting the risk for alcohol dependence, American Journal of Medical Genetics, Vol. 81, No. 3, pp207-215, 1998

Reichman, M., Alcohol and breast cancer, Alcohol Health and Research World, Vol. 18, No. 3, pp182-184, 1995

Reid, M., Cancato, J., Towle, V., Williams, C., and Tinetti, M., Alcohol use and functional disability among cognitively impaired adults, Journal of American Geriatrics, 47:854-859, 1999

Remedies, Health After 50, Vol. 11, No. 9, November, 1999

Renaud, S., Epidemiology, March, 1997

Renaud, S., Sixty Minutes Segment, The French Paradox, CBS-TV, 1991

Renaud, S., Supporting Wine Consumption, Archive of Internal Medicine, 159:1-6, September, 1999

Renaud, S., Gueguen, R., Schenker, J., and d'Houtaud, A., Alcohol and mortality in middle-aged men from Eastern France, Epidemiology, Vol. 9, No. 2, 148-188, 1998

Renaud, S., Beswick, A., Fehily, A., Sharp, D., and Elwood, P., Alcohol and Platelet Aggregation: The Caerphilly Prospective Heart Disease Study, American Journal of Clinical Nutrition, 55(5):1012, 1992

Renaud, S., and de Lorgeril, M., Wine, alcohol, platelets, and the French paradox for coronary heart disease, Epidemiology, Vol. 339, June 20, 1992

Renaud, S., Guegen, R., Schenker, J., and D'Houtaud, A., Alcohol and Mortality in Middle-aged men from Eastern France, Epidemiology, 1998

Report on the Adelaide Conference, Healthy Public Policy, Second International Conference on Health Promotion, April 5-9, 1988

Report to the President and Congress on Health Hazards Associated with Alcohol and Methods to Inform the General Public of these Hazards, U.S. DOT and USDHHS, Washington, D.C., November, 1980

Research Shows Moderate Consumption May Reduce Stroke, On Tap, Vol. 13, No. 3, December, 1999

Researchers Set Sights on Vision Disease, Harvard Health Letter, Vol. 23, No. 10, August, 1998

Revised Anti-Kidney Stone Recipe, Health After 50, Vol. 14, Issue, 3., 2002

Richman, A., and Warren, R., Alcohol Consumption and Morbidity in the Canada Health Survey: Inter-Beverage Differences, Drug and Alcohol Dependence, 15:255-282, 1985

Ridker, P., et al., Moderate Alcohol Intake May Reduce Risk of Thrombosis, News Release, American Medical Association, September 22, 1994

Ridker, P., The Pathogenesis of Atherosclerosis and Acute Thrombosis, in Prevention of Myocardial Infarction, Oxford University Press, New York, 1996

Ridker, P., Gaziano, M., Manson, J., Future Directions in Coronary Disease Prevention, "Summary and Conclusions. Table 20.1 Quality of Evidence Concerning Modifiable Risk Factors," in Prevention of Myocardial Infarction, Oxford University Press, New York, 1996

Ridker, P., Hennekens, C., et al., Association of moderate alcohol consumption and plasma concentration of andogenous tissue-type plasminogen activator, JAMA, 272: 929-933, 1994

Ridker, P., Nader, R., Rose, L., Burling J., and Cook, N., Comparison of C-Reactive Protein and Low-Density Lipoprotein Cholesterol Levels in the Prediction of First Cardiovascular Events, The New England Journal of Medicine, Vol:347:1557-1565, 2002

Rimm, E., Editorial, Alcohol and Coronary Heart Disease: Can We Learn More?, Epidemiology, 12:380, 2001

Rimm, E., Chann, J., Stampfer, M., Coldeitz, G., and Willett, W., Prospective study of cigarette smoking, alcohol use and the risk of diabetes in men, British Medical Journal, 310:555-559, 1995

Rimm, E., et al., Folate and vitamin B6 from diet and supplements in relation to risk of coronary heart disease among women, JAMA, 279:359-64, 1998

Rimm, E., Giovannucci, E., Willett, W., Colditz, G., Ascherio, A., Rosner, B., and Stampfer, M., Prospective study of Alcohol Consumption and Risk of coronary Heart Disease in Men, The Lancet, 338:464-468, 1991

Rimm, E., Klatsky, A., et al., Review of moderate alcohol consumption and reduced risk of coronary heart disease: Is the effect due to beer, wine or spirits?, British Medical Journal, 312:731-736, 1996

Rimm, E., Williams, P., Fosher, K., et al., Moderate alcohol intake and lower risk of coronary heart disease: meta-analysis of effects on lipids and hemostatic factors, British Medical Journal, 319:1523-1528, 1999

Risking It All, Time Magazine, August 29, 1983

Ritter, L., Klein, R., Klein, B., Mares-Perlman, J. and Jensen, S., Alcohol use and age-related maculopathy in the Beaver Dam Study, American Journal of Ophthalmology, 120(2):190-196, 1995

Robinson, D., Drinking Behavior, in Alcoholism in Perspective, Croom Helm, London, 1979

Robinson, J., On the Demon Drink, Mitchell Beazley Publishers, London, 1988

Roche, A., Patterns, Paradoxes and Ambiguities of Consumption, presentations at Kettil Bruun Society Meeting, February 1, 1998, Perth Australia

Rodgers, B., Korten, A., Jorm, A., Christensen, H., Hendreson, S., and Jacomb, P., Risk factors for depression and anxiety in abstainers, moderate drinkers and heavy drinkers, Addiction, 95:1833-1845, 2000

Rodgers, H., et al. Alcohol and Stroke: A Case Control Study of Drinking Habits Past and Present, Stroke, 12(10):1473-1477, 1993

Rodriguez, A., Bangas, J., Colmenero, C., and Calero, J., Lower consumption of wine and fish as a possible explanation for higher ischemic heart disease mortality in Spain's Mediterranean region, International Journal of Epidemiology, Vol. 25, No. 6, 1196-1201, 1996

Rohan, T., Jain, M., and Howe, G., et al., Alcohol consumption and risk of breast cancer: a cohort study, Cancer Causes & Control, 11:239-247, 2000

Rohan, T., and McMichael, A., Alcohol Consumption and the Risk of Breast Cancer, International Journal of Cancer, 41:695-699, 1998

Roizen, M., Real Age: Are You as Young as You Can Be?, Cliff Street Books, New York, 1999

Room for Improvement in Stroke Treatment, HealthNews, Vol. 6, No. 5, May, 2000

Room, R., in The Future of the Word Alcoholism, British Journal of Addiction, 82:1061-1071, 1987

Rooney, J., Patterns of Alcohol Use in Spanish Society, in Society, Culture and Drinking Patterns re-examined, Rutgers Center of Alcohol Studies, New Brunswick, 1991

Rorabaugh, W., Alcohol History: Personal Reflections, Social History of Alcohol Review, 932-933, 1996

Rorabaugh, W., The Alcoholic Republic, Oxford University Press, New York, 1979

Rosenberg, L., Alcohol Consumption and the Risk of Breast Cancer, Epidemiologic Reviews, 16(1):133-144, 1993

Rosenblatt, R., Alzheimer's research focus: slowing its progression, Seattle Times, October 30, 1998

Rosenfeld, I., Get Rid of Ulcers for Good, Parade Magazine, December 7, 1997

Rosenfeld, I., How to Fight Stroke, Parade, September 12, 1999

Rosenfeld, I., Live Now, Grow Old Later, Parade, May 23, 1999

Rosenfeld, I., Not Everything You Like Is Bad For You, Parade Magazine, March 22, 1998

Rosenstock, S., Jergensen, T., Andersen, L., and Bonevie, O., Association of Helicobacter pylori infection with lifestyle, chronic disease, body-indices, and age at monarch in Danish adults, Scandinavian Journal of Public Health, 28:32-40, 2000

Ross, H., Deterring the Drinking Driver, Lexington Books, Lexington, MA, 1986

Ross, P., The Futile Crackdown, Forbes, October 18, 1999

Rossing, M., Cushing, K., Voigt, L., Wicklund, K., and Daling, J., Risk of papillary thyroid cancer in women in relation to smoking and alcohol consumption, Epidemiology, 11:49-54, 2000

Roueche', B., Alcohol: The Neutral Spirit, Grove Press, Inc. New York, 1960

Rouse, R., Wine triggers attacks in asthmatics, Australian Associated Press, March 1, 1999

Rowe, J., and Kahn, R., Successful Aging, Pantheon Books, New York, 1998

Royo-Bordonada, M., Martin-Moreno, J., Guallar, E., Gorgojo, L., van't Veer, P., Mendez, M., Huttenen, J., Martin, B., Kardinaal, A., Fernandez-Crehuet, J., Strain, J., Kok, F., Kohlmeier, F., Alcohol intake and risk of breast cancer: the Euromac Study, Neoplasma, Vol. 44, No. 3, pp150-156, 1997

Rubin, E., Alcohol and Cancer: Is There a Plausible Mechanism?, Health Effects of Moderate Alcohol Consumption: Good, Bad or Indifferent, Canadian Atherosclerosis Society, University of Toronto, December, 1994

Rubin, E., An Overview of the Evidence Concerning the Hypothesis that Alcohol Causes Cancer, Department of Pathology and Cell Biology, Jefferson Medical College, Philadelphia, 1988

Rubin, E., Letter to Alcohol, Tobacco and Firearms, Department of Pathology and Cell Biology, Jefferson Medical College, Philadelphia, 1991

Ruchlin, H., Prevalence and correlates of alcohol use among older adults, Prevention Medicine, 26:651-657, 1997

Rumpler, W., Clevidence, B., Muessing, R., et al., Changes in women's plasma lipid and lipoprotein concentrations due to moderate consumption of alcohol are affected by dietary fat level, Journal of Nutrition 129:1713-1717, 1999

Russia's Anti-Drink Campaign: Veni, vidi, vodka, Economist, December 23, 1989

Russo, A., Maconi, G., Spinelli, P., et al., Effect of lifestyle, smoking and diet on development of intestinal metaplasia in H. pylori-positive subjects, American Journal of Gastroenterology, 96:1402-1408, 2001

Rutgers monograph stresses the important role of research and education on moderate alcohol consumption, Health and Social Issues Newsline, The Wine Institute, San Francisco, November, 1991

Ryan, M., Alcoholism and rising mortality in the Russian Federation, British Medical Journal, Vol. 310, No. 6980, pp646-648, 1995

Sacco, R., American Heart Association, 22nd International Joint Conference on Stroke and Cerebral Circulation, Anaheim, February, 1997

Sacco, R., Elkind, M., Boden-Albala, B., et al., The Protective Effect of Moderate Alcohol Consumption on Ischemic Stroke, JAMA 281:53-60, 1999

Saelan, H., Muller, L., and Koster, A., Alcohol consumption in a Danish cohort during 11 years, Scandinavian Journal, Soc Med, 20(2):87-93, June, 1992

Safe Alcohol Consumption: A Comparison of Nutrition and Your Health: Dietary Guidelines for Americans and Sensible Drinking, International Center for Alcohol Policies, ICAP Reports 1, Washington, D.C., 1997

Safer, M., The French Paradox, 60 Minutes, CBS, New York, 1991

Safer, M., Giuliano, E., The Story Behind the Story: Wine Enthusiast Spends 60 Minutes with Morley Safer, Wine Enthusiast, New York, May/June, 1992

Sahi, T., Paffenbarger, R., Hsieh, C., and Lee, I.., Body mass index, cigarette smoking and other characteristics as predictors of self-reported physician-diagnosed gallbladder disease in male college alumni, American Journal of Epidemiology, 147:644-651, 1998

Sakurai, Y., Umeda, T., Shinchi, K., Honjog, S., Wakabayashi, K., Todoroki, I., Nishikawa, H., Ogawa, S., and Katsurada, M., Relation of total and beverage-specific alcohol intake to body mass index and waist-to-hip ratio: A study of self-defense officials in Japan, European Journal of Epidemiology, Vol. 13, No. 8, pp893-898, 1997

Sandler, M., et al., Dietary migraine: Recent progress in the red (and white) wine story, Cephalagia, 15:101-103, 1995

Sarley, V., and Stepto, R., Wine is Fine for Patients' Morale and Helps Stimulate Their Appetites, Modern Nursing Home, Vol. 23, No. 1, January/February, 1969

Saunders, Editorial, Drug and Alcohol Review, Number 14, No. 1, 1995

Savage, G., Calvert, B., Rohde, F., and Grant B., Liver Cirrhosis Mortality in the United States, 1970-1991, NIAAA, Washington, D.C., 1995

Savolainen, V., et al., Alcohol Consumption and Alcoholic Liver Disease: Evidence of a Threshold Level of Effects of Ethanol, Alcoholism Clinical and Experimental Research, 17(5):112-1117, 1993

Sayette, M., Does drinking reduce stress?, Alcohol Research and Health, 23:250-255, 1999

Schatzkin, A., and Longnecker, M., Alcohol and breast cancer: Where are we now and where do we go from here?, Cancer, 74:(3 Supplement):1101-1110, 1994

Schepens, P., Pauwels, A., Van Damme, P., Musuku, A., Beaucourt, L., and Selala, M., Drugs of abuse and alcohol in weekend drivers involved in car crashes in Belgium, Annals of Emerging Medicine, 31:633-637, 1998

Scherr, P., LaCroix, A., Wallace, R., Berkman, L., Curb, J., Cornoni-Huntley, J., Evans, D., and Hennekens, C., Light to Moderate Alcohol Consumption and Mortality in the Elderly, Journal of the American Geriatric Society, 40:651-657, 1992

Schinka, J., Vanderploeg, R., Rogish, M., and Ordorica, P., Effects of alcohol and cigarette use on cognition in middle-aged adults, Journal of International Neuropsychol Society, 8:683-690, 2002

Schivelbush, W., Tastes of Paradise: A Social History of Spices, Stimulants, and Intoxicants, Pantheon Books, New York, 1992

Schoen, E., Abortion-breast cancer line mustn't be ignored, Seattle Post Intelligencer, October 26, 2002

Scholten, P., A Significant Comparison, Bulletin of the Society of Medical Friends of Wine, Vol. 28, No. 1, February, 1986

Scholten, P., Wine and Health, Wines and Vines, Vol. 70, No. 8, August, 1989

Schuckit, M., Daeppen, J., Tipp, J., et al., The clinical course of alcohol-related problems in alcohol dependent and nonalcoholic dependent drinking women and men, Journal of Studies on Alcohol, 59:581-590, 1998

Schulenberg, J., et al., Getting Drunk and Growing Up: Trajectories of Frequent Binge Drinking During the Transition to Young Adulthood, Journal of Studies on Alcohol, 57:289-304, May, 1996

Schwartz, B., Tension Headaches Plague Two Out of Five Americans, JAMA, 279:381-383, 1998

Schwartz, M., Fat of land getting fatter, Seattle Post Intelligencer, May 29, 1998

Schwartzberg, J., and Margen, S., The UC Berkeley Wellness Self-Care Handbook, Rebus, New York, 1998

Scientists at last identify gene linked to "healthy cholesterol," Seattle Post Intelligencer, August 3, 1999

Scientists say a bit of what you fancy does your good, Daily Express, June 16, p19, 1995

Second Special Report to Congress on Alcohol & Health, Department of Health and Human Services, Washington, D.C., 1974

Seigneur, M., et al., Effect of the Consumption of Alcohol, White Wine, and Red Wine on Platelet Function and Serum Lips, Journal of Applied Cardiology, 5:215-222, 1990

Seitz, H., Poschl, G., and Simanowski, U., Alcohol and Cancer, Recent Developments in Alcoholism, Vol. 14: The Consequences of Alcoholism, edited by Galanter, Plenum Press, New York, 1998

Selzer, R., Mortal Lessons: Notes on the Art of Surgery, Simon & Schuster, New York, 1976

Serebruany, V., Lowery, D., Fuzailov, S., et al., Moderate alcohol consumption is associated with decreased platelet activity in patients presenting with acute myocardial infarction, Thrombosis and Thrombolysis, 9:229-34, 2000

Sesso, H., Stampfer, M., Rosner, B., Hennekens, C., Manson, J., and Gaziano, J., Seven-year changes in alcohol consumption and subsequent risk of cardiovascular disease in men, Archives of Internal Medicine, 160:2605-2612, 2000

Sesso, H., Paffenbarger, R., and Lee, I., Alcohol consumption and risk of prostate cancer, International Journal of Epidemiology, 3):749-755, 2001

Setting a Steady Course for Benign Essential Tremor, The Johns Hopkins Medical Letter, Vol. 11, Issue 10, December, 1999

Shahidi, F., Naczk, M., Food Phenolics: Sources, chemistry, effects, applications, Technomic Publishing Co., Lancaster, Basel, Chapter 5:128, 1995

Shaken, not stirred? But what about the olive?, UC Berkeley Wellness Letter, Vol. 6, Issue 6, March, 2000

Sharpe, C., Siemiatycki, J., and Rachet, B., Effects of alcohol consumption on the risk of colorectal cancer among men by anatomical subsite (Canada), Cancer Causes Control 13:483-491, 2002

Sharpe, C., and Siemiatycki, J., Case-control study of alcohol consumption and prostate cancer risk in Montreal, Canada, Cancer Causes and Control, 12:589-598, 2001

Shipper, A., Alcohol and Mortality: A Review of Prospective Studies, British Journal of Addiction, Vol. 85, 1990

Shoemaker, W., Corkscrews or track shoes? Practical Winery and Vineyard, November/December, 1995

Shoemaker, W., Wine, pregnancy and fetal alcohol syndrome, Moderation Reader, March/April, 1993

Shore, E., Outcomes of a primary prevention project for business and professional women, Journal of Studies on Alcohol, 55:657-659, 1994

Shore, T., Red Wine Headaches Linked to Histamines, Wine Business Monthly, November, 1996

Should You Be Taking COX-2 Inhibitor, Harvard Health Letter, Vol. 27, No. 1, November, 2001

Should You Continue Taking Antioxidant Supplements? Tufts University Health & Nutrition Letter, Vol. 18, No. 4, June, 2000

Shughart II, W., in Taxing Choice: The Predatory Politics of Fiscal Discrimination, Transaction Books, Rutgers, 1997

Siegel, R., Intoxication: Life in Pursuit of Artificial Paradise, E.P. Dutton, New York, 1989

Sierksma, A., Sarkola, T., Eriksson, C., and Hendriks, H., Effect of moderate alcohol consumption on plasma hormone levels in healthy middle-aged men, Alcohol Research, 7:235-238, 2002

Sierksma, A., et al., Moderate alcohol consumption reduces plasma C-reactive protein and fibrinogen levels; a randomized diet-controlled intervention study, European Journal of Clinical Nutrition, Vol. 56:1130-1136, 2002

Sierksma, A., van der Gaag, M., Schaafsma, G., et al., Moderate alcohol consumption and fibrinolytic factors of pre- and post-menopausal women, Nutrition Research, 21:171-181, 2001

Silverman, D., Brown, L., Hoover, R., et al., Alcohol and pancreatic cancer in blacks and whites in the United States, Cancer Research, 55:4899-4905, 1995

Simon, J., Grady, D., Snabes, M., Fong, J., and Hunninghake, D., Ascorbic acid supplement use and the prevalence of gallbladder disease, Journal of Clinical Epidemiology, Vol. 51, No. 3, pp257-265, 1998

Simons, L., McCallum, J., Friedlander, Y., and Simons J., Alcohol intake and survival in the elderly: A 77 month follow-up in the Dubbo study, Australian and New Zealand Journal of Medicine, Vol. 26, No. 5, pp662-670, 2000

Simons, L., McCallum, J., Friedlander, Y., Ortiz, M., and Simons, J., Moderate alcohol intake is associated with survival in the elderly: the Dubbo Study, Medical Journal of Australia, 173:121-124, 2000

Sinclair, A., Era of Excess: A Social History of the Prohibition Movement, Harper Colophon Books, New York, 1964

Singer, L., et al., Mothers of Very Low-Birth-Weight Infants Experience Higher Levels of Stress, JAMA, 281:562-563, 1999

Single, E., and Pomeroy, H., Drinking and Setting: A Season for All Things, in Alcohol and Pleasure, Peele and Grant, editors, Brunner/Mazel, Philadelphia, 1999

Sixth Special Report to the U.S. Congress on Alcohol and Health, Department of Health and Human Services, Washington, D.C., January, 1987

Sizing Up the New Arthritis Drugs, The Johns Hopkins Medical Letter, Health After 50, Vol. 11, Issue 6, August, 1999

Skiing is relatively safe, experts say, Chicago Tribute, Knight-Ridder Newspapers, January 7, 1998

Skovenborg, E., Good News for Beer Drinkers, AIM Digest, Vol. 10, No. 4, 2002

Skovenborg, E., U.S. moderate drinkers live longest, Healthy Drinking, January/February, 1995

Slater, M., et al., A cluster of alcohol-related attitudes and behaviors in the general population, Journal of Studies on Alcohol, 68:667-674, September, 1999

Slater, M., Rouner, D., Karan, D., Murphy, K., and Beauvais, F., Placing alcohol warnings before airing, and after TV beer ads: effects on knowledge and responses to the ads and the warnings, Journalism Mass Communication Quarterly, 76:468-484, 1999

Smart, R., Behavioural and social consequences related to the consumption of different beverage types, Journal of Studies on Alcohol, Vol. 57, No. 1, pp77-84, 1996

Smart, R., and Ogborne, A., Beliefs about the cardiovascular benefits of drinking wine in the adult population of Ontario, American Journal on Drug And Alcohol Abuse, 28:372-378, 2002

Smart, R., et al., Drug Use Among Students in 36 Countries, Addictive Behaviors, Vol. 25, No. 3:455-460, 2000

Smart, R., et al., Heavy Drinking and Problems Among Wine Drinkers, Journal of Studies on Alcohol, July, 1999

Smith, C., The wrath of grapes: the health-related implications of changing American drinking practices, Area, 17:97-108, 1985

Smith, I., Silent and Deadly, Time, February 21, 2000

Smith, I., The Pressure's On, Time, September 11, 2000

Smith, W., and Mitchell, P., Alcohol intake and age-related maculopathy, American Journal of Ophthalmology, 122(5):743-745, 1996

Smith-Warner, S., et al., Alcohol and Breast Cancer in Women, JAMA, 279:535-540, 1998

Smoking, Drinking and thinking, Harvard Men's Health Watch, Vol. 5, No. 11, June, 2001

Snyder, C., Alcohol and the Jews, The Free Press, Glencoe, Illinois, 1958

Sokol, R,, and Martier, S., Advice to Physicians— What You Can Do to Prevent Fetal Alcohol Syndrome (FAS) and Alcohol-Related Birth Defects, NIAAA Paper, Washington, D.C.

Soleas, G., Deimanadis, E., Goldberg, D., Resveratrol: a molecule whose time has come? And gone?, Clinical Biochemistry, Vol. 30, No. 2, 91-113, 1997

Sonko, B., Effect of alcohol on postmeal fat storage, American Journal of Clinical Nutrition, 59:619-625, 1994

Speck, S., Women and Heart Disease, Healthwatch, Swedish Medical Center, Vol. 8, No. 1, Winter, 1998

Stall, R., Research Issues Concerning Alcohol Consumption Among Aging Populations, in Drug and Alcohol Dependence, 19:195-213, 1987

Stamler, J., Coronary Heart Disease: Doing The "Right Things," The New England Journal of Medicine, April 18, 1997

Stamler, J., Wentworth, D., and Neaton, J., Is the Relationship Between Serum Cholesterol and Risk of Premature Death from Coronary Heart Disease Continuous and Graded?, JAMA, Vol. 236, No. 20, November 28, 1986

Stampfer, M., Hennekens, C., et al., A Prospective Study of Cholesterol, Apolipoproteins, and the Risk of Myocardial Infarction, The New England Journal of Medicine, Vol. 325, No. 6, August, 1991

Stampfer, M., Colditz, G., Willett, W., Speizer, F., and Hennekens, C., Prospective Study of Moderate Alcohol Consumption and the Risk of Coronary Disease and Stroke in Women, The New England Journal of Medicine, 319:267-73, 1988

Stampfer, J., et al., Commentary: Alcohol, the Heart and Public Policy, American Journal of Public Health, Vol. 83, No. 6, June, 1993

Staying stout may be healthier than dieting, Seattle, Times, March, 20, 1994

Steinberg, D., Pearson, T., Kuller, L., Alcohol and Atherosclerosis, Annals of Internal Medicine, 114 (11), 967-976, 1991

Stepto, R., Clinical Uses of Wine, The New Physician, January, 1968

Stern, C., If Your Hand Trembles . . ., Parade Magazine, July 23, 1995

Stevens, J., Cai, J., Pamuk E., Williamson, D., Thun, M., and Wood, J., The Effect of Age on the Association Between Body-Mass Index and Mortality, The New England Journal of Medicine, Vol. 338, No. 1, January 1, 1998

Stewart, A., and Maddren, K., Police officers' judgments of blame in family violence: the impact of gender and alcohol, Sex Roles, Vol. 37, No. 11-12, pp921-933, 1997

St. Leger, A., Cochrane, A., Moore, F., Factors Associated with Cardiac Mortality in Developed Countries with Particular Reference to the Consumption of Wine, The Lancet, May 12, 1979

Stinson, F., DeBakey, S., and Steffens, R., Prevalence of DSM-III-R Alcohol Abuse and/or Dependence Among Selected Occupations, Alcohol Health & Research World, Vol. 16, No. 2, 1992

Stirring Up Helpful Bacteria, Health After 50, Vol. 14, Issue 9, 2002

Stoduto, G., Adlaf, E., Mann, R., Adolescents, bush parties and drinking-driving, Journal of Studies on Alcohol, 59:544-548, 1998

Strauss, S., An Historical Perspective on the Clinical Uses of Wine, Vintage, August, 1979

Stress Still Plays A Role in Ulcer Formation, Tufts University Health & Nutrition Letter, Vol. 17, No. 7, 1999

Study considered benefits to drivers and accident costs, Seattle Post Ingelligencer, Monday, December 2, 2002

Study Finds Teenage Suicides Not Due to Imitative Behavior, AMA News Release, November 16, 1989

Study Suggests doctors are ignoring guidelines, Seattle Post Intelligencer, January 14, 2002

Stuttaford, T., To Your Good Health! The Wise Drinker's Guide, Faber & Faber, London, 1997

Study finds new breast cancer clue, Seattle Post Intelligencer, December 5, 2001

Subbaramaiah, K., et al., Resveratrol inhibits cyclooxygenase-2 transcription and activity in ester-treated human mammary epithelial cells, Journal of Biological Chemistry, 273(34):21875-21882, 1998

Sugarman, C., Fortifying Food, Seattle Times, November 4, 1998

Suh, I., et al., Alcohol Use and Mortality from Coronary Heart Disease: The Role of High-Density Lipoprotein Cholesterol, Annals of Internal Medicine, 116(11):881-887, 1992

Sullum, J., Shrink Control, a review of PC, M.D.: How Political Correctness is Corrupting Medicine, Reason magazine, May, 2001

Surh, Y-J, Hurh, Y.J., Kang, J-Y, Resveratrol, an antioxidant present in red wine, induces apoptosis in human promylelocytic leukemia (HL-60) cells, Cancer Letters, 140:1-10, 1999

Sulaiman, N., du V Florey, C., Taylor, D., and Ogston, S., Alcohol consumption in Dundee primigravidas and its effects on outcome of pregnancy, British Medical Journal, Vol. 296, May, 1988

Sullivan, L., Message to Conference Participants, Healthy People/Healthy Environments Conference, DHHS, Washington, D.C., March 23, 1992

Sullum, J., How the public health lobby prescribes morality, Reason, January, 1996

Sullum, J., What the Doctor Orders, Reason magazine, January, 1996

Surh, Y., Hurh, Y., Kang, J., et al., Resveratrol, an antioxidant present in red wine, induces apoptosis in human promyelocytic leukemia, Cancer Lett, 140:1-10, 1999

Suter, P., Effect of ethanol on energy expenditure, American Journal of Physiology, 226:R1204-R1212, 1994

Suter, P., Jequier, E., and Schutz, Y., Effect of ethanol on energy expenditure, American Journal of Physiology, 266: R1204-R1212, 1994

Svetkey, L., Combination Diet Significantly Lowers Blood Pressure, Archives of Internal Medicine, 159:285-293, 1999

Swanson, C., Coates, R., Malone, K., Gammon D, Schoenberg, J., Grogan, D., McAdams, M., Potishman, N., Hoover, R., and Brinton, L., Alcohol consumption and breast cancer risk among women under 45 years of age, Epidemiology, Vol. 8., No. 3, pp231-237, 1997

Swanson, C., et al., Moderate alcohol consumption and the risk of endometrial cancer, Epidemiology, 4(6):530-539, 1993

Swartzberg, J., Speaking of Wellness, (pharmaceutical advertising) UC Berkeley Wellness Letter, Vol. 18, Issue 5, February, 2002

Swartzberg, J., Speaking of Wellness, Educated Guesses, UC Berkeley Wellness Letter, Vol. 19, Issue 1, October, 2002

Swartzberg, J., Speaking of Wellness, Facts of Life, UC Berkeley Wellness Letter, Vol.19, Issue 4, 2002

Swora, M., Review of International Handbook on Alcohol and Culture, Journal of Studies on Alcohol, 57(4):460, July, 1996

Tabak, C., Smit, H., Heederik, D., Ocke, M., and Kromhout, D., Diet and chronic obstructive pulmonary disease: independent beneficial effects of fruits, whole grains, and alcohol (the Morgen study). Clinical and Experimenta allergy, 31:745-755, 2001

Tabak, C., Smit, H., Rasanen, L., et al., Alcohol consumption in relation to 20-year COPD mortality and pulmonary function in middle-aged men from three European countries, Epidemiology 12:2329-245, 2001

Takada, H., Washino, K., and Iwata, H., Risk Factors for low bone mineral density among females: the effect of lean body mass, Preventive Medicine, 26:633-638, 1997

Take Tea Daily, HealthNews, Vol. 5, No. 4, November 20, 1999

Takkouche, B., Regueira-Mendez, C., Garcia-Closas, R., Figueriras, A., Gestal-Otero, J., and Hernan, Miguel, Intake of Wine, Beer, and Spirits and the Risk of Clinical Common Cold, American Journal of Epidemiology, Vol. 155, No. 9: 853-858, 2002

Tanasescu, M., Hu, F., Willett, W., Stampfer, M., Rimm, E., Alcohol consumption and risk of coronary heart disease among men with type 2 diabetes mellitus, Journal of American College of Cardiology 38:1836-1842, 2001

Task Force on Responsible Drinking, Final Report, Booklet 3, Education Commission of the States, Denver

Tavani, A., et al., Alcohol consumption and the risk of prostate cancer, Nutrition Cancer, 21:23-31, 1994

Tavani, A., Gallus, S., and La Vecchia, C., Risk facts for breast cancer in women under 40 years, European Journal of Cancer, 35:1361-1367, 1999

Tavani, A., Ferrarone, M., Mezzetti, M., Francheschi, Lo Re, A., and La Vecchia, C., Alcohol intake and risk of cancers of the colon and rectum, Nutr Cancer 30:213-219, 1998

Teen Drinking Study, International Communications Research, Media, Pennsylvania, June 6-10, 2001

Thakker, K., An Overview of Health Risks and Benefits of Alcohol Consumption, Alcohol: Clinical and Experimental Research, Vol. 22, No. 7, pp285S-289S, 1998

The Adelaide Recommendations: Healthy Public Policy, 2nd International Conference on Health Promotion, Adelaide, South Australia, April 5-9, 1988

The Aging Brain: Preserving Memory Through the Years, Harvard Health Letter, Vol. 23, No. 10, August, 1998

The Alzheimer's Driving Dilemma, HealthNews, Vol. 6, No. 8, August, 2000

The American Heritage Dictionary, Second College Edition, Houghton Mifflin, Boston, 1982

The bald truth about Propecia, UC Berkeley Wellness Letter, Vol. 1, No. 8, March, 1997

The Benefits for Healthcare Expenditures from Moderate Wine Consumption, Executive summary, prepared for American Vintners Association, Fairfax, VA, April 7, 1994

The Common Cold: An Update on Therapy, Harvard Men's Health Watch, Vol. 1, No. 7, February, 1997

The Facts About Drinking to Your Health, Health After 50, July, 2000

The French Paradox, CBS-TV 60 Minutes episode, November 17, 1991, New York

The Good, the Bad, and What's Healthy, Harvard Health Letter, Vol. 25, No. 1, November, 1999

The Great Cocktail Debate, The Cleveland Clinic Heart Advisor, Vol. 2, No. 6, June, 1999

The Health Benefits of Moderate Wine Consumption, Executive Summary, prepared for American Vintners Association, Fairfax, Virginia, May 25, 1993

The Herbal Medicine Boom, Time, November 23, 1998

The Johns Hopkins Complete Home Encyclopedia of Drugs, Medletter Associates, 1998

The Johns Hopkins Prescription for Longevity, Health After 50, Vol. 10, Issue 10, December, 1998

The Limits of Binge Drinking, International Center for Alcohol Policies, ICAP Reports 2, Washington, D.C., April, 1997

The Medical Advisor, Time/Life Books, Alexandria, 1996

The New American Plate, pamphlet, American Institute for Cancer Research, Washington, D.C., 2001

The New England Journal of Medicine, Editorial, Alcohol and Breast Cancer, Vol. 316, No. 19, May 7, 1987

The New Puritans and Alcohol: Robert Wood Johnson Foundation's Health Care Agenda, Foundation Watch, Vol. IV, No. 5, May, 1999

The Report on Carcinogens, 9th Edition, National Toxicology Program, National Institutes of Health, Washington, 2000

The Surgeon General's Report on NUTRITION AND HEALTH, USDHS, Publication No. 88-50211, DHHS, Washington, D.C., 1988

The Truth About Diet and Cancer, Health After 50, Vol. 12, Issue 3, May, 1999

The Wellness Encyclopedia of Food and Nutrition, Health Letter Associates, New York, 1992

The Year's Best Food News, Parade Magazine, November 11, 2001

This Bug and Booze Don't Mix, Harvard Health Letter, Vol. 24, No. 10, August, 1999

Thornton, J., Symers, C., and Heaton, K., Moderate Alcohol Intake Reduces Bile Cholesterol Saturation and Raises HDL Cholesterol, The Lancet, 2:819-822, 1983

Thornton, M., in Taxing Choice: The Predatory Politics of Fiscal Discrimination, Transaction Books, Rutgers, 1997

Thun, M., Peto, R., Lopez, A., Monaco, J., Henley, S., Heath, C., Doll, R., Alcohol Consumption and Mortality among Middle-aged and Elderly U.S. Adults, The New England Journal of Medicine, 337:1705-1714, 1997

Ticehurst, S., Elderly may benefit from daily tipple, New Zealand Press Association, April 9, 1999

Ties That Bind: Social Networks and Health, Harvard Men's Health Watch, Vol. 4, No. 5, December, 1999

Tiger, L., Harvard and Rutgers Researchers Explore the Connection between Wine, Diet, and Well-Being, News Release, The Wine Institute, San Francisco, February 22, 1993

Tiger L., Nunc Est Bibendum, Wall Street Journal, January 10, 2003

Tiger, L., The Pursuit of Pleasure, Little, Brown and Company, Boston, 1992

Tishler, P., Henschel, C., Ngo, T., Walters, E., and Worobec, T., Foetal alcohol effects in alcoholic veteran patients, Alcoholism: Clinical and Experimental Research, Vol. 22, No. 8, pp1825-1831, 1998

Tizon, A., Jobs, more than race, determine your odds of dying by violence, Seattle Times, February 21, 1999

To Err is Human, But . . ., Harvard Women's Health Watch, Vol. VII, No. 7, March, 2000

To University Health Letters at Odds Over Alcohol, Wine Issues Monitor, March/April, 1993

To Your Health: Alcohol and the Heart, Lifetime Health Letter, Vol. 7, No. 11, November, 1995

Tobe, H., Muraki, Y., and Kitamura, K., et al., Bone reabsorption inhibitors from hop extract, Bioscience, Biotechnology and Biochemistry, 61:158-159, 1997

Tough Love Rehab After Stroke, HealthNews, July, 2000

Trichopoulos, D., New Harvard Dietary Guidelines Include Wine, Wine Issues Monitor, Wine Institute, March/April, 1993

Trevithick, J., Beer cuts risk of cataracts and heart disease, Webmaster@bigfy.com, December 23, 2000

Trigg, D., Lai, M., and Wenig, B., Influence of tobacco and alcohol on the stage of laryngeal cancer at diagnosis, Laryngoscope, 110:408-411, 2000

Truelson, T., et al., Amount and type of alcohol and risk of dementia, Neurology, Vol. 59:1313-1319, 2002

Truelsen, T., Gronbaek, M., Scnohr, P., and Boysen, G., Intake of beer, wine and spirits and risk of stroke, The Copenhagen City Heart Study, Stroke, Vol. 29, No. 12, pp2467-2472, 1998

12 Ways to Reduce Your Risk of Cancer, Lifetime Health Letter, Vol. 2, No. 9, September, 1990

Tseng, M., Weinberg, C., Umbach, D., et al., Calculation of population attributable risk for alcohol and breast cancer, Cancer Causes Control, 10:119-123, 1999

Tsevat, J., Many Elderly Patients Prefer Quantity to Quality of Life, JAMA, 279:371-375, 1998

Tucker, K., et al., Bone Mineral Density and Dietary Patterns in Older Adults: The Framingham Osteoporosis Study, American Journal of Clinical Nutrition, Vol. 76:245-252, 2002

Turn of the News, Harvard Health Letter, Vol. 24, No. 11, September 11, 1999

Turner, C., and Anderson, P., Is alcohol a carcinogenic risk?, British Journal of Addiction, 85:1409-1415, 1990

Turner, R., Evans, G., Zhang, M., et al., Is resveratrol an estrogen agonist in growing rats?, Endocrinology, 140:50-54, 1999

Turner, T., and Bennett, V., Forward Together: Industry and Academia, Alcoholic Beverage Medical Research Foundation, Baltimore, 1993

Turner, T., Bennett, V., and Hernandez, H., The Beneficial Side of Moderate Alcohol Use, Johns Hopkins Medical Journal, 148:53-63, 1981

Tuyns, A., Riboli, E., Doornbos, G., and Pequignot, G., Diet and Esophageal Cancer in Calvados (France), Nutrition and Cancer, 9:81-92, 1987

Tuzcu, E., Kapadia, S., Tutar, E., Ziada, K., Hobbs, R., McCarthy, P., Young, J., and Nissen S., High Prevalence of Coronary Atherosclerosis in Asymptomatic Teenagers and Young Adults, Circulation, 103:2705-2710, 2001

Tyson, P., and Schirmuly, M., Memory Enhancement After Drinking Ethanol: Consolidation, Interference, or Response Bias?, Physiology & Behavior, Vol. 56, No. 5, pp933-937, 1994

Ueshima, H., Ozawa, H., Baba, S., Nakamoto, Y., et al., Alcohol drinking and high blood pressure: data from a 1980 national cardiovascular survey of Japan, Journal of Clinical Epidemiology, 45(6): 667-73, June, 1992

Understanding Your Triglyceride Levels, Johns Hopkins Medical Letter, Vol. 11, No. 9, November, 1999

United States has no room to brag about health care, Editorial, Seattle, Post Intelligencer, July 15, 2000

University of California, Berkeley Wellness Letter, Vol. 4, Issue 9, June, 1998

Update on Homocysteine, Cleveland Clinic Heart Advisor, Vol. 1, No. 8, August, 1998

U-Turn by WHO: Health Benefits of Moderation, in AIM, Vol. 4, No. 4, February/March, 1996

Vaccarino, V., Parsons, L., Every, N., Barron, H., and Krumholz, H., The New England Journal of Medicine, Vol. 341, No. 4, July 22, 1999

Vachon, C., Cerhan, J., Vierkant, R., et al., Investigation of an interaction of alcohol intake and family history on breast cancer risk in the Minnesota Breast Cancer Family Study, Cancer, 92:240-248, 2001

Vaeth, P., and Satariano, W., Alcohol consumption and breast cancer stage at diagnosis, Alcoholism: Clinical and Experimental Research, Vol. 22, No. 4, pp928-934, 1998

Vaillant, G., The Natural History of Alcoholism, Harvard University Press, Cambridge, 1983

Valmadrid, C., et al., Alcohol Consumption Associated With a Lower Risk of Death Due to Heart Disease for Persons with Diabetes, JAMA, 282:239-246, 1999

Valmadrid, C., Kelin, R., Moss, S., Klein, B., and Cruickshanks, K., Alcohol intake and the risk of coronary heart disease mortality in persons with older-onset diabetes mellitus, JAMA, 282:239-246, 1999

van der Gaag, M., Ubbink, J., Silanaukee, P., Nikkari, S., Hendriks, H., Effect of consumption of red wine, spirits and beer on serum homocysteine, The Lancet, 355:1522, 2000

van der Gaag, M., van Tol, Scheek, L., et al., Daily moderate alcohol consumption increases serum paraoxonase activity: a diet-controlled, randomised intervention study in middle-aged men, Atherosclerosis, 147:405-410, 1999

van der Pol, V., et al. Does alcohol contribute to accident and emergency department attendance in elderly people? Accident Emergency Medicine, 13:258-260, 1996

van der Stel, J., Drinking as a problem of civilization, Alcohol Digest, Vol. 14, No. 49, January, 1996

van der Wiel, A., Alcohol and insulin sensitivity, Netherlands Journal of Medicine, Vol. 52, No. 3, pp 91-94, 1998

van der Weil, A., van Golde, P., Kraaijenhagen, R., von dem Borne, P., Bouma, B., and Hart, H., Acute inhibitory effect of alcohol on fibrinolysis, Eur J Clin Invest, 31:164-170, 2001 van Tol, A., van der Gaag, M., Scheek, L., van Gent, T., and Hendriks, H., Changes in postprandial lipoproteins of low and high density caused by moderate alcohol consumption with dinner, Atherosclerosis, 141(Suppl 1) S101-S103, 1998

Vahtera, J., Moderate Drinkers Take Less Sick Leave, American Journal of Epidemiology, 156:969-976, 2002

Veenstra, J., et al., Effects of a Moderate Dose of Alcohol on Blood Lipids and Lipoproteins Post Prandial and in the Fasting State, Alcohol and Alcoholism, Vol. 25, No. 4, 1990

Vegetables can protect against prostate cancer, study finds, Seattle P.I., January 5, 2000

Venkov, et al., Thrombo-Haemost, 1999

Vinson, J., and Honts, B., Phenol antioxidant index: comparative antioxidant effectiveness of red and white wines, Journal of Agricultural Food Chemistry, 43:401-403, 1995

Virgili, M., and Contestabile, A., Partial neuroprotection of in vivo exitotoxic brain damage by chronic administration of the red wine antioxidant agent, trans-resveratrol in rats, Neruoscience Letter, 281:123-126, 2000

Virkkunen, M., Goldman, D., and Linnolla, M., Seratonin in alcoholic violent offenders, Ciba Foundation Symposium, 194:168-177, 1996

Vital Signs, Seattle Times, January 9, 2000

Vitamin C under attack, UC Berkeley Wellness Letter, Vol. 14, Issue 10, July, 1998

Vitamin E: E for Exaggerated?, Harvard Health Letter, Vol. 25, No. 5, March, 2000

Vitamin E: Have We Jumped the gun?, Tufts University Health & Nutrition Letter, Vol. 18, No. 1, March, 2000

Vitamins for the Heart?, Harvard Men's Health Watch, April, 2001

Vitamin E: E for Exaggerated?, Harvard Health Letter, Vol. 25, No. 5, March, 2000

Vogel-Sprout, M., Is behavioural tolerance learned?, Alcohol, Health and Research World, Vol. 21, No. 2, pp161-168, 1992

Vogler, R., and Bartz, W., The Better Way to Drink, Simon & Schuster, 1982

Volpicelli, J., Balaraman, G., Hahn, J., Wallace, H., and Bux, D., The role of uncontrollable trauma in the development of PTSD and alcohol addiction, Alcohol Research and Health, 23:256-262, 1999

Wagner, D., The New Temperance, Westview Press, Boulder, 1997

Wagner, R., in Taxing Choice: The Predatory Politics of Fiscal Discrimination, Transaction Books, 1997

Walpole, I., Zubrick, S., and Pontre, J., Is there a fetal effect with low to moderate alcohol use before or during pregnancy?, Journal of Epidemiology and Community Health, 44:297-301, 1990

Walsh, G., Bondy, S., and Rehm, J., Review of Canadian low-risk drinking guidelines and their effectiveness, Canadian Journal of Public Health, 89:241-247, 1998

Walzem, R., and Hansen, R., Atherosclerotic Cardiovascular Disease and Antioxidants, Wine in Context: Nutrition, Physiology, Policy, American Society for Enology and Viticulture, Reno, 1996

Wang, Y., and Watson, R., Is alcohol consumption a cofactor in the development of acquired immunodeficiency syndrome?, Alcohol, Vol. 12, No.. 2, pp105-109, 1995

Wang, Z., and Barker, T., Alcohol at moderate levels decreases fibrinogen expression in vivo and in vitro, Alcohol: Clinical and Experimental Research, 23:1927-1932, 1999

Wang, Z., and Fuller, G., Moderate concentrations of ethanol down-regulate fibrinogen production in vivo and in vitro, Alcohol: Clinical and Experimental Research, 23:114A(Suppl), 1999

Wannamethee, S., and Shaper A., Patterns of alcohol intake and risk of stroke in middle-aged British men, Stroke, 27:1033-9, 1996

Wannamethee, S., et al., Type of Alcoholic Drink and Risk of Major coronary Heart Disease Events, American Journal of Public Health, 89:685-690, May, 1999

Wannamethee, S., and Shaper, G., Type of alcoholic drink and risk of major coronary heart disease events and all cause morality, American Journal of Public Health, 89:685-690, 1999

Wannamethee, S., Shaper, A., Perry, I., and Alberti, K., Alcohol consumption and the incidence of type II diabetes, Journal of Epidemiology and Community Health 56:542-548, 2002

Warburton, D., Pleasure for Health, in Alcohol and Pleasure, Peele and Grant, editors, Brunnel/Mazel, Philadelphia, 1999

Waterhouse, A., Can We Recommend Wine?, Speech to Society of Medical Friends of Wine, San Francisco, October 23, 1996

Waterhouse, A., Exploring the mystery of resveratrol, Practical Winery and Vineyard, March/April 1993

Watkins, T., Heart patients benefit from a little daily wine, paper to American Chemical Society Conference, Chicago, August, 1995

Watkins, T., Yesterday's Antidote for Today's Oxygen Stress, in Wine: Nutritional and therapeutic Benefits, American Chemical Society, Washington, D.C., 1997

Weakly news, Drinking wine may halve the risk of macular degeneration, UC Berkeley Wellness Letter, April, 1998

Wechsler, H., Molnar, B., Davenport, A., and Baer, J., College alcohol use: a full or an empty glass, Journal of College Health, 47:247-252, 1999

Wei, M., Gibbons, L., Mitchell, T., et al., Alcohol intake and incidence of type 2 diabetes in men, Diabetes Care, 23:18-22, 2000

Weiderpass, E., and Baron, J., Cigarette smoking, alcohol consumption, and endometrial cancer risk: a population-based study in Sweden, Cancer Causes and Control, 12:239-247, 2001

Weight and Longevity, Harvard Health Letter, 1998

Weight Gain and Heart Risk, Harvard Heart Letter, 1998

Weill, J., Total alcohol consumption and rates of excessive use: the Ledermann model revisited, Alcohol Research Vol. 6, No. 3, p101-102, 2001

Weinberg, R., Benefits of Alcohol Use Wash Out the Costs of Use Says Noted Economist, Moderate Drinking Journal, Vol. 1, No. 5, September/October 1987

Weiner, C., The Politics of Alcoholism, Transaction Books, 1981

Weiner, L, FAS: Science, myth and other things, Speech to Joys of Wine Forum, Women for Winesense, New York City, October 21, 1993

Weiner, L., Morse, B., Garrido, P., FAS/FAE: Focusing Prevention on Women at Risk, The International Journal of the Addictions, 24:385-395, 1989

Weisse, M., Eberly, B., and Person, D., Wine as a digestive aid: comparative antimicrobial effects of bismuth salicylate and red and white wine, British Medical Journal, 311:1657-1660, 1995

Wetle, T., Aging research comes of age, JAMA, 278:1376-1377, 1997

Wellness facts, UC Berkeley Wellness Letter, Vol. 16, Issue 2, November, 1999

Wetzel, M., Many U.S. Medical Schools Offer Alternative Medicine Courses, JAMA, Vol. 280:784-787, 1998

What are your chances of developing breast cancer?, Medical Essay, Mayo Clinic Health Letter, June, 2001

What Causes Cancer?, Harvard Men's Health Watch, Vol. 3, No. 2, September, 1998

What is a "Standard Drink"?, International Center for Alcohol Policies, ICAAP Report 5, September, 1998

What is Fetal Alcohol Syndrome? What is Fetal Alcohol Effects?, AWARE, Vol. 1., No. 1, Fall, 1990

What Minerals Do We Need?, Harvard Women's Health Watch, October, 1999

What to Eat for a Long & Healthy Life, University of California at Berkeley, 1998

What You Can Do to Protect Your Eyes, Harvard Health Letter, Vol.26, No. 12, October, 2001

When Alcohol and Aging Don't Mix, Health After 50, February, 1999

Whelton, P., He, J., Appel, L., Treatment and Prevention of Hypertension, Prevention of Myocardial Infarction, Oxford University Press, New York, 1996

When Alcohol and Aging Don't Mix, Health After 50, Vol. 10, Issue 12, February, 1999

White, H, Fagan, J., and Pihl, R., Alcohol and Violence, Alcoholic Beverage Medical Research Foundation Monograph No. 2, Baltimore, 1994

White, I., The level of alcohol consumption at which all-cause morality is least, Journal of Clinical Epidemiology, 52:967-975, 1999

White, I., and McKee, M., Festive cheer for all? Headaches for alcohol policy makers, British Medical Journal, Vol. 315, No. 7123, December, 1997

Whitten, D., A Symposium on Wine, Culture & Healthy Lifestyles, New York Academy of Sciences, May 1, 1987

Whitten, D., The Truth Will Out, Wine Spectator, April 30, 1996

Whitten, D., Wine and Healthy Lifestyles, A Symposium on Wine, Culture & Healthy Lifestyles, The Wine Institute, New York, May 1, 1987

Whitten, D., and Lipp, M., To Your Health!: Two Physicians Explore the Health Benefits of Wine, HarperCollinsWest, New York, 1994

Who is Joseph Califano Anyway?, Beverage Alcohol Marketing Report, New York, 1995

Whole-Diet Approach Extends Lives, HealthNews, June, 2000

Whorton, J., Nature Cures: The History of Alternative Medicine in America, Oxford University Press, New York, 2002

Why Wine? The Latest Research on Wine's Role as Part of a Healthy Diet and Lifestyle, Research News Bulletin, Vol. 4, No. 2, September, 1996

Wiley, J., and Camacho, T., Life Style and Future Health: Evidence in the Alameda County Study, Preventive Medicine, 9:1-21, 1980

Wilkie, S., Global overview of drinking recommendations and guidelines, AIM Digest (Supplement), June, 1997

Will, G., No logic found in smoking debate, The Washington Post Writers Group, in Seattle Post Intelligencer, July 30, 1998

Will medication cure osteoporosis?, Arthritis Today, March/April, 1998

Will Stress Give You A Heart Attack, The Cleveland Clinic Heart Advisor, Vol. 1, No. 8, August, 1998

Willett, W., Harvard's New Mediterranean Diet Guidelines Include Wine, Research News Bulletin, The Wine Institute, Vol. 2, No. 1, January, 1993

Willett, W., Eat, Drink, and Be Healthy, Simon & Schuster, New York, 2001

Willett, W., and Lenart, E., Dietary Factors in Prevention of Myocardial Infarction, Oxford University Press, New York, 1996

Williams, Presentation to the National Press club, May 12, 1997 in Wine, Nutrition & Health, OIV, No. 30, 1998,

Williams, F., Road accidents third biggest killer by 2020, Financial Times, June 25, 1998

Williams, P., Interactive effects of exercise, alcohol and vegetarian diet on coronary artery disease risk factors in 9242 runners, The National Runners' Health Study, American Journal of Clinical Nutrition, 66:1197-2006, 1997

Willett, W., and Lenart, E., Dietary Factors, in Prevention of Myocardial Infarction, Oxford University Press, New York, 1996

Williamson, D., Forman, M., Binkin, N., Gentry, E., Remington, P., and Trowbridge, F., Alcohol and Body Weight in United States Adults, American Journal of Public Health, 77:1324-1330, 1987

Wine and Medical Practice, Wine Institute, San Francisco, 1979

Wine and Health, Wine, Nutrition & Health, No. 39, 1999

Wine and the heart in 1994, Practical Winery & Vineyard, San Rafael, September/October 1994

Wine and Medical Practice, A Summary, Tenth Edition, The Wine Institute, San Francisco, 1979

Wine and the heart in 1994, Practical Winery & Vineyard, San Rafael, September/October 1994

Wine, Beer and Gastrin Release, Digestion, 26:73-79, 1983

Wine Consumption May Reduce Risk for Blindness, Wine Institute NEWSFLASH, Vol. 4, No. 5, January, 1998

Wine for Skin Ulcers, Bulletin of the Society of Medical Friends of Wine, Sausalito,

Wine in Context: Nutrition/Physiology/Policy, Symposium on Wine and Health, American Society for Enology and Viticulture, Reno, 1996

Wine in Nutrition Study, Bulletin of The Society of Medical Friends of Wine, Vol. 17, No. 1, February, 1975

Wine Institute Applauds Dietary Guidelines Advisory Committee Efforts, New Release, The Wine Institutes, February 3, 2000

Wine, Nutrition & Health, Office International de la Vigne et du Vin, No. 26, Paris, 1997

Wishful thinking about diet and breast cancer, UC Berkeley Wellness Letter, Vol. 15, Issue 6, March, 1999

Wodak, A., Conditions and diseases other than cardiovascular associated with moderate alcohol consumption, Contemporary Drug Problems, Spring, 1994

Woodward, M., and Tunstall-Pedoe, H., Alcohol Consumption, Diet, Coronary Risk Factors, and Prevalent Coronary Heart Disease in Men and Women in the Scottish Heart Health Study, Journal of Epidemiology and Community Health, 49:351-362, 1995

World Health Organization, Technical Report Series 841, Geneva, 1994

World Health Organization, Wine, Nutrition & Health, Vol. 59, 2000

Women and Moderate drinking: Health in the Balance, Harvard Women's Health Watch, November, 2000

Wright, I., Vascular Diseases in Clinical Practice, Year Book Publishers, Chicago, 1952

Wright, R., McManaman, J.., and Repine, J., Alcohol-induced breast cancer: a proposed mechanism, Free Radical Biological Medicine, 26:348-354, 1999

Yano, K., Rhoads, G., and Kagan, A., Coffee, Alcohol and Risk of Coronary Heart Disease Among Japanese Men Living in Hawaii, Journal of American Medical Association, 297:405-409, 1997

Yano, K., Reed, D., and McGee, D., Ten-Year Incidence of Coronary Heart Disease in the Honolulu Heart Program, American Journal of Epidemiology, 119(5) 653666, 1984

Yokoyama, A., Muramatsu, T., Ohmori, T., et al., Alcohol related cancers and aldehyde dehydrogenase-2 in Japanese alcoholics, Carcinogenesis, 19:1383-1387, 1998

You Can Remember This– Even as Time Goes By, Harvard Health Letter, Vol. 25, No. 7, May, 2000

Young People & Drinking, The Century Council, Los Angeles, July, 1998

Your Stroke Survival Action Plan, Health After 50, Vol. 13, Issue 3, May, 2001

Yuan, J., et al. Follow up study of moderate alcohol intake and mortality among middle aged men in Shanghai, China, British Medical Journal, 314:18-23, 1997

Zantac Caution, HealthNews, Vol. 6, No. 3, March, 2000

Zang, E., and Wynder, E., Revaluation of the confounding effect of cigarette smoking on the relationship between alcohol use and lung cancer risk, with larynx cancer used as a positive control, Prevention Medicine, 32:359-370, 2001

Zarkin, G., et al., Alcohol use and wages: new results form the National Household survey on Drug and Alcohol Use, Journal of Health Economics, 17:53-68, 1998

Zavras, A., Douglass, C., Joshipura, K., et al., Smoking and alcohol in the etiology of oral cancer: gender-specific risk profiles in the south of Greece, Oral Oncology, 37:28-35, 2001

Zeegers, M., Volovics, A., Dorant, E., Goldbohn, R., and van den Brandt, P., Alcohol consumption and bladder cancer risk: results from the Netherlands Cohort Study, American Journal of Epidemiology, 153:38-41, 2001

Zeeman-Polderman, M., Drinking behaviour of various population segments in Western countries: differences and trends, Alcohol Digest, Vol. 13, No. 44, September, 1994

Zhang, Q-H, Das, K., Siddiqui, S., and Myers, A., Effects of acute, moderate alcohol consumption on human platelet aggregation in platelet-rich plasma and whole blood, Alcohol Clinical and Experimental Research, 24:528-534, 2000

Zhang, L., Wieczorek, W., and Welte, J., The nexus between alcohol and violent crime, Alcohol Clinical Experimental Research, 21:11264-1271, 1997

Zhang, S., Hunder D., Hankinson, S., et al., A prospective study of folate intake and the risk of breast cancer, JAMA, 281:1632-1637, 1999

Zhang, Y., Kreger, B., Dorgan, J., Splanksy, G., Cupples, A., and Ellison, R., Alcohol Consumption and Risk of Breast Cancer: The Framingham Study Revisited, American Journal of Epidemiology, Vol. 149, No. 2, January 15, 1999

Zinberg, N., Drug, Set and Setting, Yale University Press, New Haven, 1984

Zodpey, S. and Tiwari, R., Alcohol consumption and risk of haemorrhagic stroke: a case-control study, Alcohol Research, Vol. 5, No. 4, pp145-148, August, 2001

Zuger, A., Evidence Mounting That Moderate Drinking Is Healthful, New York Times, December 30, 2002

Zuger, A., How a Drink a Day Helps the Heart, New York Times, December 30, 2002

Zuger, A., How a Tonic Keeps the Parts Well Oiled, New York Times, December 31, 2002

Zuger, A., The Case for Drinking (All Together Now: In Moderation!), New York Times, December 31, 2002

Index

The goal of this book is to set forth a significant volume of seldom-seen drinking research. This exposure demonstrates beyond doubt that these data are neglected in conventional medical and public health media. Since this book targets the practicing physicians and other caregivers, the index features authors and publications. Through this index and the extensive reference section, physicians and researchers can check book sources and scientific references. This book represents a new effort at resolving a very old problem — inordinate fear of drinking.

B

F

G